The Battles of
King Arthur

The Battles of
King Arthur

Tony Sullivan

PEN & SWORD
HISTORY

First published in Great Britain in 2022 by
Pen & Sword History
An imprint of
Pen & Sword Books Ltd
Yorkshire – Philadelphia

ISBN 978 1 39901 530 1

A CIP catalogue record for this book is
available from the British Library.

Typeset by Mac Style
Printed and bound in the UK by CPI Group (UK) Ltd,
Croydon, CR0 4YY.

Pen & Sword Books Limited incorporates the imprints of Atlas,
Archaeology, Aviation, Discovery, Family History, Fiction, History,
Maritime, Military, Military Classics, Politics, Select, Transport,
True Crime, Air World, Frontline Publishing, Leo Cooper, Remember
When, Seaforth Publishing, The Praetorian Press, Wharncliffe
Local History, Wharncliffe Transport, Wharncliffe True Crime
and White Owl.

For a complete list of Pen & Sword titles please contact

PEN & SWORD BOOKS LIMITED
47 Church Street, Barnsley, South Yorkshire, S70 2AS, England
E-mail: enquiries@pen-and-sword.co.uk
Website: www.pen-and-sword.co.uk

Or

PEN AND SWORD BOOKS
1950 Lawrence Rd, Havertown, PA 19083, USA
E-mail: Uspen-and-sword@casematepublishers.com
Website: www.penandswordbooks.com

Contents

Acknowledgements

My thanks go to: Glenn Higgins for reading the first draft; Edwin Hustwit, who gave valuable advice on archaeology and history; Stephen Holden, who suggested some possible northern battle locations; Paul Mortimer, who kindly contributed photographs of re-enactors and whose books on Dark Age weapons and warfare are an invaluable resource; and Charles Evans-Gunther, for help with correcting many errors, and helping me avoid assumptions and leaps of logic.

A special mention to Robert Vermaat and the excellent Vortigern Studies website, which is packed with relevant information. Additionally, thanks to the many posters on numerous Facebook groups: Historia Brittonum; King Arthur and Lords of the North; King Arthur; Anglo-Saxon History and Language; King Arthur, History, Literature and Legend; Gildas, and many more.

All remaining errors are my own.

List of Maps, Illustrations and Tables

Tables

Introduction

Before beginning this investigation, it must first be acknowledged there is a possibility that King Arthur was a mythical figure. The pros and cons of the argument have been covered in my previous book *King Arthur: Man or Myth*.[1] It is fair to say at best that academic historians hold a healthy scepticism. This work is based on the assumption Arthur is indeed a historical figure. I will not go too deeply into that debate here, except to lay out the sparse available evidence. Nor is this book's primary concern one of identifying a figure from history or any genealogical tables. Instead, it is the geography, history and politics of the time that is of most interest here. From that, I will attempt to lay out some reasonable parameters within which we can place a historical Arthur, and describe the likely political, geographical and military context. The second assumption to be acknowledged is that the battle list in the eighth-century *Historia Brittonum* is a legitimate copy of an earlier oral record. This, too, is highly debatable and I will discuss that further in the relevant chapter. Identifying at least some of the battle locations will aid our understanding in placing Arthur in the correct historical context. We will also look at the nature of warfare, weapons, tactics and battles in the so-called 'Dark Ages'.

Firstly, let us narrow down our search. The earliest references, although late, place Arthur somewhere in the fifth or sixth centuries. We have plenty of contemporary sources for the Roman period up to around AD 410. This is the date the Western Emperor rejected the Britons' pleas for aid and told them to look to their own defences. Three years earlier, Constantine III had left Britain and taken a large part of the army to Gaul to seize imperial power. We should not view Roman Britain as ending at this date, rather that it evolved over the next two hundred years, fragmenting into a series of petty kingdoms. The process, speed and manner of this evolution will be vital in understanding the world Arthur was born into. One major theme will be the changing cultural identity of people living in Britain over that time. The terms Romano-British and Anglo-Saxons are both misleading and applied retrospectively.

There is no evidence whatsoever for any historical Arthur prior to the end of Roman Britain or for any specific details of the legend. What is surprising is that although Arthur (from the Greek Arturus or Arcturus) is a well-attested

Roman name, only one figure has been suggested. But the only claim the obscure Lucius Artorius Castus has is his name. A relatively minor military rank at the end of the second century, he may have been stationed in Britain and have had unsubstantiated links to Sarmatian cavalry. From inscriptions on his memorial in Croatia, we see he commanded two British legions in Armenia (or Armorica) and was a procurator (financial official) of Liburnia in Croatia. There is not a shred of evidence of any link and his story would have had to travel across hundreds of years of history to appear in the ninth-century *Historia Brittonum*, later Welsh sources and the twelfth-century *History of the Kings of Britain* by Geoffrey of Monmouth, leaving no traces in the historical record. It is this latter book, written around AD 1136, that caused an explosion of interest as well as later works, especially from French Romance writers such as Chrétien de Troyes.

Likewise, stories of Sarmatian cavalry with their legends of magic swords pulled from the earth and dragon symbology are also rather tenuous. There is simply no evidence beyond speculation and one is left to explain the complete absence of any trace of the legend between the time the Sarmatians were stationed in Britain in the second century and the appearance of some similarity in legends many centuries later. Indeed, magical swords, often fixed into the ground or trees, are fairly common in western mythology. We also have reasonable contemporary records after around AD 600, and certainly from the time of Augustine's mission to King Aethelbert of Kent in 597, initiated by Pope Gregory the Great. We begin to get reliable confirmed records concerning Anglo-Saxon kings from the end of the sixth century: Aelle (c.590–600) in Deira and Aethelfrith (c.592–616) in Bernicia (the two kingdoms later combined to form Northumbria). Raedwald (c.599–624) in East Anglia and Penda (626–655) are equally well-attested. On the continent, Gregory of Tours (c.538–594) wrote *The History of the Franks* and Jordanes completed *The Origins and Deeds of the Goths* in around 551. Yet no reference to an Arthur or any hint of any part of the legend presents itself.

One figure that does occasionally get highlighted is Artur mac Aedan of Dalraida at the end of the sixth century. In a similar way to Lucius Artorius Castus, there is no evidence whatsoever and no hints from his life of any connection with the Arthur legend. Artur apparently died at the Battle of Miathi, which occurred before St Columba's death in 596. Adomnán writing the *Life of St Columba* in around 700 gives no indication of any link. Nor do any subsequent writers such as Bede who fail to mention any King Arthur. Having said that, it may be the case that some aspects of this Arthur may have erroneously been attributed to the legend.

So, we have a window – from AD 400 to 600 – outside of which it is unlikely a historical Arthur existed. As we shall see, the earliest references do indeed place Arthur in this time frame, specifically between AD 450 and 550. The narrative is surprisingly consistent across the various sources and legends: the Romans leave and Britain is subject to instability and raids from Picts, Irish and Saxons. A council headed by a 'proud Tyrant' (later named Vortigern) invites Germanic mercenaries, said to be led by Hengest and Horsa. They are placed in the east of the island (Kent, when mentioned), and in the north to fight the Picts. A rebellion follows and barbarians take control over part of the island. Subsequently, the Britons fight back, led by Ambrosius Aurelianus, and this culminates in the Battle of Badon. It is at this point that Arthur is generally placed by the sources. A period of relative peace follows Badon before the Anglo-Saxons push westwards, eventually confining the Britons to Cornwall, Wales and the north. Or so the literary sources say.

The earliest references to Arthur begin 300 years after this period, although it is possible one or two sources may be copies of earlier documents. The eighth-century *Historia Brittonum* is the first attested reference and places Arthur after the deaths of St Patrick and Hengest (probably in the second half of the fifth century), but before the reign of Ida of Bernicia (dated to AD 547 by the same document). The possibly tenth-century *Annales Cambriae* dates two of Arthur's battles to AD 516 and AD 537. The medieval *Saints' Lives* associates him with saints who lived either side of AD 500. Finally, Geoffrey of Monmouth in his twelfth-century ahistorical *History of the Kings of Britain* gives only one date for Arthur's death at Camlann: AD 542.

Contemporary records that do exist, either from the continent or Britain, fail to hint at any historical Arthur. There are no papal letters, no records from European Kingdoms, no marriage proposals, no contemporary treaties or charters, no comments from travellers and nothing from contemporary writers such as Sidonius Appollinaris (c.430–489) or Procopius (c.500–570). There are many continental sources that refer to Britain which we will cover. One of the most important is the *Gallic Chronicle* of 452 which records for the year 440: 'The Britains, which to this time had suffered from various disasters and misfortunes, are reduced to the power of the Saxons.'[2]

Bede, writing in the eighth century, dates the arrival of the Saxons, the *adventus Saxonum*, to AD 449. We will investigate this apparent discrepancy in dates further. We only have one contemporary record that covers the period we are looking at: *De Excidio et Conquestu Britanniae*, written by Gildas in the second quarter of the sixth century. This is not a document from a historian but a sermon describing the end of Roman Britain, the coming of the Saxons and their defeat at Badon. Importantly, Gildas notes the 'unhappy partition' with the barbarians. The study of this document, and the nature of any partition in particular, is vital in assessing the situation in Britain. It is likely Gildas is writing just after, or contemporary with, a historical Arthur although he does not mention him at all. It's within this political, cultural and military context that we will attempt to locate Arthur's battles.

It is worth making two points before we continue. Firstly, in an age before modern communications, the printing press and widespread literacy, narratives lose their accuracy and reliability beyond about five generations. We must bear in mind that your grandfather might be able to relate reasonably accurately what *his* grandfather told him but beyond that, facts get distorted. We know how unreliable eyewitness statements can be or how conspiracy theories can form, even days after an event. Thus, some have suggested that beyond about two hundred years we can no longer trust an account as contemporary.[3] Secondly, much of the evidence that is used in Arthurian research – *Historia Brittonum*, *Annales Cambriae*, *Anglo-Saxon Chronicles*, sagas, Welsh legends and genealogies – are not considered credible by academic historians for this period. They are in effect 'inadmissible' as evidence[4] which is why, of course, Arthur's very existence is questioned.

The evidence

Given Arthur, if he existed, is likely a fifth- or sixth-century figure, we are forced to prioritise sources that are closer in time. This inevitably means disregarding our modern version of the legend. As much of this evolved from Geoffrey of Monmouth's fantastical book, I will ignore all the stories that post-date that. There is little value in investigating dubious versions of stories that first appear six hundred years after the time in question. Welsh legends and *Saints' Lives* give a very different picture of Arthur. While the earliest surviving copies post-date Geoffrey's work, many are thought to originate much earlier, such as the tale of *Culhwch and Olwen*. These tales describe a more fantastical and magical character and, in some cases, a warlord acting rather badly.

It is worth briefly noting the evidence that does exist. I will list it below and then look at each piece in turn:

1. One reference in a possible seventh-century poem, *Y Gododdin*, comparing a warrior to Arthur.
2. The existence of four persons called Arthur in genealogies at the end of the sixth century, suggesting the name became popular.
3. The existence and persistence of a body of stories and legends for several centuries.
4. Two references in the *Annales Cambriae* written in the mid-tenth century.
5. The list of twelve battles in the *Historia Brittonum* written in the early ninth century.

Y Gododdin is a poem reportedly by the sixth-century poet Aneirin about a battle near Catraeth (perhaps in Catterick, North Yorkshire), in around AD 600 that mentions a warrior who, although brave, 'is no Arthur'. This only survives in a thirteenth-century manuscript. If we give it the benefit of the doubt (although many don't) and assume the line referring to Arthur was not added later, and the poem is indeed a genuine early seventh-century account of the battle, this still would not prove the reference concerned a historical figure. One could equally claim someone was not Superman or Hercules, yet this reference could not be used centuries later to prove the existence of either.

Additionally, even if the phrase referred to a real person, it may be a completely different Arthur. For example, the battle concerns the northern Gododdin from the Lothian area fighting the Angles. It is possible the Artur mac Aedan of the nearby Dalriada was a well-known heroic person and the one referred to in the text. So unfortunately, this tantalising vague reference to a warrior named Arthur proves nothing at all. If we are generous, we can accept that the oral composition of the poem occurred in the third quarter of the sixth century.[5] We could be more generous and claim a seventh-century scribe copied down this earlier poem, which, in turn, did indeed include a reference to a famous warrior. This might indicate his fame had spread as far north as the Gododdin around modern-day Edinburgh. It would not necessarily follow that Arthur was confined to, or even had a connection with, the north. The most we can do is note the possibility of a northern connection.

Likewise, the existence of four persons called Arthur cannot help. They are as follows: Artur, son of Aedan Mac Gabhrain of the Gaelic kingdom Dalriada, killed in battle around 596; Artur ap Bicuir, recorded as killing an Ulster chieftain in 624; Arthur ap Pedr of Dyfed, grandson of Vortipor; and an Irish Artur, grandfather of Faradach, recorded in a law text of 697. Dyfed has extensive Irish settlement so it's worth noting that all four Arthurs have Irish heritage. However, Artorius was a fairly common name throughout Roman times and there could be scores of Arthurs hidden from us. The dates all seem far too late to be linked to any possible British Arthur fifty years either side of AD 500. We have various examples of Roman names such as Tacitus and Constantinus changing to Tegid and Custennin respectively or Gaius to Kai. Yet there are no known further uses of Arthur for 600 years until it was revived by the Norman romances. So, finding four persons named Arthur at least fifty years after he is supposed to have lived is hardly strong evidence when there are no examples from Welsh genealogies or other records nearer his floruit. Even if there was a tradition that venerated the name, again this would not prove a historical figure. They could just as likely be named after a fictional character from popular sagas and poems of the time.

The third category of evidence is the 'no smoke without fire' argument. This refers to the existence and persistence of a body of stories and legends into the Middle Ages. There are four main groups: the lives of various saints from the eleventh century onwards; Geoffrey of Monmouth's *History of the Kings of Britain* in the twelfth century; the proliferation of French Romances that were based on that book; and various Welsh legends and poems that may have predated Geoffrey of Monmouth's work, but whose earliest surviving copies are much later. These all date from at least 600 years after Arthur is alleged to have lived and are not treated as credible or valid evidence by academics and historians. The most we can say is that some people in the Middle Ages appear to have believed these stories had some basis in reality. In the absence of any hard evidence, what people believe 600 years after an event holds little weight.

The fourth category is the *Annales Cambriae* (the Welsh Annals): a twelfth-century manuscript, presumed to be a copy of a tenth-century record. It includes two entries for Arthur, although dates in the *Annales* are often unreliable and these entries could have been added later:[6]

Year 72 (c. AD 516) The Battle of Badon, in which Arthur carried the cross of our Lord Jesus Christ on his shoulders for three days and three nights and the Britons were victors.

Year 93 (c. AD 537) The Strife of Cam lann in which Arthur and Medraut [Mordred] fell and there was death in Britain and in Ireland.

There is no indication of where these battles were fought or even against whom. Unfortunately, we simply cannot trust the validity of this source. As the earliest copies of this manuscript are found with our last category, we will turn to that now.

Finally, the *Historia Brittonum*, written c. AD 830, possibly by a Welsh monk called Nennius, describing Arthur as a *dux bellorum*, fighting with the kings of Britain against the Saxons. In fact, the exact wording is '*dux erat bellorum*' (leader in battle) which is more likely a description than a title. It is similar to the description of the role St Germanus takes in leading the Britons to victory in AD 429 against raiding Picts and Saxons. We cannot translate this, as some have done, as *Dux Britanniarum*, the title of the commander of the northern military command. In Chapter 56 of the *Historia Brittonum*, the author records twelve battles, the last of which is Badon.[7]

Then Arthur fought against them in those days, together with the kings of the British; but he was their *dux bellorum* [leader in battle].

The first battle was at the mouth of the River Glein. The second, third, fourth and fifth were on another river, called the Douglas which is in the country of Lindsey. The sixth battle was on the river called Bassas. The seventh battle was in the Celyddon forest, that is the battle of Celyddon Coed. The eighth battle was in Guinnion fort, and in it Arthur carried the image of the holy Mary, the everlasting virgin, on his shoulders and the heathen were put to flight on that day, and there was a great slaughter upon them. The ninth battle was fought in the city of the legion. The tenth battle was fought on the bank of the river called Tryfrwyd. The eleventh battle was on the hill called Agned. The twelfth battle was on Badon hill and in it 960 men fell in one day, from a single charge of Arthur's, and no-one laid them low save him alone; and he was victorious in all his campaigns.

To this battle list we shall add Camlann, or *Cam lann* as it is recorded in the *Annales Cambriae*. The battles in Geoffrey of Monmouth's book will also be investigated. We won't, however, bother ourselves with anything later. Many of the legends appeared hundreds of years after Arthur and the period we are focusing on. We can see when some of the concepts we associate with Arthur were introduced into the story: Merlin, Excalibur, the sword in the stone, Avalon, Camelot, the grail and the round table all appeared from the twelfth century onwards. The original Welsh traditions have a more magical, mystical Arthur fighting giants and witches and visiting the underworld. Having said all that, many of the sources and legends have a level of consistency.

Arthur is always placed after Ambrosius and before the Anglo-Saxons renew their territorial gains. If we trust the *Anglo-Saxon Chronicles*, further Saxon expansion occurs in the south after around AD 552. Thus, the stories place him in the very period for which we have a lack of contemporary sources: 400–600. The timeline places Arthur sometime after the Romans leave Britain and before Anglo-Saxon kingdoms emerge, so we can narrow it down to 450–550. Indeed, we may be able to go further with likely dates for Badon ranging from c.480–520. I would therefore argue our evidence is reduced to two things: the *Historia Brittonum* and the fact the stories persisted over many hundreds of years. There are tenuous links to the north through *Y Gododdin* and a possibility the name Arthur was popular in Irish genealogies. But the legend persisted in Wales, Cornwall and Brittany too. The timeframe is the late antique period or the transformation of a Roman Britain into a Brittonic and Anglo-Saxon Britain.

This book will argue that the *Historia Brittonum* does indeed provide a credible narrative and also an explanation for the discrepancies between the sources and gaps in our understanding for that period. I will also argue the battle list not only has some support as an authentic battle poem, but some of the battles can indeed be identified. In addition, it will be shown there is nothing unreasonable about battles some distance from early Germanic settlement. Two important questions about Arthur need to be noted. Firstly, where exactly on our timeline do we place him? In my first book I suggested three options: an early Arthur, c.450–480; a middle Arthur, c.480–510; and a late Arthur, 510–540. Crudely, an early Arthur might have experienced a greater legacy from Roman Britain in terms of provincial and political structures. A later Arthur would be living in a world of emerging petty kingdoms and warlords.

Following on from that, what sort of man was Arthur? Later legends make him a king. Some even title him emperor and Geoffrey of Monmouth has him conquering most of Western Europe and on the verge of invading Italy. Yet the *Historia Brittonum* doesn't call him king at all. He is simply *dux bellorum*, leader of battle. Welsh legends portray a petty king, one among many or simply a warlord-type figure. The later genealogies make him the son of Uther and nephew to Ambrosius Aurelianus. The latter figure we can attest from one of the few contemporary sources we have: Gildas, writing in the second quarter of the sixth century. Gildas does not mention Arthur and one interpretation is that it is Ambrosius, 'the last Roman', who leads the Britons to victory. It is possible that Roman civilian or military positions were still influential. Thus, Arthur could have held a military or civilian command. I leave this question open to the reader but as we go forward, perhaps we will be able to judge the most likely scenario.

One vital aspect to understand is how Roman Britain evolved into the patchwork of petty kingdoms of the seventh century. How did the Diocese of Britain, made up of five provinces and many *civitates*, fragment and the later kingdoms emerge? Was there an invasion of Germanic warriors destroying cities and pushing out the Britons? Or was there more assimilation of newcomers and continuation of the indigenous population? Was there a clear boundary between different political or cultural groups? Or was the situation more mixed and nuanced? This process was no doubt complex and inconsistent across time and geography. Britain in 450 may have been very different to 550. One might expect a boundary, if it existed, to move over time and some of the battle locations to be near any borders. Seven of the battles are located by rivers, which were often natural boundaries between polities. However, battles deep within one territory might indicate who was the aggressor.

In summary then, we find the evidence for King Arthur largely poor and it could be said the entire edifice of the tradition rests upon the veracity of the *Historia Brittonum*. The purpose of this book is not to prove whether Arthur was man or myth because the pros and cons of that have been covered in my previous book, and many others. It is unashamedly based on two assumptions:

firstly, Arthur was an historical figure and secondly, the battle list in the *Historia Brittonum* is genuine. I will attempt to make a case for the most likely location of Arthur's battles based on these assumptions. To aid this we will use archaeological evidence and historical sources to try to place Arthur, and his battles, in the political, cultural, and military context. As a bare minimum, I hope to indicate parts of the country which are least likely areas for Arthur's activities. It will focus on the battles in the *Historia Brittonum* although other sources will be covered. This book will focus on three broad hypotheses:

1. There is a reasonable amount of evidence to estimate the political, cultural and military situation. From this we can attempt to draw the border or partition that Gildas alluded to and the later emerging kingdoms imply.
2. Despite claims to the contrary, some of the battles can, at least, be located on the balance of probabilities.
3. These locations will make sense in the context of the political and military situation, and the archaeological and literary evidence. They will more likely be on or near boundaries or borders within the fragmenting political situation.

We will begin with a brief look at the historical events leading up to the period in which Arthur fought. The archaeological evidence and literary sources will be investigated to aid our understanding of the nature of Germanic migration and change from *civitas* to kingdoms. The chapter on timelines will attempt to reconcile the discrepancies, both in the literary sources and the archaeological record. We will delve deeply into weapons, warfare and contemporary accounts to give a flavour of fifth- and sixth-century battles. We will then address the battle list and likely candidates. The final chapter will evaluate and discuss the evidence.

Chapter 1

Roman Britain

In order to understand Britain at the time Arthur fought his battles, we need to have a clear picture of what the political and military situation was at the end of Roman Britain. It is only with hindsight that many historians date the end to AD 410 citing the *Rescript of Honorius*, which rejected the Britons' pleas for aid. One could legitimately date it to 407 when Constantine III left for Gaul with much of the remaining troops. Alternatively, it could be as late as the 440s when an apparent appeal to the Roman Aetius was similarly rejected. For our purposes this chapter will take us up to the middle of the fifth century. Chapter 2 will cover the *Gallic Chronicle* of 452 and its entry for 440 that states: 'The Britains, which to this time had suffered from various disasters and misfortunes, are reduced to the power of the Saxons.'[1] It will also cover events recorded by Gildas, writing a hundred years later, and Bede, who points to 449 as the key date. It is possible either the *Gallic Chronicle*, Bede or Gildas are mistaken. They might be referring to different events, something we will look at in more detail later.

Julius Caesar invaded Britain twice, the first time in 55 BC and the second, a year later. But it wasn't until AD 43 when the Emperor Claudius returned and gained a large part of the island. The Romans were confronted with a patchwork of tribes ranging from friendly to hostile. In the 350 years that followed, some of these tribal areas formed the basis of *civitates* and over thirty towns and cities grew within a provincial structure. Care must be taken in assuming a direct continuity from pre-Roman kingdoms to later *civitates* and even later fifth-century kingdoms.[2] Nevertheless, there are strong hints that some, such as the Iceni and Cantii, did just that. We don't know the extent to which tribal affiliation survived over that period. Some areas at least, such as Kent of the Cantii, seemed to survive as a political entity well into the Anglo-Saxon period. Indeed, we still see echoes of this past in some of the names of our counties today. The basic building-block of the empire was the *civitas*. This is important to remember as it became a particularly important 'socio-political unit' in the fifth century and formed a significant layer of Roman identity.[3]

As Roman influence extended beyond the first century, two walls were built in the far north. The first, in AD 122, was Hadrian's Wall which took six years to complete.[4] Fronted by a ditch, it was 73 miles long, 10ft wide and 12–15ft high. To the rear was an earthwork, the Vallum, that measured 20ft wide and 10ft deep, with a 20-foot mound on each side. Every mile was marked with a castle and every five miles, a larger fort. Later it became part of the northern command under the *Dux Britanniarum*. The second was the Antonine Wall in AD 142 which took twelve years to construct. It was a shorter construction of turf at 39 miles long, 10ft high and 16ft wide. This was marked with a fort every two miles: nineteen in total. Abandoned in AD 162, it was briefly reoccupied at the end of the second century. However, Roman influence retreated back to the earlier line. As we shall see, Gildas, writing in the sixth century, misdates these walls to the early fifth century, demonstrating his lack of sources and knowledge.

In the first century the Greek geographer Strabo describes the Britons importing ivory, chains, necklaces, amber, glassware and other 'trinkets'. Exports included grain, cattle, hunting dogs, slaves, gold, silver and iron. The changes over the centuries could be summarised as follows:[5] the first and second centuries were marked by enormous increases in economic activity, levels of imports and access to trade routes. Coinage was in greatest abundance in the third and fourth centuries, but this was affected by debasement and inflation. Another important change was the Edict of Caracalla in AD 212, which gave full Roman citizenship to free men in the Roman Empire, and free women the same rights as Roman women. A hundred years later, Constantine the Great had united the empire and made Christianity the official state religion. An extensive road network of over 3,000 miles connected urban centres. The picture is one of a heavily 'romanised' south, alongside the less-developed areas of the far north and west. These two points are important. We shall see that nearly all medieval battles in England were fought close to surviving Roman roads.[6] Secondly, the more romanised south-east contains the greatest evidence of early Germanic material culture and settlement.

Ptolemy, writing in the second century, laid out the main tribal areas. He makes two possibly important points to be noted. Firstly, Londinium was part of the Cantii although there is no other evidence their territory extended north of the Thames. Secondly, the Belgae had two main towns: Venta Belgarum (Winchester) and Aquae Calidae, which is assumed to be Aquae Sulis (Bath). There is a similarly named town in modern-day Bulgaria that was also home to Roman baths. In addition to this, Caesar, writing in the first century BC in his *Gallic Wars*, describes previous immigration from a Belgic tribe with indications that he regarded both the Atrebates and Belgae as Belgic.[7] There are also hints that he viewed the Belgae as more Germanic than Celtic. This could be significant when we see evidence of languages spoken and the possible etymology of Badon.

The Regni are positioned along the south coast between the River Meon to the west of their capital at Chichester to Pevensey in the east, with the Weald separating them from the Cantii. One of the largest tribal areas was the Catuvellauni, comprising most of Hertfordshire, Bedfordshire, Buckinghamshire, Oxfordshire, Cambridgeshire and Northamptonshire. It is difficult to know exactly where the provincial boundaries were. However, we have two clues that might suggest the Catuvellauni were part of Maxima Caesariensis. Their capital was at Verulamium (St Albans), only 25 miles to the north-west of Londinium. Germanus of Auxerre had no difficulty visiting the shrine of St Alban there in AD 429. Gildas, writing a hundred years later, claimed the grave was inaccessible in his day. Secondly, in the *Historia Brittonum*, it is claimed after Hengest massacres the Britons at a peace conference and captures Vortigern, he forces him to cede Essex, Sussex, Middlesex and other regions. Given he already has Kent according to the *Historia*, this sounds very much like the entire south-eastern province.

Another interesting fact is that there appeared to be pre-Roman links between the Corieltauvi in Lincolnshire and the East Midlands, and the Parisi, north of the Humber.[8] We will find that the earliest Anglo-Saxon settlements, in what became Deira, may have been part of an expansion from south of the Humber. Indeed, further north, the name Lindisfarne may well have an etymology similar to Linnuis, which is considered to derive from Lindsey.

We don't know the exact boundaries or even the number of the *civitates* or provinces. Not a single document or source defines the provincial boundaries, let alone those of the *civitates*.[9] Our understanding of political structures, as well as boundaries, also remains poor.[10] By the early fourth century, Britain had been split into four provinces with a fifth added after AD 367. A common version for the location of the provinces is shown below.[11] It is worth noting that some sources place Flavia Caesariensis and Britannia Secunda the other way round.[12] For our purposes, we will stick with the following, as shown in Map 1:

- Britannia Prima covered the West Country and modern-day Wales with the provincial capital at Cirencester.
- Flavia Caesariensis covered the Midlands and Lincolnshire, the capital at Leicester and, possibly later, Lincoln.
- Britannia Secunda covered north of this line up to Hadrian's Wall with the capital at York.
- Maxima Caesariensis covered the south-east and East Anglia, with London being both the capital of the province and the Diocese.
- Valentia referred to the renaming of part of a province or a new province (regained from earlier centuries), north of Hadrian's Wall, after AD 367.

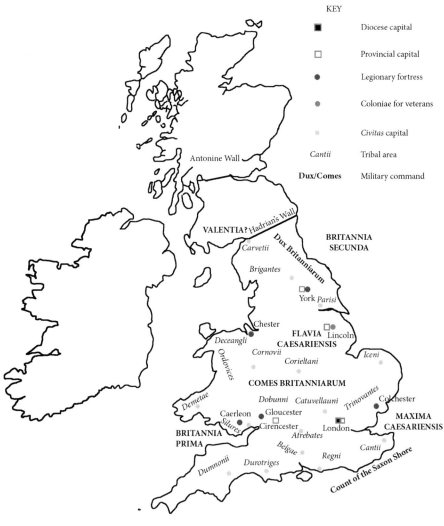

KEY

■	Diocese capital
□	Provincial capital
●	Legionary fortress
●	Coloniae for veterans
●	*Civitas* capital
Cantii	Tribal area
Dux/Comes	Military command

Map 1: Roman Britain

Two provinces were headed by consuls: Maxima Caesariensis and Valentia. Three were headed by *Presidii*: Britannia Prima, Britannia Secunda and Flavia Caesariensis. All five were headed by the *Vicarius Britanniae* who ruled the Diocese of Britain under the Praetorian Prefect of the Gauls, based at Trier. Within each of the five provinces were several *civitates*, many likely to be similar to the pre-Roman tribal areas. Each also had at least one city or large town with its own administrative structure, often headed by *decurions*.

Numerous civilian posts were likely filled by indigenous Britons:[13] *decurions* on town councils, *aediles* responsible for public buildings and services, and *quaestors* in charge of finance and magistrates. A town senate, *ordo*, consisted of up to 100 representatives from the local community. Late Roman army commands included *tribunes, praefectus* and *protectors*. This required a continuation of a civilian authority and a taxation system that paid for it. Indeed, it has been suggested the growth of urban centres and collection of taxes are inextricably linked.[14]

It is worth noting at this point how urbanisation is defined.[15] Aside from the presence of a significant population, it involves activities other than food procurement such as a hub for trade and a centre for civilian and military control. One of the most significant factors is its transformational effect on the surrounding rural countryside. This influence could be vital when we later consider the breakdown of both the tax system and urban life at the end of Roman Britain.

Later, we will see that in terms of material culture and cultural identity in the fifth and sixth centuries, it is possible to view Britain split into four zones[16] with some similarities to these earlier provinces. Zone one in the north was influenced by the fragmenting military command. Zone two, north of Hadrian's Wall, was possibly linked to the emerging Brittonic kingdoms of Gododdin, Rheged and Strathclyde. Zone three corresponds roughly to Britannia Prima. This area is marked with reoccupation of hill forts, continuation of trade links with the Mediterranean, and Brittonic language. The last zone to the south and east of the Fosse Way (the Roman road from Exeter to Lincoln) was marked by the more extensive romanisation, prevalence of Latin and larger scale of Germanic immigration. This could be crucial in considering how the provincial structure fragmented and in what political, social and military context Arthur operated. The provinces in Roman Britain were split into *civitates*, which as stated, appear to have been based on tribal areas. There were also four *coloniae* formed by ex-legionnaires: Colchester, Gloucester, Lincoln and York.

Regarding the military structure, the rank of *Magister Militum* was created in the fourth century and took over the military functions of the Praetorian Prefect; both were based in Gaul. Within Britain there were three military commands:

- *Dux Britanniarum* controlled the *limitanei* (literally 'frontier troops') in the north, including Hadrian's Wall
- *Comes Litoris Saxonici per Britanniam* (Count of the Saxon Shore) also utilised the *limitanei* across the forts along the southern and eastern coast
- *Comes Britanniarum* controlled the main field army consisting of four infantry units and six cavalry units, suggesting a mobile force to combat raiders.

The first two reported to the *Comes Britanniarum* who, in turn, reported to the *Magister Militum* in Gaul. These provinces, *civitates* and military commands are important to remember when we consider Arthur's Britain approximately fifty to 150 years later. They clearly fragmented and some disappeared but to what extent, and when, is open to question. It is a vital point when considering any likely line of partition and possible battle sites, and also what sort of title or role Arthur held.

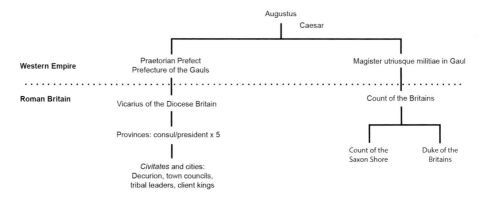

Administrative organisation of the late Western Roman Empire

Prior to the fourth century, Britain had broken away or rebelled several times from the empire. Diocletian's reforms created the tetrarchy which split power between east and west with each Augustus assisted by a *Caesar*. In AD 306 Constantine I was declared Emperor at York and after much bloodshed, he united the empire and made Christianity the official religion. After his death in 337, the empire returned to political division and civil war involving the sons of Constantine. Table 1 lists some notable events in relation to Britain within the empire.

Table 1: Roman Britain AD 43–350

Year (AD)	Event
43	Invasion under Emperor Claudius
c.60	Boudica revolt
84	Agrippa defeats the Caledonians at the Battle of Mons Graupius in northern Scotland
122–128	Hadrian's Wall constructed
142–154	Antonine Wall built
155–157	Brigantes revolt
c.164	Antonine Wall abandoned; frontier withdrawn to Hadrian's Wall
175	5,500 Sarmatian cavalry deployed to northern Britain
180	Cassio Dio records Picts breached Hadrian's Wall and a senior officer or governor was killed

Year (AD)	Event
c.184	Revolt of army in Britain; usurper governor elected; the future Emperor Pertinax sent to Britain and attacked by troops
195	Governor Clodius Albinus declared Emperor and crossed to Gaul; defeated by Emperor Aurelian
207–209	Barbarians invade northern Britain; war against Maeatae tribe of southern Scotland; Emperor Severus invades Caledonia
c.210	Britain divided into two provinces: Britannia Superior and Inferior
212	The Edict of Caracalla gives free men in the Roman Empire full Roman citizenship and free women the same rights as Roman women
259–274	Independent Gallic Empire including Britain, Gaul and Spain survives until retaken by Emperor Aurelian
c.280	Attempted uprising by British governor put down by Vandal and Burgundian troops
286–293	Rebellion of Carausius, commander of Britannic fleet, who controlled Britain and northern Gaul until killed by Allectus, his finance minister
293–296	Allectus usurps control in Britain
296	Junior Emperor Constantius Chlorus invades, defeats and kills Allectus; Britain divided into four provinces: Britannia Prima, Britannia Secunda, Maxima Caesariensis and Flavia Caesariensis
284–305	Reign of Diocletian; c.293 tetrarchy created, in which two *Augusti* would rule east and west, each with a co-emperor or *Caesar*; c.303–312 Diocletian persecution directed at Christians
306	Emperor Constantius campaigns in northern Britain but dies at York; Constantine I declared Emperor
313	Edict of Milan allows Christianity
324	Constantine becomes sole ruler after civil war; Christianity is made official state religion; created *praetorian prefectures* as the largest administrative division of late empire; *Praetorian Prefects'* military duties given to *Magister Peditum* and *Magister Equitum*
337	Death of Constantine I

Roman Britain 350–c.410

After Constantine's death in 337, instability soon returned which resulted in Magnentius having Emperor Constans murdered and seizing Britain, Gaul and Spain. Part of his appeal was his apparent tolerance of both Christians and pagans. Magnentius was defeated by Constantius II who ruled until 361. One of the first things Constantius did was send an imperial notary, Paulus Catena, to root out supporters of Magnentius. Known for his cruelty, Paulus was soon arresting people with no evidence. The *Vicarius* of Britain, Flavius Martinus, attempted to intervene to stop the injustices but was accused of treason by

Paulus. Martinus attacked him with a sword and, having failed to kill him, committed suicide. The Roman historian Ammianus describes the cruelty and how, in a later rebellion in Gaul, Paulus tortured and killed people before being burned alive during the reign of Julian the Apostate. Julian restored polytheism as the state religion although Christianity was restored after his death by Jovian.

Despite these upheavals, by 350, most inhabitants of the Western Empire, including Britain, had a sense of Roman identity.[17] Britain, in particular, was viewed as a 'prosperous diocese' economically[18] and overall 'very wealthy'.[19] There is evidence of maintenance and new construction within towns up to the mid-fourth century.[20] In addition, there is strong evidence of a 'substantial urban population'[21] although the bulk of the population, around ninety per cent, remained rural.[22] Yet within a generation, the towns became poorer and politically weaker.[23] The apparent continuation of villa-building might be a sign of a shift of political power from the city to country estates. On the other hand, many of the most luxurious and largest villas were built in this time.[24] It was the 'heyday of Romano-British villas' within a 'wealth producing agricultural economy.'[25] Both small and medium-sized villas were also very common alongside their more illustrious examples.[26] This seems to suggest the shift of power away from urban areas was already under way by the end of the fourth century.

At the same time, trade with the continent declined. For example, the domestic pottery industry, extensive in the fourth century, appears to have collapsed in the fifth. Towns were already stagnating or decaying by the late fourth century. Yet villa estates evolved and improved, as did agricultural production, especially grain. Indeed, in the 360s, the Emperor Julian ordered 600 grain ships from Britain to supply troops on the Rhine. Map 2 illustrates where the bulk of villas were located. This area is roughly to the south and east of a line from Exeter to York,[27] and this distinction persisted after the end of Roman Britain.[28] While there are isolated examples outside this zone, it is interesting to note it resembles later evidence for early Germanic settlers. It is also worth noting the relative absence of villas in the sparsely populated fenland of Eastern England and the Weald in Kent. The population of Roman Britain has been estimated at between three and four million,[29] most of which would have lived outside towns and villas and worked on the land.

Roman Britain had been through many upheavals, rebellions, civil wars and barbarian raids. These may be significant as some of our later sources mention three such major incursions as a prelude to events that lead to Badon. However, it is not clear if these raids reference ones we know about, from before 410, or as yet unconfirmed events from after that time. Picts and Scots raided Britain in 360 and four years later, they were joined by Saxons and Attacotti (the latter was possibly a north-western British tribe). In 367 a major incursion from multiple

Map 2: Major concentration of Roman villas in Britain

tribes became known as 'the barbarian conspiracy' and was said to have included Irish, Picts, Scots and Germanic tribes. Some blame for the upheaval was placed on the *arcani*, Roman spies posted in northern Britain, who sided with the barbarians.[30] Not only was the northern frontier overrun but Fullofaudes, the *Dux Britanniarum*, and Nectaridus, the *Comes maritime tractus* (possibly synonymous with the later *Comes Litoris Saxonici*), appear to have been killed.[31] Alternative explanations of an internal insurrection or exaggerated episode have not gained wide support.[32]

Valentinian I reigned from 364 to 375 and made his brother Valens co-emperor in the east. In 367 the Comes Theodosius was sent to Britain to restore order and the defences of the Diocese. After the campaign, the fifth province of Valentia was created although its location is uncertain. It may have been named for the recovery of a breakaway province or *civitas*.[33] Theodosius was named as *Comes Britanniarum* and his son, Theodosius I, went on to become the last Emperor to rule both east and west.

Further raids by the Picts occurred in 382 and 398, the former of which was subdued by Magnus Maximus. We don't know what post he held but it is possible he was the *Dux* or *Comes Britanniarum*.[34] The last raid we know about occurred in 408, twenty years after the death of Maximus, and is attributed to the Saxons. The year before, Britons are said to have revolted again and appointed three different leaders, ending with Constantine who took most of the remaining army into Gaul. The incursion of 408 and British rebellion may be connected. Their request for help to the Western Emperor in 410 was denied and this date is often viewed retrospectively as the end of Roman Britain.

It was during the reign of Theodosius I (379–395) that Magnus Maximus was declared Emperor in Britain in 383. He crossed into Gaul, taking much of the British garrison with him before being killed in 388. Many of our later sources mention Maximus, and Welsh legends know him as Mascen Wledig. He appears in various genealogies and tales, and is cited by Geoffrey of Monmouth writing in the twelfth century as settling Armorica (modern-day Brittany) with his troops. The founder of the kings of Armorica, Conan Meriadoc, is, according to Geoffrey, the ancestor of Arthur. Needless to say, there is no proof for any of this.

After Theodosius died in 395, he was succeeded by his two sons: Arcadius in the east and Honorius in the west. It was during the reign of Honorius that we get to what is essentially the beginning of the period we are interested in when trying to locate Arthur. The empire was already home to a number of Germanic tribes: the Franks in Gaul and the Goths in the East. In around 400 the *bacaudae*, provincial rebels (a more detailed description of which will follow later), emerged in Gaul. Honorius had sent General Stilicho to deal with another barbarian incursion into Britain in around 398. By 402 Stilicho had pulled troops, and much of the coinage, away from Britain and northern Gaul to deal with the Visigoth threat and the general unrest and rebellions.

In the winter of 406, multiple tribes poured across the Rhine into a relatively undefended northern Gaul. Vandals, Burgundians, Alemanni, Alans, Saxons and Gepids all threatened the Western Empire, including Britain. It was this incursion and Stilicho's apparent abandonment that caused the Britons to rebel, appointing three different leaders in quick succession. Three contemporary sources – Orosius, Olympiodorus and Sozomen – describe the following events. In Britain, the soldiers rebelled. First, they 'proclaimed' Mark but slew him. Gratian followed after this but Sozomen tells us within four months, he, too, was killed. Finally, Orosius (writing in c.417) tells us Constantine, 'a man of the lowest military rank, on account of the hope alone which came from his name and without any merit for courage, was elected.' Once elected, Constantine crossed over to Gaul with his forces and became 'master of Gaul as far as the Alps'.[35]

Initially, Honorius had little choice but to accept Constantine as co-emperor. Shortly after Constantine left for Gaul, the *Gallic Chronicle* of 452 recorded Britain as being 'devastated by an incursion of the Saxons'[36] in the year 409. With most of the army gone and Saxons attacking the country, the Britons rebelled again, this time against Constantine, and requested help directly from Honorius in 410. Zosimus, writing in around 500, records the Britons expelled the Roman civilian administration. But what does this mean? Were they replaced or removed altogether? Did the Diocese retain its political integrity? Did tribal loyalties survive 350 years of Roman rule and was there a push for independence? Did the military structure survive? How many troops were left to defend Britain? Did the provincial structure survive? Zosimus records the events as follows:[37] the barbarian assaults caused 'Britain and some of the Celtic peoples to defect from the Roman rule... independent from the Roman laws.' The Britons freed their cities from the barbarian threat and, interestingly, together with 'all Armorica and the other Gallic provinces' expelled Roman officials and set up a constitution 'as they pleased.' Zosimus blames the assaults squarely on Constantius and his 'carelessness in administration'.

The Emperor Honorius, based at Ravenna, had enough trouble fighting against Alaric, King of the Visigoths. Unable to help, he issued what is known as the *Rescript of Honorius*. Interestingly, the reply was to the *civitates*, and not to the provinces, to look to their own defences. The provincial apparatus may have broken down or could not be trusted, either by Honorius or the British *civitates*. That same year, Alaric sacked Rome and a year later, Constantine was killed. The famous *Rescript of Honorius* is much debated. It is possible the extract from Zosimus, writing about a hundred years after the events, refers to Bruttium in Italy.[38] Sozomen, writing in 439, records that after Constantine's defeat, the province returned its 'allegiance to Honorius'. Sozomen is likely referring to Gaul and makes no mention of Britain at this point. This is rather academic as Procopius, writing in 540 records: 'However the Romans never succeeded in recovering Britain, but it remained from that time on under tyrants.'[39]

The *Notitia Dignitatum* (List of Offices) records the civilian and military administrative organisation of the Western and Eastern Empires. Its date and accuracy is disputed but a date of AD 425[40] has been suggested, which would be important if we could be sure the entries reflected reality. Unfortunately, it is likely it is an early fifth-century copy of an earlier document that itself was depicting an ideal, rather than reality on the ground.[41] The original was a working document and the copy was out of date when it was completed.

It is estimated that, by the end of the fourth century, the army had dropped to between 12,000 and 20,000 men compared to a force of perhaps 50,000 in the second century.[42] In fact, one estimate places the army size as low as 6,000 by the year 400.[43] We must remember this is before Constantine crossed over to Gaul with a sizeable force. We should consider the likely military situation and how that may have evolved by Arthur's time, fifty to over 100 years later.

The coin supply had probably already stopped by around 402 when General Stilicho had taken some of the army units back to Gaul after suppressing an incursion in 398. The last mint had been closed in the time of Magnus Maximus (383–388), and no new coins appear to have been shipped to Britain after 402.[44] The main purpose of these shipments was the payment of soldiers. Low-value coins appear to have fallen out of circulation around 410–430, suggesting higher value coins followed c.450–470.[45] Constantine's further removal of troops, together with the subsequent barbarian incursions into Gaul and Britain, would have exacerbated an already significant problem. This would not, of course, mean that money ceased to be available, but the evidence does suggest the economic cycle and parts of Roman life were severely impacted.[46]

Table 2 details the major raids, rebellions and events in Roman Britain. Yet it remained relatively prosperous, despite frequent raids and political upheaval. It had gone through many periods of rebellion and insurrection, and there had been many examples of someone from Britain declaring themselves Emperor and seizing power. What seems likely is most people in Britain still had a sense of Roman identity, something we will return to later. Someone standing in Britain, Gaul or the western capital at Ravenna in AD 410 may have considered Britain's apparent independence a temporary situation.

Table 2: Timeline AD 350–410

Year	Britain	Roman Empire
350	Magnentius usurps power in Britain, Gaul and Spain	
353	Magnentius killed	
360	Raiding by Picts and Scots (Irish)	
364	Constant raids by Picts, Scots, Saxons and Attacotti	
367	The 'Barbarian Conspiracy' involving Attacotti, Scots and Saxons caused widespread destruction	General Theodosius sent to restore order
378		Romans defeated by the Goths at Adrianople; Emperor Valens killed.
379		Reign of Theodosius I begins
382	Raids by Picts subdued by Magnus Maximus	

Year	Britain	Roman Empire
383	Magnus Maximus declared Emperor in Britain; leaves with much of the army	Maximus invades Gaul and secures most of Western Empire; Emperor Gratian killed
388		Maximus executed after the Battle of Aquileia
395		Theodosius dies and is succeeded by his sons: Honorius in the west and Arcadius in the east
395–6		Goths led by Alaric rebel in the east and plunder Greece
398	Raids by Picts subdued by General Stilicho	
401		Alaric moves into Western Empire
402	Stilicho returns to Gaul with much of coin supply; no further supplies of coinage or mints recorded after this date	Alaric invades Italy
c.406	Succession of three emperors declared in Britain; the last, Constantine III, invades Gaul, taking much of the army	Various Germanic tribes cross the Rhine into Gaul; Alaric is made 'Master of Soldiers'
408		Stilicho agrees to pay Alaric but is arrested and executed by Honorius; Alaric invades Italy
409	Britain devastated by Saxon raids	Alaric lays siege to Rome
410	Britain rebels against Constantine III; sends appeal to Honorius who rejects it, telling them to look to their own defences	Alaric and the Goths sack Rome
411	'Romans never succeeded in recovering Britain' (Procopius)	Constantine III is defeated by General Constantius and killed

Chapter 2

Post-Roman Britain AD 410–450

Evidence suggests the end of the coin supply and Roman governance after the year 400 severely disrupted the economic cycle, and parts of Roman life failed suddenly and irrevocably.[1] One view is that this caused a collapse in the infrastructure of Roman Britain that was more sudden and more complete than elsewhere in the Western Empire.[2] Given the discrepancy between the 'plentiful and varied' fourth-century evidence and the dearth of later finds, the end of Roman Britain has been described as a 'mass extinction' in terms of archaeological material.[3] The question is, does this reflect historical reality?

James Gerrard in *The Ruin of Roman Britain* offers three possibilities: a systemic shock; 'slide and bump'; and a soft landing.[4] On the one hand, there was an unparalleled economic collapse seen nowhere else in the Western Empire, other than northern Gaul. Coin use, pottery and other imported luxury items declined. With taxation ceasing, urban centres deteriorated and the general fragmentation was accelerated by plague, famine and war. On the other hand, the removal of the tax burden and need to produce a grain surplus improved the lives of the general population, although it was a significant economic readjustment. The bulk of production was local and agricultural, and the 'over fixation' on visible finds skews the evidence.[5]

Towns and villas seem to have prospered more in Gaul compared to Britain in the fifth century.[6] Indeed, some have stated town life in Britain did not survive past 430.[7] Others accept that life in towns continued even if 'town life' did not.[8] Halsall argues that villas appeared to be abandoned in the early fifth century and urban life ended around the same time.[9] A layer of dark earth at many sites suggest villas and towns were transformed into small agricultural settlements.

Gildas, writing in the sixth century, implied towns were 'much reduced' but not completely abandoned. The *Anglo-Saxon Chronicle* records the towns of Gloucester, Cirencester and Bath being captured in 577 after the Battle of Dyrham, also suggesting some continuation of urban centres. Roman buildings appeared to go through a change in function in the generations either side of 400. For example, villas appear to have changed their function from elite private dwellings to become 'nodal points' of a more military nature. Metal working and grain driers appear where once dining areas and other high-status rooms and buildings existed.[10]

In the late fourth century, the security situation may have deteriorated. Some gates were deliberately blocked and projecting towers added to walls along with 'u'-shaped ditches, presumably as added defensive measures. The late fourth and early fifth centuries also produced a large number of hoards.[11] However, there is no evidence for widespread violent destruction. Also, the absence of Romano-British material in Northern Germany and Southern Scandinavia for this period suggests raiding from those areas at least was not a significant issue. With this mixed picture in mind, let us look at some of the evidence we do have for the major towns.

Towns

Pam Crabtree summarises the debate in her book *Early Medieval Britain: The Rebirth of Towns in the Post-Roman West*.[12] One view is that 'the principal towns of Roman Britain were deserted by the mid-fifth century, and remained so for at least a hundred years.' Alternatively, they 'retained a real presence and vitality in the landscape until the seventh century.' There is some evidence for surviving enclaves within areas otherwise surrounded by Anglo-Saxon finds at Lincoln, Silchester and Verulamium.[13] Lincoln shows the north gate being blocked and rubbish being dumped by the west gate in the late fourth century, which could suggest a breakdown of maintenance or governance. Some houses are abandoned and others reduced in use, contrasting with the evidence of villas in a 'prosperous part of Britain'.[14] Yet roads appear to have been kept clear into the early fifth century, although there's no evidence of occupation past the mid-fifth century.[15] However, Bede's reference to a *Praefectus Lindocolinae* in the eighth century might suggest some continuity between post-Roman and Anglo-Saxon Lincoln. We shall see further proof of continuation at Lincoln later and this may well be important when considering four of Arthur's battles 'in the region of the *Linnuis*', which is often taken as Lincolnshire.

Villas around Verulamium show a 'high level of prosperity' in the late fourth century[16] and a largely Christian community continuing in the fifth. St Germanus's visit in 429 adds further weight to this. Chichester in Sussex shows evidence of refurbishment in the later fourth century, which indicates a level of confidence for the future. There are signs of continuation into the early fifth, both in the town and at nearby Portchester Castle. However, there are also indications of decay, such as drains and roofs collapsing and not being repaired, although there are no signs of violent destruction.[17]

Silchester may be instructive as it shows evidence for the late presence of Roman military and coins dated 388–392, which are worn enough to suggest use well into the fifth century.[18] There is no evidence for early Anglo-Saxon settlement, despite extensive sites further north from Goring to Dorchester-on-Thames, which appears to be the heart of the later West Saxon expansion. Roads in other directions were maintained but not the one to the north. Dykes were built facing north although it's difficult to ascertain the date and reason. Nearby Winchester, the fifth largest town in Roman Britain, also shows signs for an early fifth-century Roman garrison with the south gate being blocked with a ditch and crude masonry wall.[19] In contrast, Crabtree argues its urban character did not last into the fifth century with town houses reduced to 'shanties'.[20] While it appears to have changed from an administrative to an industrial centre in the fourth century, Winchester ceased to exist as an urban entity early in the fifth century.

Interestingly, a line taken from Winchester north-east to Silchester would cut through modern-day Basingstoke and the village of Old Basing. This is one of the possible locations for the as-yet-unidentified River Bassus, the location of the sixth battle on Arthur's battle list. This line would also appear to be close to the boundary between the *civitates* of the Regni and Belgae. It could also be the boundary of the south-eastern province, Maxima Caesariensis. It is not an unlikely place for a battle as, at the same location, a Danish army defeated the West Saxons there in 871. On the other hand, we have no evidence of a river called Bassus in the area and any link to a Germanic tribe based on the Basingas is uncertain and not contemporary.

Cirencester shows decay alongside reduced but continued occupation into the fifth or even sixth century. To give some indication of population levels, it has been estimated here at between 8,000–12,000.[21] As this was the second largest city in Roman Britain, many of the others would have had much smaller populations. By the mid-fifth century, all the major buildings 'were in ruins'.[22] There is some indication that the amphitheatre was used for protection similar to other examples on the continent.[23] This could indicate some populations simply sought out the best defended parts of the former town. It is useful to speculate how many fighting men such a town could produce. If we take the lower figure of 8,000 due to the suspected general deterioration (and it could have been much less), then we might make the following calculation: half the population were male and half of those were children, leaving 2,000, of which half were likely to be of fighting age (roughly 1,000 men). But these were not warriors. They were the cohort from which a militia or warriors could be trained if they were willing, able and available. Should the town have been reduced to a population of, for example, a couple of thousand, then fighting-age men might have numbered in the low hundreds and a town militia drawn from that in the dozens. In such situations, a small force of well-armed and experienced warriors could prove decisive.

We will look at this in more depth in later chapters on the nature of warfare and likely size of armies of the time. The *Anglo-Saxon Chronicle* entry for 577 has Cuthwine and Caewlin capturing three towns – Gloucester, Bath and Cirencester – thus supporting the concept of continuation in some towns at least. Other examples, such as Dorchester in Dorset, show desertion rather than either continuation or any destruction.[24] Further west, Exeter shows maintained trade links with the Mediterranean[25] into the fifth century, as does Tintagel on the north coast of Cornwall.

Leicester shows a serious fire damaged much of the centre of the town in the late fourth century. The forum, basilica and market hall were all destroyed, yet none were rebuilt. Despite this, signs of occupation exist in the ruins.[26] Thus we get a picture from the middle of Britain that may be instructive. A general deterioration before the end of the fourth century exacerbated in the first half of the fifth, yet with some evidence of limited occupation. Other towns in the west such as Caerwent and Carmarthen show some continuation well into the fifth century.

Viroconium (Wroxeter) has the best evidence for continued use, although the rebuilding of the basilica appears to have been in timber rather than stone. A tombstone dating to the late fifth century suggests the presence of an Irish chieftain named Cunorix.[27] Further finds imply that Viroconium was a power base right through the time we are interested in, although Halsall states he 'expects more' from an urban site.[28] Similarly at Birdoswald Fort on Hadrian's Wall, disintegration of the masonry structure was followed by the building of two timber halls. Crabtree suggests Wroxeter may be the 'exception that proves the rule.'[29] Many fifth-century towns in Gaul became fortified centres for bishoprics and maintained some urban functions.[30] The suggestion is that in the west and north, the largely Christianised population still had a functioning church structure. Indeed, this is exactly what St Augustine finds when he arrives in Britain in the late sixth century. It is possible, therefore, that Wroxeter was the centre of a bishopric.

At York, there are signs of Alemmanic troops or civilians as early as the fourth century; in the fifth century, the legionary fortress was still occupied although evidence for survival of the town is lacking.[31] Brough-on Humber and Aldborough are similar to York in that they show a decline in maintenance even before the end of the fourth century, along with reduced occupation.

At York, evidence of a defensive ditch inside the eastern wall could indicate part of the fortifications being utilised.[32] While there is solid evidence of continuation in Britain outside urban areas, there are few signs of exploitation of Roman infrastructure by the Anglo-Saxons.[33] For example, excavations under York Minster show no activity from the fourth to the seventh century. A number of Anglian settlements and burial sites appear from the mid-sixth century such as Heslington. However, there is no evidence of structural continuation from the early fifth century.[34]

This could be significant in terms of Arthur. Geoffrey of Monmouth claims not only battles at York, but also that Ambrosius takes up residence in the city after the defeat of Hengest. This seems very unlikely given the evidence. Some theorists suggest the survival of the northern military command headed by the *Dux Britanniarum* headquartered at York. It would seem from this evidence that any surviving remnants of a military force abandoned York and either fragmented into different war-bands or were reduced to a smaller area, perhaps one centred on Hadrian's Wall.

We are left to wonder what to make of the *Anglo-Saxon Chronicle* entry for 418: 'The Romans hid their treasures in the earth.' We certainly have an increase of major treasure hoards all over Britain.[35] Some appear to be hack-silver which could suggest looted treasure from raids, although St Germanus in 429 seems to have found Britain to be reasonably stable and prosperous. The rural fabric of late Roman Britain appears to have survived into the fifth century, as did some towns and trade links.[36] Late Roman weights and measures were still used in the sixth century.[37]

Yet every significant Roman settlement of note saw deterioration in post-Roman Britain.[38] Where there was continued occupation, people appear to have been unwilling or unable to maintain the towns to previous standards. The supporting structure and services, resources and personnel were no longer available. In the early fifth century, the use of villas declined with gardens turned over to agriculture and a drastic reduction in maintenance and repairs. The last phase of occupation in many villas appears to be 'squatter occupation' of people living in ruined or semi-derelict buildings.[39] There is, however, no evidence for occupation of villas by Anglo-Saxons or any other 'barbarian' invaders.[40]

What, then, of the largest city in Roman Britain, Londinium? The archaeological record suggests London was deserted by 500 and not reoccupied until Alfred the Great in 886. Crabtree goes further and states London was abandoned soon after c.410.[41] No evidence of Anglo-Saxons has been found within the city walls for the fifth century.[42] Following the Battle of Crecganford in 457, the *Anglo-Saxon Chronicle* claims the Britons 'forsook the land of Kent and fled to their stronghold at London.' We do have some evidence of continued Romano-British activity within London up to the year 450, as well as Anglo-Saxon settlements outside and around London after that date.[43] Lundenwic grew up a mile to the west of the city walls. Links between the Diocese and the church in Rome appear to have continued into the mid-fifth century. The British church was using the Easter dates computed in the time of Pope Leo around 454, suggesting these links continued until then. However, later changes do not appear to have got through, suggesting that contact was lost some time after this.[44] After c.454, the British church appears to evolve distinct and separate from the continent. There is therefore nothing unreasonable about the *Anglo-Saxon Chronicle* entry for 457. The next we hear of London is that a bishopric was established in 604 and Bede describing it as an important market.[45]

In general, the archaeological record appears to suggest a decline of town life prior to the end of the fourth century. The apparent ending of the coin supply coincides with a significant impact on economic activity. This seems to accelerate into the fifth century and some towns are at least partly abandoned. Evidence for 'urban functioning' declines rapidly and one view is that Roman towns had lost most of their populations by the first decades of the fifth century.[46] However, the picture is more nuanced and some researchers describe late Roman Britain as 'a very wealthy Diocese'[47] and that a substantial urban population remained, despite a reduction in town life.[48] Communication links certainly still existed, especially within the church. The visit of St Germanus and the letter of appeal to Aetius support this. Prosper of Aquitaine considered Britain to still be a Roman island in the 430s.[49]

St Augustine's mission to Kent in 597 finds an established British church and that Christianity had survived on a 'considerable scale'.[50] Towns were the 'last bastions' of Romano-British civilisation and aside from treachery, famine or disease, fifth-century fortifications were 'more than a match' for barbarian raiders.[51] So it's unlikely fully functioning and populated towns could be destroyed on any great scale. Archaeological evidence concerning settlements, structures, burials and artefacts continue into the first third of the fifth century.[52] This concept of a 'collapsed state' may be relevant but it's debatable if Anglo-Saxons were the cause or exploited it.[53] Thus, it would seem that the infrastructure of Roman Britain, the economy and town life had all been much reduced prior to, and separate from, significant Germanic settlement.

Crabtree summarises the likely situation as follows:[54]

- Reduced activity continued in some Roman towns into the first half of the fifth century
- However, they lost their 'urban character' in the first decades of the fifth century
- The primary function of Roman towns was tax collection; the end of Roman administration, the tax system, collapse of the economy, and reduction in international trade and coinage caused the contraction of urban sites
- The resultant depopulation would take a generation or two.

We will now look at two of the three military commands controlled by the *Dux Britanniarum* in the north and the *Comes Litoris Saxonici* in the south.

Hadrian's Wall and the northern military frontier

Neither archaeology nor contemporary literary sources suggest Hadrian's Wall was abandoned at the end of the fourth century.[55] Several forts all show continuous occupations and activity well into the fifth century: South Shields, Vindolanda, Birdoswald, Carlisle and south of the wall at Binchester, Piercebridge and York.[56] In fact, Piercebridge on the River Tees shows the defences were used until the late sixth century.[57] There is evidence for a change in material culture in East Yorkshire in the mid-fifth century and this spreads through the eastern half of the wall in the sixth century.[58] So we have some evidence of Germanic presence, even if we lack significant Anglo-Saxon burials. Both the *Historia* and Geoffrey of Monmouth claim Hengest's son Octha was settled near the wall from Deira up to the border with the Picts. The archaeological record doesn't fully support that assertion. But absence of evidence isn't evidence of absence and the *Historia* also states that after Hengest's death, Octha came down from the north to Kent. If Germanic mercenaries were present, who or what drove them out? If there were no settlements or forces, how did Ida become the first king of Bernicia in 547?

With no evidence for the collapse of the northern frontier in the fifth century, we are left to consider how it may have evolved up to the time of Arthur.[59] At the beginning of the century, the garrison under the control of the *Dux Britanniarum* was likely separate from provincial and diocesan authority. It was, however, dependent on logistical needs being met in terms of resources, food, raw materials and coinage. A breakdown of this may have eventually led to fragmentation into local war-bands. Yet we appear to have a continuation of Romano-British control, certainly in the fifth century. Unfortunately, we have little evidence to confirm, date or even locate the early kingdoms that may have emerged.

The literary sources go further. The *Historia* describes how four British kings unite to push the Bernicians back to the Island of Lindisfarne as late as c.570. All this suggests the Brittonic kingdoms of Rheged, Alt Clut and Elmet, or their predecessors, were powerful polities at the time Arthur lived. The *Anglo-Saxon Chronicle* has Elmet being conquered as late as 616. The Gododdin in the Lothian area were strong enough to launch an attack against both Deira and the Bernicians in around 600 if the epic *Y Gododdin* is to be trusted. They didn't fall to the Angles until 638 after a siege at Edinburgh. We thus have a strong tradition for the survival of Brittonic authority in the north.

The border between the later kingdoms of Deira and Bernicia was traditionally at the Tees and we do see a marked difference in early Germanic presence either side of this line. There is evidence for an Anglo-Saxon presence just north of the

Humber, even though the name Deira has a Brittonic etymology and appears to cover the same area as the *civitas* of the Parisi. The forces would have consisted of the *limitanei* which were the border troops. In *Hadrian's Wall and the End of Empire*, Collins lays out four scenarios:[60]

- There remained an effective imperial garrison into the fifth century
- Major changes and decline in the fourth century left a skeleton force and the frontier became a military backwater
- Major changes in the fourth century left a more regional or localised force that remained effective
- Changes in the fourth century caused the frontier to evolve into local command/polities served by militia or barbarian *foederati*.

Of these four choices, the first two are deemed unlikely and the evidence points to a fragmentation of the northern command into local polities before the time of Arthur. This is at odds with the picture Geoffrey of Monmouth paints in

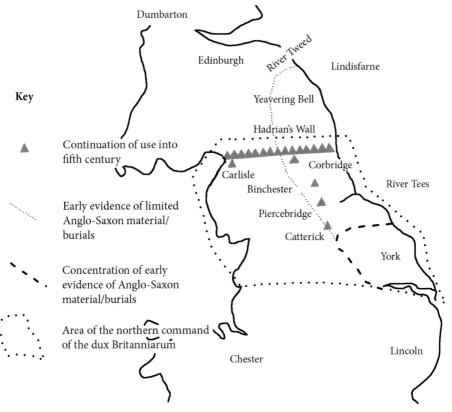

Map 3: Continued use of fifth-century northern command sites

the twelfth century of a king ruling a wide area. However, it is in line with the ninth-century *Historia* claim that Arthur fought with the kings of the Britons. Map 3 illustrates some of the sites that showed continuation. Evidence exists at other places, especially along Hadrian's Wall. Also added is a rough guide to early evidence of Anglo-Saxon material[61] and burials.[62]

South Deira has a concentration of such finds. This makes sense in the light of extensive early settlement in the Lindsey area south of the Humber expanding northwards. However, we also have finds in the north as far as the Tweed. Later, we will see unconfirmed literary evidence of Soemil, who is said to be the first to separate Deira from the Bernicia. In the genealogy tables, he is placed five generations before the first known king of Deira, Aelle, who reigned in the last quarter of the sixth century. Given Ida, the first king of Bernicia reigned in 547, Soemil could only have separated it from British control in perhaps around 500. Moreover, the five-generation gap would likely place him in the last quarter of the fifth century, exactly when Bede claims Ambrosius was active (in the time of Zeno 474–491) and possibly when Arthur fought his battles. We shall see that many of the likely suggestions for battles are in the north or Lincolnshire, which would be compatible with an expansion of Angle influence from Lincolnshire to north of the Humber. Indeed, many of the battle sites have suggestions as far north as Edinburgh and at least one is likely to be north of Hadrian's Wall.

Saxon Shore Command

During the third century, the Romans constructed a series of forts in the south-east, known as the Saxon Shore Forts (their positions are shown in Map 4). They formed part of a wider Gallic coastal system, including northern Gaul. Pearson, in *The Roman Shore Forts*,[63] emphasises the economic and social purposes. The Saxons were a minor and intermittent threat, especially in the third century when the forts were built. Indeed, nine out of the eleven forts were constructed two centuries before the fifth century and may be related to trade rather than defence. It is only through the early fifth-century *Notitia Dignitatum* that we see the phrase *Comes Litoris Saxonici per Britanniam* (Count of the Saxon Shore in Britain).

Some of the Saxon Shore Forts show early abandonment (Lympne, Reculver, Caister and Burgh), as do many of the Yorkshire signal stations.[64] Richborough in Kent may have been one of the last sites garrisoned by troops in late Roman Britain. Not only is it recorded as the base for the *Legio II Augusta* in the *Notitia Dignitatum* but a huge number of bronze coins (20,000) have been found, suggesting some fiscal function.[65] Of the Saxon Shore Forts, only Portchester in Hampshire shows occupation well into the fifth century and a later Saxon presence.

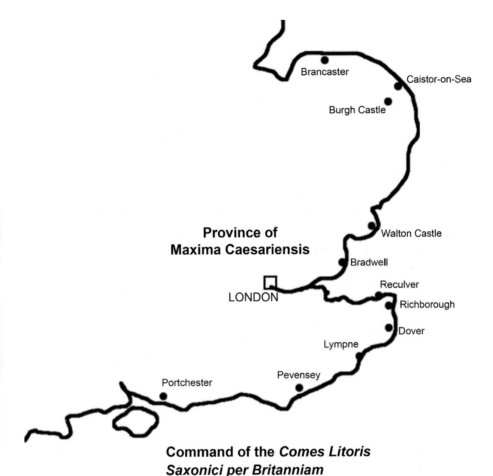

Command of the *Comes Litoris Saxonici per Britanniam*

Map 4: The Saxon Shore Forts

There have been suggestions that the Saxon Shore Forts may indicate Germanic *foederati* troops or immigrant settlements. Interestingly, there is no example of any Roman defensive system anywhere being named after an enemy.[66] Unfortunately, there is no evidence of Saxons being stationed there either. The title of the Southern coastal command, *Litoris Saxonici*, remains unexplained. The fact the title appears so late in Roman Britain suggests the presence, at least, of Saxons. We can tentatively suggest either Saxons were attacking, trading or settling the coast for the Romans to refer to it in that way. It follows that with no evidence of continued use, Portchester aside, there would be little in the early fifth century preventing an increase in Saxon settlement or raiding.

The *Gallic Chronicle* entry for 440 suggests any military command in the south-east was lost to the Britons, as well as the Romans, possibly through a political change in the province or wider Diocese. Alternatively, it could reflect a realignment or insurrection of the south-east province or shore command forts. The *Historia Brittonum* has an interesting point in its narrative. Vortigern is captured and forced to cede Essex, Sussex, Middlesex and other regions to Hengest, who already controlled Kent. This sounds remarkably like the entire south-eastern province of Maxima Caesariensis, which conceivably included the former Saxon Shore Command. Whether the Command extended into neighbouring provinces is unknown. The likely boundary near the River Meon at least suggests Portchester may have been in Britannia Prima and it's possible the province did not reach as far as Norfolk. This is worth remembering when we consider not only what forces Arthur may have commanded, but also where he fought his battles. The implication is clear. If any of the military commands survived in any form, it is unlikely the southern Saxon Shore Command was available to him. If it continued until the end of the fourth century, it was probably caught up in the events of the mid-fifth century. If it survived past that date, it was likely controlled by groups hostile to western or northern polities.

Rural life

The bulk of the population of post-Roman Britain remained rural, perhaps around ninety per cent.[67] In the fourth century, rural Britain had been 'booming' and a thriving villa culture still existed at the end of the century.[68] Additionally, the rural fabric of the Diocese survived into the fifth century.[69] The removal of the tax burden allowed the agricultural economy to transform. With the need for a grain surplus to supply the empire removed, conditions likely improved for some rural communities. They may well have changed production to less efficient but more localised pastoral activities. There is even evidence for an improvement in diet for the period, resulting in an increase in height across much of Western Europe of up to 3cm for men and 2cm for women.[70]

The more productive farming communities were in the south and east. However, the use of villas declined with gardens turned over to agriculture and a drastic reduction in maintenance and repairs. We then get the evidence mentioned previously for 'squatter occupation' in 'semi-derelict' buildings.[71] Yet there is also significant continuation of occupation and land use in rural areas across post-Roman Britain. Farming practices at West Stow in Suffolk appear to have continued into the Anglo-Saxon period.[72] Lincolnshire also has evidence of occupation from Roman through to the Anglo-Saxon period with Roman field systems lasting until the Middle Ages.[73] Interestingly, the population of the area appears to have remained stable and relatively high.

In general, farming practices in Roman Britain were more intensive compared to the early Anglo-Saxon period but field patterns were maintained.[74] Recent studies found a 'duality of continuity and change', and no widespread abandonment of agricultural land with two-thirds of sites showing maintenance of boundaries.[75] Rippon finds a 'substantial surviving native population' and high continuity of land use. However, he views direct continuity from tribal/*civitas*/petty kingdoms as 'unlikely'. What there is evidence for is community-based continuity within 'spheres of socio-economic interaction'. It may be that Roman Britain's coherence was 'constructed and imposed.'[76] Once removed the Diocese dissolved into local powers based around a people, warlord or mercenaries, or a location such as a villa, town or hill fort. Indeed, the literary sources from St Germanus, St Patrick and Gildas suggest a level of continuation of Roman culture and lifestyle.

In summary, the fifth-century landscape remained 'fully occupied and exploited' for both arable and pasture.[77] There continued a 'treeless central belt' in the fifth century stretching as far as the Vale of York up to the ninth century, which suggests significant continuation of occupation.[78] Romano-British settlements largely carried on as before, but were saved from the burden of taxation.

I will conclude with the following findings:[79]

- Relatively rare for fields to be abandoned
- Shift from high- to low-intensity forms of farming
- Villa sites remained centres of economic activity despite some buildings falling to ruin
- Stability of agriculture sector.

This should hardly be surprising. The former Diocese supported a relatively large population of low millions through two centuries of economic and political upheaval, war, pestilence and famine. At the end of the period, the island was stable and prosperous enough to support several emerging kingdoms of different cultural and political hues. There must have been sufficient agricultural production and economic activity to support it.

Hill forts

Hill forts were also reoccupied: South Cadbury, Crickley Hill near Gloucester[80] and other strongholds such as Tintagel and Cadbury-Congresbury too.[81] Yet it is difficult to ascertain by whom, and for what purpose, such places were occupied. Dinas Powys was occupied from the fifth century, fortified in the sixth and abandoned by around 700.[82] Reoccupied hill forts are a feature of fifth-century Britain in the south-west too, such as a stone enclosure at Trethurgy in Cornwall.[83] As far north as Dunadd hill fort, an important centre of power in Dal Riata, there is evidence of trade links with post-Roman Southern Europe.[84] We get similar evidence from Tintagel in Cornwall.

By the sixth century, settlements in the north and west were distinctive and often could be described as 'family forts' in a well-defended position such as a hill.[85] There was a clear distinction between the area north and west of a line from Tees to Exeter and the more romanised south-eastern areas.[86] Many locations show links to the Roman past.[87] There is also a striking amount of Mediterranean and continental imports.[88] This is in contrast to areas associated with Germanic material culture and settlements in the south and east. It suggests these areas had a break with Mediterranean trade and appear to have had stronger trade links with the North Sea coast.

The interesting point is that this practice of reoccupation of hill forts occurred in the less romanised and urbanised parts of Britain. Perhaps in these areas it was simply the easier option. Or maybe it reflects some cultural difference between east and west. Whatever the case, an Arthur operating from the north or west would have been aware of hill forts. Whether he defended or attacked one is open to question. But some of the later legends do indeed connect him to certain sites such as Cadbury or Tintagel. The battle at Castello Guinnion implies a Roman fort but Badon is described as a siege, so it could conceivably be a hill fort.

St Germanus

We do have three contemporary records that suggest some sort of continuity in the province. Firstly, Constantius of Lyon (born c.420) writing in 480 describes the visit of St Germanus of Auxerre in 429. His journey is in response to the Pelagian heresy. Pelagius, described as a British monk, favoured the concept of free will over that of original sin. Anti-Pelagian legislation appeared in 418 and Prosper of Aquitaine, writing in the mid-fifth century, records how Agricola, a Pelagian supporter, fled to Britain where it appeared to be safe for followers.[89] Prosper, writing in 455, then states the following:[90] 'at the persuasion of the deacon Palladius, Pope Celestine sent Germanus, bishop of Auxerre, as his representative, and having rejected the heretics, directed the British to the catholic faith.' He also mentions another deputation in 431, indicating the presence of Christianity in Ireland prior to St Patrick's later mission: 'Palladius was sent by Pope Celestine to the Scots who believed in Christ, and was ordained as their first bishop.' Latin writers often used the term 'Scots' to mean Irish, and that's certainly the case here.

Constantius, writing a generation or more after Prosper, tells of crowds welcoming Germanus and his winning of a debate with the apparently wealthy Pelagians. This suggests a religious schism between the aristocracy and the bulk of the population. Three notable events then occur.

He cures the blind daughter of a tribune, suggesting a continuation of Roman administrative or military structures. He visits the shrine at St Albans, implying that travel in this area was still viable. There then follows an incursion of Saxons and Picts, and the army requests help from Germanus. On arrival, he baptises many of the soldiers and appoints himself *Dux Proelii* (leader for battle), which has echoes of Arthur being labelled *dux bellorum* (leader of war) in the *Historia Brittonum*. Germanus is able to win the battle without bloodshed by hiding and shouting 'Alleluia' repeatedly, scaring the enemy, many of whom drowned in a river. The 'most wealthy island' now secure, Germanus returns to Gaul.

It's worth briefly looking at some of the details of this battle as reported.[91] Rather than show the 'worthlessness' of the Britons as Gildas would have it, they had already marched out, located the enemy and were in camp when Germanus was sent for. What form this camp took is unstated but it is at least possible some vestige of Roman practices survived. The request came from their apprehension of the numbers rather than being panic-stricken or cowardly.

The raid perhaps consisted of a couple of hundred warriors, although this is speculative. Germanus, apparently some distance away, arrives and preaches daily before taking command. Perhaps a week or more has passed. The barbarians learn of the Britons' location and advance to attack. But the Britons once again show 'decisive superiority in reconnaissance' and lay an ambush. Germanus leads lightly-armed men across country, presumably leaving the bulk of the heavy infantry behind. They then successfully ambush the raiders. One is left to wonder why the retreating enemy were not pursued. What is clear is that the Britons were organised, able, confident and willing to take the initiative with or without Germanus. At the very least, we have a near contemporary account of some sort of organised military force still in existence.

The heresy returns and this time, Germanus is able to banish the heretics. Three different years have been suggested for this second visit: 437, 442 or 448. We know he visited Armorica to settle a dispute around 436 and that he passed through Vienne during the pontificate of Pascentius, who died before 441. Thus, despite some sources accepting the later dates, the earlier one is the most likely and supported by the events in Gaul at the time.[92] This is especially so given the *Gallic Chronicle* entry for 440, which would have likely impacted Germanus's activities yet it is not mentioned. Some more recent studies agree with this position.[93] Alternatively, if he did witness such events, this could be where the *Gallic Chronicle* author received his information. Perhaps tellingly, Constantius, writing in around 480, claimed by the end of the visit this 'opulent island' was secure and peaceful.[94] The visits of Germanus suggests a number of things:

- Britain in the first half of the fifth century was reasonably stable enough to travel to and across – twice
- There were still links within the church between Britain and Gaul at this time
- The Pelagians are portrayed as being richly dressed and so might be aristocratic
- The religious division between Pelagians and the Church suggests a possible political divide too
- In the first visit the Pelagians are 'confounded' but in the second, they are condemned and exiled, suggesting a shifting of power towards the Roman church
- Britain was subject to at least one raid by Saxons and Picts twenty years after barbarian raids are recorded for 408. This could suggest an ongoing problem in the intervening years.

The picture is one of a romanised province, if not a Roman one. This view is enhanced by our contemporary writer, Prosper. He praises the Pope, Celestine, for freeing Britain from the disease of the Pelagian heresy and for sending a bishop (Palladius) to the Irish: 'while he [Celestine] labours to keep the Roman island Catholic he has also made the barbarian island Christian.'[95] Later, we will discuss the *adventus Saxonum*, the arrival of the Saxons and their subsequent revolt. There will be some debate whether to date this to 440 as the *Gallic Chronicle* states, 449 as Bede suggests, or even later as some modern scholars believe. This affects our understanding of where Arthur is on the timeline. We have seen evidence of deterioration in urban and villa life, but here we have sources implying that in the 430s at least, Britain is considered 'opulent', 'peaceful' and essentially Roman in nature, if not politically.

St Patrick

The next source concerns St Patrick who wrote two works, the *Confessio* and *Epistola*. From the *Confessio* we learn the following: Patrick was born in Bannavem Taburniae (unknown location), a small country estate. His father, Calpornius, was a *decurio* (member of a town council) and a deacon in the church, and his grandfather, Potitus, was a priest.[96] All this suggests functioning town councils and an established Christian community in Britain at the beginning of the fifth century. Patrick is captured by Irish raiders at the age of sixteen and escapes six years later. He returns to Ireland as a bishop to become the 'apostle of the Irish'. There is no provable date for his activities[97] and it should not be confused with the mission of Palladius. Perhaps importantly, the author of the *Historia Brittonum* appears to do just that. Traditional dates for Patrick's death differ between either the 450–460s or the 490s. This dating is also important as the first written source for Arthur places him at the time of, or after, Patrick's death. One theory suggests that St Patrick's arrival has indeed been confused with Palladius and his floruit was a generation later, with his death being recorded in the Annals of Ulster as 493.[98]

Patrick's letter to King Coroticus is in response to a raid by the king's soldiers killing or capturing the 'newly baptised' to be sold to their allies, the 'apostate Scots and Picts'. Coroticus could come from the Strathclyde area around 450 but this is not certain.[99] To be labelled neither Christian nor a Roman citizen is used as an insult, suggesting people in one part of Britain at least still considered themselves to be both. A letter sent the next day asking for the return of the captives was ignored. Patrick mentions sending a priest he 'had taught from infancy', suggesting he had been in Ireland some time at this point. If he had sent the letter to a *Vicarius*, Governor or *Dux Britanniarum*, we would at least have clues that the provincial structure persisted. The most we can say is that by the mid-fifth century, some areas at least were Christian and considered themselves part of the Roman world, and that petty kings ruled and were not averse to raiding neighbouring territories.

So, from Constantius and St Patrick, we learn that there are still echoes of the Roman past. There are possibly *tribunes*, *decurions* and a functioning church, one that was sufficiently influential to reach out from Gaul and cause heretics to be exiled from Britain. Both Constantius and St Patrick report at least one raid suggesting it was commonplace. Ammianus Marcellinus records that raids by Franks and Saxons were continuous in the late fourth century.[100] Sidonius Apollinaris, writing in the late fifth century, makes similar comments concerning Saxon attacks on Gaul. A hundred years later, Gildas writes looking back over that time and lists major raids prior to the appeal to the Romans. It is to Gildas we will now turn. He was writing about a hundred years after Germanus and was in a good position to provide details of the period we are interested in. Unfortunately, his main purpose was not a faithful recording of history but a religious polemic castigating the worthlessness of the Britons.

Gildas

We can't be sure exactly where or when Gildas was writing but scholars believe it was between 524 and 547.[101] His style of Latin demonstrates a good level of training[102] and thus suggests more of the fabric of Roman civilisation survived later than first thought.[103] While he denounces five kings for various evils, paganism is not one of their faults. Gildas's audience is Christian and he appears to appeal to the Romano-British as a whole. Whether this means one polity or many is unclear, although he does state there are kings, governors, magistrates and priests, all of whom receive his condemnation. He clearly sees the Saxons as different, describing 'the unhappy partition with the barbarians' and implying it affects the whole of Britain.[104] There is some debate whether this partition is a boundary or refers to some other type of separation, such as the breaking of a treaty. He decries the fact 'our citizens' cannot visit the graves of the holy martyrs and names St Alban of Verulam. The location of the martyrs Aaron and Julius are often translated as being from Caerleon in South Wales but this is not certain. However, it is their graves that are mentioned, not where they were from, so whether they were from Caerleon or elsewhere may not be relevant to the location of their graves. We will discuss this point in more detail later.

The timeline Gildas provides is equally ambiguous and at odds with the *Gallic Chronicle*, which we will also cover later. He provides one of the few datable events with the death of Magnus Maximus in 388. Constantine is not mentioned but he states the army, military resources and governors have been 'despoiled'. He talks of three attacks by Picts and Scots, misdating the building of both Hadrian's Wall and the Antonine Wall. The last attack results in the north being lost 'up to the wall' which is abandoned along with the towns. He later states towns are occupied but not 'as they once were', implying some urban life continues. There is then an appeal to 'Agitius, thrice consul' which most scholars agree is Aetius, who was consul for the third time from 446 to 454. It is possible Gildas added 'thrice consul' and the appeal was earlier with Aetius being active from the 420s and rising to his powerful position in the 430s. Equally, he could mean someone completely different such as Aegidius who was active in northern Gaul as late as 464. This would have the result of pushing the date of the appeal back or forwards by a generation, given the likely alternatives.

However, the consensus is that it is indeed Aetius and sometime in the 440s. Aetius spent much of his career campaigning but we have little information for the period 447–450. There does appear to have been another *bacaudic* revolt in northern Gaul a few years after Britons likely emigrated into the region.[105] Jordanes lists the Armoriciani as being allied to Rome in the war against Attila. There is also a record of pestilence in 442 that 'spread over almost the entire world.'[106] Both the Justinian plague of the sixth century and the Black Death of the Middle Ages took a few years to reach Britain, so it's possible that Gildas references the mid-fifth-century plague, just after the appeal. He also refers to a famine and indeed, we have one recorded for Italy in 450 although for Gildas, the famine comes before the pestilence. We must remember Gildas is writing a hundred years after these events and his sequencing is perhaps inaccurate.

We will look at the text in more detail in the chapter discussing timelines. For our purposes at this point, it is sufficient to consider the text relevant to the period from Magnus Maximus to the revolt of the Saxon mercenaries. Table 3 outlines the key events from this timeline.

Table 3: Gildas's timeline AD 383–c.450

Chapter	Date	Content
13	383–388	Revolt and death of Magnus Maximus
14		Army despoiled, attacks by Picts and Scots 'for many years'
15		Envoys are sent, first appeal made, a legion is despatched, the barbarians defeated and a turf wall is built
16		The Romans leave and the Picts and Scots return
17		Envoys sent for second time and Romans help again
18	410?	Romans return to deal with threat but say they can no longer help (possible confused reference to *Rescript of Honorius* of 410); they build stone wall and towers (possibly another confused explanation for Hadrian's Wall and Saxon Shore Forts)
19		The Scots and Picts return and seize part of the north 'up to the wall'; the towns and 'high wall' are abandoned
20		Appeal to 'Agitius' denied; Britons fight back and for 'the first time… inflict a massacre on them'
21		The Irish return home and the Picts settle the 'northern part'; a period of truce followed by famine and then a 'period of abundance'; 'Kings are anointed'
22		Picts and Scots rumoured to return; a council is convened
23		The council, led by a 'proud tyrant,' invite the Saxons; three warships arrive and settle in the 'eastern part of the island'. A second, larger group arrive to help; supplies are granted 'for a long time' (suggests *foederati* status); and the Saxons revolt
24		The revolt causes 'fire from sea to sea… burned nearly the whole island… licking the western ocean with its fierce red tongue' and all the major towns are 'laid low'. Many are killed, enslaved or forced to emigrate

If we take Gildas at face value and assume Agidius is indeed Aetius, then we must conclude some sort of diocesan structure existed up to the mid-fifth century. A council is able to hire mercenaries and place them in one part of the island. This might suggest a Roman identity was still prevalent and perhaps Roman administrative and military structures persisted too. It's the changing cultural identity we will turn to next.

Germanic settlement

This section will focus on evidence for the earliest period up to the middle of the fifth century. There were already Germanic and other settlers in Britain prior to Constantine leaving the country for Gaul in 407. An archaeological site at Mucking, Essex, shows evidence of Saxon settlement and graves as early as the year 400. While there is no evidence of high levels of Germanic immigration in the fourth century, it is clear some Germanic troops were already present before 410.[107] Similar to the Sarmatian force in AD 175, contingents from across the empire would have periodically been posted to Britain. In fact, as early as the third century, the field army of Allectus in Britain consisted of many Germanic mercenaries and his predecessor, Carausius, was himself a native of the Belgic coast in Gaul.[108] Alamanni troops based in Britain in the 370s were said to be 'distinguished for their numbers and strength'.[109] We have already noted the Saxon Shore Command and the possibility of Saxon *foederati* or settlers.

There is clear evidence for a significant level of migration in the fifth century, particularly into central and southern England. In the second quarter of the fifth century, increased Germanic material culture appears notable in the south. Cremations, common in northern Europe, appear in the east, areas later associated with Angle settlement. Some of the first evidence appears from about 425 with materials from the North Sea coast found in the Thames Valley.[110] Much of this early evidence points to river valleys and coastal regions.[111] Other areas that seem correlated with an early presence are those of Romano-British economic and political activity which suggests some possible continuity.[112] However, the area south of the Thames retained significant Roman material culture.[113]

There is a marked increase in finds after the middle of the fifth century. This is broadly in line with the narrative in the sources. An initial settlement is followed by a rebellion after which their presence increases. However, we should not assume this archaeological evidence proves the presence of Germanic settlers. It could just as easily show the adopting of certain fashion or cultural practices. Where the DNA does provide evidence, it often produces a range of possibilities. Additionally, modern DNA results often prove difficult to distinguish between fifth-century Germanic contribution and the later Viking period. However, the contribution seems to be from as little as ten per cent to a high of forty per cent. Where numbers are estimated, they tend to be in the low thousands a year into a population of low millions. All the studies show a significant continuation of the indigenous population. We can therefore be confident in dismissing the notion of a widescale displacement and destruction of the Romano-British. Initially, the evidence suggests assimilation and integration rather than displacement by force.[114]

The other assumption we should be wary of is any shared identity between the various 'Germanic speaking' peoples.[115] They were not a homogenous group any more than the indigenous Romano-British population. Indeed, Bede describes a number of other tribal groups aside from the often-quoted Saxons, Angles and Jutes. However, something happened in the mid-fifth century to cause a Gallic chronicler to view Britain as being lost to the Saxons. Gildas seems to have a distinct 'them and us' view of the world with a partition separating Christian Romano-British from the barbarians. We should not take these at face value as it could simply reflect a political change. It could also reflect a cultural evolution that Gildas found unpalatable. It is to this topic of shifting cultural identity we will turn to next.

We will finish with Map 5 which shows the earliest evidence of Germanic material culture and burials. The provincial and *civitas* boundaries are very rough estimates. The very earliest evidence appears confined to an area between the Thames and the Humber, but south and east of the Trent. The literary sources then place mercenaries into this context. Gildas claims they were in the east of the island while the *Historia* points to Kent and in the north near

Map 5: Pre-mid-fifth-century evidence of Germanic culture

Hadrian's Wall. Later, we will see the spread of culture and DNA evidence expands after the mid-fifth century to affect much of the two eastern-most provinces. Roughly speaking, the partition Gildas alludes to appears to involve the south-east province at least and possibly further north. The map reflects the situation before what Bede calls the *adventus Saxonum*. A generation later is the earliest of our options for Arthur's floruit. Gildas is writing a hundred years after this and marks the latest timeframe for our hero.

Cultural identity

Tribal affiliations may have persisted and remained a major factor throughout the Roman period and even into post-Roman Britain. In fact, distinctive types of villas and socio-economic material culture show discernible different identities that support the continuation of tribal differences throughout the Roman period.[116] We cannot say if these persisted but certainly the importance of the *civitas* was central to cultural identity in the fifth century.[117] Sidonius Apollinaris mentions a Briton in 471, referring to him as *Regiensem*.[118] Perhaps one's *civitas* was as central to fifth-century cultural identity as someone's country is today. Obviously, referring to someone today as an Englishman, for example, would in no way describe his political, religious or social context. A modern nation state likely contains a similar mixture of competing influences as a fifth-century *civitas* or tribal group. One of the major overriding influences was the sense of Roman identity that was fostered throughout the empire.

Two examples from early Roman Britain are instructive. After Boudica's rebellion in AD 61, the new procurator, Julius Classicianus, worked towards reconciliation. Julius, a Gallic-Roman, was a descendant of the very people Julius Caesar had conquered 100 years before. Within four generations, Gaul was sufficiently romanised to produce men for high office embedded in Roman civic life. Tacitus (AD 98) records the British king, Tiberius Claudius Cogidubnus, as being loyal 'down to our times'. He goes on to describe a policy of gradual romanisation: temples, public squares, Roman baths, arcades, towns and houses. Roman dress and manners were copied and their children were encouraged to learn Latin. Tacitus calls this gradual acculturation 'enslavement'. We have seen how two major changes affected attitudes in the empire. Firstly, the Edict of Caracalla in AD 212 expanding citizenship, and secondly, Constantine's adoption of Christianity in the early fourth century as the official religion. Ethnicity can therefore be complex and often socially constructed.[119]

One of the features of Roman identity was its multi-ethnicity and Roman law as its defining feature.[120] In the fourth century, barbarians were seen as being outside this law and thus beyond civilised behaviour. Roman attitudes towards those labelled barbarians were generally negative. The term was used pejoratively to mean uncultured, unreliable and undesirable and, on occasion, compared to the rebel *bacaudae*. There was even an imperial law laying out punishments of exile and confiscation for the wearing of barbarian breeches.[121] The Emperor Gratian was criticised for preferring the company and dress of 'barbarian comradeship'. Mixed marriages were discouraged, sometimes by law, although there were important exceptions such as the marriage of the Gothic King Athaulf and the Empress Galla Placidia in 414.[122] This was a marriage criticised by the Byzantine chronicler Philostorgius as a 'union of iron and clay'.

In the late fourth century, most people in the Western Empire still saw themselves as Roman but within 150 years, many of their great-great-grandchildren viewed themselves very differently. The influx of a large number of different tribal groups with a diverse range of cultures had a significant effect. Barbarians in the fifth century were not a homogenous group. The Vandals in Africa were described as a 'huge mob of diverse savage enemies' which included Alans, a 'mixed company of Goths' and others of 'diverse backgrounds'.[123]

While we have little evidence from Britain, there are various contemporary reports from Gaul that give some clue as to how cultural identity evolved. Indications from some sources suggest there was a decline in culture and 'Latin learning'.[124] The importance of literature was 'second only to a blood tie' and there was a distinctive difference from barbarian culture.[125] Every major Gallic city had a literary circle while barbarians did not take part in such 'literary activities'. The aristocracy had already begun to withdraw from the Rhine region at the end of the fourth century as the threat from barbaric raids increased.[126] Further departures occurred from south-west Gaul with the arrival of the Goths in Aquitaine in 412.[127] Birth and merit were the two primary routes into the senatorial order.[128] Society was hierarchical and 'everyone knew their place' in a system of obligations and favours.[129] By the mid-fifth century, there was a growing disinclination to hold state office. During the reign of Petronius Maximus in 455, over 1,000 Gauls refused to hold imperial offices.[130] This was at the same time the imperial administration was contracting and the number of offices reducing significantly.[131] The ties between the Gallic and Italian aristocracy had also become remote.[132] It is likely, then, that the ties with Britain had declined too. The cornerstone Gallic aristocratic lifestyle became a 'quest for local influence'.[133]

Reports from the mid-fifth century suggest Gallic Romans were dissatisfied with Roman rule. Salvian of Marseilles claims the Romans under barbarian rule desire to never again 'pass under Roman authority.'[134] He further reports that many 'even those of not obscure birth' prefer to live among the barbarians or even flee to the Goths or, notably, the *bacaudae*. The reasons given are to avoid Roman 'iniquity and cruelty'. This view is especially common among the 'Roman plebs' or free Roman citizens. A law by the Emperor Majorian in 458 gives further clues. It mentions the flight of inhabitants of cities to avoid 'the injuries caused by the tax collectors.' Paulinus of Pella reports that 'many are flourishing through the favour of the Goths.'[135] He also relates how Bazas in 414 was affected by violence where a 'servile faction mixed with the insane fury of a few young men and even freeborn men which was armed in particular for the slaughter of the nobility.'[136] One fifth-century playwright was able to include the line: 'It is in fact common knowledge and manifestly clear that all lords are wicked.'[137]

By the second half of the fifth century, senior Roman figures were comfortable plotting with barbarians against Roman rule: Agrippinus with the Burgundians and Arvandus with the Goths. Barbarian rulers also changed their attitudes. Athaulf, King of the Visigoths, is reported to have first wanted to obliterate the Roman Empire and replace it with a Gothic one.[138] The difficulty of ruling a fractious people convinced him to defend the Roman name by Gothic arms, helped by his Roman wife, Galla Placidia. Similarly, Anglo-Saxon kings from the fifth to eighth centuries often claimed to be heirs of Rome and could still be 'regarded as culturally late Roman.'[139] As power shifted away from Roman rule in the second half of the fifth century, barbarian rulers made efforts to protect Roman subjects and aristocrats.[140]

As early as the 460s, the laws of the Burgundians addressed several mutual concerns. Laws of Theoderic (453–466) and his son Euric (c.476) tried to preserve the status of Romans and Goths in place at the time of the initial settlement in 418. One example decreed 'ancient boundaries are to stand.' Land held for more than fifteen years could be kept if voluntarily given in the first place. Land taken by force could be recovered within thirty years through the courts. The Burgundian Law code of the early sixth century commanded that 'Romans be judged under Roman Laws', discouraging the transfer of Roman matters to Burgundian advocates.[141] Social laws also applied. The prohibition of mixed marriages from the late fourth-century Theodosian Code still existed in the Burgundian Code. A Roman girl who married without the consent of her parents could have none of their property. In 506, the Council of Agde, south-west France, declared mixed marriages with heretics were improper. But these attempts could just demonstrate how prevalent mixed marriage was. Since the marriage of the Gothic King Athaulf and the Roman Empress Placidia in 414, evidence of Roman and Germanic names within immediate families increased.[142] Perhaps the concept of Ambrosius Aurelianus having a brother called Uther and the latter naming his son Artorius is not so unlikely. It is interesting to note that under the Burgundian Code, Romans and Burgundians had roughly equal status but barbarians were still considered outsiders.[143] This should not be surprising as many of the laws were written by Romans themselves, now working under barbarian kings.[144] One example is Leo, an aristocrat from Narbonne, who was 'counsellor of the most powerful king', Euric of the Visigoths. What may be important is that Euric had conceded the language of law was Latin written by a Gallic-Roman.[145]

Another important change was the increase in the use of violence. In Germanic society there was a 'legal concept of self help'. With much of the legal machinery gone along with ties that bound Roman elite behaviour, factionalism and quarrelling increased. The system of *Wergeld* formalised in Germanic law codes began to look like a price worth paying if it settled a dispute quickly and in your favour. The use of violence and the risk of banditry and hostage-taking increased.[146] Some profited from barbarian patronage to such an extent that it began to be reflected in barbarian law codes. By the end of the sixth century, aristocrats can be said to have adopted a new ideology.[147]

It was also difficult to tell how much 'barbarian ethnic identity' remained.[148] At the same time, contemporary sources indicate Roman attitudes towards them had changed too.[149] They no longer saw them as outsiders. Indeed, Gallic bishops wrote to Clovis after he conquered Soissons and advised him having 'undertaken the administration of *Belgica Secunda*.'[150] Halsall argues ethnicity is multilayered: fluid, dynamic, performative, cognitive and situational.[151] This does not reduce its importance. Roman identity in sixth-century Gaul was 'elastic' but an increasingly important component was adherence to Chalcedonian Christianity (adhering to the definitions and resolutions of the Council of Chalcedon, the Fourth Ecumenical Council held in 451).[152]

In summary, then, we can use the example of Gaul to tentatively speculate on conditions in Britain. Crabtree describes the early fifth century as a 'post-colonial period' and 'a number of aspects of Roman economy and material culture appear to be actively rejected, especially in south-eastern England.'[153] Social and cultural identity in post-Roman Britain can be divided among three significant groups:[154] the indigenous elites, Germanic migrants and the indigenous peasantry. None of these groups were homogenous. Thus, we have a number of different overlapping groups, each with multiple layers of cultural identity that were constantly changing. Halsall estimates a change in ethnic or cultural identity to take a 'generation or so.'[155]

It is worth considering what this might mean in practice. Imagine a rural farmhand living at the time of Arthur, working on a villa estate somewhere in southern Lincolnshire. The area has experienced decades of significant migration from various Germanic tribes. The largest are the Angles but Saxons, Friesians, Jutes and many others are also represented. Mixed marriages have been common and our farmhand probably has friends or even relatives from various backgrounds. If he descends from indigenous Britons, he is likely Christian. However, there is no guarantee he feels loyalty towards the local bishopric, which was probably at Lincoln. Perhaps his family were Pelagians or Arians. His attitude will likely be influenced by multiple factors: his economic situation; his relationship with the local landholder at the villa; the political situation in the *civitas* and wider province; and the various layers of cultural identity. Nor is the situation static; he may well alter his view and loyalty as the situation changes. Should conflict erupt and he is forced to take sides, what decision does he make? Does he support the villa owner or use it as an excuse to help destroy him? Similar decisions arise for *civitas* and church authorities. Does ethnic identity trump economic considerations? Which decision is safer for himself and his family in a dangerous world?

Hopefully, this exercise, if repeated with sufficient examples of competing identities and influences, will demonstrate an interesting possibility. Arthur's Britain may have been far more complex and nuanced than the simple Romano-British versus Anglo-Saxon country that is often portrayed. The visit of St Germanus suggests that religion may have been one of the important influences affecting cultural identity. It's to this topic we will turn next.

Religion

We have already seen how Constantine I made Christianity the official state religion of the empire in the year 324. Christianity thus thrived in Britain in the fourth century. In 359 the Council of Arminium in northern Italy records three British bishops attended, although they were so poor, they had to beg for financial help. In the late fourth century, bishoprics in Britain numbered as many as twenty.[156] When Constantine III took much of the remaining military force to Gaul, not only was the population 'mostly Christian' but the majority of major urban centres had large churches.[157]

Some have claimed Christianity failed to emerge in the first half of fifth-century Britain and there remained dozens of pagan shrines.[158] One such is to the Celtic deity Nodens at Sydney Park in Gloucestershire. However, while paganism was also widespread in the fourth century, by the end of Roman Britain, Christianity was dominant and there are no pagan sites found after 450.[159] The visits of St Germanus in 429 and c.437 describe a schism with Christianity but no hint of paganism. The Pelagians are 'richly dressed', suggesting perhaps parts of the aristocracy sympathised. The reference to giving mass to the army prior to the 'Alleluia victory' implies that much of the military were also Christian. At the end of the second visit, the heretics are this time condemned and exiled, suggesting not only a shift in power but that the ability to judge and pass sentence was on the side of the church.

The links with the continental church can be seen in another example. Prosper praises Pope Celestine, both for ending the Pelagian heresy and for sending Bishop Palladius to Ireland c.431, stating he 'labours to keep the Roman island Catholic he has also made the barbarian island Christian.'[160] The implication is there is already a Christian community in Ireland that need a bishop. We get further confirmation of surviving Christianity from the letters of St Patrick. While we cannot date him precisely, it does appear he preached in Ireland around the middle of the fifth century. Both his father and grandfather held positions in the church while his father was a *decurio* on a town council as well.[161] Patrick's second letter to Coroticus strongly indicates both Christianity and Roman identity were positive influences. To deny someone was either was an insult perhaps similar to calling someone a barbarian or *bacaudae* in early fifth-century Gaul.

Contact with the church in Rome appears to have broken down after the mid-fifth century. Easter dates calculated in c.454 in Rome were utilised in Britain. But after that date, the British church appears to evolve distinct and separate from the continent. This break in contact is surprising given the continued trade links between western Britain and the Mediterranean. There may have been political or religious doctrinal differences. Whatever the reason, the church clearly survived in western Britain and Ireland.

It is quite possible that St Patrick was a contemporary of Ambrosius Aurelianus. It is unlikely Gildas would have praised him if he was not a good Christian. He places Ambrosius and/or Badon forty-four years before he puts pen to paper. He also comments on his grandchildren, alive at the time of writing though 'greatly inferior'. Gildas goes on to castigate tyrant kings for various crimes but paganism isn't among them. He also appears to talk over their heads to one polity. His audience is clearly Christian and he makes a distinction with the barbarians, whom he describes in withering terms. He doesn't allow for nuance or the complexity of cultural identity. He is portraying a clear dichotomy that may not reflect the political or social reality. His purpose is a religious message, not historical accuracy. However, what is clear from St Germanus and Gildas is that a strong Christian identity and British church continued from the fifth into the sixth century and beyond, at least in the west and north.

What then of eastern areas that experienced migration and the mercenary revolt narrated in the literary sources? What is clear is that many migrants were Germanic pagans. St Augustine was sent to Kent in 595 precisely on a mission to convert. King Aethelbert had married a Christian Frankish princess but he initially remained pagan. Pope Gregory alludes to the 'bishops of the British', implying the presence and continuation of a significant Christian community within Kent at least. Additionally, some Anglo-Saxon rulers seem to have tolerated different religious practices. Evidence from fifth-century Gaul shows Christianity thrived, despite the presence of the barbarians.[162] As the later Anglo-Saxon kingdoms converted from the seventh century, there remained a chasm between the Celtic and Roman church that was partly alleviated by the Synod of Whitby in 664. Bede, looking back from 731, adds this to the crimes Gildas levels at the Britons of his day: 'they never preached the faith to the Saxons or Angles who inhabited Britain with them.'[163]

Differences in religion did not necessarily equate to conflict. Arians and Catholics coexisted in the fifth century in Gaul relatively peacefully.[164] Many of the barbarian tribes were Christian Arians such as Goths, Vandals and Burgundians. It is possible some of the Germanic immigrants were similarly disposed. This might suggest areas with the most significant immigration were possibly the most diverse, both ethnically and in terms of religion with different Christian denominations and pagans living alongside each other. We can see how this distinction with the west might influence the evolution of cultural as well as religious identity. Additionally, in Gaul, since the time of Constantine, the great ecclesiastical offices increasingly became synonymous with high-ranking status and a hereditary right.[165] Surviving bishoprics in eastern Britain might suggest an aristocratic elite allying themselves with incoming Germanic elites.

In summary, we can be reasonably confident that western Britain remained largely Christian with a functioning church structure. In eastern Britain, we have evidence of significant continuation of land use, occupation and an indigenous population. The evidence from Augustine's mission at the end of the sixth century suggests similar levels of continuation, although alongside a dominant Germanic pagan culture. These differences would have formed one of many layers of cultural identity. We recall the reference to Arthur's eighth battle: 'in Guinnion fort, and in it Arthur carried the image of the holy Mary, the everlasting virgin, on his shoulders.' It's worth noting the similarity to the *Annales Cambriae* record for Badon: 'in which Arthur carried the cross of our Lord Jesus Christ on his shoulders for three days and three nights and the Britons were victors.' These could be later additions by Christian scribes. However, on balance, any Romano-British warrior, warlord or king fifty years either side of the year 500 would likely have been Christian. But we should not assume all his allies and warriors were. Nor should we assume all his enemies were pagan.

The contemporary record regarding Britain falls silent after the visit of St Germanus. It appears once more a hundred years later with Gildas. Arthur is perhaps slightly nearer to Gildas than Germanus in time. Other than the narrative Gildas provides, we are largely blind. We do, however, have much more information concerning fifth-century Gaul and we will turn to that next.

Fifth-century Gaul

It is worth reminding ourselves what the situation in Gaul was after the fall of Constantine III in the year 411. The first half of the fifth century was dominated by the increasing presence of Germanic tribes. Franks had been present in the north for many decades but a generation after the incursion in 407, Burgundians were settled in the south-east of Gaul and Alemanni in the east. The Visigoths were officially settled in Aquitaine, south-west Gaul in 418. Constantius, the *Magister Militum* and later Emperor, had defeated Constantine and regained control over much of the Diocese. We recall Sozomen's contemporary report regarding the province returning its allegiance. It is possible the reference to the break with Roman rule could in part be connected to the *bacaudae*. This was a colloquial term meaning bandit, synonymous with rebel.[166] While the peasant freeholder might have been a likely recruit, contemporary reports suggest they were from the lesser aristocracy to whom 'the oppressed flee'.[167] No distinction is made between these and barbarians. Drinkwater suggests the burdens of heavy taxation, economic contraction, the arrival of significant barbarian peoples and warfare caused social unrest.[168] It is at least possible whatever regime now existed in Britain may have been regarded as *bacaudae* by some in Rome. Perhaps some in Britain viewed themselves the same way.

Aetius was made the *Magister Militum* in Gaul in 425 and became one of the most powerful men in the West. He spent the next two decades trying to maintain Rome's power and played the different tribes off against one another with the extensive use of *foederati* troops. He also used Hunnic mercenaries long before the war against Attila. The Hunnic threat ended with the death of Attila in 453. Unfortunately for Rome, Aetius was murdered a year later and Rome was sacked by the Vandals in 455. The Western Empire descended into a succession of nine emperors which ended in 476 when the General Odoacer deposed the last Western Roman Emperor, Romulus.

Gaul had already started to fragment after the death of Aetius. In the early 460s, an area of northern Gaul had broken away as the Kingdom of Soisson, ruled by the Roman General Aegidius (a possible alternative for Agidius of Gildas). He had served under Aetius and was also *Magister Militum* of Gaul. The final disappearance of Roman authority from Gaul occurs in this period.[169]

Evidence of Saxons in the Loire and Saxon pirates on the coast in the 460s can be seen in both the archaeological and literary records.[170] Gregory of Tours describes a 'great war' between Romans and Saxons resulting in the latter being 'cut down and pursued' by the Romans, who appear to have been aided by the Franks as they took many of the islands in the Loire from the Saxons. He goes on to describe Bretons being defeated by the Goths at Bourg-de-Deol in central Gaul and being expelled from Bourges near the Loire River. Jordanes in *The Origin and Deeds of the Goths*, also writing in the sixth century, possibly describes the same war.

The Emperor Anthemius (467–472) made one last-ditch attempt to exert Roman authority in Gaul against increasingly powerful Germanic tribes. A letter was sent requesting aid from a 'King Riotimus of the Brittones' to fight the Visigoth king Euric. Riotimus is sometimes suggested as a possible candidate for Arthur but we have no evidence to support this. However, it is evidence of Brittonic or Armorican forces fighting in Gaul, possibly around the time Ambrosius Aurelianus fights back against the Saxons in Britain. Riotimus arrives with 12,000 men 'by way of the ocean'. This has often been used to support the notion they came from Britain. But it is just as likely it means he sailed from Armorica down the west coast and entered the Loire River near to the area Gregory of Tours says many Britons were killed. There Riotimus is soundly beaten as he disembarks and flees to the land of the Burgundians in the east, never to be heard of again. The Goths were later pushed back by the Franks who expanded their dominance after Clovis was crowned at the age of 15 in the year 481.

In Soissons, Aegidius was succeeded by his son, Syagrius, in 465. The kingdom fell to the Franks in 486 but what is interesting for our narrative is that Armorica (modern-day Brittany) retained its independence for some time. Archaeological and literary sources support the presence of British immigration into this area in the fifth century, and later Arthurian stories and literature flourished there. In fact, much of Geoffrey of Monmouth's twelfth-century story is taken up with Arthur's exploits on the continent. The presence of Britons in north-west Gaul, then, is at the very least confirmed, although not to the extent of Geoffrey's lurid imagination. In addition, the events of the 460s onwards supply a reason, independent of British sources, for migration of Germanic peoples away from Gaul and towards Britain.[171]

After the capture of Soissons, the Roman/Breton border now became a Frankish/Breton one. Clovis went on to defeat the Thuringians in 491, the Goths in 507 and the Alemanni in 508. The relationship in the sixth century between Britons and Franks was said to be one of peace and there may have been a treaty around 497.[172] However, Procopius, writing a hundred years later, describes the Armoricans fighting off the Franks so that they were forced to make them 'their companions and relations by marriage.'[173]

Despite these events there was no 'sharp break' between Roman and Germanic administrations.[174] The Western Roman Empire had become socially and economically fragmented, causing political vacuums.[175] The barbarian migrations of the fifth century were the product of this and not the cause. Gallic unity only existed as a result of Roman authority and once removed, it fragmented into separate states.[176] The Roman state had become inefficient and corrupt.[177] The loss of the Rhine frontier was perhaps one of the most significant events which led to them losing military control of large areas of Gaul. Moving the prefecture headquarters from Trier in central Gaul to Arles, near Marseille, also shifted power further south.

Despite the upheavals, the administrative structure survived well into the fifth century, importantly even in areas under barbarian control.[178] As late as 469 there was a certain Evantius, of the rank of *praeses*, responsible for maintaining the road between the Visigoth capital at Toulouse and Clermont.[179] Additionally, there was still a resident count at Triers in the 470s and Clovis retained the Belgic provincial organisation after he conquered Soissons in 486. Christianity still thrived and bishops became virtually monarchal in fifth-century Gallic cities.[180]

A number of important factors are worth noting. Firstly, if we are to even consider Geoffrey of Monmouth's claim that Arthur invaded Gaul and fought against the Romans, we have to think about what event he might have exaggerated to fit his narrative. There are only a limited number of possibilities which we will look at in more detail in a later chapter. Secondly, the various barbarian leaders used existing Roman political and administrative structures, which raises the question as to whether something similar happened in Britain. Lastly, cultural identity evolved and changed for both Romans and barbarians. Table 4 lists the most notable events in fifth-century Gaul and beyond.

Table 4: Fifth-century Gaul

Year	Event
c.409–417	Bacaudic rebellion in Armorica and parts of northern Gaul
411	Death of Constantine III; Constantius becomes *Magister Militum* and starts to restore order to the west
413	Constantius campaigns against Goths who begin to be settled in Aquitaine
416–419	Romans and Goths defeat Vandals and Alans in Spain
418	*Anglo-Saxon Chronicles* record: 'This year the Romans gathered all the gold-hoards there were in Britain; some they hid in the earth, so that no man might find them, and some they took with them to Gaul.'
423	Death of Honorius
425	Valentinian III crowned Western Emperor; Aetius made *Magister Militum* in the west

Year	Event
426	Aetius defeats Goths
427	Civil war in Africa
428	Aetius defeats Franks
429	Vandals cross to North Africa with approximately 80,000 people
429	St Germanus's first trip to Britain to combat Pelagian heresy
430	Aetius defeats Goths
431	Prosper of Aquitaine records 'Palladius was sent by Pope Celestine to the Scots who believed in Christ, and was ordained as their first bishop'
432	Aetius is consul for first time, and defeats Franks; steps down after defeat in civil war by Boniface
433	Aetius returns and is appointed *Magister Militum* again
435	Aetius defeats Burgundians and signs treaty; Vandals given parts of North Africa and agree treaty; Bacaudic revolt in Armorica; Aetius becomes *patricius* making him the most powerful man in Western Empire
436	Aetius sends army to Armorica to fight *bacaudae*
437	Possible date of St Germanus's second visit to Britain
440	*Gallic Chronicle* in 452 records: 'The Britains, which to this time had suffered from various disasters and misfortunes, are reduced to the power of the Saxons.'
441	Bacaudic revolt in Spain
442	Pestilence across empire; treaty with Vandals; Alans settled in northern Gaul
443	Burgundians settled in Savoy; treaty between Aetius and Attila
444	Attila has brother Bleda assented and takes control of Huns
445	Aetius defeats Franks
446	Aetius declared consul for the third time
c.446	Gildas writing c.540 cites a letter to Agidius, thrice Consul
447	Huns attack Eastern Empire
448	Peace treaty with Huns; Bacaudic revolt in northern Gaul
449	Bede, writing in 731, dates the arrival of Saxon mercenaries
451	Attila invades Gaul; Aetius leads coalition to victory at the Battle of Catalaunian Plains; famine in Italy
452	Attila invades Italy but is forced to retreat
453	Death of Attila leads to Hunnic civil war; Goths attack Alans in Gaul
454	Aetius assassinated
455	Western Emperor Valentinian III assassinated; Vandals sack Rome; Goths declare Avitus as Emperor

Summary

In summary, the evidence is rather more nuanced than is often portrayed. There is no archaeological 'smoking gun' demonstrating a catastrophic end to Roman Britain. Life continued with disruptions and deterioration in urban life and the economy. International trade was drastically reduced, although links between the west of Britain and the Mediterranean continued. A fully functioning urban life may have ended but life in towns survived in places. Similarly, villas changed and the economy became more local. Raids from Picts, Irish and Saxons continued and *The Life of St Germanus* appears to confirm the narrative from Gildas. The *Anglo-Saxon Chronicle* adds support when it records for the year 418: 'The Romans hid their treasures in the earth.'

Germanic material culture and burials appear from around 425, mainly down river valleys, coastal areas and locations associated with Romano-British economic activity. Cremation and inhumation practices give some support to Bede's claim that Saxons settled in the south and Angles in the east. Evidence for this material culture increases after the mid-fifth century. Yet just prior to this, Britain still retained a Roman identity. Germanus reports there is still a military force. The existence of a council able to hire and post mercenaries would indicate the Diocese and provincial structures survived to the middle of the century. We end this chapter with the *adventus Saxonum*. The *Gallic Chronicle* dates this to 440 while Bede places it a little later. This is just the beginning of the events that culminate in the Battle of Badon. Two or three generations lie between these two events. In that time, I would suggest significant forces changed the cultural identity of parts of Britain. One of those influences was the further migration of various Germanic peoples. The *Historia Brittonum* is quite clear – it is precisely these people Arthur was fighting. It may be that the author is mistaken and erroneously labelled all the battles as being against Saxons, but that is what it states. The next chapter will look at this migration in greater detail.

Chapter 3

The Anglo-Saxons

So, who were these Anglo-Saxons that Arthur is said to have fought? The first thing to point out is the term Anglo-Saxon is a much later invention. The earliest reference to Anglo-Saxons as a distinctive group was by eighth-century Carolingian writers.[1] No-one in the fifth century would have described themselves in these terms. In reality, there were a variety of Germanic peoples who traded, lived and settled in Britain over many centuries. They cannot be viewed as a homogenous group, all arriving en masse at one point in history. They did not share a sense of common identity.[2] They were as complex and fractious as the indigenous population into which they moved. Nor can we assume the presence of material culture equates to the presence of Germanic settlers. Much of it could represent the adoption of practices by Britons. With that in mind, it will be useful to see what generalities can be gleaned from the archaeological and historical record.

Germanic origins

Language gives us some clues as to the origins of the people known by the Romans as Germanic. The Proto-Indo European group of languages originated during the Copper Age on the European steppe, north of the Black and Caspian Seas. Proto-Germanic developed no later than 500 bc and later split into West, North and East Germanic; West Germanic later evolved into Old English.[3] Pytheas, writing in the fourth century bc, describes the Germani as amber collectors likely located on the banks of the Baltic who were later pushed south by climate change.[4]

The name *Saxones* first appears in Ptolemy's *Geography* in AD 150.[5] Tacitus, writing in the second century, classed the Anglii as coming from the Suebi tribe originating from the area that is now modern-day Germany. By the end of the fourth century, archaeological evidence shows Saxons moving westwards towards the north-western European coast.[6] By the mid-fifth century, Saxons had settled in the Loire Valley and the Germanic Roman General Odacer used them to fight against the Goths in around 460. Gregory of Tours records a 'great war' between the Romans and Saxons and at the same time, Britons were being expelled from Bourges. The Saxons appear to have lost this war as they are described as being 'cut down and pursued', losing many of their islands in the Loire to the Franks. Sidonius Apollinaris, writing in the last quarter of the fifth century, complains of Saxon pirates off the Gaulish coast.

The Romans, and Britons, often used 'Saxon' to describe Germanic settlers in general. Celtic speakers also conflated Saxons with Angles and other Germanic people, hence *Saeson* (Welsh), *Sasanaigh* (Irish) and *Sassenach* (Scottish Gaelic) when they were more likely referring to Angles. The archaeological evidence shows Germanic presence before the end of Roman Britain, but then increasing in the south from around 425. This appears to have accelerated from the middle of the fifth century and included the eastern areas of the island.

Writing in the sixth century, Procopius describes Britain as populated by three 'populous nations' with each ruled by their own king: Anglii, Frissones and Britonnes. He learns this from Angles accompanying a Frankish embassy to Byzantium in around 553. The implication is that the Angles viewed the Saxons as Frisians, or perhaps so assimilated into the British population as being indistinct with the Friesians as a separate group. Tacitus referred to the Jutes as *Eudoses* while *Eote* is the Anglian name used in the poem *Beowulf.* In the West Saxon dialect, it became *Yte* and the New Forest area was called the land of the *Ytene* in later Old English. Indeed, Bede states the land opposite the Isle of Wight was named for the Jutes. We can identify their homeland prior to the migration period as shown in Map 6: Jutes in the north of modern-day Denmark; Saxons around the River Elbe in Germany; and Angles in the Schleswig-Holstein region between modern-day Germany and Denmark and the island of Fyn.

The origin of settlement can be identified by pottery, metalwork and burial goods and rites.[7] Archaeological evidence broadly supports Bede's description of 'three Germanic tribes': Saxons in Wessex, Sussex and Essex; Jutes in Kent and Hampshire; and Angles in East Anglia, Mercia and Northumbria.[8] He describes their original homeland of Angeln as still being unpopulated in his day.[9] It follows other examples of historical migrations: exploration, second wave and a third establishment phase.[10] Gildas describes the first settlement as 'in the east' and Nennius specifies Thanet in East Kent. Recent scholars have suggested the first settlements were in East Anglia and spread westwards towards Dorchester and Oxford,[11] although others cite Yorkshire and Lincolnshire as well.[12] The archaeological evidence can be summarised as follows:[13]

- Saxons from west of the River Elbe in Germany settle in the Thames Valley and the south from the early fifth century
- Jutes from Jutland in the mid-fifth century settle in East Kent

Map 6: The origins of the Angles, Saxons and Jutes

- Angles from the Schleswig-Holstein region between modern-day Germany and Denmark and the island of Fyn settle in central, eastern and north of England with some Saxons
- There is a further late-fifth century influx from western Norway into Norfolk and Humberside.

We do have evidence for some Germanic settlement in the early part of the fourth century or even much earlier. Additionally, the late Roman title of the Count of Saxon Shore seems to imply Saxons were present, either as mercenaries or settlers along the south coast, even before the end of Roman Britain. Four centuries earlier, Caesar implied the Belgae in the Hampshire area were possibly a Germanic people. The widespread presence of a Germanic language during the Roman period could be extremely important in identifying the location for

Badon. What is often forgotten is that Bede also lists other peoples who settled in Britain: Frissians; Rugians; Danes; Huns; Old Saxons; and Bructeri.[14] This would suggest a far more complex and nuanced situation.

Cremation, more associated with Angles, was prevalent in the east with inhumations more common in Saxon areas.[15] A whole range of grave goods show a marked difference between southern and eastern England and western areas: amber beads, ivory rings, rock crystals and glass vessels.[16] The earliest Germanic cruciform brooches appeared in Wessex in 425. A wider range of goods spread throughout southern Britain in the second quarter of the fifth century.[17] However, the largest volume of finds appear in the Midlands and eastern areas.[18] We also find differences in the distribution of inscribed stones and rune markings appearing in Angle and Jutish areas, but not supposed Saxon ones.[19] Other examples of distinctive Jutish material are found in Kent.[20] Interestingly, the majority of Anglian finds occur in Flavia Caesariensis which covers Lincolnshire, the East Midlands and possibly Norfolk. Saxon finds predominate in Maxima Caesariensis, which includes Kent, Sussex and Essex.[21]

Areas of Germanic settlement appear to have occurred in regions of Romano-British economic and political activity, suggesting continuation of occupation.[22] Sixth-century Anglo-Saxon and British kingdoms do show some similarity with Roman provinces and *civitates*.[23] Yet settlements also appear in the fifth century in previously unoccupied areas with evidence of wooden buildings and apparent Germanic material culture.[24] Bede's description of Saxons in the south and Angles in the east and north may well have appeared reasonable in the early eighth century looking back 250 years, but we will now look more closely at the details.

Burial and cremation evidence

Cremation, common across northern Europe, was rare in Roman Britain.[25] This allows us to see the marked change in the archaeological record in the fifth century. In the homeland of the Angles and Saxons in northern Germany, cremation was normal until the fifth century when inhumation appeared, possibly from the influence of returning soldiers from the Roman army.[26] In general, Angles tended towards cremation and Saxons to inhumation.[27] Where Saxon cremations do occur, they are similar to finds in the Elbe-Weser triangle in Germany. Anglian types are similar to an area just north of this in the German/Danish border region of Schleswig-Holstein.[28] An Anglian cemetery in the Vale of Pickering, North Yorkshire show equal numbers of males and females[29] which suggests, in this area at least, it was more than simply the activity of a 'warrior elite'. In Cambridgeshire, high-status British burials are found with Anglo-

Saxons of the same period suggesting assimilation and integration rather than displacement by force.[30] In the south in the *civitas* of the Atrebates, cremation burials appear in the late fifth century at Pewsey, Mildenhall, Abingdon and Andover.[31]

Map 7 combines a number of different concepts from various sources: fifth-century cemeteries;[32] the extent of cemeteries by the seventh century;[33] the main towns and cities; and the concentration of sites up to the seventh century to the east of a line from Lyme Regis in the south and Sunderland in the north.[34] It's not a definitive list and there are outliers, so we should not view the line as an exact or political boundary. What is important to note is that within these areas, there was still a continuation of a significant indigenous population. There are also areas where no graves have been found, such as the Weald in Kent or the Fens.

The evidence so far allows us to be confident about the following points concerning the second quarter of the fifth century (425–450):[35] artefacts found in grave sites north of the Thames undeniably originate from the Northern

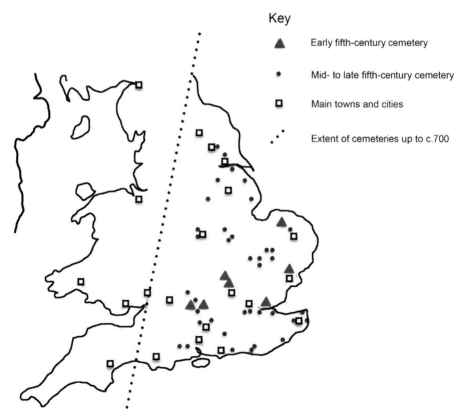

Map 7: Fifth-century Anglo-Saxon cemeteries

Germany and Denmark regions; the spread of cremation practice is clear evidence of significant migration; and the regions with the most Roman villas are remarkably similar to areas with inhumation furnished with Germanic material culture. Additionally, the burial evidence remains constant throughout the early Anglo-Saxon period including sharing the same gaps with villas in the Weald and the Fens. The area south of the Thames appears to have retained significant Roman material culture in this period.

The distribution of fifth-century finds and graves also highlights the importance of the river systems in the early settlement process. Broadly, we can split fifth-century Britain into three zones.[36] The east faces the North Sea, and East Anglia and Lincolnshire are especially relevant with the Trent forming a possible boundary, at least in terms of settlements and finds suggestive of Angles. The Thames Valley and south coast contain predominantly Saxon finds. To the west, the Irish Sea and Atlantic Ocean zone remained under Romano-British control, although we do see some Irish incursions and settlements in this area. These systems roughly correspond with the predominance of inhumation and cremation cemeteries. Map 8 is also a very rough guide to the distribution of material culture such as Saxon brooches.

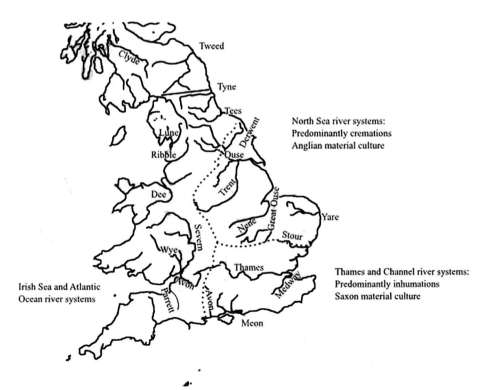

Map 8: River systems and settlements

We can see a passing resemblance to the former provincial boundaries. The Thames Valley and south coast roughly corresponds with Maxima Caesariensis. The North Sea river systems derive in part in Flavia Caesariensis. When we combine this with the distribution of Anglian versus Saxon finds, there is the faint hint of provincial differences in ethnic make-up and potential evolution of culture identity. We can go no further than that but by the end of the sixth century, the outcome is a clear differentiation between east and west. It must be repeated that material culture and burial methods do not necessarily prove ethnicity or identity. For example, one study from Oxfordshire found the data suggested the indigenous population adopted Anglo-Saxon burial customs in the fifth century.[37] To explain this, we must turn to DNA studies.

DNA evidence

The debate about the so-called Anglo-Saxon invasion has two broad schools of thought. One theory suggests a large-scale movement of people, possibly tens of thousands, took over significant areas by force. Alternatively, small warrior groups took over towns, *civitates*, hill forts or other localised areas, adding up to the low thousands over several decades. Another option is the acculturation, assimilation and evolution of Romano-British-Germanic identities involving both the indigenous Britons and the various groups of settlers and mercenaries. The population of post-Roman Britain has been estimated at between one and four million.[38] Recent estimates are of approximately three million, although there is some debate as to population decrease from famine and disease in the fifth century.[39]

The British Isles as a whole remains 'stubbornly Celtic.'[40] Indeed, the majority of DNA contribution was made after the last ice age.[41] With the evidence that does exist for migration, it is difficult to accurately assess exactly when this occurred, and over what timescale.[42] However, studies also show a significant difference between western areas such as Wales, Devon, Cornwall, Cumbria and Scotland, and eastern areas which experienced the most settlement.[43] In the north-east, East Anglia and the Thames Valley, 'continental influences' could account for as much as 38 per cent of DNA content.[44] However, they are 'impossible to distinguish genetically' from later Viking contribution.[45] This would imply the actual scale of immigration was far less than 38 per cent and was initially confined to these areas. Archaeology, too, suggests continuity of use in terms of settlements across the British/Anglo-Saxon divide.[46] More localised studies have suggested a male immigrant population of 10 per cent in the Wessex area compared to 20 in East Anglia.[47] Interestingly, one study found a warrior elite of only 10 per cent, spread over many decades, could account for up to 50 per cent towards the gene pool within five generations due to reproductive advantages.[48]

Estimates for the total Germanic immigrant population in the mid-fifth century suggest 100,000 to 250,000 in a population of two million, while skeletal data for just the south and east estimates the percentage of immigrants range from around 15–25 per cent.[49] Cunliffe summarises the evidence, stating both the genetic and archaeological finds suggest 'a significant level of immigration into south-eastern England during the fifth century in the order of between 10 and 20 per cent.'[50] We have already seen the distribution of cemetery and material culture, and this is located in the south and east of the island. The regions of the island with the highest level of DNA contribution from northern Europe were the relatively densely populated romanised, urbanised areas.

A computer simulation showed that a migrating population of 250,000 using twenty boats in the May-August sailing season would take thirty-eight years to complete.[51] I described in my previous book how a typical Saxon *keel* carried thirty people, which would imply 1,500 boats would be necessary to transport a population of 50,000. That equates to thirty boats a week for a year, or just one boat a week for thirty years. This suggests that a few thousand people arriving each year to specific areas is a reasonable hypothesis. It's a significant but certainly not an overwhelming invasion displacing the population.

Early settlers or raiders would have put to sea between March and October, and likely avoided the winter months to make best use of prevailing winds and tides.[52] Travel times were roughly 80 miles a day under sail, compared with 40 by oars. This compares with average times of 30 miles a day by horse and 15 on foot.[53] The travel distances on land could be improved upon by a well-trained disciplined army. To give an idea of distances, the sea route from Denmark to Lincolnshire is about 370 miles. From the coast of the Netherlands to East Anglia, it's a little over 100 miles, and from Belgium to Thanet, it's only 64 miles. The shortest distance is from Calais to Dover at only 20 miles. Thus, the shortest distances could be sailed or rowed in a day from the north coast of Gaul.

With the DNA evidence there are gaps in our understanding and much that is 'not yet proven'.[54] However, one source makes the following points:[55]

- The DNA evidence supports significant migration over time, although it is difficult to be precise about numbers, timescale, or cause and effect
- There is a greater concentration of Northern-Western European DNA in the east of the country than the west, but the incomers were still a minority
- There was significant British continuity across all areas with some estimates as high as 90 per cent

- The Germanic migrants were not a homogenous group but came from a variety of different tribes; they are likely to have numbered far less than the 200,000 Goths who settled in fifth-century Gaul (compared to the 80,000 Vandals that crossed from Africa to Spain in 429)
- The evidence suggests widespread assimilation of newcomers into the existing Romano-British landscape
- One estimate is of between 50,000 to 100,000 assimilating into a population of around 1.5 million Britons over several decades.

More recent evidence supports higher numbers:[56] regional differences put DNA contribution in some areas between 24.4 and 72.5 per cent linked to Dutch Frisia, Northern Germany and Denmark. In terms of numbers, this could point to as high an average as 50/50 in some eastern areas. Alternative estimates of overall immigration are calculated between 250,000 and 500,000 men and 100,000 women into an estimated population of 3.7 million. This would have occurred over a hundred years or more and after a few generations, a shared identity of Angle or Saxon evolved. If we take the higher estimate of 600,000, then we can estimate 6,000 a year over one hundred years, which seems rather low. However, we must remember William the Conqueror arrived with a similar number of troops and was able to take the throne of England. It is unlikely early fifth- or sixth-century kingdoms could have mustered more than 1,000 warriors, so it would depend on the type, number and intention of the immigrants.

Three explanations are proposed:

- An apartheid system: Germanic immigrants living alongside but separate from the Britons
- War-band model: immigrant males arriving and marrying British women
- Elite transfer model: small band of Germanic immigrants take over a *civitas* or kingdom.

The reality was likely far more complex and dynamic with all three playing a role to different extents across time and place.

In general, the archaeological and DNA evidence do not support a military invasion and widespread population displacement.[57] It should also be noted that ethnicity is complex and is as much socially, rather than biologically, constructed.[58] It is dynamic, evolving in different ways across age, gender, belief, status and geography. It is thus clear that Arthur lived in a Britain that already had significant numbers of Germanic immigrant groups. Some groups would have been present before the end of the empire and intermarried over several generations. These were groups as diverse as Alemanni, Friesians and many others besides, some long forgotten. Angles, Saxons and Jutes are perhaps the main and most memorable examples from the fifth century. Any partition or border would have had pockets of Romano-British and Germanic settlers on both sides. Even in areas with high numbers of immigrants, the Romano-British population is still very likely to have been the majority. Into this context, mercenaries arrive and are positioned by a council. What this says about the breakdown and fragmentation of the provincial system is open to question, but we shall have to look at the change from *civitates* based on tribal areas to later Anglo-Saxon and Brittonic kingdoms to get an idea of the political and military situation in the fifth to sixth centuries. Next, we will look briefly at language.

Language

Only 3 per cent of Old English contains non-Germanic loan words compared to 70 per cent of modern English.[59] Language and place name studies could support the idea of a mass migration, however, there are examples of a 'subgroup' taking on the language and culture of an elite such as the Normans after 1066. [60] The presence of the Belgae at the time of Caesar, Germanic mercenaries within the army, and the Saxon Shore Forts along the south coast mean it is at least possible an early form of Friesian (the closest linguistically to English) may already have been present at the beginning of the fifth century.

Looking at place names in England, we do indeed see a continuation of Brittonic names the further west one goes.[61] But while those in the east were small in number, some Brittonic names survived. We can see from Map 9 that it roughly mirrors the distribution of both villas and early Germanic material culture and settlement. The question arises, then about the difference between linguistic and genetic evidence. Even the higher estimates of Germanic immigration into specific areas still allow for the Romano-British population to be in the majority. It would thus appear more likely the population adopted the language of the immigrant culture, rather than it being forced upon them through violence and displacement. How and when this happened is open to question.

The evidence suggests British enclaves persisted in Bernicia, the Pennines, North Yorkshire, Sussex and Essex, and between the Tees and the Tyne.[62] Brittonic names persisted in king lists both in Wessex and Lindsey. Interestingly, a survey of place names in the Fenlands in the early Middle Ages suggests an even distribution of Brittonic late Latin and Old English place names and no evidence of the region being divided between distinct language groups.[63] There is therefore good evidence of multi- or bilingualism being common across some parts of southern Britain in the post-Roman period,[64] with Brittonic, Latin and

Key

Significant presence of
Brittonic place names
alongside English
place names

Predominance of
Brittonic place names

Low number of
Brittonic place names

Map 9: Brittonic place names

Old English all being present. This will be of vital importance when we consider the evidence for the location of the battles such as Badon. One could conclude there was a 'massive language shift' from the fifth century to Old English.[65] However, it is important to acknowledge we have no idea what language was spoken in the fifth century in areas that later became the earliest Anglo-Saxon kingdoms.[66] It is quite possible a proto-English was already prevalent in the south and east.

Summary

While it is difficult to interpret the presence of material culture, the archaeological evidence does seem to fit the literary sources up to a point. From c.425, evidence of Saxon presence increases in the south. From the middle of the fifth century, we find a further, mainly Anglian, presence in the east and north. There is nothing to undermine Bede's statement of where Saxons, Angles and Jutes settled. However, there is no support for a large-scale invasion and displacement of the original population. Instead, there appears to be significant continuation in line with the previous chapter concerning land use. There is evidence for a significant level of immigration and settlement, largely based on navigable rivers and previous Romano-British settlements. This might suggest something rather different from previous views of Arthur fighting with the Romano-British to push back the Anglo-Saxons. It may be closer to the truth to view Arthur and the Western Romano-British fighting against the Eastern Romano/Germanic-British. Or perhaps competing and fragmenting *civitates* and provinces descended into civil war with the presence of significant Germanic settlers on one side highlighted much later.

Map 10: Area settled by c. AD 500

We will conclude this chapter with Map 10 which shows one estimate of the extent of Anglo-Saxon settlement at the end of the fifth century.[67] I have added the region of the Parisi north of the Humber, which later likely formed the basis of the kingdom of Deira. A number of things need to be considered in relation to Arthur:

- The presence of Germanic settlement isn't necessarily an indication of control or power
- Significant continuation and pockets of Britons existed in the east
- Some limited Germanic material culture and graves have been found west of this line
- A historical Arthur would have lived a generation or two either side of the year 500, thus the line in his time may have been significantly different.

While this line might not reflect the political, cultural or military situation at the time, it is worth remembering both the partition mentioned by Gildas and our original hypothesis. Any difference between this early settlement line and a partition would create a corridor. It is our hypothesis that this corridor is the most likely area where conflict might occur. This does not negate battles far away from this area. That in itself would be interesting and cause us to radically rethink the likely scenario in which Arthur fought.

Chapter 4

Timelines and Partitions

We shall look at the sources in chronological order and then compare and evaluate them. First, let us remind ourselves of the general narrative.

After the Romans left Britain for the last time, the British suffered barbarian incursions which eventually caused them to request help once more. This being rejected, a council of sorts hired Saxon mercenaries, who were settled in the east of the island, to help fight against the Picts and Scots. They then rebelled and caused widespread bloodshed and destruction which ended in, what Gildas describes as, a 'partition of the island.' Ambrosius Aurelianus led a fightback which culminated at Badon. There then followed a generation or more of relative peace before Anglo-Saxon expansion resumed. The key dates are the arrival of the Saxons (the *adventus Saxonum*), and the Battle of Badon. There are significant discrepancies between the sources and differences in the length of timeframe. We will address these points and attempt to reconcile where we can. The first source is the *Gallic Chronicle*.

Gallic Chronicle

The author of the *Gallic Chronicle* is anonymous. Both the records we have – the *Gallic Chronicle* (AD 452) and the *Gallic Chronicle* (AD 511) – appear to be ninth- or tenth-century copies of the original.[1] The *Chronicle* is fairly accurate after around 446. Earlier dates are often slightly inaccurate. For example, it records Carthage as being captured by the Vandals in 444, five years after the actual date. We can reduce this error to two years if the entry refers to the official cession of the city.[2] It would be unlikely the *Chronicle* of AD 452 misdated an event that occurred two or three years before. Thus, if the given date is inaccurate, it is more likely to be too late than too early. Here is a comparison of the two records describing the same event in Britain:

Gallic Chronicle (AD 452)
Entry for 441: 'The Britains [i.e. the five provinces], which to this time had suffered from various disasters and misfortunes, are reduced to the power of the Saxons.'

Gallic Chronicle (AD 511)

Entry for 440: 'The Britains, lost to the Romans, yield to the power of the Saxons.'

The earlier *Chronicle* notes disaster and misfortunes. They could possibly be a reference to repeated raiding which *could* equate to those in Gildas. Perhaps the increase in Germanic material culture in the first half of the century reflects significant migration similar to that in Gaul. Two of our sources for the first half of the fifth century display major differences in this regard.[3] For Prosper of Aquitaine in 433, the barbarians are peripheral to events and he focuses on Roman matters. The writer of the *Chronicle* of AD 452 views their arrival as the most important event. He seems to know little of the Franks or northern Gaul. This leaves us to wonder about the accuracy of the record concerning Britain. We recall the second visit of Germanus and the debate over when exactly this was. If Germanus did indeed die in 437 rather than the later date of 448, we can tentatively accept the *Gallic Chronicle* is not more than a couple of years in error. The authenticity of the content is perhaps more reliable than the date and it is generally accepted to have a contemporary origin.[4]

Two questions will present themselves as we go forward. Firstly, what does the phrase reduced to, or yield to, 'the power of the Saxons' mean? If it refers to a military takeover, then we know it did not involve the entire island as the west held out for centuries. Perhaps it affected the south-east province containing the Diocese capital at London or the military command of the south coast. If the English Channel was inaccessible due to piracy, a chronicler in southern Gaul might assume the whole province was lost. We can only guess if the author gleaned any information from the second visit of Germanus. There is one intriguing further possibility: it refers to a political situation such as Germanic personnel in prominent positions of power. This could be a pro-Germanic faction taking control of the council or military, or even a marriage cementing an alliance with a barbarian group.

The second question is how do we reconcile the date with the later sources such as Bede that give a date of 449 for the Saxon arrival? One or both could be mistaken. Alternatively, they could be referring to different events. Gildas gives us no dates but the implication from his narrative differs from the *Gallic Chronicle*. There is an earlier entry in the *Chronicle* that relates to Britain. In 409/10, 'The Britains were devastated by an incursion of the Saxons.'

Gildas

We do not have reliable contemporary records to date Gildas.[5] However, the academic consensus is his text can be dated to approximately 534–547.[6] It is not a document concerned with the accurate recording of history. *De Ecidio et Conquestu Britanniae* (The Ruin of Britain) is a sermon in three parts: a historical narrative importantly covering from the death of Magnus Maximus to the Battle of Badon and beyond; a denunciation of five tyrants; and lastly, he aims his ire at his fellow clergy and the church in general. The key parts of the text are summarised here:[7]

After the death of Magnus Maximus, there follows attacks by Picts and Scots 'for many years'. Envoys are sent with a first appeal. A legion is despatched, the barbarians defeated and a turf wall built. The Romans leave, and the Picts and Scots return. After a second appeal for help, the Romans deal with the threat a second time. They tell the Britons they can no longer help, but build a stone wall and towers and leave 'manuals for weapon training'. The Scots and Picts return and seize part of the north 'up to the wall'. The towns and 'high wall' are abandoned. There is an appeal to 'Agitius, Thrice Consul'. The appeal is denied. The Britons fight back and 'for the first time… inflict a massacre on them'. The Irish return home and the Picts settle the northern part. There follows a period of truce. Famine is followed by a 'period of abundance' and 'kings are anointed'. Rumour of further raids is followed by a plague, killing so many the 'living could not bury the dead.' A council led by a 'proud tyrant' invite Saxon mercenaries to deal with 'repeated invasions and plunderings'. Three warships arrive and settle in the 'eastern part of the island'. A second, larger group arrive to help. Supplies are granted 'for a long time'. The Saxons revolt and 'fire from sea to sea… burned nearly the whole island… licking the western ocean with its fierce red tongue' and all the major towns were 'laid low'. Many are killed, enslaved or forced to emigrate. After 'a time' Ambrosius Aurelianus, whose parents had 'worn the purple', leads a fightback. An initial triumph leads to victories going 'back and forth' up to the siege of Badon Hill nearly 'the last defeat of the villains and certainly not the least'. Gildas states 'that was the year of my birth… the forty fourth year since then has passed.' The adult grandchildren of Ambrosius are 'inferior' to their forebear. Earlier he describes the 'partition of island' which makes visiting shrines of Saints Alban, Julius and Aaron impossible. There has been a time of peace from 'external wars' though civil ones persist. Cities are not populated as they were and are 'deserted, ruined unkempt'. The generation who experienced the wars have died. The age that succeeded them are 'ignorant of that storm'. He goes on to castigate five kings: Maglocunnus; Vortipor 'tyrant of Dematae'; Cuneglasus 'bear'; Aurelius Caninus; and Constantine of Damnoniae.

The only reliable date we have is the death of Maximus in 388. Gildas appears ignorant about when Hadrian's Wall and the Antonine Wall were built. The raids could be those prior to Constantine III, who Gildas fails to mention, which would equate the phrase 'tell the Britons they can no longer help' with the

Rescript of Honorius of 410. Perhaps the Britons' first victory is synonymous with the Saxon incursion in 408 mentioned by Zosimus: 'The Britons therefore took up arms and, braving the danger on their own behalf, freed their cities from the barbarian threat.'[8] The 'proud tyrant' could then be Constantine III. Indeed, the mercenary revolt that 'spread from sea to sea' could refer to the incursion of 409 and may have been confused with a political upheaval in the mid-fifth century. Given the confusion over the origin of the Antonine Wall and Hadrian's Wall, the whole chronology for the early part could be mistaken. However, some of the chronology remains secure if we can trust the reference to 'thrice consul', and Agitius is synonymous with Aetius.

The earliest Aetius could have been in a position to receive an appeal is 425 when he was made *Comes et Magister Militum* of Gaul.[9] He was the junior partner in the west until his first consulship in 432. It is possible Gildas added the title 'thrice consul' and the actual appeal was in the 430s. The following narrative would then tie in with the *Gallic Chronicle* entry for 440. We could then accuse Bede and the *Anglo-Saxon Chronicle* of simply following this mistake and later misdating events.[10] However, if we take Gildas at face value, then the appeal was after Aetius was made consul for the third time in 446 and before his death in 454. Other possibilities include Aegidius (*Magister Militum* from 458) or Avitus, Western Roman Emperor (455–456). However, Agitius is generally accepted by historians to be Aetius.[11]

We then get a period of truce, famine, 'abundance', the appointment of kings and rumours of further attacks, followed by a dreadful plague. The council and 'proud tyrant' then invite the Saxons. It's difficult to fit all that into a period between the third consulship of Aetius in 446 and when Bede claims the Saxons arrived in 449. It's also difficult to fit the events into the period between the first consulship of Aetius in 432 and the *Gallic Chronicle* entry for 440.

The problems with this timeline have been addressed by Professor Dumville in an extensive study.[12] The appeal to Aetius in 446–454 is accepted. He then allows a more likely sounding generation for the other events leading up to *foederati* being hired in the 480s. This would suggest the provincial and Diocese structure survived into the late fifth century. It would, however, shorten the time for the acculturation and adoption of English for much of the indigenous population in the south-east. This may all be academic as Dumville, like Bede, places Badon at approximately 500.

This section is one of the most hotly debated.[13] Gildas relates the fightback led by Ambrosius Aurelianus. He is described as a 'gentleman who, perhaps alone of the Romans had survived the... storm'. His parents had 'worn the purple' and were slain. This could mean an imperial family or a consular rank. Ambrosius leads a fightback and the Britons win an important first victory. The war goes back and forth 'up to the siege of Badon Hill, pretty well the last defeat of the villains and certainly not the least. That was the year of my birth; ... one month of the forty-fourth year since then has already past'.

The difficulty here is that Gildas is not clear when the forty-four years start. He could be dating it to the appearance of Ambrosius, the first victory or the siege of Badon Hill. If he is writing between 534 and 547, this gives us a range from 490 to 503. A more literal translation does not make things clearer:[14] 'now the citizens, now the enemies were victorious ... up to the year of the siege of Mount Badon almost the last defeat of the rascals and by no means the least one month of the forty fourth year as I know having passed which was of my birth'. So, we have two possible options. Either Gildas is writing forty-four years after Badon, or forty-four years after some other event and Badon occurred in the intervening period.

Gildas goes on to describe a period of relative peace, although civil wars are still prevalent. This would suggest at least a generation had passed since Badon. The grandchildren of Ambrosius appear to be adults and worthy of condemnation. Perhaps one of the five kings, Aurelius Caninus, is among them. Forty-four years is a likely timeframe for grandchildren to reach adulthood.

Further content is worth noting. Firstly, Gildas describes an 'unhappy partition' with the barbarians. It is not clear if this is a physical boundary or simply a reference to the breaking of the treaty. Whatever the case, it results in being deprived of the graves of St Alban and Aaron and Julius, 'citizens of Caerleon'. We know from St Germanus that St Alban's grave was indeed in Verulamium. However, we cannot assume the graves of Aaron and Julius were in their alleged home town. It could be the graves and shrines have been destroyed. But the possibility remains there is now some political boundary.

The second point is he does seem to be talking to one polity, despite the various kings. In terms of cultural identity, the narrative has a distinct dichotomy: a Christian Roman community with civil and church administration on one side, and on the other 'ferocious Saxons, name not to be spoken, hated by man and God.'[15] Elsewhere they are called barbarians, a savage enemy, wolves, dogs and heathens. If the partition involves an area lost to Saxon control, then it is somewhere in the 'east of the island' which extends inland far enough to include St Albans.

We don't know where Gildas is writing from. Later, *Saints' Lives* links his family to the far north, yet his five tyrant kings all seem to be from the (perhaps) former province of Britannia Prima. Only Vortipor, 'tyrant of Dematae', can be firmly placed (in Dyfed, South-west Wales). But there is an acceptance that Maglocunnus is Maelgwn of Gwynedd (c.534–547). There is a similar debate over what part of the island suffered the Saxon revolt 'from sea to sea'. A raid from Kent to the Bristol Channel; the east coast of Northumbria west along Hadrian's Wall; or Lincolnshire to Wales are all possible. But Gildas is more rhetorical than accurate and, in any case, the underlying narrative implies the revolt and war affected the whole island.[16]

Lastly, Gildas's use of Latin suggests some, at least, received a classical education.[17] He also notes Britain has governors, watchmen, judges, public persons and a functioning church with priests, churchmen, ministers and clerics. The general content suggests the fabric of Roman Britain, or part of Britain, survived much later than expected.[18] Gildas may well have lacked accuracy for events a hundred years or more before, but Badon certainly occurred in his lifetime and he may well have met people who fought there.

In terms of dating Gildas himself, there is some debate. The later *Saints' Lives* suggests two different periods. A ninth-century *Life of Saint Gildas* by a monk of Rhuys makes him a son of the king of Alt Clut and associates him with figures from both the second half of the fifth century and first half of the sixth. Confusingly, it mentions a small boy who is also called Gildas. Caradoc of Llancarfan in the twelfth century names Gildas's father as Nau, king of Scotia and there are hints at sixth-century links. The *Annales Cambriae* gives his date of death as 570.[19] These seem to be derived from Irish annals. This conventional dating for Gildas's career is not wholly accepted.[20] Higham argues for a late fifth-century Gildas.[21] Others give more weight to Irish annals and the bulk of the evidence.[22] On balance, the consensus is he wrote *De Excidio* between approximately 534 and 547. If accurate, we have another piece of intriguing evidence from a surprising source.

Tree rings, all from Europe to America, show a marked reduction in growth and evidence for a drop in temperatures. Ice core studies from both the North and South Poles show high sulphate levels, suggesting an acidic dust veil that would corroborate the contemporary sources. The evidence points to a meteorite or volcano with the latter the leading contender. The main suspect is Krakatoa in South East Asia, although the blast may have been many times that of the famous 1883 eruption. A detailed study by David Keys, *Catastrophe: An Investigation into the Origins of the Modern World*, finds not only references in Chinese sources, but evidence for an extreme climatic event c.535. Leaving aside his analysis of the historical consequences, there is no doubt this event occurred.

Writing in late 536 in Italy, Cassiodorus tells of a dust veil or fog darkening the sky for about a year. The sun lost its 'usual brightness'. Procopius too records a 'most dread portent' in 536 and the sun gave forth light 'without brightness'. The phenomenon is confirmed by John Lydus, writing in Constantinople in the 540s. Clouds 'dimmed the light of the sun' over Europe and the produce was destroyed. The *Annals of Ulster* record a 'failure of bread' for 536 and the *Annals of Inisfallen* date this to 536–539. Widespread crop failures are reported from China to Europe.

Gildas states 'a dense cloud and black night of their sin so loom over the whole island' [23] and uses many images of light and dark throughout the text. David Woods argues it is possible Gildas is alluding to this and thus likely writing in 537.[24] Interestingly, a forty-four-year-period before 537 would place Gildas's birth, and possibly Badon, in 493. However, the alternative interpretation is just as interesting.

If Gildas had experienced this phenomenon, one would have expected him to make more than subtle allusions. He would have likely used it to support the general thrust of his argument that the Britons were suffering due to their wickedness. Thus, we get a real possibility he was writing before 536. This provides us with a very tight range if we accept the academic consensus. A date of 534–536 would put the appearance of Ambrosius and/or Badon in 490–492. This is interesting as it is almost exactly when Bede places them and it's to his work we will turn to next.

Bede

Bede wrote *Historia ecclesiastica gentis Anglorum* (The Ecclesiastical History of the English People*)* in 731. He copied much of the same narrative from Gildas, but also had access to continental and Anglo-Saxon sources. In the preface to his book, he alludes to various Kentish, Wessex, Northumbrian, East Anglian, Mercian and Lindsey sources that stretch back to the time of Pope Gregory's mission to Kent. He is far more respected as a historian compared to Gildas.[25] Where he is unsure, he says so. For example, he says the 'first leaders are said to have been two brothers, Hengist and Horsa', rather than making a more definitive statement.[26]

Bede dates the appeal to Aetius and states the previous year, Attila's brother Blaedla had died. We know from other sources that Blaedla died c.444, implying Bede accepts the appeal was c.445/6.[27] He names the 'proud tyrant' as Vortigern. An early version of the name, *Uuertigerno*, is suggested to be evidence of a fifth-century source.[28] He dates the arrival of the Saxons in three ships to the time of Marcian and Valentinian (449–456) on two occasions (Chapters 1.15 and 5.24). On two other occasions (Chapters 1.23 and 2.14) he implies 446 but as both times he uses the phrase 'about 150 (180) years after', we can trust the more definite date. One could interpret the section on settlement as meaning Hengest and Horsa are the first leaders of the Angles only. Alternatively, he could mean the Saxons, Jutes and Angles in general, or simply the first group that arrived. They are settled in the east, but rebel and 'lay waste to every part of the island.'

The Saxons return home (presumably to their 'settlement in [the] eastern part of the island') but the Britons fight back, defeating them under Ambrosius Aurelianus. Victory then goes back and forth up to the siege of Mount Badon which he dates to forty-four years after their arrival (493–500).

This is interesting as Bede seems to have misinterpreted Gildas or he had access to a copy that differs to the ones that survived. He usually rounds lengths of time up to the nearest five or ten years. He clearly has copied his narrative so the forty-four years phrase is very likely to have originated from Gildas. He may well have made a mistake but Bede is usually very careful and he had access to other documents. If he already had other sources that placed Badon in 493–500, then this would explain why he might interpret Gildas in the way he did. Additional evidence comes from Bede's *Chronica Majora* in 725 where he dates Ambrosius to 'in the time of Zeno', who was Eastern Emperor from 474 to 491. He continues following Gildas in describing a period of 'rest from foreign wars', but cities remain abandoned. He describes the visit of St Germanus (in 429) as being 'a few years before' the arrival of the Saxons and follows Constantius of Lyon's account in *The Life of St Germanus*. He then jumps to the year 582 and continues his history.

It has to be acknowledged that two leaders with alliterative names are very common in Germanic sagas, as is an arrival event involving three ships. Some have suggested Bede rewrote Gildas's narrative to fit eighth-century knowledge.[29] We are left to consider some likely possibilities concerning the *adventus Saxonum*:

1. The *Gallic Chronicle* date of c.440 is accurate and Gildas and Bede are both mistaken
2. The *Gallic Chronicle* is wrong and Bede's date of 449 accurately reflects Gildas
3. They have all slightly misdated the same event to c.444/5
4. They are all mistaken and the transformation of Britain occurred at a different time and process than any of them represent
5. The dates of 440 and 449 are both roughly accurate but they represent two different events and situations.

We must bear in mind that the revolt obviously occurred sometime after the arrival. Thus, it is even more difficult to reconcile the *Gallic Chronicle* date with that of Bede. We must also remember that the *Gallic Chronicle* is fairly accurate after about 445 and its content is not in doubt, even though some dates are. I would suggest one of the two most likely options is that the *Gallic Chronicle* date of 440 is accurate and Bede has misinterpreted Gildas, although this relies on the 'thrice consul' title being added by Gildas or some other copyist.

The second alternative is perhaps the most intriguing – they are both accurate but reflect two different events. The *Gallic Chronicle* notes a shift in power while Bede records a treaty with *foederati*: a treaty that is later broken, *si non lugubri divortio barbarorum*.[30] Without a source that describes such events, it is easy to dismiss. This would require perhaps more than one arrival and a period of time to allow these events to play out. It might start with the ceding of territory similar to fifth-century barbarian settlement or an alliance tied by marriage, such as King Athlauf and Empress Galla Placidia in 414. An initial arrival might be followed by more troops and then later official *foederati* status. This last date could be remembered distinctly from the original. After these events, a rebellion causes major destruction and political upheavals. It is to such a document we will turn to next. It is a story full of treachery, murder, incest, battles and, at the very least, provides both a credible and entertaining explanation of events.

Historia Brittonum

The *Historia Brittonum* is generally dated to c.830 and attributed to a monk, Nennius, although this only appears in a later version.[31] Other manuscripts name Mark the Anchorite as author or interestingly, Rhun, son of Urien, suggesting a northern and much earlier provenance of c.600. It begins with the ages of the world and the origins of Britain with an unlikely tale of Trojan immigrants. It then covers Roman Britain before reaching the main part of the book.

Some view the text as 'synchronised history' written for political purposes in a ninth-century context.[32] Others believe that the author is 'actively manipulating his text to create a synthetic pseudo-history' although it is accepted that it shows Arthur was considered historical in the ninth century.[33] However, Charles-Edwards states 'if such history is unhistorical, so also are all the major histories of the early middle ages.'[34] Chadwick views Vortigern as the most important figure in the text and concludes there is 'no reasonable doubt' he is historical.[35] Another important figure is Ambrosius/Emrys (Emrys is simply the Welsh version of the name); this is undoubtedly the same figure Gildas highlights and is later used by Geoffrey of Monmouth to construct his figure of *Merlinus*. The story in the *Historia Brittonum* goes as follows:

After the death of Maximus and the end of the Roman Empire in Britain, 'the Britons went in fear for forty years.' Vortigern reigned in Britain and in his fourth year, three ships led by Hengest and Horsa arrived and were settled in Thanet, East Kent. Sixteen more ships arrived along with Hengest's daughter. In return for her hand in marriage, Vortigern gave Kent to Hengest. Forty more ships arrived with Hengest's son, Octha and nephew, Ebissa, and they settled 'near the wall' to fight the Irish. St Germanus and the council condemned

Vortigern for having a child with his own daughter and Vortigern fled. There then follows a strange tale of a young boy, Emrys Ambrosius, the son of a Roman consul. Vortigern attempted to build a castle in Gwynedd, North Wales, but it repeatedly collapsed. His wizards advised him to sacrifice a 'child without a father'. They found Ambrosius in Glywysing in South Wales and took him north. The boy told of two worms lying underneath the castle, one red, one white, causing the collapse. These were discovered, Ambrosius made various prophecies and from this, the legend of the two dragons is born. Vortigern then ceded the fortress and the western part of the island to 'Emrys the overlord' before heading north to the region called Gwynessi.

Vortigern's son Vortimer then fought the Saxons and drove them back to Thanet three times. Hengest summoned more men and battles went either way. Vortimer fought four battles and three are named: Deguentid (possibly Darenth in Kent); Episford (Aylesford, Kent) where Cateyrn, Vortimer's brother died along with Hengest's brother Horsa; and a third, a victory, in 'open country by the inscribed stone on the shore of the Gallic Sea' (possibly the south-east coast). The fourth battle is not named. Soon afterwards, Vortimer died. The Saxons returned and Hengest asked for peace which Vortigern persuaded the council to accept. At a peace conference, the Saxons treacherously killed 300 British nobles, captured Vortigern and forced him to cede Essex, Sussex and Middlesex. Followed by Germanus, Vortigern fled to a fortress in Dyfed where he was destroyed by fire 'with all his wives' although 'others have different versions' of his death. Afterwards, St Germanus returned to his own country.

The author then describes the life of St Patrick who died at the age of 120 after preaching in Ireland for 85 years. Then 'at this time' the *Saxones* increased their numbers. Hengest died and his son Octha came down from the north to Kent and from him 'sprung the kings of the kentishmen.' We then get the famous important passage: 'Then Arthur fought against them' and his twelve battles are listed in which he was victorious. However, they (the *Saxones*) then sought help from Germany and brought over their kings to rule over the mercenaries until the time when Ida reigned (approximately 547), the first king of Bernicia.

Halsall finds the structure 'a mess' and the fifth-century dates 'worthless'.[36] On this, he has a point. A number of different dates are given for the *adventus Saxonum* within the text:

- Chapter 16: 'From the year when the Saxons first came, to the fourth year of King Mervyn, 429 years are reckoned', i.e. the year 399
- Chapter 31: 'the British went in fear for 40 years.' It's unknown if this means from the death of Maximus (388), the killing of the 'generals' (407), or the end of Roman Britain (410). It points to 428/447/450

- Chapter 31: When Gratian ruled for the second time with Equitius, the Saxons were received by Vortigern, 347 years after the Passion of Christ, i.e. the year 375
- Chapter 66: Vortigern, however, held empire in Britain in the consulship of Theodosius and Valentinian and in the fourth year of his reign the English came to Britain, in the consulship of Felix and Taurus, in the 400th year from the Passion of our Lord Jesus Christ, i.e. 428
- Chapter 66: From the year when the English came to Britain and were welcomed by Vortigern to Decius and Valerian are sixty-nine years. Unidentified figures and unknown date
- Chapter 66: From the reign of Vortigern to the quarrel between Vitalinus and Ambrosius are twelve years, that is Guoloppum, the battle of Guoloppum (possibly Wallop in Hampshire), an unknown date

A number of things are worthy of note concerning Vortigern:[37] he holds power over the whole island; his role is similar to a *vicarius* or civil governor; and he is connected to eastern central Wales. He is said to be a descendant of Gloiu, who built the city of the same name meaning Gloucester, thus connecting Vortigern to areas further east.[38] There is a reference to him on the 'Pillar of Eliseg', a ninth-century stone in Denbighshire, Wales, commemorating the Kings of Powys. It reads 'Britu son of Vortigern, whom Germanus blessed and whom Sevira bore to him, daughter of Maximus the king who killed the king of the Romans.' This would place Vortigern earlier in the fifth century. If Vortigern is a title and not a name, or there was more than one person called Vortigern, then this might explain things. The fact the later Vortigern is called in Welsh legends 'Vortigern the thin' suggests there may have been a more rotund Vortigern a generation or two further back. This could explain some of the confusion. However, while lifespans were shorter, it is not impossible for a figure to be born in c.390, marry a daughter of Maximus, take a tribal throne in 425, lead a council and still be alive to suffer a Saxon revolt in 440 or the 450s.

The text also tells us some interesting things about Ambrosius. He is from South Wales and is a young boy when Vortigern is an adult. The author is clearly referring to the same Ambrosius as Gildas but has nothing to say about his later exploits, save a battle that sounds like a civil war against Vitalinus at Guoloppum twelve years from the reign of Vortigern. This is possibly Wallop in Hampshire. Interestingly, a ninth-century record names Amesbury in Wiltshire Ambresbyrig, possibly 'the burgh of Ambrosius' and it was certainly a 'royal villa' later used by the kings of Wessex.[39] It's recorded as Amblesberie in the Domesday Book. There are other sites in the south such as Ambrosden in Oxfordshire and Amberley in both Gloucestershire and Herefordshire. This is all speculative but would point to Britannia Prima as a significant area for many of the events described.

Another important point to note is the references to St Germanus and St Patrick. Constantius of Lyon has none of this narrative in his *Life of St Germanus*. One theory is that the author has confused St Germanus with the Welsh St Garmon, who was active in Wales in the 460s and died on the Isle of Man in 474.[40] This obviously makes a big difference to the chronology. An early Vortigern likely leads to the early Arthur of our three options. A Vortigern alive in the 460s suggests a middle or late Arthur. The author also seems to conflate the arrival of St Patrick in Ireland with that of Palladius in 431. He goes on to claim that Patrick had preached in Ireland for 85 years before he died at the unlikely age of 120. We then go directly to the passage about Arthur and his battles. We are left to wonder what 'at that time' means. If it means at the time of his death, then we have already seen the *Irish Annals* suggest 461 or 493 with the latter shown to be the most likely. The earlier date could refer to Palladius. The *Historia*, however, claims Patrick, too, was sent by Pope Celestine, who died a year after sending Palladius in 432. If we add eighty-five years, we arrive at 516/7.

This is significant because it gives a clear method by which the author of the later *Annales Cambriae* arrived at his date for Badon. Another clue is that prior to Arthur's battles, Hengest died and Octha came down from the north to Kent. This is dated in the *Anglo-Saxon Chronicles* to 488. At this point the *Historia* is clear in its chronology. It is after Hengest's death and Octha beginning his reign in Kent when we read 'then Arthur fought against them'.

In summary, there is nothing far-fetched about the narrative in the *Historia*, whether it is the granting of *foederati* status, ceding of territory, or a marriage to cement an alliance. But the dates for the *adventus Saxonum* seem very insecure, as are those for Vortigern. What the *Historia* does is provide a plausible explanation to reconcile the *Gallic Chronicle* date with Bede. Vortigern being reliant on Germanic mercenaries, making Hengest his father-in-law and handing over control of Kent might well cause a chronicler to view Britain as being under Saxon control. We then get the separate arrivals of three, sixteen and forty ships. Vortimer, Vortigern's son, fights against his father's allies, suggesting civil war that may have prompted an appeal for help to Aetius. Hengest returns and requests a 'permanent treaty'. Perhaps this is where Bede gets the date of 449 from. The subsequent massacre ends with the Saxons in control of much of the south-east.

While the exact dates are uncertain, two things stand out from the story. Firstly, the upheavals leave a physical partition with the Saxons controlling what sounds like the south-eastern province Maxima Caesariensis. Secondly, the Arthur of the *Historia* is placed firmly after St Patrick and Hengest. We will now turn to the *Anglo-Saxon Chronicle* to assess, among other things, how credible the date of 488 is for Hengest's death.

Anglo-Saxon Chronicle

The *Chronicle* was possibly commissioned by Alfred the Great in around 891. A number of manuscripts survive and for the entries below, I have referred to Swanton's translation unless otherwise stated. It dates the appeal to the Romans to the year 443. The denial is blamed on Attila who was more of a threat a few years later. In the same year, they then sent an appeal to 'the princes of the Angle race'. It is interesting that once again, the Angles are singled out. It follows Bede in dating the reign of Martianus and Valentinus (Valentinian) who ruled together for seven years from 449: 'In their days Hengest and Horsa, invited by Vortigern, king of the Britons sought out Britain'. They landed at Ebba's Creek (Thanet, Kent) and were given land in the south-east in return for fighting the Picts. The *Chronicle* then repeats Bede's description of three tribes. Their numbers increase but there is no mention of a revolt.

The fifth- and sixth-century entries focus mainly on the south. If we separate them out, we can see the echoes of three foundation stories. Firstly, in Kent:

- In 455, Hengest fights Vortigern at Agelesford (possibily Aylesford, Kent), and Horsa is killed. Hengest and son Aesc 'succeeds to the Kingdom' (possibly Kent).
- In 456, Hengest wins victory, killing 4,000 at Caegansford (possibly Crayford, Kent). Britons flee to their stronghold at London and 'abandon Kent'.
- In 465, Hengest and Aesc fight the Welsh at Wipped's Creek (unidentified) and twelve Welsh chieftains are killed along with 'one of their thegns' called Wipped.
- In 473, Hengest and Aesc fight the Welsh and they 'fled from the English like fire'.
- In 488, Hengest dies and is succeeded by Aesc who rules for 24 years.

The first two battles seem synonymous with those in the *Historia*. Here, only Horsa falls whereas the *Historia* records Vortimer's brother Cadeyrn's death too. That text has battles moving from west to east and the Britons victorious. The *Chronicle* on the other hand has the first two battles going east to west with a victory to Hengest. We recall Gildas saying victories went first 'to our countrymen now to their enemies.'[41] There is no revolt or massacre but the 465 entry is interesting as it does not claim a victory. It has been suggested

Wippedsfleot is Ebbsfleet in East Kent. This would then make it one of Vortimer's final battles that drove Hengest out.

Perhaps it is an exaggeration of the massacre at the peace conference in the *Historia*, claiming 300 nobles were treacherously killed. We will leave that speculation to one side and look at Sussex.

- In 477, Aelle and his three sons land at Cymen's shore (probably Selsey, Sussex) with three ships. He fights a battle, driving the Welsh into the Weald.
- In 485, Aelle fights the Welsh near the 'margins of Mearcred's Burn' (unidentified).
- In 491, Aelle besieges Anderitum (the coastal fort at Pevensey, Sussex). He kills 'all who live there'.

Here, the battles appear to go west to east and are confined to the *civitas* of the Regni. Yet Aelle is described as the first Bretwalda by Bede with the next, Caewlin of Wessex, several decades later. This would imply he has authority over a much larger area than a strip of coastline. The South Saxons are not mentioned again until a battle with Wessex in 607. We hear no more about Aelle or his sons, and are left to ponder what happened to him after his initial victories. If the dates are accurate, his floruit is similar to Ambrosius and Hengest but there is no tradition linking him to Badon. The *Chronicle* then turns to Wessex. The preface lists a genealogy for Wessex which states two *ealdormen*, Cerdic and his son, Cynric, conquered the West Saxons' kingdom six years later and were the first kings.

- In 495, Cerdic and Cynric arrive with five ships at Cerdic's shore and fight the Welsh.
- In 501, Port and his two sons, Bieda and Maegla, arrive with two ships at Portsmouth and kill a 'noble British man'.
- In 508, Cerdic and Cynric kill a British king called Natanleod along with 5,000 men (near Charford and Netley in Hampshire).
- In 514, West Saxons Stuf and Whitgar arrive with three ships at Cerdic's shore and fight Britons, putting them to flight.
- In 519, Cerdic and Cynric succeed to the kingdom of West Saxons, and fight the Britons at Cerdic's Ford.
- In 527, Cerdic and Cynric fight Britons at Cerdic's Wood.
- In 530, Cerdic and Cynric take the Isle of Wight.

However, the regnal dates within the *Chronicle* when added together do not match the arrival date of 495. Additionally, there seems to be a duplication with arrivals at Cerdic's Shore in 495 and 514 with a battle thirteen years after both. The consensus is the more likely date for Cerdic's arrival would be 532.[42] If the academics are correct, then Cerdic took the throne of the West Saxons in around 538. If true, this suggests that at the start of Arthur's likely floruit, the Wessex area, Isle of Wight and Hampshire coast were all under British control. Perhaps it was his death at Camlan that allowed Cerdic to take power. Cerdic was also fighting Britons in an area with links to Kent and the Jutes.

Alternatively, if the dates are accurate, this suggests military action in the south at the likely time for Badon. However, there is a distinctive defensive feel about these early battles with action confined to Hampshire and moving further south to the Isle of Wight. Cerdic and Cynric are both British-sounding names, as are many in the later Wessex king list. Hampshire is associated with Jutish settlement while the West Saxons seem to have expanded from the Thames Valley area. Bede says they were originally called the Geuissæ. It is often assumed these groups and individuals are all the same. However, Cerdic and Cynric, Stuf and Whitgar, the Geuissæ (or Gewisse, Gewissae) and the West Saxons might not all have homogenous origins.

Leaving that aside for later, we then get entries suggesting an expansion of power. In 547, Ida, from whom the 'royal family of the Northumbrians first originated', succeeds the kingdom. In 552 the West Saxons capture Salisbury and then expand out from the Thames Valley in a series of battles against the Britons in the second half of the sixth century. These battles have been plotted on Map 11 to illustrate which areas might have been under British control at the time of Arthur. The *Chronicles* mention neither Arthur nor Badon. This could mean both are far away from the areas of initial Germanic control. However, if

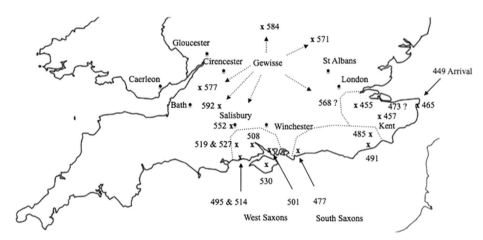

Map 11: Early battle sites of the *Anglo-Saxon Chronicles*

the origins of Wessex began after Arthur died, then it may be unsurprising. But we should not assume whose side the Geuissæ, Cerdic or other group of Saxons might take in a conflict between Arthur and his opponents, whoever they were. We will expand on this point later in the chapter.

We know the *Chronicles* become more accurate from the late sixth century onwards. However, there is a point that gives us some hope for the earlier dates. Two entries for eclipses are dated to 1 March 538 and 20 June 540. In fact, there were eclipses on 15 February 538 and 20 March 540.[43] While we should not accept sources without supporting evidence, perhaps we should not be so quick to dismiss them out of hand either.

Annales Cambriae

The earliest manuscript of the *Annales Cambriae* is a twelfth-century copy of a tenth-century text likely created in St David's, South Wales in c.954.[44] The entries related to Arthur are also thought to be mid-tenth century.[45] As the earliest copy is found with the *Historia Brittonum*, it is thought the contents may derive from that. The two surviving manuscripts, known as the A and B texts, record Badon and Camlan but the B text also records the *adventus anglorum*, along with *Wortigerni regis* and *Horsi* and *Hengisti*. Some entries appear to have derived from Irish annals and sources from Britons in the north.[46] This opens a debate about the origins of the entries concerning Arthur:[47]

> 516 The Battle of Badon, in which Arthur carried the Cross of our Lord Jesus Christ for three days and three nights on his shoulders and the Britons were the victors.

> 537 The battle of Camlann, in which Arthur and Medraut fell: and there was plague in Britain and Ireland.

Similar to the narrative in the *Historia* the content is viewed as unhistorical by academics.[48]

However, it is important to point out that there are no knowingly fictitious figures in the annals.[49] A similar statement could be made for the *Historia*. Additionally, a second Battle of Badon is recorded for the year 655 but frustratingly, we get no indication of where or who fought it. We have already seen how a tenth-century copyist could have derived the Badon date from the confusion in the *Historia* concerning St Patrick's floruit. Alternatively, he might have seen Bede's dating of Ambrosius, in the time of Zeno, and added Gildas's forty-four years to the start of Zeno's reign, which comes to the year 518.[50]

However, there are other interpretations. Firstly, this is the first reference to a battle at Camlan. As we shall see, later sources seem to confirm its historicity. If the annals derived from a lost northern source, it could be the dating is completely independent of the *Historia*. One option is the copyist had details of Camlan and not Badon, and attempted as best he could to place one battle at the start of Arthur's career and the other at his death. It may well be he was mistaken and Badon in the c.490s is more accurate, meaning Camlan should be dated to twenty years later coincidentally c.516/8.

However, there is another intriguing possibility that has significant consequences for our hypothesis. In the vast majority of legends, poems and Welsh tradition, Arthur is never associated with Saxons or Badon at all.[51] If Badon was erroneously added to Arthur's exploits, we are free to accept a late Arthur option placing him in c.510–540. In this scenario, an original version of that part of *Annales Cambriae* would have had details of this Arthur falling at Camlan. A later copyist added the Badon entry as the tradition grew. This would then leave eleven battles on the list. It would also make the case for a northern Arthur more compelling. Perhaps one operating from the remnants of the northern command of the *Dux Britanniarum*, fighting battles on and either side of the borders of the northern province, from *linnuis* to the forest of *celidon*. We are getting ahead of ourselves and over-speculating. One could argue, even with some understatement, over-speculating is exactly what Geoffrey of Monmouth was guilty of and it's to him we will now look.

History of the Kings of Britain by Geoffrey of Monmouth (1136)

The *Historia Regum Britanniae* (The History of the Kings of Britain), was written in 1136. This fantastical mythical tale is full of historical errors, contradictory dates and magic. It inspired all the later French Romances and formed the basis of the Arthurian legend we know today. It is from this story and after that many elements of the legend were added: Merlin; round table; sword in the stone/anvil; holy grail and many others. It also corrupted many of the Welsh tales although they appear to have derived from a much earlier tradition. Prior to this the stories around Arthur were more mythical and magical in style.[52] The merits and drawbacks of this text has been covered in my previous book.[53] Needless to say it wasn't seen as credible even by contemporary writers in the twelfth century. Our purpose here is to take the chronology and compare it with the other sources. The basic story is as follows:

He gives a garbled and ahistorical version of Magnus Maximus and the end of Roman Britain. Maximus makes Conanus Meridiadocus first king of Armorica when he invades Gaul. Geoffrey repeats Gildas's narrative of further raids and a subsequent appeal but names the recipient Agicius, thrice consul. This appeal having been rejected, the Archbishop of London, Guithelinus, travels to Armorica and enlists the help of the brother of King Aldroneus, great-grandson of Conanus. Constantine is crowned and reigns in Britain for ten years, followed by his son Constans. His other two sons are Aurelius Ambrosius and Uther Pendragon.

Vortigern, leader of the Gewissei, arranges for the assignation of Constans then takes power. Hengest and Horsa arrive and are given land near Lincoln. Vortigern marries Hengest's daughter, Renwein, and gifts him Kent in return. Octa and Ebissa arrive with a further 300 ships and settle in Northumbria. St Germanus is introduced as in the *Historia*.

Vortigern is deposed and Vortimer fights four successful battles before being poisoned by his new mother-in-law, Renwein. Hengest returns with 300,000 men and Vortigern regains the throne. A peace conference is called near Salisbury and the Saxons slay 460 nobles. Vortigern is captured and forced to cede London, York, Lincoln and Winchester. Geoffrey then copies the story of Emrys Ambrosius from the *Historia* but renames him Merlin.

Aurelius and Uther come of age and return to lay siege; they then burn Vortigern in his castle. Ambrosius defeats the Saxons at Maisbeli and Kaerconan, and becomes king, ruling for four years. Hengest is executed and Octa and Ebissa are given Bernicia in Northumberland. There is then the tale of Merlin and Uther transporting stones from Ireland to form Stonehenge, built to re-tomb the nobles slaughtered by the Saxons.

After this, another son of Vortigern and an Irish king invade. While Uther defeats them, Ambrosius is poisoned and a 'two-headed comet resembling a dragon' gives Uther his title, Pendragon. Octa and Ebissa rebel and are defeated. There then follows the first version of Uther's seduction of Igraine, assisted by Merlin, from which Arthur is born. Years later Uther is poisoned while fighting another Saxon rebellion and Arthur is crowned at the age of 15 (supposedly in the year 505, working back from the date given for his death).

He defeats the Saxons at the River Douglas and then besieges York. He retreats to Lincoln and gets assistance from his nephew, Hoel, the son of King Budicius of Brittany. Earlier, Geoffrey has Arthur's sister Anna also marrying Loth and having two sons, Mordred and Gawain. Arthur then wins two victories at Kaerluideoit (Lincoln) and the Caledon Wood in Strathclyde. He then defeats the Saxons at Badon, which Geoffrey places at Bath. His cousin Cador pursues the Saxons to Thanet.

Arthur then fights three battles against the Picts, one at Loch Lomond and another against a king of Ireland. He marries Guinevere before invading Ireland and receiving the surrender of the Orkneys and Gotland. Twelve years later he invades Norway, Denmark and Gaul, defeating a tribune, Frollo, outside Paris.

Nine years later a Roman delegation arrive at his court in Caerleon-on-Usk and demand tribute. Supposedly in the time of Leo (Eastern Emperor 457–474 or Pope Leo 440–461), the story also names Lucius Hiberius which could refer to Western Emperor Glycerus (473–474). Arthur refuses and invades Gaul, leaving Mordred in charge. After killing a giant at Mont St Michel, he fights a huge battle near Dijon in Eastern France.

Before his planned invasion of Italy, Arthur learns that Mordred and Guinevere have betrayed him. He then returns, winning battles at Richborough and Winchester. Mordred is finally defeated at Camlan in Cornwall and Arthur, fatally wounded, is taken to the Isle of Avalon. This supplies the only date in the whole narrative of 542, placing Badon after Arthur's crowning in 521.

Geoffrey appears to equate his Constantine with Constantine III although this is not clear. This would begin our narrative at the beginning of the fifth century. However, the name, and that of his son Constans, could be a coincidence given both have very different deaths from their apparent namesakes. We are reminded of Gildas after the appeal to Aetius was rejected: 'Kings were anointed.' This would begin our narrative forty years later. Regarding dates, Geoffrey seems to pull in two directions. Firstly, the Briton-Roman war is associated with people in the second half of the fifth century. In fact, it is possible he has used the figure Riothamus and exaggerated it.

Yet the only date Geoffrey gives is 542. Indeed, many of the figures he associates Arthur with, such as St David, point to the sixth century. It is possible he got the 542 date from the *Annales Cambriae*. To confuse things further, he also includes late sixth-century figures such as Urien, presumably Urien of Rheged. It would be easy to dismiss Arthur's continental exploits because none of the Welsh traditions allude to them. However, there is one source that causes us to pause. The life of a sixth-century saint, Goeznovius, a Bishop of Léon in Brittany, was written in 1019. The date is debated but it would predate Geoffrey by a hundred years. It describes Vortigern, the arrival of the Saxons and how 'their pride was checked by Arthur, king of the britons'.[54] It goes on to recall his 'many victories which he won gloriously in Britain and in Gaul'.

If we accept this, then we need to re-evaluate Geoffrey's narrative. He undoubtedly exaggerates, misrepresents and fabricates parts of his story, from Trojan emigrés defeating giants at the start of his book to using the historical sack of Rome by the Gallic chieftain Brennus in 387 BC as the basis for his fictional Belinus and Brennius (two Briton brothers who also conquer Rome). However, let us at least look at the possibility of Arthur fighting in fifth- or sixth-century Gaul. We have good evidence for much of this time and can be quite confident there were no rampaging British or Roman armies in the time or places Geoffrey claims. But could he have taken a real historical event and exaggerated or twisted it beyond recognition?

The alleged Roman war

According to Geoffrey of Monmouth, the spark that caused Arthur's invasion of Gaul was the arrival of a Roman delegation demanding tribute. Geoffrey names the Emperor as Leo and there are a few possibilities: the Eastern Emperors Leo I (457–474); Leo II (474); or Pope Leo I (440–461). Geoffrey also names Lucius Hiberius, sometimes called Lucerius, which could refer to Western Emperor Glycerus (473–474). Prior to this, he mentions the reign of Pope Sulpicius which could only be Pope Simplicius who held the office from 468–483. On the balance of probability, it does appear he is associating Arthur at this point with the same timeframe as Riothamus. Of course, none of this fits in with the only date he does give: Arthur's death in 542.

Assuming for a moment we cannot trust the date, there are only a limited number of potential scenarios that *could* have been the basis for this part of the legend. The wars in the Loire Valley in the 460s or the Emperor's request of aid to Riothamus c.471 are possibilities. A request for help from either Clovis or Syagrius in c.486 could have resulted in Arthur aiding one side. Possible border wars against the Franks may have resulted in a treaty dated to 597.[55] In 508, Clovis was given the consulship by the Eastern Roman Emperor. One could speculate about an embassy from Emperor Anastasius or Clovis to Britain. After the death of Clovis in 511, the Frankish kingdom was shared between his four sons.

Consolidation was followed by further expansion against the Thuringians in 531, the Burgundians in 534, the Provence region in 537, the Visigoths in northern Spain in 542 and a Saxon war in 555–56. The Thuringian war might be relevant to our investigation as there is some evidence of Saxon emigrants from Britain being used as mercenaries by the Franks. The line of argument suggests there was pressure in Britain prior to this, driving Anglo-Saxons out. The Frankish kingdoms were finally unified once more under Clothar in 558. After Clothar's death in 561, his four sons inherited the four separate kingdoms again. Two wars involving Britons are worth mentioning: firstly, in around 560, Clothar's son Charm rebelled and joined forces with a Breton leader, Conomer resulting in the death of both Conomer and Charm. Secondly, there were wars between the Breton Waroch II and the Frankish Kings Chilperic in 578 and Guntram in 589.

Another curious event that may be relevant is the siege of Rome in 538. Vitiges led an Ostrogoth army in besieging General Balisarius who had been sent by the Eastern Emperor Justinian to reconquer Italy. Procopius records that during the siege, the Goths were made a surprising offer: 'And we on our side permit the Goths to have the whole of Britain, which is much larger than Sicily and was subject to the Romans in early times.' The question arises how the Romans could have offered such terms? After all Britain had been lost to them for over a hundred years. Perhaps it was simply a ruse but it is interesting to wonder what the response might have been if the Britons had heard this. This is around the same time that Gildas was writing his polemic. One wonders what kind of reception a visiting Byzantine ambassador might have got with the suggestion the Romans were now taking back control and had promised 150,000 Goths they could settle in Britain. It is interesting that it ties in with a date for Camlan in 542.

A number of later sources do support a fifth-century date for Arthur, the early option from our three:[56]

- Fontium, writing in the thirteenth century, dates Arthur's reign to AD 459–475.
- The tenth-century *Salzburg Annals* has a notation added beside the reign of Pope Hilarius in 461: 'At this time Arthur, of whom many stories are told, reigned in Britain.'
- Jean de Pries accepts a sixth-century date but records a Martinus Polonus, who claimed Arthur reigned when Pope Hilarius died in 468.
- Jacques de Guise, writing in the fourteenth century, records his country of Hainaut (modern-day Belgium) suffered in the time of 'Arthur and the Goths, Huns and Vandals', thus suggesting a mid- to last quarter fifth-century date.

All this may be unlikely and it could be easier to dismiss the whole idea and put it down to Geoffrey's imagination. However, if we put aside the narrative and dates, implied or stated, we are left with the following possible derivations for the story:

- The Roman-Saxon or Gothic/Breton wars of 460–471.
- The war between Clovis and the rump Roman state of Soissons in 487.
- Frankish/Breton border clashes leading up to a treaty in 497.
- Clovis receiving the consulship in 508.
- Border clashes with Clovis's sons after his death in 511.
- The offer of Britain to the Goths in 538.
- The war between Conomor and the Franks in the 560s although this is likely too late.

My suspicion is that it is a fictional addition similar to Belinus and Brennius to show the historical authority of the rulers of Britain to please his Norman patrons. If there is any truth in it, I would suggest the most likely scenario is the border wars in Armorica, probably against the Franks.

Miscellaneous

Various *Saints' Lives* connected with Arthur were written from the eleventh century onwards. They often portray Arthur as a petty sinful warlord or king who is brought to heel by the hero saint. The stories often result, quite coincidentally, in some proof of land rights in perpetuity for the medieval reader. Bartrum's detailed and extensive study of historical and legendary Welsh figures allows us to estimate the birth year of the relevant saints:[57] Illtud (470); Carannog (470); Padarn (480); Gildas (490); and Cadoc (495). St David, said to be a cousin of Arthur, is dated to c.485. To Arthur, Bartrum gives the date of c.480 for his birth, thus choosing the middle Arthur option and allowing him to be of fighting age at a Badon in around 500. It is interesting that the saints Arthur is associated with are all linked to South Wales and the West Country, and the same time period. One exception is the life of St Efflam (448–512).[58] Here, the saint helps Arthur defeat a dragon in Brittany. It is worth noting, despite the plethora of Irish and Welsh saints in the fifth and sixth centuries and beyond, no other saints, in other geographical areas lay claim to Arthur. These tales are all likely literary inventions.[59] They are also all consistent with an Arthur living c.480–520.

Regarding genealogies, the sources are all very late. We can summarise them in the following way. On one side, many of the Welsh kings and saints descend from Cunedda, whom the *Historia* states came from the Manaw Gododdin to Wales to expel the Irish. Cunedda married Gwawl, a daughter of Coel Hen, from whom many of the kings of the north descend. Vortigern's line is separate. Igraine is a granddaughter of Cunedda and thus Uther marries into the line of Cunedda and is not listed as a king in any of the early kingdoms. If we are to believe Geoffrey of Monmouth, Arthur's father and uncle are the sons of a Breton immigrant, albeit one who is given the throne.

Maelgwn's death is dated to 547 and in much later genealogy tables, he is of the same generation as Arthur, both being great-grandsons of Cunedda. However, as Cunedda had nine sons and at least one daughter, his children could have been born a generation apart and so on. The sources are as below:

- *Bonedd Y Sant* (Descent of the Saints): thirteenth to eighteenth century.
- Harleian genealogies in the *Historia Brittonum* and *Annales Cambriae*: MS 3859 c.1100.
- *Bonedd Gwyr y Gogledd* (Descent of the Men of the North): Peniarth MS 45, late thirteenth century.
- Jesus College: MS 20 manuscripts, late fourteenth century.

None of these can be trusted but in my last book, I attempted to place them alongside each other.[60] Assuming a fifty-year lifespan with offspring halfway through, I started with generation 1 in 350–400 and generation 2 in 375–425, and so on. Placing Magnus Maximus in generation 1, Arthur appeared to be five generations later in c.475–525.

Similar to the *Saints' Lives*, it is interesting that the sources all point to the same timeframe. Of course, medieval copyists and compilers would be trying to do exactly what we are attempting. So, it's hardly surprising there is a strong correlation. What may be worth noting is that none seem to point to any other period, such as the early fifth or late sixth centuries. A historicised fictional character might be expected to have a much greater range of associations.

There are a number of genealogies for the Anglo-Saxon kingdoms: the *Historia Brittonum*, an eighth-century Anglian Collection and the *Anglo-Saxon Chronicles*. Their origins are in the late eighth century.[61] Unfortunately, there are no figures associated with Arthur. Neither the *Historia* or the *Annales Cambriae* name his enemies directly. The *Historia* hints at Octha of Kent but it is not certain. Geoffrey does supply names – Colgrin, Baldulf and Cheldric – from Arthur's first battle to Badon. No such names occur in any of the king lists.

Comparing the sources

We have a number of narratives that each produce a different timeline and, in turn, imply a different floruit for Arthur: early, middle or late in a range from 450–550. Firstly, the *Gallic Chronicle* suggests an *adventus Saxonum* in 440 and offers nothing more. Gildas gives much more detail, though confused and contradictory, but no definite dates. Bede, taking much from Gildas, supplies us with dates of 449 for the *adventus Saxonum*, 474–491 for Ambrosius and 493–500 for Badon. The Welsh sources seem to pull us all ways. The multiple dates in the *Historia* for the *adventus Saxonum* could support the *Gallic Chronicle* date. Yet the dates in the *Annales Cambriae* and *The History of the Kings of Britain* point to Arthur c.510–540. However, Arthur's alleged war against the Romans pulls us back to c.470. The genealogies and *Saints' Lives* appear to support a middle Arthur c.480–520.

We get little help with other major characters. Vortigern in the *Historia* invites the Saxons in 375, 428 and/or c.450, as with Bede. Ambrosius, generally, is a generation after Vortigern but the *Historia* states he fights a battle against Vitalinus who is listed as Vortigern's grandfather. This has led many to suggest an older and younger Vortigern and Ambrosius. The confusion, contradictions and discrepancies between the sources have resulted in various theories involving two or multiple Arthurs. However, I would argue this is overly complicated. The reference to 'Vortigern the thin' and the discrepancy with the implied dates between Bede and the Pillar of Eliseg might support the idea of two Vortigerns. However, a lifespan of c.390–460 or even longer would be unusual for his day, but not impossible.

One approach would be to lay all the sources alongside each other and attempt a 'line of best fit'. We then need to factor in the archaeological evidence and known historical record for the Western Empire. The *Gallic Chronicle* entry for 440 seems secure although its meaning is open to interpretation. Our nearest contemporary source is Gildas but his chronology is highly unreliable. Bede is far more trustworthy and thus much of the debate is academic if we can place Ambrosius in the last quarter of the fifth century and Badon in the last decade.

With the *Annales Cambriae* we get support for a late Arthur but also a possibility that Badon has been mistakenly dated. This could suggest both Badon and Camlan should be dated a generation earlier, making Arthur's death c.510–520. Alternatively, it might support the notion that by the ninth century, Badon had been erroneously attributed to Arthur causing a perhaps northern copyist to bring it forward in time to fit with a known floruit of c.510–540. Geoffrey of Monmouth likely obtained his date of 542 from the *Annales Cambriae* but is generally not to be trusted. However, despite the flaws in Geoffrey's book, 'history keeps peeping through the gaps'.[62]

This brings us to the *Historia Brittonum*. I would claim we have here a fascinating ninth-century view of fifth- to sixth-century events, a view that may have originated as early as c.600 if the Chartres manuscript was accurate in assigning the authorship to Rhun, son of Urien. It also gives us a perfectly reasonable explanation for the discrepancy and confusion between, and within, the sources, specifically the *Gallic Chronicle*, Gildas and Bede. We have a number of options concerning the veracity of the text: it could be a complete fabrication by the author; the author could have used known mythical figures and events from sagas; he may have erroneously believed in the veracity of legendary and mythical figures and events; he may have used historical characters and events but made errors of fact and timing; or the author may be accurately recounting actual events with the historical figures involved.

I attempted a process of 'line of best fit' in my last book and was able, up to a point, to reconcile and cross-reference multiple entries between sources.[63] This leads me to conclude that out of the three options, the early Arthur (c.450–480) is the least likely. It causes us to dismiss or change too much from the dates in Bede, Badon and floruits of figures associated with him. I am tempted by a late Arthur dying at Camlan in c.537. But this requires one of two things: the forty-four years of Gildas starting with the first victory of Ambrosius in c.491 and not Badon, which would be in the intervening period fitting in with the *Annales Cambriae* c.516 and with Gildas writing in c.536. Alternatively, a copyist or chronicler knew Arthur's floruit was c.510–540 and he, or tradition, had erroneously attributed Badon to him. However, my preferred option is a middle Arthur (c.480–510). This produces the 'line of best fit' and does the least damage to the sources.

I will end this section with Table 5, which compares timelines in the sources, and leave the reader to attempt the 'line of best fit' process.

Table 5: Comparison of timelines

Known sources	Gildas and Bede	*Anglo-Saxon Chronicles*	*Historia Brittonum,* Geoffrey of Monmouth and *Annales Cambriae*
388 Death of Maximus 410 End of Roman Britain 411 Death of Constantine III	Death of Maximus		425 Vortigern King 428 Hengest and Horsa arrive
423 Aetius *Magister Militum* 429 St Germanus visit 431 Palladius sent to Ireland	Three incursions from Picts and Scots, seize north 'up to wall'. Britons abandon cities Civil war Famine		Vortigern marries Renwein, cedes Kent, Octha given land in north St Germanus confronts Vortigern
437? St Germanus second visit 440 *Gallic Chronicle:* Britain falls to power of Saxons 446 Aetius third consul	Appeal to Agitus/Aetius Victory over Picts, time of plenty, Kings anointed, disease/plague.	443 Appeal to Aetius	Vortimer drives Saxons out in four battles. Catigern and Horsa killed Hengest returns. Peace conference massacre.
454 Aetius dies 460s Roman/Saxon war 471 Riothamus dies in Gaul 476 End of Western Empire	449 Arrival of Saxons Rebellion 474–491 Ambrosius Aurelianus fights back	449 Hengest and Horsa arrive 455–473 Hengest (four battles), Horsa dies 477–491 Aelle arrives (three battles) 488 Hengest dies	Saxons take Essex, Sussex, Middlesex (or London, York, Lincoln and Winchester) Vortigern dies St Germanus returns to Gaul
488 Last Roman enclave in Gaul falls 493? St Patrick dies 507 Clovis made consul of Rome	c.490–500 Battle of Badon	495–514 West Saxons arrive	Hengest and St Patrick die *Arthur fights against them* 516–521 Battle of Badon
531 Saxon emigration to Frankia	c.534–547 Gildas writes *De Excidio*	519–530 West Saxons (three battles)	Floruit of saints connected with Arthur 537–542 Battle of Camlan
550s Expansion of Anglo-Saxon kingdoms		547 Ida first king of Northumbrians 552 West Saxon expansion	

The rebellion and partition

Regardless of the exact chronology, it is clear the end result of this period of upheaval was the emergence of petty kingdoms by c.600 that had distinctive cultural identities. On the one side, we have Anglo-Saxon kingdoms such as Kent, Wessex, Northumbria and East Anglia. On the other, there are Brittonic kingdoms of the west and north such as Gwynedd, Powys, Rheged and Gododdin. Several factors contributed to this: the break with the empire at the beginning of the fifth century; the increase in Germanic material culture and settlement from c.425; significant migrations of various barbarian tribes into the west; the apparent significant increase in settlement in Britain in particular; or the collapse of the Western Empire. But the pivotal moment is the event Gildas alludes to in his tract.

It is important to attempt to estimate what areas may have been affected by an initial revolt. It may well be that this situation changed after Ambrosius. The war, and perhaps any border that existed, went 'now to our countrymen, now to their enemies'. This culminated at Badon and the 'partition' possibly stabilised as Gildas records that 'external wars' had stopped. An Arthur before or after Badon would be fighting in this political context. We will thus attempt to estimate the time and location of the partition.

The *Gallic Chronicle* states it is Britain that has 'fallen to the power of the Saxons'. If they mean the whole island, this surely refers to some political event. If it is a military take-over, then we can only speculate about the south-eastern province, the Saxon Shore Command or areas directly facing the Gallic coast. Gildas states the Saxon mercenaries initially 'fixed their dreadful claws on the east side of the island.' Then, during the subsequent rebellion, a fire 'spread from sea to sea' lasting 'until it burned almost the entire surface of the island and was licking the western ocean with its fierce red tongue.' The clear implication is that the whole island is involved as 'all the major towns are laid low'. But then we hear 'after a time, when the cruel plunderers had gone home'. We are left to wonder where exactly? Presumably back to the east of the island. But the 'unhappy partition' has resulted in Verulamium at least being inaccessible. The graves of *Aaron et Iulium Legionum urbes cives* are unknown, regardless of whether they were indeed from Caerleon. We could simply draw a vertical line down the country which places St Albans to the east of it, but that would be too crude.

Bede states they were granted 'a place of settlement in the eastern part of the island'. First, they attacked the enemy from the north (i.e. the Picts) then 'the newcomers received from the Britons a grant of land in their midst', a literal definition of which would suggest within, or in the middle of, British areas. We are reminded of the map of early Anglo-Saxon cemeteries and settlements which are fairly widespread alongside southern and eastern river systems. The initial rebellion involved 'every part of the island' but then they returned 'home', presumably to their settled areas.

The *Historia* gives more detail. The Saxons are first settled in Thanet in Kent, which was later ceded to Hengest in return for his daughter's hand in marriage to Vortigern. His son, Vortimer, drives them out completely but after his death, they return though it's not stated where to. There follows the infamous massacre where three hundred British nobles are killed at a peace conference. Vortigern is captured and forced to cede Essex, Sussex and Middlesex and other districts to Hengest, who presumably retains Kent as well. This strongly suggests the entire south-east or former province of Maxima Caesariensis was taken over. We are reminded of fifth-century figures in Gaul breaking away similar-sized areas: Theodoric; Euric; Aegidius; Syagrius; or Clovis.

If we take the *Anglo-Saxon Chronicles* at face value, then Kent and Sussex are under Germanic control before the likely date for Badon. This seems to corroborate the *Historia*. The gap between Bede's *Bretwaldas* would also support the idea of containment between c.490s–560. The 'fly in the ointment' are the entries for Wessex. If the academics are correct, the dates are miscalculated and should begin c.532 with Cerdic taking control in c.538. This happy coincidence immediately removes the discrepancy between Gildas's period of peace and the dates for arrivals and battles in the *Chronicles* for the period 495–530. It would mean the Hampshire area and coast was controlled by Britons in the key time period. However, even if the dates are accurate, this would not undermine the narrative too greatly. Firstly, the battles recorded between 495 and 530 do appear confined to a relatively small area. Secondly, there is no guarantee whose side they fought on. The etymology of Geuissæ meaning 'certain' or 'sure' could be interpreted as meaning they were reliable. The question is: who were they reliable to? Geoffrey of Monmouth names Vortigern as leader of the Gewissei which raises an interesting sub-plot. If Vortigern and Ambrosius were embroiled in a civil war, perhaps Gildas would have regarded a conflict between Cerdic and Britons as a civil, not external, war. It follows we should not assume Arthur and Cerdic, if their paths crossed, would have been enemies.

Geoffrey of Monmouth claims Hengest landed in Kent, but Vortigern first granted lands in Lindsey, Lincolnshire to him. He later builds a fortress there called Castrum Corrigie, in Latin, Kaercarrei in Welsh or Thanceastre in Saxon. Some have identified this as Caistor (Thwangcastre in 1322), north-east of Lincoln. He follows the *Historia* in describing Vortigern giving Hengest Kent in return for marriage to Renwein. Later, Octa and Ebissa are given lands near the wall 'between Deira and Scotland'. The Britons desert Vortigern causing him to flee and Vortimer drives the Saxons back to Thanet; eventually, the warriors leave (without their women and children) although whether this is just Kent or the north is not made clear. After Vortimer's death, Vortigern is king once again and there follows the slaughter of British nobles resulting in the Saxons seizing London, Winchester, Lincoln and York.

Putting all this on a map, as shown in Map 12, gives a fairly complex picture. We must remember the revolt supposedly affected the 'whole island' and it reached the 'western ocean'. Much ink has been spilled attempting to determine where Gildas wrote, and whether a raid from sea to sea is more likely in the north or south. This may be academic as it affected the whole island and they returned to their base or 'home' as Gildas tells us, presumably in the east. So, the important thing to determine for our purposes is where 'home' was.

If this seems overly complicated, we can simplify matters further if we make some assumptions. We can draw two lines, the first on the basis of the initial settlement and partition, which at its minimum probably contained Kent and part of the south-east, including Verulamium. The second line can be drawn

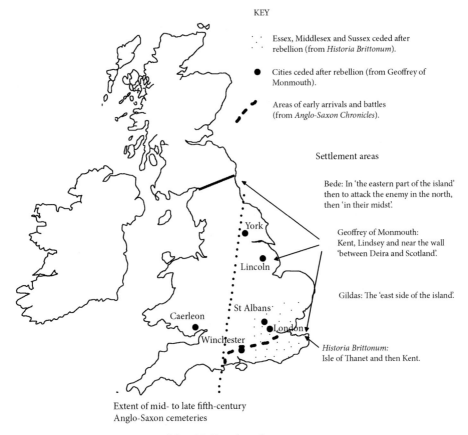

KEY

⋰ · Essex, Middlesex and Sussex ceded after rebellion (from *Historia Brittonum*).

● Cities ceded after rebellion (from Geoffrey of Monmouth).

⦙ Areas of early arrivals and battles (from *Anglo-Saxon Chronicles*).

Settlement areas

Bede: In 'the eastern part of the island' then to attack the enemy in the north, then 'in their midst'.

Geoffrey of Monmouth: Kent, Lindsey and near the wall 'between Deira and Scotland'.

Gildas: The 'east side of the island'.

Historia Brittonum: Isle of Thanet and then Kent.

Extent of mid- to late fifth-century Anglo-Saxon cemeteries

Map 12: Revolt and partition

at the furthest extent of early Germanic material culture, cemeteries and settlement combined with likely postings of mercenaries. We would thus expect to see conflict in this corridor.

We should also consider the areas that were definitely under British control at the time. We know present-day Devon, Cornwall and Wales held out for many hundreds of years. It wasn't until the Battle of Peonnum in 660 (possibly Penselwood, Somerset) that the Britons were pushed back to the River Parrett in Somerset. The present-day boundary between Dorset and Hampshire appears to be roughly the same as the fifth-century one between the *civitates* of the Durotriges and Belgarum, with present-day Dorset being firmly Romano-British. The area around Dorchester and Poundbury hill fort shows signs of post-Roman occupation into the seventh century.[64] Only Romano-British graves have been found in the *civitates* of the Durotriges.[65] In 658, the Britons suffered defeat again and were driven back to the River Parrett.

As we travel north, West Wiltshire, Somerset and Gloucestershire also show a relative absence of early Anglo-Saxon finds and evidence for continued Romano-British control. Hill forts at Cadbury and Cadbury-Congresbury show occupations into the sixth century, as do areas around Glastonbury and Athenley, Bath, Cirencester and Gloucester. In 577 at the Battle of Dyrham, there were three kings with Brittonic-sounding names: Conmail, Condidan and Farinmail. Gloucester, Cirencester and Bath were taken by Caewlin of Wessex, strongly suggesting the area was under British control at the time Gildas was writing, thirty years earlier. All Anglo-Saxon material culture from the sixth century is found to the east of Teffont in South Wiltshire.[66] A little further north, Pewsey and Avebury appear to be a 'late fifth century frontier zone.'[67]

Yet to the east of this line, Salisbury is not 'taken' until 552 according to the *Anglo-Saxon Chronicle*. We also have some evidence for continuity around Silchester and Winchester. There is evidence for a 'notable degree of population continuity', alongside a limited amount of male immigration from the mid-fifth century around Winchester of about 10–20 per cent.[68] On the other hand, 'managed cemeteries' appear to have ended abruptly in the early fifth century.[69] At Silchester, occupation continued into the fifth and one find is an inscription of an apparently British name: *Tebicato*, dated to AD 550 at the earliest.[70] There are early Anglo-Saxon cemeteries around Salisbury alongside evidence of Romano-British occupation to the north in the fifth century.[71] Thus we have the impression of an area under Romano-British authority but with significant Anglo-Saxon immigrants. There were Jutes in the New Forest area, Saxons in the Thames Valley and confusing and possibly misdated literary sources concerning the arrival of the first West Saxon kings.

What all this suggests is significant Germanic presence in the tribal areas of the Atrebates and Belgae but continued British presence and control of some towns and cities. Additionally, it implies a clear distinction between the east and west of Wessex, which leaves some to wonder what became of the *civitas* of the Atrebates and who was in control around 500? This mixed picture across the south is especially interesting when considering some of the more likely candidates for Arthur's battles, especially Badon.

Towns in Oxfordshire were recorded as captured in the late sixth century, implying this area was also under British control at the time of Arthur. As we head north, the Fosse Way Roman road (connecting Exeter, Ilchester, Bath, Cirencester, Leicester and Lincoln) appears to have been a very important boundary line.[72] It seems to increase in significance the further north one goes until it meets the Trent Valley which passes north of Leicester. The Trent itself was a very important route for immigration and we see early Anglo-Saxon settlements mainly to the east and south of this line.

The Lincoln area is especially interesting as it shows both significant early Germanic settlement and a continuation of Romano-British authority. To the north-west of Lincoln lay the British kingdom of Elmet, around the Leeds area, which was overrun by Northumbria in the early seventh century. So, we can be fairly confident that the area was under British control in Arthur's time. Further north we come to York. We can see early evidence of Anglo-Saxon burials, materials and settlements is confined to Deira, just north of the Humber, possibly covering the *civitas* of the Parisi. Across the north, outside the modern-day East Riding of Yorkshire, there is an absence of early Anglo-Saxon burials and settlements.

North of Hadrian's Wall, the evidence supports a strong British Gododdin kingdom centred on the Lothian region.[73] East of this, Rheged is likely to have spanned both sides of the Wall. If the *Historia Brittonum* is to be believed, the British kingdoms were strong enough after Ida (and thus Arthur), to combine and push the Bernicians back to Lindisfarne. Rhydderch Hen, Gwallawg, Urien and Morcant are named and if later genealogies are correct, it involved the kingdoms of Strathclyde, Rheged and Elmet. Their opponent was Theoderic, one of Ida's sons who reigned (again, if we accept the genealogies and reign lengths in the *Historia*) in the 570s. We can tentatively suggest that the Romano-British position would have been even stronger at the time of Arthur. Importantly, the archaeological evidence would suggest that the area covered by the *Dux Britanniarum* and the *civitas* of the Brigantes maintained a strong British polity or military force.[74]

We can use the archaeological evidence to draw a third line between the maximum and minimum. Some have suggested a line running roughly from

Berwick to Poole.[75] However, that may be too crude and I have tried to place my 'likely line of conflict' to reconcile it with the archaeological evidence just covered. It's a 'line of best fit' rather than an accurate boundary, as shown in Map 13.

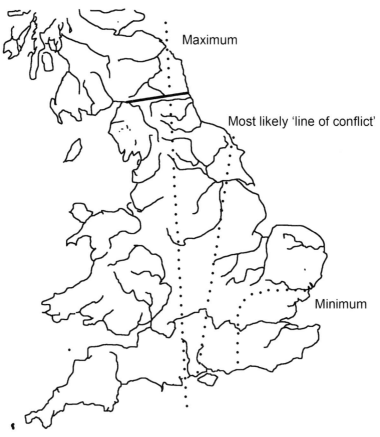

Map 13: Minimum and maximum likely partition lines

It has to be accepted we have little evidence of the political reality north of Hadrian's Wall for the late fifth and early sixth century. It may well be the literary sources are correct, despite the lack of archaeological evidence, and Germanic mercenaries were indeed posted somewhere in the north. We have seen evidence for significant numbers of early migrants in specific areas: East Anglia, the Thames Valley and Lincolnshire. These areas may well have remained under the control of the Britons. Map 14 might therefore be more accurate. Firstly, I retained the line containing the south-eastern province of Maxima Caesariensis representing the area first affected by Hengest seizing control. Secondly, I have added areas of significant Germanic presence that may have resulted in conflict, along with the former northern command where mercenaries may have been posted.

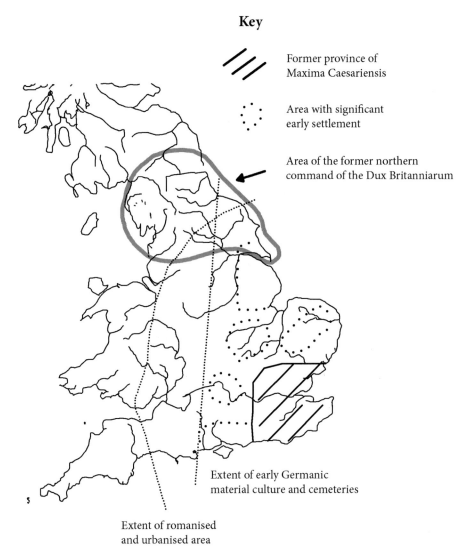

Key

Former province of
Maxima Caesariensis

Area with significant
early settlement

Area of the former northern
command of the Dux Britanniarum

Extent of early Germanic
material culture and cemeteries

Extent of romanised
and urbanised area

Map 14: Likely areas of conflict

Summary

In conclusion, we have a number of sources that, in spite of discrepancies and contradictions, have an element of consensus and consistency. Roman authority ends but a romanised Britain continues despite a decline in the economy and urban life. An increase in Germanic immigration adds to a general cultural change alongside religious, political and social friction. A distinctive difference exists with a romanised, urbanised, and more ethnically and culturally diverse south and east. Cultural identity begins to shift for some. The Diocese structure appears to survive long enough for mercenaries to be placed in the east, very likely Kent, and an area of the northern command. Sometime in the mid-fifth century, a revolt occurs.

'After a time', Gildas states, Ambrosius Aurelianus leads a fightback that culminates with 'pretty well the last defeat of the villains' at the siege of Badon Hill. It also results in a partition and a period of peace from 'external wars' that have lasted to his day. The exact date of the *adventus Saxonum* remains open to debate but the *Historia* gives a very reasonable, if not highly entertaining, explanation. Regardless of this, the evidence points to Badon falling between 490 and 520, and more likely, 490–500. On this basis, one could argue that the middle or late Arthur are more likely options. Some scholars, such as Arthur W Wade-Evans, have argued for the earlier option. Leaving that debate to one side, we now have some reasonable clues pointing to where conflict might have occurred: roughly, a corridor either side of a line from the Humber to the Solent.

To be clear, this is where we would expect to find locations for battles. This would not negate battles far from this zone. It would raise some interesting questions and require some explanation, but it would not be impossible or even unreasonable as we shall see. Having now reached the time of Arthur, we will now go beyond to the emergence of kingdoms at the end of the sixth century. Knowing what happened immediately after Arthur's time will be just as instructive and useful as the historical background of the early fifth century.

Chapter 5

Civitas to Kingdom

The previous chapters have brought us up to the very earliest time a historical Arthur could have lived. We began with three rough options, an early, middle or late Arthur within a timeframe of c. AD 450–550. The evidence so far suggests the earlier option is the last likely. We can have more confidence in placing the battle at Badon Hill between c.490 and 520. To be more precise, we can reduce this to a Badon in c.490–500 or Ambrosius winning a victory c.490 with Badon a generation later in c.516. In both cases, Gildas is writing between 534 and 547, and it is more likely to be either side of c.536. This would be either before the climatic events noted by contemporary writers across the empire or prompted by their manifestation or as a response. We recall the reports from 536 of dust veils or fog darkening the sky from Cassiodorus, a 'most dread portent' from Procopius and the *Irish Annals* recording a 'failure of bread'.

The traditional chronology is not undermined by any of the evidence so far: the Romans leave and there is an increase in raids and migration; a council, led by Vortigern, invites Saxon mercenaries who later revolt sometime in the mid-fifth century; and Ambrosius Aurelianus, c.474–491 (from Bede), leads a fightback that culminates in the victory at Badon either side of the year 500. We are left with two likely timeframes for Arthur. The first, c.475–525, has him reaching fighting age in time for a Badon in the 490s, perhaps with the senior Ambrosius in charge. The second places him c.500–540 with Badon either misattributed to him or occurring just as he comes of fighting age.

Putting that to one side, we have seen how Britain evolved over the fifth century. While economic and urban life declined, Roman identity did not collapse overnight, rather it evolved. Significant Germanic settlement occurred disproportionally in precisely those areas that had been more romanised and urbanised. These places were associated with river valleys and coastal areas but also sites of significant economic activity near to, and surrounding, towns and villas. The Diocese structure likely survived to the mid-fifth century but had probably broken down by 450–475.[1] Whatever occurred in the mid-fifth century contributed to distinctive cultural identities forming. In the east, by the seventh century, the former Roman identity had evolved into a Germanic Anglo-Saxon one, despite most of the indigenous population remaining and land use continuing.

The question then is what happened to the provinces and *civitates* during and after the Saxon revolt and later war with Ambrosius? The provincial structure was clearly long gone by the year 600. Some *civitates* appear at face value to have evolved into petty kingdoms. However, it is not certain that pre-Roman tribal areas corresponded with Roman *civitates* or that those *civitates* were the basis of Anglo-Saxon or Brittonic kingdoms.[2] The debate about the nature of *civitates* offers two possibilities:[3] they were either based on tribal areas covering the whole province; or a complex pattern with only some based on tribal areas and others on Roman administrative organisations with some areas outside the direct control of Roman authority. There was also likely a distinction between military, urban and rural areas.

We recall from fifth-century Gaul one's *civitas* was a central part of cultural identity, even after Roman identity was diminished. In 471, Sidonius Apollinaris refers to a Briton as *Regiensem*, thus demonstrating the concept of *civitas* was still important to some Britons too.[4] *Civitates* in Wales appear to show continuation, as do the West Country. We can say with some confidence the later Welsh kingdoms were based on the former Romano-British political identities.[5] In the east, Britons certainly retained authority over some areas as immigrants became assimilated.[6] Enclaves appear to have existed for a time at London, Lincoln and York although ringed by Germanic burials and settlements.[7] Yet there appears, for example, to be a link between the *civitas* of the Cantii to the emergence of the kingdom of Kent. In general, the boundaries of the Roman *civitates* appear to be very relevant to the pattern of later settlement and thus the later emerging Anglo-Saxon kingdoms.[8] A fair summary would be a patchwork of polities consisting of different ethnicities, culture, religion and assimilation rates,[9] with significant levels of assimilation of Germanic peoples alongside acculturation among the indigenous Britons. At the same time, in what later became England, kings up to the eighth century often portrayed themselves as heirs to Rome and regardless of any partition, they could still be 'regarded as culturally late Roman.'[10]

We have seen which areas were probably affected by the initial Saxon revolt. We have also considered the likely line partition or corridor of potential conflict. Investigating the emerging kingdoms of the late sixth century may give further clues. Many appear just after Arthur's floruit but some could have much earlier origins. It may be worthy of note that none of the theories for locations of Arthur's battles appear to suggest London, the largest and most important of Roman Britain's cities, as well as the former Diocese capital. In fact, while a multitude of theories place Arthur's battles from Scotland and Wessex through to Wales and Lincolnshire, it's interesting to see which locations don't feature. Very few put the battles in the south-east where the *Historia* claims Octha came after Hengest's death. We will begin with the earliest of the Anglo-Saxon kingdoms.

Kent

Kent claims to be the first English kingdom and it is certainly the first Anglo-Saxon kingdom to convert to Christianity. It also has the first written English law codes from Aethelbert in the early seventh century.[11] The weight of evidence suggests migration was the prime factor in its formation.[12] Archaeological evidence demonstrates Jutes were present in East Kent and that Saxons were in West Kent, and while Frankish material is found all over the south it is more prominent in Jutish areas.[13] The case for Jutish origin is supported by pottery and other artefacts.[14] We will see Frankish links were still influential at the end of the sixth century through marriage and a Roman mission. We will also recall Procopius's tale of a Frankish embassy to Constantinople in 553 accompanied by Angles.

By the end of the fifth century, Germanic material culture was dominant and was associated with Roman sites of continued occupation.[15] In a survey of late Roman towns, the greatest evidence for continued fifth- and sixth-century activity came from Canterbury.[16] We thus have some archaeological evidence to support the literary sources. DNA evidence also shows significant immigration with one study suggesting 20 per cent with similarities in genetic markers with Friesland.[17] It is noted the kingdom's name seems to have persisted from a pre-Roman tribal area, settled by the Cantii, or the Cantiaci as Caesar called them. It then evolves through Cantware or Centrice in the Anglo-Saxon period to the modern-day Kent. It is likely the kingdom grew out of the former Romano-British *civitas*.[18] There is also support for a political divide between West and East Kent.[19] It is unique for having had two bishoprics at Canterbury and Rochester. So, we have evidence for early settlement, continuation of administrative boundaries and a distinction between east and west Kent.

The *Historia* states the first mercenaries were granted Thanet in East Kent. It continues by explaining how it was transferred from the British King Gwyrangon to Hengest as the price for the hand of Hengest's daughter to Vortigern. This sounds like the story of a legal transfer similar to many other examples across the Western Empire. There's no record of Gwyrangon's feelings. Later Vortimer, taking the crown, fights a series of battles driving them out of Kent. It is worth recording what is claimed:[20] 'Vortimer fought vigorously against Hengest and Horsa...expelled them and besieged them as far as the island called Thanet'. Three times he 'shut them up and besieged them, attacking, threatening and terrifying them.' Hengest and Horsa then send envoys to Germany to 'summon a vast number of fighting men'. We then hear of a period where they 'sometimes victoriously advanced their frontiers, sometimes being defeated and expelled'.

This sounds very much like Gildas's account of Ambrosius: 'From then on victory went now to our countrymen, then to their enemies.' It's also interesting that they were 'sometimes expelled'. Another notable similarity is with the description after Arthur's battles: after their defeats the 'English sought help from Germany and continually and considerably increased their number.'

While the *Historia* implies British victories from west to east, the *Anglo-Saxon Chronicles* record victories going east to west. However, Vortimer is only stated as victorious after the third battle on the list – the others are simply described as 'keen' battles. Whatever the case, Hengest returns after Vortimer's death. Details of the battles in Kent from both sources are summarised in Table 6.

Table 6: Battles in Kent

Battle	Vortimer's battles from the *Historia Brittonum*	Hengest's battles from the *Anglo-Saxon Chronicles*
1	*flumen Derguentid* translated as the River Darenth, near Dartford.	In 455, Hengest and Horsa fought Vortigern at *Agelesford*; Horsa was killed. Aesc succeeded to kingdom. Translated as Aylesford.
2	At a ford called Episford in their language. Horsa and Vortigern's son, Cateyrn, fell.	In 457, Hengest and Aesc fought the Britons at Crecganford, killed 4,000 men. Britons abandoned Kent and fled to their stronghold of London. Translated as Crayford which feeds into the Darenth a mile to the north.
3	In open country by the inscribed stone on the shore of the Gallic sea. Barbarians defeated: 'They fled to their keels and were drowned.'	In 465 Hengest and Aesc fight the Welsh near *Wippedesfleot* (Wipped's Creek) killing 12 chieftains and a thegn called Wipped. Possibly Ebbsfleet, East Kent.
4	Unstated.	In 473, Hengest and Aesc fought the Welsh and seized countless war loot. The Welsh fled like fire.

The first two battles can be viewed as correlated, though in reverse order. In the *Chronicles*, Hengest's first battle is against Vortigern rather than Vortimer, but there appears to have been a cross-cultural tradition about where Horsa was killed. Perhaps only the Britons were aware a son of Vortigern fell. Hengest's second battle also suggests London was still a functioning urban centre: 'the Britons then abandoned the land of Kent and in great terror fled to the stronghold of London.' This is interesting as Ptolemy, writing in the second century, attributes three towns to the Cantii: London, Canterbury and Richborough. It would appear that at some point, Hengest controlled East Kent and left the Britons in parts of West Kent with London.

The third battle on both lists could be the same. Equally, Hengest's last two battles could have occurred after Vortimer's death. Either could be synonymous with the massacre of three hundred nobles at the peace conference after which Hengest takes control of Sussex, Essex, Middlesex and 'other regions', presumably as well as retaining Kent.

Various sources list the genealogy for the early kings of Kent, which is summarised in Table 7. We can see some small differences but a fair amount of consistency. Importantly, Hengest is consistently four or five generations before Aethelbert, who reigned at the end of the sixth century.

Table 7: Early Kentish kings

Historia c.830	*Anglo-Saxon Chronicles* c.900	Bede 730	Anglian Collection Eighth century
Hengest and Horsa	Hengest and Horsa 455 Hengest and Aesc succeed to kingdom	Hengest and Horsa 449	Hengest
Octha	Aesc 488 succeeds to kingdom of Kent and rules for 24 years	Oisc	Ocga
Ossa	512?	Oeric Oisc	Oese
		Octa	
Eormenric		Eormenric	Eormenric
Aethelbert	Aethelberht 465, rules for 53 years	Aethelbert 596 Pope Gregory sends St Augustine	Aepelberht

Bede names Hengest's son as Oisc and implies he was the founder of the royal house as the descendants were known as the Oiscingas. The first attested king is Aethelbert at the end of the sixth century although Bede names his father as Eormenric. Gregory of Tours, writing in the seventh century, refers to Aethelbert's marriage to a Frankish Christian princess, and describes his father as being the King of Kent without naming him. The implication from Gregory is that Eormenric was still king at the time of the marriage in around the 580s. Given Aethelbert's death in 616, it is likely the entry for 565 in the *Anglo-Saxon Chronicle* is actually his birth, rather than the start of his reign. We can thus be fairly confident that Eormenric is actually the first attested King of Kent and Aethelbert, born in 565, married a Frankish princess in c.585 and came to the throne between 589 and 593.[21]

What the genealogies strongly suggest is that the earliest dates given for Hengest's arrival in the *Historia* are very unlikely. If we take an unusually long average of twenty-five years for each reign, then we must count back five generations from Aethelbert's known death in 616. This would get us back to 491, close to Hengest's death in 488. A Hengest arriving fighting fit in 428 might live an unusually long life but would not be expected to be fighting battles fifty years later. A date of AD 375 is certainly out of the question.

Therefore, the narrative in Bede and the statement for Hengest's death in the *Anglo-Saxon Chronicles* is not implausible. One interpretation of the passage in the *Historia* is that Arthur came to fight them, that is Octha, in the land of the Kentishmen, i.e. in Kent. However, the whole passage is as follows:

> On Hengest's death, his son, Octha came down from the north of Britain to the Kingdom of the kentishmen, and from him are sprung the kings of the kentishmen. Then Arthur fought against them in those days, together with the kings of the British; but he was their dux bellorum.

So, one could interpret it as Arthur fighting the descendants of Octha such as Ossa. In Welsh legends 'Osla big-knife' is described as one of Arthur's men in the tenth-century tale of *Culhwch and Olwen* and as Arthur's opponent at the Battle of Badon in the twelfth-century *Dream of Rhonabwy*. This could be a confusion with the eighth-century Mercian king Offa, who was recorded as Offa 'Great-Knife' in some genealogy tables. Geoffrey of Monmouth in the *History of the Kings of Britain* names two of Arthur's earlier opponents as Octa and Eosa although at Badon he names Colgrin, Baldulf and Cheldric as the Saxon leaders.

One could also interpret it as fighting them in the north from where Octha had just come. Or simply that he fought the Anglo-Saxons wherever he found them. The important thing to take from this is that according to literary tradition, Kent and subsequent lands lost in the rebellion were firmly under Anglo-Saxon control prior to the time of Arthur. Secondly, there is nothing in the archaeological or later historical record that undermines the tradition in the *Historia*.

I will finish this section with an interesting addition from J.R.R. Tolkien, author of *Lord of the Rings*. He made a detailed study of the *Finnesburg Fragment* which forms part of the heroic poem *Beowulf*, one of the oldest and most important examples of Old English.[22] The story is set in the sixth century and features various Danish, Geatish, Jutish and other characters, and a warrior called Hengest. Tolkien estimates the timeframe for the characters involved and equates his Hengest with that of the *Historia*. It's an interesting tale of a Jutish leader, Hengest, fighting in a Danish-Geat war in Friesland. Tolkien dates him to c.425 and his arrival in Britain to c.453.

Essex, Sussex, Surrey and Middlesex

We have already seen a heavy concentration of Saxon settlement around the south-east. Stretching eastwards, the *civitas* of the Trinovantes seems to have evolved into the later kingdom of Essex.[23] However, recent analysis shows a lack of early Germanic material culture around major urban sites such as London, St Albans, Rochester, Canterbury and Colchester.[24] In the Northern Thames Basin, evidence is largely confined to coastal areas and waterways.[25] Rippon finds an absence of evidence for early Anglo-Saxon settlement within 'all but the fringes' of Catuvellauni and Trinovantes areas.[26]

The site at Mucking, in southern Essex, demonstrates settlers were arriving in the early part of the fifth century. It suggests the inhabitants were confined to a small area, possibly a grant of land peripheral to existing Romano-British communities.[27] It would appear that in this region, at least, it was sparsely populated that formed tribal, and later *civitas*, boundaries such as fens, woodland, high ground and rivers.[28] Thus, an increase in Germanic material in these areas might indicate settlement on unoccupied land or positioning of mercenary forces to protect strategically important areas. Indeed, Rippon finds the following concerning the distribution of cemeteries and *Grubenhauser* (sunken houses) in the Northern Thames Basin in the mid-fifth century:[29] it suggests 'immigration may have occurred within the context of Romano-British socio-political control.'

Yet the first known king recorded was Sledd as late as 587. He was married to Ricula, the sister of Aethelbert. It does appear that Kent had some control over the East Saxon kingdom at the end of the sixth century. Bede states it was Aethelbert who built and endowed St Paul's and it is interesting to note the extent of the early East Saxon See, founded in 604. The original London Diocese included Middlesex, Surrey and south-eastern Hertfordshire.[30] This suggests two things. Firstly, the original East Saxon kingdom was much more extensive than the modern-day county of Essex. It spread west and south, surrounding London. Secondly, the Kentish kingdom was the dominant partner, at least at the end of the sixth century. There is no evidence of any fifth- or sixth-century royal power. While the area appears to be under Saxon control by the end of the sixth century, St Albans may have remained an enclave controlled by Britons. The likely date for absorption into the East Saxon kingdom is thought to be late sixth century.[31] We have already seen the East Saxons were initially heavily influenced by Aethelbert of Kent. This is very interesting in light of the contents of the *Historia Brittonum* regarding Essex and Middlesex being ceded to Hengest, which could be taken as the *civitas* of the Trinovantes that then becomes the East Saxon kingdom.

The origins of Surrey appear lost; either it was a collection of separate groups or a southern region of Mercia, Essex or Middlesex. Similar to Surrey, the first mention of Middle Saxons is through a land grant in 704.[32] This was given to a certain *Frithuwold*, of 'the province of the men of Surrey', a 'sub-king of Wulfhere, king of the Mercians.'[33] Bede called Surrey *Sudergeona* which translates as the 'Southern District'.

To the south, the *Anglo-Saxon Chronicle* records Aelle as landing in 477 at 'Cymen's Shore and there killed many Welsh and drove some to flight into the wood which is named the Weald.' Cymen's Shore (or 'Cymenes ora') has been possibly identified as Selsey in West Sussex, which is nine miles south of the former capital of the Regni at Noviomagus Regnorum, Chichester. The next recorded battle at Mearcredes burnan (or Mearcred's Burn) is unidentified but the direction appears to be west to east as the next location, unlike so many in our sources, is firmly identified. In 491, Aelle and Cissa besieged Anderitum, the Roman-Saxon Shore fort at Pevensey. They 'killed all who lived there, there was not even one Briton left there.'

Bede also names Aelle as the first *Bretwalda*, the etymology of which is more likely to be 'wide ruler' rather than 'Britain ruler'. If this title held any weight, then it is unlikely to refer to just the Sussex area. There is no further mention of any Sussex kings until the middle of the seventh century. Archaeology does, indeed, show early evidence of Saxon settlement along the south coast between Chichester and Pevensey. The border of the Regni may have been the River Meon to the west of Portsmouth, some 20 miles to the north-west of where Aelle likely landed. Studies suggest the borders of the Sussex area stretched from the territory of the Meonware in the west to the River Cuckmere in the east.[34] There are hints that the initial settlement involved the eastern half centred at Pevensey, and later the western half, incorporating the former *civitas* capital at Chichester, was consumed.[35]

We hear no further of Aelle, his sons or Sussex until 607 when Ceolwulf of Wessex fights against them. The next reference is for 661 when Wulfhere, Penda's son, leads the Mercians as far as Ashdown. He follows this by giving Wight to Aethelwold, King of the South Saxons and receiving him at baptism. This conversion is recorded in the *Annales Cambriae* for 665: 'The first celebration of Easter among the Saxons'. Interestingly, it also records, 'the second Battle of Badon, Morgan dies'. Who Morgan was and what, if any, connection there was is unknown. It's worth noting the reference to Badon and whether there is a link to Wulfhere's raid 'as far as Ashdown.' We will cover this further in the chapter concerning Arthur's battles. It is one of the few indications of likely locations near to Octha's 'Kingdom of the kentishmen'.

Another clue is contained in a later entry of the *Anglo-Saxon Chronicles*. In 825, the West Saxons conquer what is referred to as the 'East Kingdom' which included Kent, Sussex, Essex and Surrey.[36] Admittedly, this is three centuries later but it is at least curious that the same territory is mentioned in the *Historia*, had significant early Saxon settlements and cemeteries, and is likely to be within the old Roman province of Maxima Caesariensis. It also demonstrates, along with numerous other examples from the *Chronicles*, that the Gewissae or West Saxons were just as likely to be at war with their eastern neighbours as the Britons.

Further West Saxon expansion initially occurs after 550 and in 568, Caewlin, Bede's second Bretwalda, drives Aethelbert back into Kent. This could suggest Wessex and Kent were the two major powers in the south at the time at the expense of Sussex. Perhaps Hengest's descendants controlled the 'eastern kingdom' with Aelle producing only a brief period of Sussex control. If Aelle's floruit has not been misdated, then one is left to speculate why he disappears from the record and why there is a 50–year gap between Bede's Bretwaldas.

East Anglia

This region is probably the earliest to be settled by significant Germanic immigration from early in the fifth century.[37] The first attested king of East Anglia was Raedwald who died in 627. The genealogies name his father as Tytil and grandfather as Wuffa, from whom the royal family are known as the Wuffingas. Nennius goes back one further generation claiming Webha was the first to rule. Roger of Wendover, writing in the thirteenth century, dates Wuffa's reign to 571. The archaeological evidence suggests it has Scandinavian influences, especially from Sweden. The later kingdom covered roughly the area of the Iceni but the names Norfolk and Suffolk (literally North and South folk) imply two initial areas or polities. We therefore again have a substantial gap between evidence of early settlement and records for the first kings. However, we have some tentative clues of continuation of farming practices at West Stow in Suffolk covering this gap.[38]

There are some interesting links with the earliest written Anglo-Saxon epic poem *Beowulf.* While the language in the surviving ninth-century copy is West Saxon, there are strong hints it originated in East Anglia as early as the seventh century.[39] There is a suggestion that one of the main characters, Queen Wealhpeow married to King Hrodgar, was a Wuffinga princess from Southern Sweden. The context of the storyline has been placed in the early sixth century[40] although Tolkien placed it earlier. Archaeological evidence, not least the royal ship funeral and Sutton Hoo, demonstrates that East Anglia had the strongest links to Scandinavia than any other Anglo-Saxon kingdom.[41] Additionally, the Wuffingas, with its links to south-west Sweden and south-east Norway, is 'etymologically identical' to the Wylfingas in Beowulf and Wulfingas in another tenth-century Anglo-Saxon poem, *Widsith*.[42] There are also interesting parallels in *Beowulf* with stories of Anglian saints' lives, folklore tales of fenland monsters and place names.[43] This evidence from literary sources, poems and folklore suggests an interesting change over time. An early Anglo-Saxon audience listening to *Beowulf*, perhaps in an early seventh-century hall, still regarded their ancestral homeland as overseas with stories set around modern-day Denmark and the surrounding regions. By the time of the tenth-century poems like *Battle of Brunanburh* and *Battle of Maldon*, the 'ancestral lands are no longer overseas.'[44] They considered themselves English and their homeland England.

Recent analysis suggests the East Anglia region had a separate socio-economic identity as early as the first half of the fifth century.[45] There is a consistent difference in terms of material culture between East Anglia and further south, such as the area occupied by the Trinovantes.[46] Examples include sleeve clasps and the position of weapons in cemeteries. Additionally, unlike in other areas, early immigrants are spread out across the landscape rather than confined to specific areas.[47] Dykes in South Cambridgeshire appear to show a fluctuating boundary between the East and Middle Angles.[48] Their construction and positioning show they were likely built by the locals defending attacks from the west, rather than facing east and defending raids from Angles or Saxons.

We can summarise as follows: the *civitas* of the Iceni and surrounding areas experienced significant early Germanic immigration, but it differed significantly to that in other areas with heavy Scandinavian influences. There was a considerable gap between settlement in the mid-fifth century and the formation of the known Anglo-Saxon kingdoms in the late sixth. There may well have been lost and forgotten lines of rulers but it's precisely in this gap that Arthur would have been active. Finally, the East Angles of the sixth century likely considered themselves to be culturally distinct from Britons but also other Germanic tribes such as the Saxons.

Lincolnshire

The earliest Germanic immigrants appear to have been present by the year 400 but there are then signs of new Anglian communities from before 500 which expanded considerably over the next two centuries.[49] By the seventh century, Lindissi was an Anglo-Saxon kingdom with Bede, writing in the early eighth century, describing the people as 'Lindisfaran'. However, there is evidence for a surviving British authority well into the sixth century. Archaeological evidence such as cremation cemeteries form a ring around Lincoln but did not encroach its hinterland unlike other fifth-century evidence at York, Leicester or Caistor.[50] This suggests the Romano-British retained control and thus possibly invited the Germanic settlers or mercenaries. It may be worth noting that Geoffrey of Monmouth states that Hengest, leading the first band of mercenaries, is given land near Lincoln. This is not inconsistent with Gildas, who simply says they were first settled in 'the east of the island' although the *Historia* names Thanet in Kent.

There was a thriving Christian community in the area and a bishop of Lincoln attended the Council of Arles, southern Gaul, as early as the year 314. We also have evidence of post-Roman church-building alongside some very British-sounding names in the later Anglian Collection detailing the genealogy of the kings of Lindsey such as Caedbaed, likely derived from the British *Cataboduos*.[51] There is also significant place name evidence across the region for a continuity of British communities.[52] The eighth-century *Life of St Guthlac* talks of Brittonic-speaking communities in the area at that time. In fact, there is evidence of a distinct British community in Cambridge as late as the eleventh century.[53] Thus, not only does there appear to have been a significant British power up to the mid-sixth century but a 'substantial British element to the population' remained into the later centuries.[54]

Bede records that St Paulinus visited Lincoln after being appointed Archbishop of York in 627.[55] His first convert was Blaecca, a Reeve or *Praefectus Lindocolinae civitas*. This suggests a survival of a Romano-British administrative title.

Archaeology and genetic studies suggest the following: the majority of people in the later centuries were descendants of the Romano-British population; there was considerable continuity of demographic and agricultural activity; and newcomers were largely assimilated into existing communities.[56]

In the East Midlands, early presence of Germanic culture and cemeteries appear to be restricted to river valleys.[57] The Trent in particular has significant finds to the south and east with kingdoms north and west of this, such as Elmet and Powys remaining under Romano-British authority into the seventh century. Further south, there are no substantial migration period cemeteries in central or southern Hertfordshire.[58] We can tentatively suggest that Lincoln may have been under British control at the time of Arthur, although with significant pockets of Germanic settlers. This may prove very relevant when we look at the battle locations as probably a third and up to half the battles on our list could reasonably be located there, in the region of the Linnuis, though a River Dubglas is unknown in the area.

Northumbria

Another area containing a number of likely battle locations is the north. Northumbria consisted of two kingdoms, Deira and Bernicia, both with British etymologies *Bernech* and *Deura* (the latter deriving from the River Derwent). Deira, perhaps covering the *civitas* of the Parisi just north of the Humber, was first settled before the more northern Bernicia.[59] The boundary between the two is likely to have been the River Tees[60] with Bernicia beginning south of Hadrian's Wall and eventually extending all the way to Lothian in modern-day Scotland. This is exactly where both the *Historia* and Geoffrey of Monmouth place Hengest's son, Octha, and cousin Ebissa. Perhaps they took their whole force with them and settlers followed. Perhaps the reference to Arthur fighting against them refers to any remnants left in the north. It's left frustratingly unclear.

However, neither linguistics nor archaeological material reveals much of an Anglo-Saxon presence before the seventh century, especially north of the Tees and west of the Vale of York. The largest concentration of cemeteries in Bernicia are in the extreme south and there is little evidence of any Anglo-Saxon materials in the fifth or sixth centuries aside from isolated burials.[61]

Evidence of material culture does exist in the second half of the fifth century from York to Catterick.[62] These are often associated with Romano-British military centres,[63] although the later Bernician royal palace site at Yeavering confirms the reality of great halls similar to ones depicted in poems such as *Beowulf* (Hrodgar's Hall).[64] Angle mercenaries could have been driven out of Bernicia by a powerful Brittonic force. Or perhaps the evidence between York and Catterick in the second half of the fifth century is indeed a faint whisper of Octha and Ebissa's force.

The first king of Deira we can confirm is Aelle who reigned from c.568 to 598.[65] The *Historia* names Soemil as being the first king to separate Deira from Bernicia, which could mean wresting it from British control before the time of Ida. He is listed as five generations before Aelle by both the *Historia* and the eighth-century *Anglian Chronicles*. This could push his date back to the fifth century yet if we take examples from the sixth, seventh or eighth centuries for the kings of Northumbria, there would be nothing unusual about six kings spanning anything from 30 to 70 years. This would then place Soemil firmly in the early sixth century. Given this date, the implication is that he separated Deira from British control and placed Angles there and around York, just when early archaeological evidence presents itself. Indeed, Carver describes 'the creep of Anglo-Saxon burial grounds' north of the Humber after 475.[66]

The first king of Bernicia is named as Ida by both Bede and the *Historia*, and is given the date of 547 for the beginning of his reign. A surviving French document from c.850 states that Oesa and Eosa were the first of the Bernician royal dynasty to arrive.[67] As the grandfather of Ida, this would place Oesa around 500.[68] The *Historia* names Ida's father as Eobba. Interestingly, it also states Hengest's son Octha and Octha's cousin Ebissa campaigned against the Picts and were given land 'near the wall'. On Hengest's death, Octha comes south but no further mention is made of Ebissa. A corruption of Ebissa to Eoppa in the Vespasian genealogy list would not be difficult and from that to Eobba a simple step.[69] If there is any truth in this, we would have a link between Hengest's descendants and Ida's dynasty. Three slightly different genealogies can be seen and compared below. It is worth noting Ida's grandfather's name, Oesa, Ossa or Esa, which also could be corrupted to the 'Osla big-knife', the name given to Arthur's enemy at Badon in the fourteenth-century Welsh poem *The Dream of Rhonabwy*.

Anglian Collection, eighth century: Oesa, Eoppa, Ida
Historia Brittonum, early ninth century: Ossa, Eobba, Ida
Anglo-Saxon Chronicle, late ninth century: Esa, Eoppa, Ida

The *Historia* records Ida as joining Din Guaire, the British name for Bamburgh, to Bernicia. Bede claims Bamburgh is named after the British-sounding Queen Bebba. This could suggest a nascent Angle kingdom pushing northwards from the eastern end of Hadrian's Wall in the second quarter of the sixth century. This again implies the British were in control of this area in the time of Arthur a generation or two before.

The *Historia* records a combined British force fighting against Theodoric, one of Ida's sons, and besieging him on Lindisfarne. Urien of Rheged, Rhydderch Hen of Alt Clut, Gwallawg (possibly Elmet) and Morcant blockaded them for three days and nights, similar to the duration claimed in the *Annales Cambriae* for Badon. A similar phrase to Gildas and Bede is used: 'sometimes the enemy, sometimes the Cymry were victorious.' Given the reign lengths outlined in the *Historia* and elsewhere, Theodoric's reign can be estimated as between 572 and 579. The kingdoms of Alt Clut, Gododdin and Rheged likely emerged from the mid-fifth century after the Picts were driven back.[70] This would suggest they flourished through the time of any historical Arthur and were still a dominant force in the north after he was gone.

In the epic Welsh poem *Y Gododdin*, three hundred warriors from the British kingdom centred around Lothian were still powerful enough to launch an attack on their southern Anglo-Saxon neighbours at Catraeth, possibly Catterick, towards the end of the sixth century, before the kingdom fell in around 638. The older 'B' text of *Y Gododdin* never mentions the Bernicians, only the Deirans.

This might suggest an earlier date for the battle than first thought.[71] Yet if we accept the line referring to Arthur, then the battle occurred sometime after his exploits.

What all this strongly suggests is that even in the mid-sixth century, the embryonic kingdoms of Deira and Bernicia were surrounded by powerful British-controlled polities: Rheged, Alt Clut, Gododdin, Elmet and later Pictish and Dal Riata kingdoms. The final dominance of Aethelfrith, (c.593–616), was in no way guaranteed at that point. The evidence from Hadrian's Wall and military forts in the north suggests some continuity into the fifth century. So, we have archaeological evidence for continuation of military forts; some Germanic settlement confined to Deira; literary sources placing Octha and Ebissa by the wall; and Bede who states the Saxons 'made a temporary treaty with the Picts', suggesting they were close by geographically.

How likely is it that evidence is missed in the areas the literary sources point to? The *Historia* claims Octha went to the north with forty *keels*, each of which

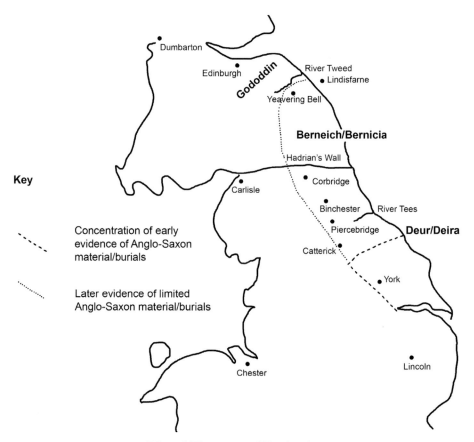

Map 15: The origins of Northumbria

carried around thirty men equating to 1,200 troops. Geoffrey of Monmouth claims an unlikely three hundred boats implying 9,000 troops and later claims Hengest returns with an army numbering an even more unlikely 300,000. But 1,200 is a late Roman legion-sized force which could be posted to two or three locations. It is quite conceivable such a relatively small force over just a few years, confined to a small area, would leave no discernible trace.

In conclusion, we can make the following points: there is a strong suggestion that Brittonic military strength in the north continued throughout and beyond Arthur's likely floruit. Evidence for Germanic settlement around AD 500 is confined to Deira, just north of the Humber; and literary sources place mercenaries as far north as Hadrian's Wall. We are thus left to speculate about which areas might likely have been points of conflict: much of the former Parisi *civitas*, perhaps the coastal area up to north of Hadrian's Wall, plus any of the forts in the old northern command where mercenaries might have been posted by a council led by a 'proud tyrant'. Map 15 shows early Deira based on the earliest Anglo-Saxon finds and burials. You will note it does not extend to the River Tees, which is the traditional border with its northern neighbour.

Wessex

Bede tells us in 'the early days', the West Saxons called themselves the Gewisse although he uses both terms himself writing in the early eighth century.[72] Many of their earlier kings have distinctly Brittonic names and Geoffrey of Monmouth describes Vortigern as the leader of the Gewissei. They settled in the territory of the former Atrebates tribal area and possibly part of the Belgae. This would place them on the western borders of the Trinovantes and the Regni, and that of the former Roman province Maxima Caesariensis. The name Gewissae means 'sure' or 'reliable', which might suggest they were considered loyal to at least one power at one time. But loyal to Vortigern would not necessarily mean loyal to Ambrosius or Arthur.

We have seen previously that the arrival date in the *Anglo-Saxon Chronicles* for Cerdic and Cynric of 495 is not certain. It may be a duplication of that for the West Saxons Stuf and Whitgar in 514. In any case, the regnal dates do not fit the chronology and historians have suggested a date of c.532 is more accurate.[73] Asser's *Life of Alfred the Great* in the late ninth century makes Creoda son of Cerdic and father to Cynric, which would make the 495 date more likely although this is not universally accepted. The alleged landing sites and battles against Britons along the south coast are also suspect. From Bede, we find the Isle of Wight and the land opposite were Jutish up to the late seventh century until 686 when Caedwalla of Wessex conquered the area.[74] The evidence for the origins of West

Saxon power is actually the upper Thames Valley.[75] Archaeological evidence points to the Abingdon area and the first site of a West Saxon Episcopal See was Dorchester-on-Thames. The battles of 552, 556 and 571 seem to suggest an expansion from the Thames Valley area and not the south coast.

In 568, Caewlin and Cutha defeat Aethelbert at Wibbandun (Wibba's mount, unidentified) and drive him back into Kent. Here then is a record of the Gewisse fighting against the Kentish kingdom. There is no reason to assume this was the first time or a one-off. The 571 entry is also illuminating: 'Here Cuthwulf fought against the Britons at Bedcanford and took 4 settlements: Limbury, Aylesbury, Benson and Eynsham and in the same year passed away.' They are unidentified but all settlements have modern place name equivalents west, east and south of Oxford. The implication is the Britons still held areas in what later became southern Mercia at the time of Arthur's floruit.

The archaeological record shows a marked contrast between west and east Wessex:[76]

- There is an extensive Saxon presence in the fifth century in east Wessex.
- The earliest settlements around the River Meon in east Hampshire.
- Artefacts dated prior to 475 are only found in eastern Wessex and the earliest is 425.[77]
- The finds are centred on the *civitas* of the Atrebates, as well as eastern Belgae and western Regnenses.
- The towns of Abingdon and Winchester are especially notable for early settlement, as well as Reading, Mildenhall, Andover, Pewsey and Maidenhead.
- Anglo-Saxon cemeteries as early as the second quarter of the fifth century are found at Abingdon and, from around 475, at Wallingford, Reading, West Hendred, Harwell, East Shefford and Long Wittenham with a more isolated case at Market Lavington.[78]

In summary, early Wessex appears to be a complex area in terms of ethnic and cultural differences. To the east are the emerging kingdoms of Kent and Sussex; to the west and north there is a fragmenting Romano-British provincial structure. Within the Atrebates and Belgae tribal areas, there was significant Germanic settlement. There were Jutes on the south coast of Hampshire, and Gewisse in the Thames Valley area, particularly around Abingdon; but there were also significant pockets around declining urban centres such as Winchester and Silchester. If Bath was part of the Belgae as Ptolemy stated in the second century, then we have an interesting piece of evidence. Bath is not taken by the West Saxons until 577. This might suggest the *civitas* structure had broken down as well, at least for the Belgae.

In a time of changing cultural, political and economic influences with warfare and social upheaval, it would not be surprising if, as some *civitates* consolidated power, others fragmented. We have already seen a distinct difference between east and west Wessex in terms of material culture and burials. Stronger regions such as Kent, and the Britons further west, might try to carve up a neighbouring area. They might be asked to help by particular towns or tribal groups. But power abhors a vacuum and out of the upheavals, new powers emerge from the ashes of the former tribal areas and *civitates* with perhaps new and evolving cultural identities. We get perhaps a hint of this from Bede when he tells us the West Saxons were originally called the Gewisse (the reliable). Together with the Jutes of south Hampshire and the indigenous Britons of the Atrebates and Belgae, they settled in what became Wessex. From such beginnings, centuries later, they defeated the Vikings and united the Anglo-Saxons to form England.

In *From Roman Civitas to Anglo-Saxon Shire*, Eagles attempts to map the 'unhappy partition with the barbarians' that Gildas refers to.[79] Using archaeological evidence and place name studies, a number of locations have been identified as forming the boundary by the mid-sixth century when Gildas was writing: Teffont, Bokerley Dyke, Charlton, Kemble, Pewsey, West Ashton and Market Lavington. The latter site has burial evidence from as early as 475 and is only 20 miles, or a day's march, from Bath. The other evidence I have used is the battles listed in the *Anglo-Saxon Chronicles*. The locations, or towns captured, cannot all be located exactly but they give us a reasonable idea of the extent of later expansion. Lastly, I have used the evidence of early burial and settlement down the Thames Valley, Chilterns and North Downs. This information is collated in Map 16 illustrating early Wessex.

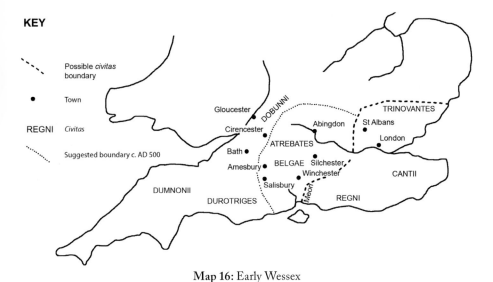

Map 16: Early Wessex

The implication from this is that in Arthur's time, to the east of this region was an established Anglo-Saxon controlled area centred from Kent, and to the west was a Romano-British domain including the Dobunni and Durotriges. But a nascent Gewisse kingdom nestled among the Atrebates and Belgae tribal areas which included significant continuity and Germanic settlement. We also have a significant difference between early east and west Wessex in terms of archaeological finds. A simple line bisecting this area might not paint an accurate picture. Romano-British continuity in the east at Silchester contrasts with early Saxon finds down the Thames Valley south-west of Abingdon. Other interesting facts are tentative links to Ambrosius from place names such as Amesbury and the various suggestions for Badon which litter this area.

Mercia

Mercia seems to have been the last kingdom to coalesce into a single unit, possibly a hundred years after some of the others such as Northumbria or Wessex.[80] Whether the smaller groups or minor kingdoms were born in the sixth or the fifth century is unknown. The Mercian royal family claimed descent from the kings of Angeln. The earliest common ancestor according to the genealogies was Pybba, father of the first historically-attested figure, Penda, who died in 655. Bede states Ceorl was king before Penda, and also that Edwin of Northumbria married Ceorl's daughter and had children while in exile from the reign of Aethelfrith, which places their births before 616. The general consensus according to legend is that Icel was the founder of the dynasty five generations before Penda. Taking 25 years per generation would thus place Icel at the start of the sixth century. However, the ten kings from Penda's son, Wulfhere, cover a period of 165 years and a rough estimate of sixteen and a half years per 'reign' would place Icel in the 550s, just after Ida took control in Bernicia.

Later medieval writers such as Roger of Wendover, Matthew Paris and Henry of Huntingdon suggest Mercia began in 585 under Creoda or Crida, who was succeeded by Pybba in 593.[81] The former two record this expansion as coming from East Anglia. A Dark Age cemetery in Wasperton, Warwickshire gives some interesting clues as it shows Romano-British graves alongside later Anglo-Saxon ones. Twenty-two were cremations dated to around 480. It suggests continuity of use, possible adoption of material and cultural behaviours, and later assimilation of Anglo-Saxon settlers. This is about 27 miles south-east of Birmingham and suggests Anglo-Saxon settlers had spread surprisingly far west at such an early date.

Just over 70 miles north-west of Wasperton is the Roman city of Viroconium at Wroxeter near Shrewsbury. We have already seen how archaeological evidence suggests Romano-British control continued there into the sixth century. We can see strong evidence for early Anglo-Saxon cemeteries on the east coast of the Trent and in Lincolnshire and Nottinghamshire. The Roman city of Ratae Corieltauvorum (modern-day Leicester) is still listed in the *Historia* as one of the twenty-eight cities of Britain. Yet it appears to have suffered much decline by the fifth century and to have been surrounded by significant settlement.

Bede tells us that in around 605, St Augustine met with the bishops of the neighbouring British kingdom at Augustine's oak on the borders of the Hwicce and the West Saxons.[82] We learn that when the South Saxons and their king, Aethelweah, were baptised in c.661, their queen, Eafe, was from the Hwicce and she and her family were Christian, 'as were their people'.[83] As late as 680, Hwicce has a king, Osric.[84] There is strong evidence the Hwicce evolved from the territory of the Dobunni whose *civitas* capital at Cirencester was also the provincial capital of Britannia Prima.[85] Within its territory lay the *colonia* at Gloucester. Worcester became the seat of the bishopric. Given that towns further south at Bath, Gloucester and Cirencester were not taken until 577, it is likely the Hwicce was under British authority prior to that time and the archaeological evidence supports this.[86] Bede also lists the bishoprics in his own day which might indicate administrative boundaries.[87] Kent and the West Saxons have two bishops, while Essex, Lindsey and Wight have one. Interestingly, Mercia and the Hwicce are separate bishoprics with a bishop each, along with a bishop of those who 'dwell west of the River Severn'.

Further north, clues may exist in the Welsh poem *Canu Heledd*, the songs of Heledd. Surviving in fourteenth-century manuscripts, it may date to the ninth century although there is debate about the veracity. It refers to Cynddylan, a prince of Powys slain in battle defending Pengwern, a subkingdom of eastern Powys. He was defeated by the English in the seventh century. It follows that Powys may have covered much of Shropshire and penetrated into Staffordshire, but there is another reason to take an interest in this poem. It includes several references to Eglwysseu bassa, the church of Bassa. It was a resting place for the prince and his ancestors, and was destroyed by the English. Not only is this associated with one of the battles, at the River Bassas, but it is close to other sites allegedly linked with Arthur.

In our time period, c.450–550, much of Central England appears to have been still under the control of the Britons. The Gewisse expanded north from the Thames Valley only in the second half of the sixth century. Another interesting point is the apparent alliances between later Mercians and Britons. In the sixth century, Penda fought with Cadwallon of Gwynedd against their common enemy, the Northumbrians. We learnt that there was extensive settlement in the east of the Trent Valley and spreading westwards from East Anglia. Bede gives the origins of the Mercians as from Angulus along with the 'East Angles, the Middle Angles, and all the Northumbrian race'.[88]

We get some idea of how Anglo-Saxon kingdoms emerged from a seventh-century document, *The Tribal Hidage*. It is easy to focus on the small tribal groupings and imagine them coalescing into the powerful Mercian kingdom of Offa in the eighth century. But it is far more difficult to go back in time and determine the political, cultural and military situation a hundred or two hundred years before. We must remember the whole region had significant continuation of the indigenous population.

The Tribal Hidage

The Tribal Hidage is an eleventh-century document thought to have been compiled in the seventh century. There is some debate as to whether it originated in Mercia or Northumbria. The absence of any reference to Northumbria could indicate it was a tribute list, although there is a consensus it is Mercian. Thirty-five tribes or territories are listed with the number of hides assigned to each one. A hide should be considered a unit of taxation rather than an exact geographical area. The area varied and depended on the quality of land. However, on average, one hide is roughly 30 modern acres or 120,000 square metres. This equates to about seventeen football fields. If we take an example, Kent has 15,000 hides compared to modern-day Kent which covers double that. It could just be East Kent but it is more likely a reflection of uninhabited or uneconomical areas. Not all the tribes can be identified or located but it does suggest an early presence of Anglo-Saxon peoples as far west as the Severn. The tribes and territories in the Tribal Hidage are shown in Table 8 and also in Map 17.

Table 8: The Tribal Hidage

Myrcna landes (Mercia) 30,000	North Gyrwa 600	Gifla 300	Hendrica 3,500	West Willa 600
Wocensaetna 7,000	East Wixna 300	Hicca 300	Unecungaga 1,200	East Engle 30,000
Westerna 7,000	West Wixna 600	Wihtgara 600	Arosaetna 600	East Saxena 7,000
Pecsaetna 1,200	Spalda 600	Noxgaga 5,000	Faerpinga 300	Cantwarena 15,000
Elmedsaetna 600	Wigesta 900	Ohtgaga 2,000	Bilmiga 600	South Saxena 7,000
Linesfarona 7,000	Herefinna 1,200	Hwinca 7,000	Widerigga 600	West Saxena 100,000
Suth Gyrwa 600	Sweordora 300	Cilternasaetna 4,000	East Willa 600	

Map 17: The Tribal Hidage

An interesting football-related metaphor has been used to explain the context of the Tribal Hidage.[89] It is a fiercely contested knock-out competition like the FA Cup. In the earlier rounds, various small non-league teams vie to progress, perhaps representing far less than the 300 hides of the smallest tribal areas listed above. As the competition moves forward, smaller groups are 'knocked out' and consumed into larger groupings. Eventually we reach the heptarchy of seven Anglo-Saxon kingdoms. Later still, Kent, Sussex and Essex give way to Wessex, Mercia, Northumbria and East Anglia. In the end, Wessex takes the cup, possibly at Brunaburh in 937, thus ending a 400–year competition.

It is possible to expand this analogy to ask some interesting questions. What happened to the ethnic, social and cultural identities of these smaller groups?

What about the indigenous Romano-British and pre-Roman tribal identities? We could speculate that they became as irrelevant as a 'Jutish identity' is today. One usual analogy might be the big bang theory. The universe is seen to be expanding and by imagining reversal of the process, we arrive at a small singularity over thirteen billion years ago. In our case, we have the opposite in that a single entity, England, can be traced back to a myriad of competing groups. Yet these groups themselves derived from a fragmenting whole: the Diocese of Britain. What we must be wary of is assuming the fragmentation was uniform across time and geography. We should also be wary of assuming social and cultural identity based on the outcome hundreds of years later.

Summary of Anglo-Saxon kingdoms

We have seen that for many kingdoms, dynasties appear to start well after the evidence for significant immigration. Outside Kent they mostly appear to begin from the mid- to late sixth century. Even Wessex appears to have been altered to create an earlier beginning. Of course, a new dynasty does not negate the presence of a previous one. In general, there is a consensus within the literary sources which is broadly supported by the archaeology: Saxon material culture in the south from c.425, then significant Anglian material culture in the east and north from c.450.

Table 9: Founders and kings of Anglo-Saxon kingdoms

Kingdom	First alleged founder of dynasty or arrival	First alleged king	First confirmed historical king
Kent	Hengest 449	Octa 488	Edilberht 589–616
Bernicia	Oesa (grandfather of Ida)	Ida 547	Aethelfrith 592–616
Deira		Soemel (five generations before Aelle)	Aelle 560–600
East Anglia	Wehha (father of Wuffa) c.550	Wuffa 571	Raedwald 599–624
Wessex	Cerdic 495 (or 532)	Cerdic and Cynric 501 (or 538)	Ceawlin 560 (or 580)
Mercia	Icel (grandfather of Creoda) c.540	Creoda 585	Penda 626
South Saxons	Aelle 477		Aethelwealh 660

If we take the sources at face value, a south-east 'kingdom' is already in place by the time of Arthur. This likely includes Kent, Essex, Surrey and Sussex. The king lists suggest Hengest's death is in line with the *Anglo-Saxon Chronicle* entry for c.488, rather than an early arrival as part of the *Historia* implies. This also supports the middle or late Arthur hypothesis. The picture elsewhere is mixed. East Anglia had significant early settlement yet Lindsey appeared to remain under British authority into the sixth century. Mercia may have been an even more complex mix of small tribal groups intermingled with fragmenting British polities. Carver argues that the archaeological and documentary evidence points to kings and kingdoms in what became England being an innovation of the late sixth century.[90] What we seem to have is the former Diocese fragmenting into provincial and *civitas* polities, and then some areas collapsing further into disparate groups before coalescing again into larger units. Some of these were based on former *civitates*, administrative or economically-active zones or tribal areas. There is much continuation alongside significant destruction and collapse.

In one of the latest studies, Carver describes the periods as follows:[91]

- 400–475: migration period with evidence of Irish and Pictish pressure and 'dispersed settlement by English.' At the same time, evidence from cemeteries is mainly one of continuation.
- 475–550: land claiming period with evidence of burials south of the Humber suggesting settlement increases after 450 but 'becomes more marked' after 475. Accompanied by appearance of Anglo-Saxon presence north of the Humber.
- 550–630: rise of warlords, emergence of a 'flourishing aristocracy' and 'insular equestrian class' by the late sixth century.

An alternative study by Gerrard suggests two phases for western areas:[92]

- Early phase 350/370 to 430/470: late Roman material culture; villas and urban centres still important.
- Late phase: 430/470 to 550/600: reoccupation of hill forts; decline in importance of urban centres; change of use of villas; increase in Mediterranean material culture.

In the first phase, elites governed through 'economic relationships' such as tax collectors or landlords.[93] They shared a *paideia* or social identity formed through education, speech, material culture, world view and built environment. There was an acceptance of a 'civilian ideology'. However, the second phase involved a shift to a more martial power. Material culture and symbols reflected a more individual and paramilitary world view.

The most likely time for Arthur is in the 'land claiming' period and 'late phase', with increased settlement and expansion of Germanic material culture north of the Humber. At the same time, the Britons were reoccupying hill forts while retaining links with the Mediterranean. Importantly for our view of Britons, a cultural shift is evident. Alongside signs of adoption of Germanic culture, we see a shift from a Roman identity with a civilian ideology to a more military-influenced individual culture. At the start of the fifth century, Britain still possessed a Roman character. By the end of the century, this had been swept away.[94] It is likely the age of the warlord had arrived just as Arthur arrived on the scene. We cannot, however, assume Arthur was such a man. Some elements of Roman identity and structure remained evident. Gildas refers to 'governors', 'watchmen' and 'judges'. The parents of Ambrosius had 'worn the purple', possibly of senatorial or imperial rank. After Badon, 'public and private persons, priests and churchmen, kept to their own stations'.[95] But he also tells of 'kings', 'tyrants' and their 'military companions'. We are left to ponder into which group Arthur would fit. Perhaps more than one, or none. We will now turn to the emerging Brittonic kingdoms.

The north

The northern province of Britannia Secunda had its capital at York. This also served as the military headquarters of the northern military command centred on Hadrian's Wall and commanded by the *Dux Britanniarum*. Collins found no support that Hadrian's Wall had been abandoned at the end of Roman Britain.[96] However, Clarkson sees 'widespread abandonment' by c.420 with the exception of Birdoswald Roman fort on the wall a few miles east of Carlisle.[97] Contrary to that, Collins states several forts show signs of continued occupation: South Shields, Vindolanda, Birdoswald, Carlisle and south of the wall at Binchester, Piercebridge and York.[98] Piercebridge on the River Tees shows the defences were used until the late sixth century.[99] Clarkson sees the 'appearance of small political units centred on individual forts.'[100] Collins says something similar, pointing out the frontier evolved into local commands or polities served by militia or barbarian *foederati*.[101] We could perhaps reconcile these two views by saying there are signs of both abandonment and continuation, which is likely to have led to a fragmentation of the northern command structure. Importantly, there is no evidence for the total collapse of the entire northern frontier in the fifth century.[102]

At some point in the following century, the northern province fractured into several polities, many based on tribal areas. The Votadini, or Uotadinoi, retained their 'core territory intact' and were known as the Gododdin.[103] Their main centre of power was the fortified settlement on the site of Edinburgh Castle known as Din Eidyn or the fort of Eidyn. We have mentioned the *Y Gododdin* as giving rather weak evidence for a historical Arthur, stating a warrior was 'no Arthur' in a battle against the Deirians. Dumville places this battle in the mid-sixth century.[104] One surviving version of the poem doesn't mention the Bernicians at all, suggesting they may not have been significant. Charles-Edwards agrees, placing the battle before the reign of Ida in c.547.[105]

The *Historia* claims Ida joined Din Guayroi (Lindisfarne) to Bernicia,[106] suggesting the border with the Gododdin stretched as far south as the Tweed and possibly at one time, Hadrian's Wall.[107] Irish annals mention the siege of Din Eidyn in 638 and this likely resulted in the end of the kingdom.[108] We will discuss *Y Gododdin* in more detail later. However, both the poem and other sources name other foes at the battle besides Deirians. Firstly, the poem tells us the Gododdin were opposed to the descendants of Coel, 'an evil people'.[109] The Coelings are included in very late and doubtful genealogical tables and feature in many of the northern kingdoms. One of their descendants is Urien of Rheged. In the poetry of Taliesin, he is described as the 'Ruler of Catraeth'.[110] We are thus presented with a different picture from heroic Britons vainly holding back invading barbarians. This sounds more like a civil war with Urien holding territory right on the edge of the border with Deira, and possibly in alliance with them.

Rheged has proved difficult to place although most historians centre it on Carlisle. Clarkson finds this possible but 'not proven'.[111] It may have stretched north into Galloway, south to the Eden Valley and also east as far as Catterick.

To the north was the kingdom of Alt Clut centred on Clyde Rock, Dumbarton. This likely evolved from the Dumnonii in the Clyde Valley. We recall that in the ninth-century *Life of St Gildas*, he is said to be son of the king of Alt Clut. It is thought very likely that the King Coroticus, who St Patrick castigated, was a fifth-century king of Alt Clut identified in the genealogies.[112] The capital of Alt Clut, later Strathclyde, was sacked by the Vikings in 870 and one might expect direct links or records of Arthur might have survived. Between and slightly north of Alt Clut and Gododdin, we have Manau and Manau Gododdin. They were probably derived from the Maeatae tribe that gave the Romans so much trouble in the second and third centuries.

To the south, the kingdom of Elmet in West Yorkshire was likely centred on the *civitas* capital of the Brigantes at Aldborough.[113] Various place name evidence still survives around the Leeds area such as Sherburn-in-Elmet. The kingdom was conquered by Edwin of Northumbria in c.616. This strongly suggests that Elmet and the other northern kingdoms were able to hold their own for many decades. Indeed, the *Historia* tells how four kingdoms combined to attack the Bernicians. From the genealogies, we can name Urien of Rheged, Rhydderch Hael of Al Clut, Gwallawg of Elmet and an unknown Morcant. They fought against a son of Ida, Theodoric, who we can calculate from the dates given to c.572–579. The words the author uses are familiar:[114] 'During that time sometimes the enemy, sometimes the Cymry were victorious.' Urien blockades them at Lindisfarne for an equally familiar 'three days and three nights'. Once again, the Britons are defeated by division. Urien is assassinated on the 'instigation of Morcant, from jealousy'.

It would appear Rheged was annexed by Northumbria in the seventh century. Oswiu married a princess from Rheged – Rieinmelth, granddaughter of Rhun who was a son of Urien. Rhun is reported in some sources to have baptised Edwin of Northumbria in 627 and this is accepted as the same Rhun who the Chartres manuscript claimed was the author of the *Historia*.[115] If we combine this with a potential northern influence for the *Annales Cambriae* and references in *Y Gododdin* and other Welsh poems such as *Pa Gur*, then we have some thin evidence of a link to Arthur. It is, of course, not sufficient but it is at least possible a figure active in areas later taken over by Anglo-Saxon polities could leave no discernible trace, but still be remembered in literary sources of surviving kingdoms.

Thirty years after Ida had established his kingdom, the Angles had made 'little or no progress'.[116] While many assume total collapse of the northern command, we see something rather different. There are at least four powerful Brittonic kingdoms alongside two nascent Anglo-Saxon kingdoms, both with Brittonic etymologies for their names. One last point concerns Deira, the only area with significant Germanic evidence, in addition to finds between Catterick and York.[117] We have learnt previously that Soemil was the first to separate Deira from Bernicia. Dumville finds it likely he detached it from British rule rather than Angles and dates this to the mid-fifth century.[118] This is on the basis that Aelle, the first attested king of Deira, dated to 568–598, was the great-great-great-grandson of Soemil.

Both the *Historia* and eighth-century Anglian Collection agree on this. However, it is rare to see an unbroken line of kings from father to son across six generations. It's not uncommon to see six kings cover as little as fifty years with death in battle, assassination, illness and political upheavals breaking the line of succession. If we take the regnal list at face value and accept direct descent, then one estimate would be 25 years per generation; this would assume having offspring at 25 years and living for approximately 50 years. This would then agree with Dumville and place Soemil c.425–475. However, lifespans were shorter and the minimum generation could have been 20 years. This would place his birth in c.450 and his coming of fighting age from around 470 onwards. It's difficult to accept a sixth-century date unless we doubt the veracity of the genealogical record. This is significant.

If the *adventus Saxonum* occurred between 440 and 450 then the fightback by Ambrosius is likely to be just when Bede says, in the time of Zeno (474–491). We have seen that the expansion into Deira, and settlement of Lindisfarne, likely came from the region of Lindsey. Yet we have also seen evidence for continuation of British authority in this area, alongside some very Brittonic-sounding names in their king list such as Caedbaed and Bisceop. This seems like an important area, especially as four of the battles were in the region of the Linnuis and there is more than one battle site with a likely location in the north. If Urien was indeed allied to Deirians and fighting a force from Gododdin at Catterick, there is no reason to assume similar alliances did not occur in Arthur's time.

Map 18: The North

One last point concerns the region of the Manau Gododdin. There are allusions to this area in Welsh sources including *Y Gododdin*. We will now turn to Wales and start with its links to the north.

Wales

In general there is evidence that the emergence of kingdoms in the fifth and sixth centuries were based on Romano-British political identities.[119] *Civitates* were usually based around distinct peoples or kingdoms.[120] Gwynedd likely evolved from the *civitas* of the Ordivices[121] and Powys, from the Cornovii centred on Wroxeter.[122] Activity here, a century before Anglo-Saxons had penetrated this far west, suggests a British-controlled area into the sixth century.[123] The Silures evolved into Gwent, the Demetae to Dyfed, and further east, Ergying at some point likely split from the Dobunni, perhaps after the emergence of the Hwicce along the Severn Valley.

Post-Roman Wales probably experienced friction between the *civitas* and the *pagus*.[124] Urban, economic and administrative centres struggled to retain control over the surrounding rural hinterland. The *civitas* of the Demetae appears to have fractured into three: its core, Dyfed; in the east, Brycheiniog; and Ceredigion to the north.[125] The first two have significant Irish settlement and early genealogies appear linked to the migration of the Déisi from Ireland. The *civitas* of the Silures appear to have similarly split into the later kingdoms of Gwent and Glywysing.[126]

Gildas refers to Vortipor as a 'bad son of a good king'. We can identify him from the genealogies as probably Guortiper of Dyfed, which we will see later had significant settlement from Ireland and possible links to Irish genealogies. A monument of the period stands at Castell Dwyran, Carmarthenshire. It translates as 'Monument of Voteporigis Protector' and includes both Latin text and an Irish ogham inscription. The epithet 'protector' was often given by the late Roman Empire to barbarian princes who were given *foederati* status on frontiers.[127] So we have the hint of a king of part-Irish heritage ruling in South-west Wales. Gildas describes him as near the end of his life and his hair as whitening, so we can deduce Badon was in his lifetime. Of the other kings, Maglocunnus is identified with Maelgwn of Gwynedd and we have some clues for the other three: Aurelius Caninus is possibly from Powys; Cuneglasus is perhaps Cynlas Goch, son of Owain Danwyn, another descendant of Cunedda; and Constantine of Damnoniae is thought to be from Dumnonia, which is roughly Devon and Cornwall.

It has to be noted that the genealogies and annalistic evidence are all from many centuries after the events and as such, lack credibility.[128] However, we can tentatively claim Gildas provides contemporary evidence of kingdoms based on late Roman *civitates*. We have already noted it is probable he is writing in the province of Britannia Prima and appears to be addressing one people. He mentions kings but also governors and judges, and the impression is of a functioning civic and church structure.

The *Historia Brittonum* has this to say about Maelgwn of Gwynedd, whom Gildas described as the 'dragon of the island': 'his ancestors, Cunedda with his sons to the number of eight had come from the north, from the country called Manaw Gododdin 146 years before Maelgwn reigned and expelled the Irish from those countries with immense slaughter so that they never returned.' Cunedda's sons traditionally founded many of the Welsh kingdoms such as Ceredigion and Dunoding. The twelfth-century Harleian genealogies make Cunedda the great-grandfather of Maelgwn. If Maelgwn's floruit is c.500–547, then we could calculate his father as c.475–525 and so on, placing Cunedda in c.425–475. It is very difficult to reconcile the 146 years reference which would place him arriving in North Wales in the last quarter of the fourth century.

The genealogies are interesting, although they might be late and untrustworthy.[129] Cunedda's wife is Gwawl, a daughter of Coel Hen, and his daughter Gwen, the mother of Eigr, known to many as Igraine, the wife of Uther and mother of Arthur. But they suggest there was a tradition that saw North Wales as distinct from other parts. Eastern central Wales, Shropshire and beyond formed the territory of Powys which appears to have grown out of the *civitas* of the Cornovii. We recall the capital Wroxeter had significant signs of continued occupation in the fifth century. Welsh tradition associates this area with Vortigern and we recall the Pillar of Eliseg with its reference to Vortigern and Sevira, daughter of Magnus Maximus. A number of different genealogies for Powys exist and while they differ significantly, either Vortigern or one of his sons appear.[130]

The *Historia Brittonum* could reflect two separate dynastic foundation stories between Gwynedd and Powys, with the former being shown in a good light at the expense of Powys.[131] Within the section on St Germanus, there is a tale about the 'wicked king Benli' whom the saint defeats and then gives the kingdom of Powys to a certain Cadell. Indeed, some have found Vortigern is the most important person in the text.[132] The author certainly pours much of the blame for the events on him. It also provides convenient examples of Vortigern's line ceding power to others. Ambrosius is given the fortress in Gwynedd and Vortigern flees to Caer Gwrtheyrn in South-west Wales. After his death, his son needs permission from the 'overlord' Ambrosius to retain Builth and Gwerthrynion in Central Wales.

Ambrosius is said to be from Glywysing in South Wales and this area is where many of the *Saints' Lives* that feature Arthur are located. The *Saints' Lives* are all very late and historical but give an interesting picture of the traditions that existed from the eleventh century at the earliest. The *Life of Saint Cadoc* begins with the saint's father, Gwynnllyw, a great-grandson of Cunedda and thus related to, and of the same generation as, both Arthur and Maelgwn if we trust the genealogies. He abducts Brychan's daughter, who is the future mother of St Cadoc. Both kings give their names respectively to the kingdoms of Gwynlliog and Brycheiniog in South Wales. Arthur, nearby with Cei and Bedwyr, takes sides and assists Gwynnllyw. In adulthood, he confronts Arthur at the River Usk and is conveniently granted land rights. Bartrum dates Cadoc to c.495, tying in with his floruit for Arthur at c.480. Arthur is a young man prior to the saint's conception but twenty years or more later when Cadoc is an adult, he is called a king and leads a 'great force of soldiers'.

In the *Life of Saint Illtud*, Illtud travels from Armorica to visit Paulentus in Glamorgan and his cousin, Arthur who is presumably close by. Genealogies name Illtud's father Bicanus of Armorica and his mother Rieingulid, daughter of Anblaud (Amlawdd Wledig) and thus sister to Eigr (Igraine), Arthur's mother. The *Life of St Padarn*, in Ceredigion on the west coast, has the 'tyrant' Arthur attempting to steal a red cloak. In a similar way to Cadoc, we find the saint interacts with Maelgwn as well.

We cannot accept any of these stories as historical. However, a consistent thread runs through and we can conclude with two points, one based on evidence, the other on legend. Firstly, sometime after Roman authority ends the *civitates* of Wales evolve, fragment to some extent and kings emerge. In Arthur's day, there is still the remnants of a civic and church structure but alongside there are petty kings, warlords and according to Gildas, civil wars and some very un-kingly behaviour. Map 19 illustrates the emerging kingdoms in Wales.

Secondly, several hundred years later, two traditions have emerged, neither of which can be relied upon. One suggests competing polities existed at the time of Arthur with different foundation stories: Gwynedd founded by the sons of Cunedda who came from Manaw Gododdin in the north; Powys connected to Vortigern though with various versions of regnal lists to choose from; Dyfed in the south-west with significant Irish influence; and Gwent and the south with links to various Welsh saints. The other tradition concerns those very saints. By the Middle Ages, Arthur is associated with these saints in this area. Interestingly, he is not associated with any saints from the north or in Ireland, despite the rich tradition and amount of surviving written material. The earliest Welsh legend, *Culhwch and Olwen*, is thought to have originated in the eleventh century although the earliest surviving copy is from the fourteenth. This mythical tale

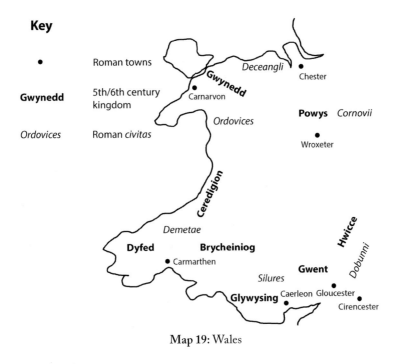

Map 19: Wales

involving a giant and magic sends our hero to Ireland to steal a cauldron and through South Wales and Cornwall to hunt a giant boar. So, in addition to the faint whispers of a northern connection from the previous section, we now have a late alleged link with South Wales. However, *Saints' Lives* and Arthur also reach across the Bristol Channel and it's to there we will turn next.

The West Country

In the south-west, two Roman *civitates* became the core territory of Dumnonia. The Dumnonii, in modern-day Devon and Cornwall, had their *civitas* capital at Isca Dumnoniorum, Exeter. The Durotriges had theirs at Durnovaria, Dorchester on the Dorset coast. Further north the small town of Lindinis, Ilchester, suggests a subdivision as inscribed stones on Hadrian's Wall attest to the *civitas Durotragum Lendiniensis*. There is some indication that at one point part of the western Belgae *civitas* incorporated Bath.[133] It is also possible that Bath, along with Cirencester and Gloucester, formed the core territory of a later Dobunnic civil authority that was conquered by the Gewisse in 577. But whatever the case, there is no evidence of 'intrusive groups' into the south-west prior to the second half of the sixth century.[134]

As late as 600, the region of the Durotriges was likely untouched by Germanic settlement or incursions.[135] It was not until 658 when the *Anglo-Saxon Chronicle* records the Britons were pushed back to the River Parrett in Somerset. The area is marked by the reoccupation of hill forts such as South Cadbury, Congresbury and Cannington. Towns may have become indefensible due to depopulation and it's worth noting the proximity of Cadbury, for example, to Ilchester. Sub-Roman kingship likely derived from an urban context near functioning towns such as with the Dobunni.[136] We recall some evidence of continuation in towns such as Cirencester. Additionally, the Hwicce, a later apparently Anglo-Saxon subkingdom of Mercia, was centred a little further north at Worcester. It is possible this reflects a fragmenting *civitas*. Map 20 illustrates the origins of Dumnonia.

The situation could be summarised as follows:[137] political centres were transferred from towns to hill forts while towns remained episcopal centres. This is possible even in Anglo-Saxon areas. We recall St Augustine meeting bishops of the Britons and Aethelbert of Kent allowing churches in Canterbury and London. In highland, rural and less romanised regions, such as Cornwall, native dynasties were restored. For the *civitas* of the Dumnonii we can make the following observations:[138] there were no towns west of Exeter and no functioning fifth-century villas; Irish immigration was limited; native Romano-British elites appear to have retained their position; the site at Tintagel suggests a Brittonic power; and the dynasty and region centred on Tintagel was sub-Roman in character.

Two of the *Saints' Lives* refer to this area.[139] The twelfth-century *Life of Saint Carannog* has the saint come across the 'Severn sea'. Then, 'in those times Arthur and Cadwy were reigning in that country'. Their castle was at Dindraithov, possibly Dunstan Castle in Exmoor. Eventually, the saint receives a land grant in Carrum, possibly Carhampton in Somerset.[140] The second *Life of Saint Gildas*, written in the twelfth century, has Gildas intervening when King Melvas abducts Guinevere and Arthur besieges him at Glastonbury in Somerset. While these tales are not in any way credible, they do demonstrate a tradition in the twelfth century onwards linking Arthur to this area.

It is Geoffrey of Monmouth, in the beginning of the twelfth century, who first places Arthur's activities here. Badon is set outside Bath and Camlan on the River Camel in Cornwall. Further association with sites such as Glastonbury come after this date. In 1191, monks at the monastery carried out what is accepted was an elaborate hoax in finding Arthur's grave with a lead cross. Unfortunately, the letter forms are decidedly tenth-century and there is much doubt as to the details and their motives.[141] In the sixteenth century, John Leland recorded a tradition that Cadbury was Camelot. Unfortunately, Camelot was introduced by Chrétien de Troyes after Geoffrey of Monmouth, who places Arthur's base at Caerleon. Welsh tradition gives him three courts: Celliwig in Cornwall, St David's in South-west Wales and Pen Rhionydd in the north (unidentified).

Bonedd Y Saint, genealogies from the thirteenth century, place Arthur in the dynasty of Dumnonia.[142] The genealogies in general are late and untrustworthy, often used as dynastic propaganda.[143] But belief in King Arthur and prevalence of the tradition existed before Geoffrey of Monmouth. In 1113, French canons from Laon, France, nearly caused a riot in Bodmin, Cornwall when they professed their scepticism that Arthur was still alive.[144]

In summary, we can say the south-west retained a strong Roman identity and trade links through sites such as Tintagel and reoccupied hill forts. The *civitates* may well have fractured along urban/rural lines, but the region was powerful enough to retain independence for a considerable time. There is little or no evidence of Germanic presence for the time period we are looking at. Much of the later tradition associating Arthur with the south-west is very late and not historical. There is no solid evidence supporting any early link with Glastonbury or Cadbury. The most one can say is there was an early tradition connecting Arthur with Cornwall that was accepted in the area as early as the twelfth century.

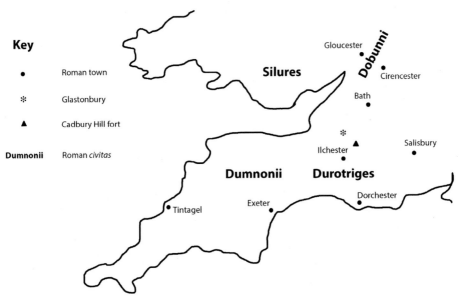

Map 20: Origins of Dumnonia

Brittany

In the early medieval period, there were close links between the south-west and Brittany which lay on the trade routes between the Irish Sea zone and the Western Empire and Mediterranean. We have already seen how imports continued into western Britain through important settlements such as Tintagel. Aside from the Breton language, there are similar named areas in Brittany such as Domnonia in the north and Cernew in the south-west.

Originally Armorica stretched east, along the northern bank of the Loire towards the Seine. The establishment of the kingdom of Soissons by Aegidius in 464 would have created a boundary with the Bretons. In the 460s, we hear from Gregory of Tours about Britons fighting in the Loire Valley and being expelled from Bourg-de Deols.[145] Odovacer captured Angers, followed by the Franks. There follows a great war between the Saxons on one side and the Romans and Franks on the other, which the Saxons lose. All this suggests the Britons were now north of the Loire. Jordanes places Riothamus in the same area, being defeated by the Visigoths at around the same time. Letters from Sidonius Apollinaris in the late fifth century suggest Riothamus likely came from Armorica.[146] A generation later, the Franks under Clovis had conquered Soissons and pushed west and south. By the sixth century, it is thought the 'normal relationship...was peace not war', possibly as a result of a treaty in c.497.[147]

Map 21 illustrates the origins of Armorica. We can make the following points about borders:[148] in the sixth century, Nantes and Rennes were outside Brittany but subject to raids from the west. Dol in the north-east was the furthest extent of Domnonia. In the south-east, Vannes would have been just inside the extent of Breton authority. Just south of Vannes is Rhuys, where one of the two versions of *Life of St Gildas* was written, which also claims to hold his resting place. Gregory of Tours states that from the time of Clovis, the Bretons 'ceased to be called kings but were merely counts subject to the Franks'.[149] A likely interpretation of Gregory of Tours is that he views the Britons in Armorica of his own day, in the sixth century, as the descendants of the ones who fought in the Loire a hundred years before.[150] This leads us to ask: when did Britons arrive in north-west Gaul?

Gildas tells us that after the Saxon revolt, some 'made for lands beyond the sea'.[151] This may have occurred by the mid-fifth century. By the sixth century, there is significant evidence of British migrants in Gaul. Hughes places this migration in the 440s.[152] The largest concentration of Britons in the sixth century was in the west in the *civitas* of the Ossimii, suggesting this could have been the core of initial settlement in the fifth century.[153] In 461, we hear of Mansuetus, 'bishop of the Britons' at the council of Tours.[154] A short time later, Riothamus was able to lead a force of 12,000 against the Goths to aid the Romans. If these were indeed all Britons, this would require a substantial population to support that number of warriors, certainly tens of thousands.

The lowest estimate might make the following assumptions: half of the population would be adults and half of those men. Another half might be too old or infirm. We would therefore need to double our force three times, giving nearly 100,000 people. This is significant given that the Vandals crossed to Africa with 80,000. Additionally, a force sent to aid the Romans would only have consisted of a proportion of able-bodied available manpower so the actual Briton population could have been much more. This is, of course, assuming the figure of 12,000 and the label of Britons is accurate.

Both Geoffrey of Monmouth and the fourteenth-century poem, *The Dream of Macsen Wledig*, contain elements of a foundation story for Armorica. Magnus Maximus is claimed to have settled supporters in the region. We have no evidence for this. According to Geoffrey, Arthur is a direct descendant from the kings of this region. After Geoffrey of Monmouth's book, we see the beginnings of Arthurian tradition in the area. Brittany was the sole route by which the legend reached the continent to inspire later writers.[155] Similar to Cornwall, we get an indication of its popularity from a contemporary source which reminds us of the view across the Channel. Adam of Tewkesbury in 1170 stated that if one was to go to the villages and market places of Armorica and claim Arthur 'died as other men die' you would likely be 'cursed or stoned by your hearers'.[156]

In summary, we can say there is support for significant levels of immigration from Britain to Armorica in the mid-fifth century. That likely affected the

Map 21: Origins of Armorica

political, cultural and military situation and we know that at one point in c.470, the Britons were a significant force. As Gaul fragmented, boundaries shifted. By the sixth century, the border was roughly between Dol and Vannes. In Arthur's time, it may well have been further west. Tradition has his family coming originally from the area so it's not unreasonable to imagine military aid being sent to Armorica to hold back the Franks. Unfortunately, we have no evidence except that by the twelfth century, there was a common belief in Arthur across Brittany similar to that in Cornwall and Wales.[157]

The Irish and Picts

Some of the proposed battle locations are far in the north and suggest Arthur may have been fighting Picts as well as Angles. This would come as no surprise given the well-documented raids from both the Picts and Irish. We recall that Gildas claimed the Picts captured the north 'up to the wall' and the later appeal to Aetius was in response to Pictish raids. So, too, was Vortigern's hiring of Saxon mercenaries. Geoffrey of Monmouth has Arthur fighting as far north as Moray and, as well as defeating Pictish armies, he fights an Irish army just as his father Uther is said to have done a generation before.

The first historical record of the Picts occurs at the end of the third century.[158] They spoke a Brittonic language and lived in small, scattered, rural communities. Tacitus, writing in the first century, describes their ancestors as having 'reddish hair and large limbs'. Describing the campaign of Agricola in AD 83, he calls the land north of the River Tay, 'Caledonia', but the people are Britanni or Britons. We get an interesting account of the Battle of Mons Graupius. The Caledonians mustered a large force with over 30,000 men under many kings, one of whom was named Calgacus. The front rank was on level ground with the rest lined up on the slope behind. Chariots manoeuvred on the flat ground in front. The Romans lined up six cohorts of Germanic auxiliaries in the centre with cavalry on the flanks. The rest of the legion was held in reserve. Tacitus, no doubt embellishing the scene, states the battle started with a rain of spears from both sides. Then the Roman war-hardened auxiliaries in the centre attacked, pushing the Caledonians backwards up the hill, striking them with the 'bosses of their shields and stabbing them in the face.'[159] We can compare this to later tactics where the sword was used more as a cutting weapon and the edge of the shield would be more effective than the boss. The cavalry easily dispersed the chariots and then outflanked the enemy and attacked the rear. Many broke and fled, while others conducted small counter-attacks throughout the day until Tacitus tells us 'our soldiers were tired of killing.' He estimates 10,000 Caledonians lay dead with Roman losses below 400.

Agricola returned south but the fleet continued north around Scotland and down the western side of Britain. The information they gathered later assisted Ptolemy, a second-century Greek geographer, in constructing a map. It shows sixteen tribes occupying Scotland, twelve north of the Forth-Clyde isthmus. Roman rule was consolidated south of the Solway-Tyne after briefly extending to the Antonine Wall between the Forth and the Clyde in central Scotland. However, within a generation, the Romans abandoned that wall and retreated back to Hadrian's Wall running between Carlisle and Newcastle.

In the late second century, Cassius Dio records Hadrian's Wall being overrun. Two main tribes, possibly confederations, were to blame: the Caledonians and the Maeatae, the latter being from the Stirlingshire area. In AD 208 Emperor Severus crossed the Forth-Clyde isthmus to attack the Maeatae and Caledonians who had launched another invasion. Severus died on campaign and the appointment of his son, Caracalla, in AD 211 marked a change in politics. He made peace and retreated south. No Roman general would ever march north of the Forth-Clyde isthmus again.

A hundred years later, documents record two main foes. The first were the Hiberni from Ireland. Agricola had briefly considered an invasion back in the first century, but decided it wasn't worth the trouble. The second were the Picti from 'the woods and marshes of the Caledonians.'[160] By 360, Ammianus Marcellinus states the Picts were divided into two peoples: the Dicalydones and the Verturiones. The former are clearly the Caledonians and the latter likely one of Ptolemy's other twelve northern tribes. So, we can see the evolution of the tribal identity and names into the Picts.

Ammianus goes on to mention a series of serious raids from Picts, Saxons, Attacotti and Scots. We recall the barbaric conspiracy that devastated much of Britain in 367, especially in the north. But we also recall the Romans on several occasions, from Theodosius in 367 to Maximus and Stilicho dealing decisively with raids. What this suggests are two interesting possibilities. The first is that Hadrian's Wall was not a significant military deterrent and did not prevent major incursions at various times throughout the Roman period. Gildas tells us, after the Picts had seized up to the wall, a force was stationed on 'the high towers' to oppose them. Then perhaps lyrically, he states 'barbed spears flung by their naked opponents which tore our wretched countrymen from the walls'. Afterwards the 'citizens abandoned the towns and the high wall.'[161]

The second point is that the Picts were not invulnerable. The Romans had demonstrated this with various punitive campaigns through the centuries. Gildas records some Britons fought back and inflicted 'a massacre on them'. The Irish returned home and the Picts are then described as 'in the far end of the island'. They 'kept quiet...though they occasionally carried out devastating raids.' We can see how a strong military-based authority north of the Wall could exert itself at the same time as Pictish and Irish raiding continued.

This seems to be exactly what Gildas is implying. The Picts reach as far south as the Wall but are then defeated, presumably north of the Wall. They then retreat, possibly back beyond the Clyde/Forth rivers. This could be the point at which the kingdoms of Gododdin and Alt Clut emerged as significant powers. Chronologically, the victory of the Britons occurs after the appeal to Aetius so we can date this roughly to the estimated time period for St Patrick and King Coroticus.

'Scots' was a broad term for Gaelic speakers, whether from Ireland or Britain. The Picti is Latin for 'Painted People.' Among fourth-century Britons, the term was Priteni. Originally, the early Roman and Greek travellers had referred to all Britons as Pritani which translates as 'The People of Designs' or 'Painted People'. Julius Caesar later used the word Britanni, which was eventually used to denote only those tribes under Roman rule, later evolving into Britonnes and Britons. He wrote that all the Britons painted themselves in woad, producing dark-blue patterns. In the third century, the Greek Herodian talks of the barbarians of northern Britain covering their skin in designs and pictures of animals. Other references to body painting or tattooing include the poet Claudian in 400:[162] 'There came the legion, shield of the frontier Britons, check of the grim Scot, whose men had watched the life leave the designs on the dying Pict.'

Evidence suggests all the people of Scotland spoke a common Celtic language during the Roman period. It was part of a group known as P-Celtic which included Britain and Gaul.[163] Q-Celtic languages spread to Scotland from Ireland. The Picts' language was more closely related to other Brittonic languages such as Welsh, Breton and Cornish.

The tribes that dwelt between the walls were long regarded as subjects or allies of Rome: the Novantae and Damnonii in the west, the Selgovae in the centre and the Votadini in the east. The Damnonii centred on Dumbarton and became Alt Clut, later the Kingdom of Strathclyde. The Votadini evolved into the Gododdin. Both kingdoms bordered the Picts but likely had more in common culturally with the Britons south of Hadrian's Wall. Certainly, by the fifth century, the tribes north of the Forth-Clyde isthmus had developed a common identity and were known as Picts.

Brude, son of Maelchon, was the first Pictish king attested by history reigning from 554.[164] There could be an interesting link here with Maelgwn, King of Gwynedd, also known as Mailcun. He is often identified as the *Maglocunus* whom Gildas castigates but calls *insularis draco*, 'dragon of the island.' In one Pictish king's list, Bridei son of Maelchon, reigned after the mid-sixth century. Maelchon is also known as Mailcon or Maelcon. With dynastic marriages commonplace, it is not impossible Bridei was the son of Maelgwn. We are reminded of another connection between the north and Wales. In the *Historia*, Cunedda is said to have left Manau Gododdin and come to North Wales with eight of his sons to drive out the Scotti.

Irish raiders were settling in western parts of Britain. One such group were the Scots of Dalriada. Or at least according to the origin legend, sometime around 500, Irish kings moved from Antrim in Northern Ireland to Argyll in Western Scotland. Bede describes their leader Reuda acquiring lands in Pictish territory by 'treaty or the sword' and were known as Dalreudini. Other tales have Fergus mac Erc as the founder of Dal Riata or Dalriada. Unfortunately, there is nothing in the archaeological record to support this[165] or any other significant migration into Western Scotland from Ireland.[166]

Bede describes four nations in Britain: English, Britons, Picts and Irish, the latter of which includes the Dal Riata. Earlier writers often used the term 'Scot' to describe Irish. The Romans knew both the Picts and Scots as 'sea raiders' while Gildas describes them as 'wandering thieves who have no taste for war.'[167] Ammianus Marcellinus records several incursions by bands of Scotti and Picts in the fourth century. Certainly, by the time of Arthur, there were two distinct powers north of Alt Clut and Gododdin: the Dalriadan Scots and the Picts.

Alongside literary records of raiding, there is evidence for distinct areas of Irish migration in the fifth century:[168]

- from North-East Ireland to Western Scotland
- from South-East Ireland to Gwynedd and Dyfed in North and South Wales respectively
- from South-East Ireland to Devon and Cornwall.

One group, the Déisi (meaning vassals), moved from South-East Ireland into South-West Wales and left a tradition of Irish kings of Dyfed.[169] We recall Vortipor, King of Demetia, well-attested in Welsh genealogies as Guortepir. His memorial stone, *Memoria Voteporigis protictoris*, has similar Irish links to the Cunorix Stone at Wroxeter with a Celtic inscription 'Cunorix son of Maqui Coline' dated to 460–475. It is possible this is the gravestone of an Irish warrior or warlord.

A tenth-century record states the Irish were in control over parts of Cornwall 'as far as the English Channel…for a long time… after the coming of St Patrick'. Two Irish strongholds are mentioned, Dind Tradui and Dind map Lethain in the 'land of the Cornish.' According to legend, Arthur's mother, Igraine, was originally married to Gorlois, Duke of Cornwall, and Arthur was conceived at Tintagel. We have a tentative link to Irish mythology with the original name of Arthur's sword, Caledfwlch, likely stemming from the Irish Caladblog (hard cleft), the sword of Fergus mac Roich in the Ulster Cycle mythology. We also have Irish elements in various Arthurian tales such as *Culhwch and Olwen*.

It is interesting that the four early Arthurs in Dark Age British history all have Irish links: Arthur, son of Aedan Mac Gabhrain of the Gaelic kingdom Dalriada, killed in battle around 596; Artur ap Bicuir, recorded as killing an Ulster chieftain in 624; Arthur ap Pedr of Dyfed, grandson of Vortipor dated to the later sixth century; and the grandfather of Faradach recorded in a law text of 697. The most likely etymology of the name is from the Roman Artorius or Arturus and, in fact, it is this latter spelling that is first recorded in the earliest *Historia*. While this is the simplest explanation, it is also possible the name stemmed from a Brittonic name or nickname translated as 'bear-man'. However, it is worth noting that the name doesn't appear in any of the other early Welsh genealogies. None of this amounts to any evidence beyond a nagging feeling there *might* be an Irish connection. What is clear is we have not a single contemporary or near contemporary reference to Arthur from Ireland.

What we do have is an 'extraordinary amount' of annalistic evidence mainly stemming from marginal notes in Easter tables.[170] The earliest set of annals likely derive from Iona in the mid-sixth century.[171] A significant number of entries relating to Scotland also likely stemmed from Iona in the seventh and eighth centuries before being transferred to Ireland and annals there.[172] Many of the entries may have derived from English or British sources. For example, Slebine, the abbot of Iona from 753 to 766, visited Ripon monastery in northern England and may have obtained information about the *adventus Saxonum* and other events from Bede.[173] The first reliable date in the annals is for the arrival of Palladius in 431.

We get little information from St Patrick. We have seen there is no provable date for his time in Ireland.[174] The debate over his year of death suggests 493 is possibly more likely than the earlier alternatives, although nothing would rule out an early fifth-century or even fourth-century date for his career.[175] We learn from him, as well as the earlier mission of Palladius, that there are Christians in Ireland as early as 430. Yet the slaves are to be sold to 'apostate Scots and Picts.' We get few further clues as to the political or military situation. But when he is captured, it is with 'many thousands.' This would indicate a major raid and ties in with the 'forty years of fear' from the *Historia* and the narrative in Gildas.

While we get no evidence from early Irish or Pictish sources, Geoffrey of Monmouth does place Arthur fighting both Picts and Irish in the far north. One of the possible identifications for battles two to five, in the region of the Linnuis, is Lennox rather than Lincoln. It is to military matters we will now turn. A carving of three warriors on a slab from Birsay shows three infantrymen with spears over six foot in length and square shields just large enough to cover a man's chest. Sculpted stones depict spears, axes, crossbows, swords and decorated shields, both round and square.[176] Gildas describes the Scots and Picts as being 'different in their customs' yet alike in their greed. He also claims they were both more likely to cover their faces than their 'private parts'. The picture is one of constant raiding yet they are powerful enough to seize the whole extreme north 'right up to the wall'. The Picts have 'hooked weapons' or 'barbed spears... tore our wretched countrymen from the walls and dashed them to the ground'. The Pictish warriors are described as 'naked opponents'.

Earlier accounts of Celtic warriors don't fully support this. Caesar describes the Suebi as wearing 'no clothing except skins'. Diodorus, also in the first century BC, describes colourful shirts, breeches and striped coats, as well as bronze helmets and sometimes iron cuirasses with shields as tall as a man. Yet some were satisfied to go into battle naked. Earlier, Polybius describes trousers and light cloaks but some warriors stood before the whole army naked but for their weapons. Yet Pictish warriors on the Birsay slab wear tunics down to the lower leg. Other carvings show various lengths for men and some warriors appear to have cloaks or tunics fixed by a shoulder brooch. By Arthur's time, it's very likely the weapons, armour and clothing were similar whether Pict, Irish, Briton or Angle.

In the first century, Tacitus describes the Celts' strength as being infantry. They also had strong cavalry that the Romans utilised. Both Tacitus and Caesar describe chariots being used by some, especially the Britons. However, there are no records of chariot use in later centuries in Britain. A battle in 563 at Moin Dain in Ireland records perhaps one of the last historical references to chariots in warfare, although it only refers to its use as a means of escape by a defeated king.[177]

Involvement of Irish warriors in Britain can be seen with a Northern Ui Neill prince fighting with Aedan Mac Gabrain at Desgastan against the Angles in 603. Despite the defeat, he escaped and lived to tell the tale.[178] This great victory by Northumbria did not end Irish or Dalriadan power completely. In 623, the Irish Annals record a possible raid by Fiachne mac Baetan on Bamburgh.[179] However, Bede records about Dagestan, 'from that day...no king of the Irish in Britain has dared to do battle with the English'. But the English were not invincible. In 685 at the Battle of Dunnichen (in English, Nechtanesmere), Bridei, son of Beli, destroyed an Anglian army.

One of the more common theories names Arthur mac Aedan as our hero. Yet nothing in Adomnán or Bede suggests this. The *Historia* is quite clear about when Arthur lived and who he fought against: between the deaths of Hengest and St Patrick and the reign of Ida, fighting against the Angles of Octha.

Where he fought is open to debate. Another point is the *Saints' Lives*. None of these can be taken as historically accurate. Yet it is again interesting that most of them place Arthur in South Wales and the West Country. None of the northern *Saints' Lives* mention Arthur at all: Saints Boethius, Kessog, Bride or Brigid, Ninnian, Kentigern, or Columba.

Later writers do, however, associate Arthur with Scotland. The Liber Floridus of Lambert of St Omer writing before 1120, and thus pre-Geoffrey of Monmouth, copies much from the *Historia* but adds details of his own:

> There is a palace, in Britain in the Picts' land, of Arthur the soldier, built with wondrous art and variety, in which may be seen sculpted all his acts both of construction and in battle. It shows in fact the 12 battles against the Saxons who had occupied Britain. ... In that time the Saxons grew strong and multiplied in Britain. At the death of Hengest, his son Octa moved from the left part of Britain to the kingdom of Kent and from him arose the kings of Kent. Then Arthur the leader of the Picts, directing kingdoms inland in Britain, with strong men, this fiercest soldier, seeing Anglia everywhere beaten in battle, good lands taken away, many enslaved and redeemed and expelled from their inheritance, with the kings of the Britons he came against the Saxons with a ferocious attack and rushing upon them fought manfully, the leader in 12 battles...

The palace could be a round Roman temple near Falkirk, Scotland, which was destroyed in 1743. It was known as Arthur's O'on (Arthur's Oven) about 25 miles east of Edinburgh. Arthur is called *dux Pictorum interioris Britanniae*, the 'dux' of the Picts of interior Britain. Holinshed's *Scottish Chronicles*, written in the sixteenth century, Arthur's reign from 521 and name Loth as King of the Picts and uncle to Arthur, having married Anne, sister of Ambrosius and Uther. The son of this union, Mordred, is thus a Pict. This latter account, being 1,000 years after events and heavily influenced by Geoffrey of Monmouth, cannot be trusted. But the earlier account is interesting. It too is late and not supported by any evidence. But it demonstrates a tradition placing Arthur in a different location contrary to the *Saints' Lives*.

It may seem odd that Britons could venerate a Pict given the narrative laid out in Gildas and other sources. But we have seen how cultural identity and allegiances change over even a single generation. If Cunedda did come from Manaw Gododdin in the north, he came from an area and time when labels such as Pict or Briton may not have been so clear-cut. The Gododdin raid on Deira was made up of warriors from all over Britain. One such was 'Bubon... beyond the sea of Iddew', which is thought to mean the Firth of Forth.[180] This would make him a Pict fighting for the Britons of the Gododdin, hundreds of miles south of his homeland against the Deirians and possibly Urien of Rheged, 'the Lord of Cattraeth'. There is nothing impossible about a different figure, with a mixed or Pictish heritage, being remembered with favour by the Britons of the north. This could, in turn, have influenced a northern chronicle from which the *Historia Brittonum* and the *Annales Cambriae* obtained their information. Such a figure may also have been remembered favourably enough by the Gododdin to earn a mention in their surviving poem. To try and build a coherent theory, one would also have to explain the presence of the name in areas affected by Irish migration and the absence of the name in early Pictish and Welsh sources.

However, Welsh legends never portray him as Irish or Pictish. In *Culhwch and Olwen*, one of his tasks is to take the Cauldron of Diwrnach. Arthur is portrayed as travelling there and fighting against the Irish. Similarly, in the hunt for the giant boar, Twrch Trwyth, Arthur travels to Ireland but there's no hint of friendly relations or family ties. The thirteenth-century poem *Pa Gur* seems to suggest Arthur and his men fought near Edinburgh but also in North Wales. In the two late biographies of St Gildas, the saint is described as a son of Alt Clut or the Scotia. From the latter, we hear the sons of Nau rebel against Arthur and he kills the eldest brother of Gildas, Hueil. Gerald of Wales, c.1190, claims this as the reason Gildas did not mention Arthur in *De Excidio*. So here we have tales of Arthur, the earliest copies of which all post-date the twelfth century, fighting against Picts and Irish with even later sources claiming a Pictish connection.

In summary, we can make some observations. There were strong links between Britain and Ireland through immigration, the church and myths that may have influenced later legends. There is good evidence of both British and Irish links with Rome in the fifth and sixth centuries.[181] None of these are strong enough to suggest any Irish connection with Arthur. The *Historia* is reasonably clear about when and who Arthur was fighting. After the death of St Patrick and Hengest, he fights against *them* with the kings of the Britons, *them* being the English who have 'increased their numbers and grew in Britain'. It is possible, and even likely, someone leading 'the Kings of the Britons' may have fought Picts, Irish raiders or even settlers. But there is no evidence from any source that Artur mac Aedan is connected with the Arthur of either the *Historia* or Welsh legends.

What does remain is a faint whisper of an Irish or Pictish connection. Something that makes a northern poet refer to Arthur in *Y Gododdin*, allows four Irish dynasties to name their princes Arthur, connects Arthur with Welsh saints and maintains a tradition from Wales to Cornwall and Brittany. We mustn't look upon these groups through the lens of previous Roman propaganda. These were no naked barbarians. They were militarily advanced enough to cause major problems for the Romans and later Romano-British. There were

Key

• • •   Areas of fifth-century
• • •   Irish settlement

1   Manau Gododdin

Picts

Dal
Riata

Maetae
1

Alt Clut

Gododdin

Northern
Ui Neill

Ulain

Connacht

Southern
Ui Neill

Gwynedd

Powys

Laigin

Munster

Déisi

Dyfed

Dumnonia

Map 22: Fifth-century Irish settlement and the Picts

also significant links between Irish saints and the north from the time of
St Columba (c.521) onwards. Alliances and marriages were also not uncommon
if we accept Adomnán and Bede's account of events in the sixth century among
other sources. We will finish with Map 22 that details the main areas of fifth-
century Irish settlement.

Summary

At the start of the fifth century, Roman Britain consisted of functioning towns and *civitates* within a provincial structure controlled by a central authority at the Diocese capital in London. This, in turn, lay within the prefecture of the Gauls in the Western Empire. By the end of the fifth century, the Diocese structure had disappeared, as had the Western Empire. It is possible elements of the provincial structure survived in some regions. However, in other areas the *civitates* themselves fractured, sometimes along rural and urban lines. Cultural identity also changed from a largely dominant widespread Roman identity to a far more complex and nuanced situation. By the end of the sixth century, post-Roman Britain is dominated by the emergence of petty kingdoms and warlords with the beginnings of distinctive Anglo-Saxon and Brittonic cultural identities. It is between these two extremes that Arthur fought on the cusp between post-Roman Britain and the early medieval period. The main social groups within Arthur's Britain were the indigenous elites, rural peasants and a number of different Germanic migrant groups.[182] We must remember these were not homogenous and no doubt there were multiple political, religious and other divisions within each.

Regarding migration, there is genetic, linguistic, literary and archaeological evidence for Germanic peoples in Britain before the year 400. Evidence for an increased presence of Anglo-Saxon or Germanic settlers in the east and the Thames Valley is found from 425 onwards.[183] Later, Anglian, Jutish and Saxon levels of immigration increased from the east and down the river valleys of the south, east and north from the Solent to the Humber. These would have been inconsistent and irregular with complex and different timescales.[184] Indeed, Anglo-Saxon ingress appears to be 'patchy and opportunistic'.[185]

On the one hand, Germanic material culture from the early to mid-fifth century was relatively homogenous.[186] However, regional differences appear within Britain from the late fifth century. This might suggest a fragmentation economically, culturally or politically, or indeed a combination of all three. But in general, we see a rough correspondence with Bede's description: Saxons in the south, Angles in the east and north, and Jutes in East Kent, the New Forest area and the Isle of Wight. Yet Bede, and the more contemporary Procopius, lists a number of other tribal groups including Frisians. The reality in Arthur's time was thus far more complex. Our understanding remains poor concerning boundaries and political structures.[187]

It is worth noting that modern county boundaries were formed in the tenth century and not the sixth. However, territorial identity appears to have been established in the Iron Age and continued into the Roman period.[188] Some *civitates* appear to be based on those tribal areas.[189] During the Roman period, the trend was towards romanisation with subtle regional differences linked to tribal areas, though we cannot assume separate ethnic identities.[190] Nor can we assume a clear evolution from all pre-Roman tribal kingdoms through *civitates* to early petty kingdoms.[191] Yet the early Anglo-Saxon kingdoms do correspond closely with socio-economic Romano-British tribal zones.[192]

Let us now attempt to take a step-by-step guide through the fifth century to Arthur's likely timeframe. The late Western Empire was increasingly socially and economically fragmented, leaving political vacuums at local and regional levels.[193] The empire had become inefficient and corrupt.[194] There was friction between the late imperial government and local elites.[195] The subsequent significant migration of different groups was the product of the decline and not the cause.[196] The upheavals in Britain from Magnus Maximus onwards suggests it was no different. The first half of the fifth century saw economic and urban decline, and significant migration down the Thames Valley and east coast river systems south of the Humber.

A pivotal political and/or military event occurred in the mid-fifth century. Evidence for Germanic settlements increased significantly in the east. A shift from a civic to a military model of identity starts to be seen.[197] While ethnic and social identity was multilayered, the importance of *civitas* or local identity increased.[198] The end of the Western Empire, and thus Roman Britain, could be described as a 'complex scrabble to maintain, reinforce and acquire position and economic control.'[199] In Britain the 'council' and 'Proud Tyrant's' authority likely collapsed. At this point, it might be useful to split Britain into various regions. In all areas, it should be remembered there is significant evidence for high levels of continuation of occupation, land use and the indigenous population. We will begin with the former provinces. While we cannot be sure of the exact boundaries, one common theory for provincial borders shows a strong correlation with later patterns of migration.[200] This can be seen in Map 23. This, in turn, can be linked to the three coastal and river drainage systems shown earlier in Map 8: Thames Valley and south coast river systems; North Sea river systems; and the western and south-west coastal area.

However, that may be far too simplistic given the different patterns of migration, the potential continuation of Brittonic control in some areas and the literary sources. It is worth remembering the evidence for pre-mid-fifth century Germanic burials was confined to river valleys between the Thames and the Humber and south-east of the Trent. Yet the literary sources point to the south-east. Therefore, Map 24 of post-provincial Britain might be more instructive. It is split into four zones as follows:

Map 23: Provinces and migration

Zone A, the south-east: marked by high levels of urbanisation, romanisation and good transport links. It is also marked by early evidence for Germanic material culture and settlement in river valleys and coastal areas, specifically Saxon immigration down the Thames Valley, and Angle and Scandinavian migrants into the *civitas* of the Iceni. The literary sources suggest this was the first region that 'broke away' from the Diocese structure. Likely centred on Kent, it appears to have included the whole of the former province of Maxima Caesariensis. *Civitates* appear to have evolved into Anglo-Saxon kingdoms with a strong correlation with former boundaries. It extends into the tribal area of the Catuvellauni to include their *civitas* capital at Verulamium, St Albans.

Zone B, an 'eastern corridor': contains much of the former province of Flavia Caesariensis and south down the Trent Valley to the *civitates* of the Atrebates and Belgae and the Isle of Wight. It is also marked by high levels of urbanisation, romanisation and good transport links. There is additionally early evidence for Germanic material culture and settlement in river valleys and coastal areas.

Former Roman provinces

1. Maxima Caesariensis

2. Britannia Prima

3. Flavia Caesariensis

4. Britannia Secunda

5. Valentia?

Map 24: Post-provincial Britain

There is specifically Angle immigration in Lindsey and Saxon immigration in the Thames Valley centred on the modern area of Abingdon in the *civitas* of the Atrebates. The *civitates* in this zone appear to have fractured at some point and later groups coalesced into larger polities.

Zone C, a 'western and northern corridor': incorporating the urbanised and romanised portion of Britannia Prima along with the former northern military command. There is little early evidence of Germanic culture and no indication of burials or settlements in the south. There is also limited material culture on the eastern end of Hadrian's Wall and a literary tradition placing early mercenaries there in the mid-fifth century. The zone is marked by deteriorating urban centres and reoccupation of hill forts. It also contains some signs of continuation of use at some forts in the north and along Hadrian's Wall. The *civitates* appear to form the basis of some early Brittonic kingdoms, some of which are based on continuation in urban sites such as Wroxeter and Cirencester. But some *civitates* are fragmented, possibly along urban and rural lines such as the Brigantes and Silures. This presents a continuation of strong Roman identity with added martial identity in the north.

Zone D, Western zone: highland and rural areas with emerging kingdoms based on tribal identities, and few urban centres of villas. There is a reoccupation of hill forts and continued trade with the Mediterranean area from sites such as Tintagel. There is a limited amount of Irish migration in some areas but an element of Roman identity is retained. It is possible the Brittonic kingdoms of Gododdin and Alt Clut could be included in this group if Roman cultural identity had spread north, and there was a greater cultural difference with the Picts to the north. Zone D contains the regions which retained a tradition of Arthurian legends that persisted for 600 years before Geoffrey of Monmouth wrote *The History of the Kings of Britain*. This zone could be extended south across the channel to include Armorica.

Map 25: Provinces of Britain in a European context

Alternatively, we could combine these two previous maps and look at things from a wider North European viewpoint. In this version, Zone A includes the Atrebates and Belgae. Zone B is the former province of Flavia Caesariensis which, in this example, includes the *civitas* of the Iceni. It correlates the river systems with the provinces within the zones detailed above. We recall Tolkien describing how Hengest, a Jute, came from Friesland after the battle at Finnsburgh in the *Beowulf* epic. We can see how much easier a journey from that area would be compared to Jutland.

But what of the average person who lived through these times? Most would have lived in rural communities. They may have been ambivalent about the cultural identity of the elite they served. For these elites, society was changing rapidly. The political decline of the Western Empire reduced the civic options of aristocrats in the fifth century.[201] They were more likely to be locally-based, armed and to have a warrior following. By 500, in the rural communities of northern Gaul, social standing relied on gift-giving, purchase of support, and networks of marriages and alliances.[202] It is unlikely Britain was dissimilar. The process of identity change is estimated to take as little as a generation or more.[203] There is therefore enough time from the mid-fifth century for a coalescence of diverse groups to support a small aristocratic core. This process was likely well underway by the time Arthur arrived on the scene. A fifth-century peasant living in, say, the Thames Valley might have a very mixed heritage. His Friesian father might work at the local garrison of Gewissae, themselves protecting the borders of the Atrebates as internally it fractures into civil war. His mother from the neighbouring Durotriges tends the farm which trades some of its produce with the South Saxons living across the Meon Valley in the *civitas* of the Regni. When war comes, who does the peasant fight for? Artorius, leading the kings of Britain from the north or west? The 'Easterners' from the former Maxima Caesariensis? Or some other group?

To summarise, Arthur's Britain is a patchwork of petty kingdoms emerging from the fragmentation of Roman provinces and significant Germanic settlement. This partition certainly involves the south-east but how much of the east coast from East Anglia, Lincolnshire and Northumbria is open to question. While there is much evidence for continuity, the Anglo-Saxon polities were based on people rather than a territory.[204] The later expansions after the mid-sixth century, which led to the formation of Anglo-Saxon kingdoms, can give us clues as to which areas were still under Romano-British control in Arthur's time. A line running roughly from Southampton to Newcastle might be a fair approximation for the partition Gildas refers to. This, of course, would be too simplistic. Firstly, neither the Britons nor the Anglo-Saxons were homogenous groups. Tribal, language, cultural and religious differences existed on both sides.

Secondly, significant pockets of Britons coexisted in Anglo-Saxon areas and vice versa. It is this scenario in which Arthur fights his battles. If Arthur is fighting Angles, Saxons and Jutes, then we now have an indication of where exactly these people were although it would not negate defensive battles deep inside Romano-British territories. Nor would it negate a complex political situation or, indeed, civil wars with Germanic mercenaries on both sides.

I will finish this chapter with one last map – Map 26. This reflects my personal opinion of one likely scenario and is based on a number of assumptions for the situation in c.500:

- In the first half of the fifth century, a significant number of small disparate Germanic groups migrated into Britain, settling near economically-active areas and along river valleys and coasts.
- This movement added to the evolving cultural identity that was already changing rapidly.
- The groups were settled within the civic, economic and military structures that already existed.
- The Diocese and provincial structures survived to the mid-fifth century.
- Around the mid-fifth century, the south-east province broke away under Hengest.
- The *civitas* of the Iceni, with some of the earliest and most extensive levels of migration, allied themselves with the south-east province or became practically autonomous.
- The second half of the fifth century was marked by further immigration into the east and south.
- A weak Diocese-level council and provincial structure still existed for the remaining provinces.
- Flavia Caesariensis contracted into a civic authority centred on Lindsey which developed a separate identity.
- The remaining mainly rural areas of the province experienced significant levels of Germanic immigration, most notably Angles.
- Soemil, expanding north from Lindsey, first separated Deira from Bernicia before Arthur's timeframe.
- The former northern military command retained a significant military influence.
- Jutish/Angle mercenaries were indeed posted to the northern command and a significant group was still present in 500.
- Britannia Prima retained a provincial structure.
- Significant levels of Germanic settlers were present within the eastern side of Britannia Prima especially the *civitates* of the Atrebates and Belgae.

Most notably, there were Saxons along the Thames Valley and Jutes on the Hampshire coast.

- Romano-Brittonic cultural identity had spread north to include Gododdin and Alt Clut.
- Immigration and political fragmentation resulted in conflict.
- Ambrosius's fightback was to stabilise and regain control in the fragmenting provinces and *civitates*, and to push out any Germanic groups opposed to that control.
- This involved leading forces from the fragmenting former northern military command.

Former Roman provinces

1. Maxima Caesariensis
2. Britannia Prima
3. Flavia Caesariensis
4. Britannia Secunda
5. Valentia?

Former northern military command

Powys Emerging kingdoms

- Important urban centres

Corridor of significant fragmentation. Likely areas of conflict.

Map 26: Arthur's Britain c. AD 500

- There were Britons and Germanic groups on both sides although distinct cultural identities began to be formed.
- Arthur was born into this political, cultural and social context and carried on where Ambrosius left off.

The areas of particular interest for our purposes are the *civitates* of the Atrebates and Belgae; the fragmenting province of Flavia Caesariensis, most notably the settlements of Lincolnshire and the Trent Valley; Deira; and the east coast of Northumbria near Hadrian's Wall. As the war ended in a victory at Badon, it is unlikely it occurred in areas that remained under Germanic control at the time Gildas wrote. This must mean at least Verulamium but includes *civitates* which later formed the basis of the earliest Anglo-Saxon kingdoms. For that reason, I have determined Kent, Sussex and Essex are not the likeliest locations for battles. With the scene now set, we can turn to the weapons and warfare of the day. We shall see we have a reasonable amount of evidence and contemporary records for battles to give us a good feel for how a fifth- or sixth-century battle would have looked.

Chapter 6

Weapons, Armour and Warfare

I will now turn to the sort of army Arthur would have commanded in the fifth or sixth century. In terms of weapons, a number of changes had taken place by the fifth century.[1] In the Western Roman Empire the familiar rectangular Roman *scutum* shield had been slowly phased out, as had the *gladius* sword. Shields had become round or oval and the short *gladius* had been replaced by the longer *spatha* sword at between 75–100cm. The *spiculum* spear replaced the *pilum* and was slightly shorter and better as a handheld weapon. Indeed, thrusting spears in general became more common like the *lancea*. Shorter javelins were used too, such as lead-weighted darts (*plumbatae*), five of which could be carried in the rear of a shield. They had a range of 30–60m. The large 5,000–strong legions of the past had been reduced to smaller, more mobile forces of between 1,000 and 1,200 men, and the previous 480–strong cohorts may have reflected a paper strength with the reality of perhaps two-thirds of that number.[2] There were two main types of units: the *comitatenses* were the main field army units while the *limitanei* literally meant soldiers in the frontier districts. There was no particular difference in equipment or training.[3] Scale or mail armour replaced the *lorica segmenta* of the early Roman army. Helmets evolved to include ridges on top, cheek pieces, a neck protector and even the first nose guards. Similarly, trousers and covered boots became more common.

In general, the overall strategy became more defensive and they deployed a 'strength in depth' strategy across the Western Empire to react to small raiding parties. There was a general influx of Germanic recruits during the fourth and fifth centuries, and armies often adopted the '*barritus*', a Germanic war cry.[4] Whether this was because their often-Germanic enemies found it intimidating or because of the presence of Germanic soldiers in the ranks is unknown. Battlefield tactics had also become less aggressive with barbarian charges being met 'at the halt' to maintain close order.[5] We are reminded of *The Life of St Germanus*, where he takes control of a British force and ambushes a Pictish and Saxon force with the cry of 'Alleluia!', which forced them to flee.

Cavalry became more important.[6] These units generally became larger and more armoured with a force of up to 500–600 strong, although again this possibly reflected a paper strength only.[7] By the mid-fifth century, most *alae* or cavalry units of the *limitanei* border forces, had reduced from twenty *turmae* (thirty men each) to just ten.[8] It might be interesting to compare this with the famous Welsh poem, *Y Gododdin*, set in the sixth century, which describes a calvary force of 300 attacking the Angles at Catraeth, possibly identified as Catterick. Evidence suggests that the percentage of cavalry in the army increased from 20 to 35 per cent between the early principate and fifth-century empire.[9] However, the ideal was still a balanced force with cavalry in the minority.[10] While heavy cavalry increased, they were still outnumbered by their lighter counterparts and trained to fight with missiles as much as mounting a charge.[11] Scouting and chasing down retreating forces would have been their main tasks. The use of cavalry as a missile platform would have been well known to the Romano-British and Germanic immigrants, as well as any other ethnic groups in fifth-century Britain.[12]

The *Notitia Dignitatum* mentions two units of interest in the *Equites Catafractarii*, one stationed with the Count of the Britons and the other in the north. These were copied from the cataphracts of the east such as the Parthians or Sarmatians. They were armed with a 4-metre-long lance, a *contus*, that was used two-handed by the Romans. Horses and riders were covered in mail or scale armour and, to the untrained eye, may have looked similar to much later armoured cavalry. Having said that, there is no evidence of Sarmatian cavalry after the deployment of 5,500 to Britain in the second century, aside from two tombstones at Ribchester that have since been lost and are undatable.[13] Indeed, there is no evidence for 'true' horse armour in Western Europe for this period.[14] There are also no references to light horse archers in Western Europe similar to examples in the east.[15] There is, however, plenty of evidence of cavalry, most notably from Sutton Hoo with some similarities to finds in Southern Sweden. Cavalry was used throughout Europe and there is no good reason why Germanic immigrants would not have been aware of their advantages in warfare.[16]

Post-Roman armies relied on horses, regardless of whether the majority of fighting was done on foot. Stirrups were not introduced into Europe until the late sixth century by the Avars. However, it is not the stirrups but the development of the saddle that enabled a 'crashing shock charge' with a lance.[17] Specifically, it is a supporting saddle with a high back and front panels that makes this possible and this didn't develop until much later. The stirrup does allow strikes to the left and right in a melee. But a rider, or more likely a horse, would be vulnerable to a spear thrust. Even in the eleventh century, at the Battle of Hastings, cavalry could not, and often would not, charge a body of densely-packed infantry. In 1066, they were confined to riding up close and hurling javelins. In the fifth and sixth centuries, it is likely cavalry were used for scouting, skirmishing and flanking. They would be ideal for chasing down a retreating army. Arthur would have ridden to battle but it's likely he fought on foot, or if mounted, waited behind the lines to direct operations. A cavalry unit may well exploit an opening like Alexander the Great leading the companions. But we must forget the idea of Arthur with armoured knights of the later Middle Ages, charging en masse with heavy cavalry. We will now turn to the Roman army in Britain.

There were three commands at the end of the Roman period with the following units:[18]

Table 10: Military commands of Roman Britain

	Cavalry units *(alae)*	Infantry cohorts
Count of Britons	6	4 (*comitatenses*)
Count of Saxon Shore	2	7 (*limitanei*)
Duke of Britons (York) Along Hadrian's Wall Reserves	5 3	18 (*limitanei*) 11 (*limitanei*)
Overall total	16	40

A rough estimate of the maximum strength of units in Britain around the beginning of the fifth century can be made: Count of the Britons (3,000 cavalry and 2,000 infantry); Count of the Saxon Shore (1,000 cavalry and 3,500 infantry); and the Duke of the Britons based at York (4,000 cavalry and 15,000 infantry). So, there was a paper strength of 20,000 infantry and 8,000 cavalry, although the reality may be closer to two-thirds of these numbers. This ties in with other evidence that suggests by the end of Roman Britain, the entire force was estimated at 20,000 troops and possibly as low as 12,000 available at any one time, compared to a force of perhaps 50,000 in the second century.[19] Other estimates give a figure as low as 6,000, which would have been further depleted by Constantine in 407.

Elsewhere across the Western Empire, it is estimated between c.380 and 420, the Western field army had lost half its strength.[20] Let us now put this into the context of our timeline. In 407, Constantine III left Britain for Gaul with much of the military force. Both Magnus Maximus and General Stilicho had done the same a few years previously. There is an assumption that Constantine took the bulk of the army, but in truth we don't know. So, the force represented in the *Notitia Dignitatum* was depleted by 408, after which there was a major Saxon incursion which partly caused the British to eject Constantine's administration. The coin supply had already dried up which no doubt affected numbers of troops available, as well as morale and loyalty. Yet they had sufficient troops to defeat the attack of 408 and retain some form of power for a generation at least. We could speculate that the higher estimate of 20,000 assorted troops had now become less than half that number. For the years 410–440, we are left to wonder how the remaining troops were replaced and new ones trained and equipped. If we accept Constantius of Lyon in *The Life of St Germanus*, there was at least some military force left in 429. According to Gildas, the Britons were able to defeat the last attack by Picts and Scots, and sometime later, defeat the barbarians twice: the first victory of Ambrosius and 'nearly the last' at Badon.

Yet Gildas also describes the Britons at the very beginning of his tract as 'unwarlike' then later as, 'ignorant in the ways of war' and a 'leaderless and irrational mob'. They were 'too lazy to fight, too unwieldy to flee' and sat about 'day and night rotting away in their folly'. Rhetoric perhaps, but by 441, the *Gallic Chronicle* states Britain fell to the power of the Saxons. Certainly, by the mid-fifth century, a significant part of the Diocese had been lost and, at least from the point of view of Gildas, his 'countrymen' were unable militarily to maintain access to certain areas.

Perhaps there was a rebellion of the *limitanei*, either along the Saxon Shore or in the north. Gildas believed the Picts seized land 'up to the wall'. So, it is quite possible that by the middle of the fifth century, the available forces numbered just a few thousand, having been halved by Constantine then halved again by the loss of the Saxon Shore and part of the north. Lack of coinage, deterioration of training and equipment, and problems with recruitment and retention would have depleted the forces further. All this was before the fightback by Ambrosius and later by Arthur. Yet parts of Britain did not fall, so significant British forces must have existed.

Size of armies

Following the failure of the request for help from Rome, Gildas states the Britons were strong enough to defeat the enemy (the Scots and Picts) for the first time. But on rumours of further incursions, they felt the need to request help. However, at first, only three *keels*, or ships, were sent. These Saxon boats would have been around 23m long and carried approximately thirty men, so this was a small force.[21] Later, a larger force was sent for, although Bede simply states 'their numbers increase'. The *Historia Brittonum* gives a number of sixteen ships, so 480 men and later forty ships with around 1,200 men who are settled 'near the wall'. If true, it implies the British didn't have a legion-sized force spare and this last group was to replace those lost in the early 440s. We can compare this to Geoffrey of Monmouth, writing in the twelfth century, claiming that Octa arrives with 300 ships, implying 10,000 men with Hengest's army later being 300,000 strong. This seems an exaggeration on the same scale as his claims of Arthur conquering Ireland, Norway and Gaul.

The *Anglo-Saxon Chronicles* also suggest relatively small numbers of men: after Hengest's arrival, Aelle and his three sons, Cymen and Wlencing and Cissa, also arrive with three ships at a place named Cymen's shore (probably Selsey Bill, West

Sussex), and 'there killed many Welsh and drove them into the wood which is named the Weald'. Then, in 495, Cerdic and Cynric appear with five ships in the Hampshire area and 'fight against the Welsh'. Port arrives next with two ships in the Portsmouth area and kill a 'noble man'. The West Saxons Stuff and Whitgar appear in 514 with three ships and fight against the Britons putting them to flight. None of the entries in the fifth or early sixth centuries can be verified, but they describe relatively minor conflicts involving less than 200 men. Under the law codes of King Ine (688–725), a body of over thirty-five men was described as a *here* or army.[22] The 755 *Chronicle* entry describes a war-band of eighty-four attacking and killing the King of the Wessex. The Battle of Finnsburg includes the phrase 'sixty war bears' when describing a young prince's war-band.

On the other hand, some records describe larger-scale conflict. The entry for 457 in the *Anglo-Saxon Chronicle* has Hengest and Aesc killing 4,000 Britons at Creaganford (possibly Crayford in Kent) causing the Britons to abandon Kent and flee 'in terror' for their stronghold at London. This suggests London was still active and in British control, and that Kent, at least, was now outside their influence. Another entry for 508 describes Cerdic and Cynric defeating Natanleod, a British king, killing 5,000 at Netley in the modern-day New Forest. Similarly, the Battle of Beandun dated to 614 records 2,065 Welsh being killed. These three battles would suggest large-scale conflicts on a par with the Battle of Hastings in 1066, which involved armies of around 7,000 and casualty rates of around half on the English side.

A battle in 878 in Devon has a half-brother of Ivar the Boneless being killed, along with 800 men plus 40 of his own war-band. This, perhaps, indicates how a relatively small army was made up of individual war-bands or ships' crews. For the Battle of Maldon in 991, we have four sources: a 325–line fragment of a poem; the *Anglo-Saxon Chronicle*; the *Life of St Oswald*; and the twelfth-century *Book of Ely*. These sources describe a Viking army of 93 ships, which suggests 2,800 men. The poem implies roughly equal forces. The earlier Tribal Hidage gives Essex 7,000 hides of land which, at one armed man per five hides,[23] would give 1,400 men. If we add the local burgh levies and hearth troops of nobles and the leader, Earl Byrhtnoth, then this gives a good indication of the size of the armies in the early Middle Ages. What we don't have evidence for in later Anglo-Saxon England is larger pitched battles such as Cannae in 216 BC, where Hannibal and 50,000 troops defeated a much larger Roman force.

So how does this compare with evidence from the continent? Large-scale pitched battles had become less common so armies had become smaller and more mobile to respond to small raiding parties. In 357, two Alemannic kings mustered a force of 35,000 from various tribes and subkings, and this was considered a very large force.[24] Even one of the king's immediate war-bands of 200 was unusual. A far more common example occurred in the same year when the Western Caesar Julian spent two months besieging 600 Franks in an abandoned Roman fort in Gaul, rather than attacking them. When the Franks surrendered, they were conscripted into the army and sent to the east. Battles the size of Attila's fight against Aetius in 451 at Chalons, which numbered tens of thousands on both sides, became rarer. General Belisarius, of the Eastern Roman Empire in the sixth century, commanded armies of 16,000 in Africa and 8,000 in Italy. A late sixth-century manual described armies of 5,000 to 15,000 but viewed those nearer the lower end as the norm.[25] Research suggests that it is unlikely any post-Roman kingdom could raise armies of 10,000 to 20,000 and a few thousand would have been the norm with 5,000 to 6,000 at the upper end of the scale.[26] We must bear this in mind when considering Arthur's battles.

If we take the Battle of Mount Badon as an example, there are tentative clues as to numbers. Firstly, Gildas, in c.540, describes it as 'pretty well the last defeat of the villains and certainly not the least', implying it wasn't the largest battle. Bede in 731 simply describes it as 'no small slaughter of the invaders'. The *Historia Brittonum* in c.830 states: 'The twelfth battle was on Badon hill and in it 960 men fell in one day, from a single charge of Arthur's, and no-one laid them low save him alone.' Whether this means 960 Saxons were killed or if this is just Arthur's contribution is unknown. But it's interesting that this number is exactly two cohorts or thirty-two ships' crews. Geoffrey of Monmouth in 1136 describes the 'vast numbers' of the enemy and 'many thousands' being killed, with Arthur personally slaying 470 men in one charge alone. We can compare this to Bernard Cornwell's excellent *Excalibur*, written over 800 years later, whose story involves armies numbering less than 2,000 men at Badon; we can conclude with some confidence that Mr Cornwell is more likely to be nearer the truth. It is worth noting that if the Saxons are the besieged in this battle and lost, then it is likely the opposing force was larger. An army of 3,000 overrunning a hill fort defended by 960 men is not an unrealistic scenario.

Danish bog finds have unearthed evidence of fifty major battles for the third to the fifth centuries.[27] One at Illerup is especially instructive. The 40 per cent excavated so far has revealed about 350 warriors, five of which appear to be high-ranking and forty of a middle rank based on armour, dress and weapons. If we double these figures for a rough estimate, once the whole site is investigated, then we come to 700 fallen in one battle. These could represent a defeated army disposed of or the fallen from both sides. The forty better-armed warriors could represent a war-band with the bulk of the remainder being conscripted farmers. From these figures, estimates of about 1,500 have been made for armies from the regions which many of the later Germanic settlers to Britain came from.

So, the next question is: what was the population size of Roman Britain at the time? Estimates range from 1 million to as high as 4 million.[28] Climatic changes, and an increase in plagues, famines, civil wars and raids, all put downward pressure on population in the fifth century.[29] An estimate of 2 million is not unreasonable and, from that, we could speculate on numbers of able-bodied fighting men. If we reduce this figure by half, then half again to estimate adult males, reducing it by half a third time might remove the elderly and infirm. One could argue that women, the young and the elderly can man ramparts and throw things down upon an attacking enemy. But in terms of fighting battles or any hand to hand combat, then a 10 per cent rule of thumb is a reasonable estimate, which would give a rough guide of 200,000 fighting-age men spread across post-Roman Britain. From this group, a much smaller number might receive training and be regarded as soldiers or local militia.

The Tribal Hidage may well have been written a couple of hundred years after Arthur fought. However, it gives some idea of the land controlled by certain groups which include some of the larger petty kingdoms. It is thought that later in Anglo-Saxon England, it took about five hides to support one armed warrior.[30] If this is accurate, it gives us some idea of possible numbers so I have adjusted the earlier table to reflect potential numbers of warriors. This should be taken with a large pinch of salt as it bears no resemblance to fifth-century Britain. However, it is an interesting counterbalance to the argument for very small armies. For example, the south might have had a population of over 1 million which, using the previous rule of thumb, would give 100,000 men of fighting age. Table 11 gives us a figure of over 64,000. This would suggest, in theory at least, that it is possible to have had large armies *if* there was an authority strong enough to organise and resource them.

Table 11: Estimation of warrior numbers from the Tribal Hidage

Myrcna landes (Mercia) 6,000	North Gyrwa 120	Gifla 300	Hendrica 700	West Willa 120
Wocensaetna 1,400	East Wixna 60	Hicca 300	Unecungaga 240	East Engle 6,000
Westerna 1,400	West Wixna 120	Wihtgara 600	Arosaetna 120	East Saxena 1,400
Pecsaetna 240	Spalda 120	Noxgaga 5,000	Faerpinga 60	Cantwarena 3,000
Elmedsaetna 120	Wigesta 180	Ohtgaga 2,000	Bilmiga 120	South Saxena 1,400
Linesfarona 1,400	Herefinna 240	Hwinca 7,000	Widerigga 120	West Saxena 20,000
Suth Gyrwa 120	Sweordora 60	Cilternasaetna 4,000	East Willa 120	

Taking a more localised view, London, as an example, had a population of 60,000 at its height in Roman Britain. This appears to have reduced from the fourth century to the end of the fifth century when it seems abandoned, not to be reoccupied until the time of Alfred the Great in the ninth century. One estimate for the number of men required to defend the 5 kilometres of walls is 2,700.[31] This could indicate the reason why it was eventually abandoned. They may simply have not had enough men to man the walls. One can thus visualise a town or city of a few low thousand with several hundred able-bodied fighting men, of which only a small percentage may have had training, weapons and armour. Perhaps there was a town militia as the first defence, but with what was left of the Romano-British forces numbering the low thousands and spread across the provinces. We can see how a small force of heavily-armed and battle-hardened warriors could make a substantial difference in specific locations. A smaller town such as Gloucester had a population at its height of around 10,000. If this had been much reduced in the fifth century, we could have a fighting-age male population of a few hundred, which might allow for a militia numbered in dozens.

We can thus imagine how a smaller fifth-century town, isolated in a fragmented political and military situation, would be vulnerable to two or three ship loads of experienced warriors. Equally how advantageous it might be for a province (e.g. Maxima Caesariensis) or even a *civitas* (e.g. Cantii) to hire them as mercenaries. Despite the literary sources, there is no archaeological evidence to back up Gildas's narrative of destroyed cities. There is no burnt layer similar to London which evidences Boudicca's revolt in AD 60. What the evidence demonstrates is there was no destruction of the Romano-British population and replacement by hundreds of thousands of Anglo-Saxons arriving en masse.

In summary, we can say that the original Romano-British forces had been depleted, even before the end of Roman Britain in 410. If we accept *The Life of St Germanus*, then an army of sorts still existed in 429. No doubt recruitment, retention, training, equipment and maintenance all deteriorated. Towns declined and the political structure fragmented with power becoming decentralised, all of which makes the organising of military forces more difficult. In fact, it is possible that none of the provincial or military structures survived up to Arthur's time. The literary, archaeological and DNA evidence all point away from a large-scale invasion replacing the population. All this supports battles between armies numbering in the hundreds. Having said that, the size of the population was still considerable. Thus, accounts in the *Anglo-Saxon Chronicles* implying armies in the thousands are not impossible. What is less likely are large-scale battles of many tens of thousands in Geoffrey of Monmouth's epic.

Weapons, armour and tactics

For the Anglo-Saxons, the spear was the most common weapon with the shield the next most prevalent piece of equipment. A common form of fighting stance would have been with a shield in one hand and a spear held, either over or under arm. Spearheads differed, as did shaft lengths. Some heads had angular cutting blades as much as 50cm in length, suggesting they may have been used two-handed; indeed, a Pictish relief shows just that.[32] The effect of shorter, barbed-headed spears, known as 'Angons', are described by a sixth-century source.[33] If striking flesh, the head cannot be pulled out without terrible pain and the injured man often dies. If it hits a shield, it is also difficult to remove or cut off because of the barb and iron cover near the head. The warrior can then tread on the shaft, pulling the shield down and exposing the neck or head. To pierce mail armour, a narrow needle-shaped head is required, as with arrows, which will pierce one of the rings pulling them apart and allowing penetration of the spearhead. The effective range of the shorter spears or javelins was around 12–15m[34] although re-enactments do demonstrate twice that distance was achievable.

In general, missile weapons became more important and there was an increase in light troops and mounted archers in the fifth century.[35] However, finds of bows are rare in Britain although literary and artistic sources regularly depict them. Germanic bows were 'longbows' made from a single piece of wood in contrast to composite Asiatic bows. Forty were found in Nydham, Denmark 6 foot in length with shafts of 74–94cm and leaf-shaped or barbed arrowheads. The maximum range was about 150–200m but with few casualties at over 100m. They were accurate at around 50–60m.[36] Archers, whether mounted or on foot, would have carried thirty to forty arrows.[37] Throwing axes were popular with the Franks, and both Procopius and Gregory of Tours describe these short-handled axes as being thrown prior to a charge, with a range of 12m. These differed from the normal axes used in day-to-day work or the longer axe hammer found at Sutton Hoo with a shaft of 78cm. They are rarely found in graves or mentioned in the sagas for this period.[38]

So, in terms of range weapons, we can imagine the following scenario. A standard football pitch is around 100m long by 75m wide. A war-band of five ships, full of men, would number about 150 and could stand two deep at one end, four deep if only covering the width of the goalkeeper's box. A similar force of Romano-British facing them at the other end might stand their ground in a defensive position. At this range, arrows would begin to have minimal effect, enough to make you want to retreat out of range or advance quickly. At the half way line, the bows become accurate. As you advance to the edge of the centre circle in the opponents' half, javelins start to rain in and at the edge of the 18–yard box they become accurate. In the thirteenth-century *Dialogue of Taliesin and Myrddin*, we have the vivid lines concerning the Battle of Arfderydd dated 573 in the *Annales Cambriae*: 'A host of spears fly high, drawing blood. From a host of vigorous warriors. A host, fleeing; a host, wounded. A host, bloody, retreating.'

To continue our football pitch analogy, at the penalty spot, anyone carrying a Frankish axe would unleash this too. The longer 9-foot spears, held 3 feet from the end, would start to touch tips and as the shield-walls drew together, warriors would attempt to thrust their spears over the shields or through gaps. How good your shield and armour were might affect how fast or keenly you covered this distance. The shield-walls would push and shove while trying to land blows with spear or sword. Warriors in the rear would hurl javelins, darts or sling shot. Cavalry might lurk at the flanks, ready to exploit openings. The first shield-wall to break would be extremely vulnerable.

Aside from spears, one of the most common weapons was the *seax*, a single-edged blade ranging from 8–31cm. Longer examples of between 54 and 76 cm are not found until the later eighth century.[39] It is likely a fifth-century Saxon would have had the shorter version, at up to a foot long, carried horizontally on his belt. The blade would not have been suited to piercing mail. The more iconic weapon was the sword, even if only the elite may have possessed one. We will cover swords in more depth later.

Germanic tribes mainly used round or oval shields, 60cm to 1 metre in height.[40] The early Anglo-Saxon shield, in particular, was smaller than those on the continent and later Viking shields, being one and half to two and a quarter foot in diameter. Their thickness was 6–8mm and weighed 3–5kg. Poems and art sometimes depict a convex shape, which might be better for deflecting blows, but all the archaeological finds are of flat shields. Lime wood or pine were the most common material used but in reality, a variety of wooden boards glued together would suffice. They were often covered in rawhide, which added further protection from arrows and spears, and could mean the difference between it penetrating the shield by several inches or not at all. The covering was obviously important enough for King Athelstan in the tenth century to prohibit the use of sheepskin on shields.[41] The boss was often larger than imagined at 20cm in height to protect the hand grip in the centre. A strap was attached for carrying purposes. The boss acted more as protection for the hand and balance than any offensive capabilities. In reality, the edge of the shield was more effective in delivering a blow to knock the opponent's shield aside or to strike the warrior. The edges of the shield would also have been covered in leather in the early period. Literary sources suggest shields often suffered damage in battle after repeated blows, with one saga describing a sword blow severing a shield in two and embedding itself in the warrior's head.[42]

Mail armour offered excellent protection against most weapons and was most effective against cutting blows. In the late Roman army, both *lorica hamata* (ring mail) and *lorica squamata* (scale armour) were used. Lamellar armour could also be made from leather scales while a sculpted cuirass was generally worn by officers.[43] Ring mail was also used by Germanic warriors. Only one example has been found in Britain at the Sutton Hoo burial. An example from Vimose in Denmark is hip-length with sleeves to just above the elbow, which includes 20,000 8mm iron rings weighing about 11kg. Alternate rows of welded and riveted rings made it extremely strong. Rings of softer metal or butted (without rivets), as is sometimes seen in re-enactments or in the movies, could be torn apart by hand and would not withstand a blow. It is estimated it would take several weeks to produce a good quality mail shirt, hence the high price compared to a sword. It was prone to rust and some sources mention them being stored in leather cases when not in use.[44] While they were excellent for defensive purposes, they did have the disadvantage of being heavy and tiring over long distances or prolonged use.

It was not an item one would normally wear day to day as can be demonstrated by the Viking army at Stamford Bridge in 1066, who were caught unprepared without their mail shirts. The reason why the Vikings were still prepared to stand and fight without mail is because other materials offered reasonable protection as well. Deer hide, for example, was nearly as strong as mail but lighter and more flexible.[45] Several layers of linen within leather formed a quilted material that would also be surprisingly effective. The *gambeson* quilted leather armour worn in the later medieval period was just an extension of earlier examples. The late Roman *supermalis* worn under armour was simply two layers stuffed with sheep's wool. Some form of under armour would have been essential when wearing metal armour, but a thicker version covered in rawhide would have been a reasonable alternative for the average warrior. A battle re-enactor for that period has found five layers of linen is enough to stop an arrow even at close range.[46] By the late Roman period, muscle cuirasses are depicted on monuments as well as lamellar armour and segmented armour for arms and legs of heavily armoured horsemen.[47] In the early medieval period, in Arthur's time, both chainmail and swords were probably rare for the average warrior.[48] Certainly, even in the late Roman army, light units, whether infantry or cavalry, generally had no armour.[49] Most fighters would have been armed with a spear and protected by a shield and a leather padded jerkin.

Very few helmets have survived with only four found in Britain. A usual design would be four or six metal plates held together with riveted bronze bands. Hinged cheek plates feature, as do nose guards. Neck guards of plate or mail gave added protection. Ridge protection similar to late Roman helmets would protect from overhead sword blows. The most common examples on the continent are *spangenhelms*, with two dozen being found from France to the Balkans. They also included hinged cheek pieces and nasal guards, with some adding eye protection as well as neck protection with mail attached to the rear. The Sutton Hoo helmet takes this one step further, having a full face-guard, and shows significant parallels with the description of helmets in epic poems such as *Beowulf*.[50] The ridges of helmets may have been adorned with an animal crest such as a boar, or a plume. Given the nature of such warfare, the one item of protection that would be a priority after a shield would be a helmet.

Unlike their continental Germanic counterparts, Anglo-Saxons do not appear to have fought on horseback to the same extent.[51] In the Battles of Maldon in 991 and Hastings in 1066, the army appears to have travelled on horseback, but fought on foot. An entry in the *Anglo-Saxon Chronicle* for 1055 records the Herefordshire *fyrd* fleeing before the battle because they had been ordered to fight on horseback 'against their custom'. This might have put them at a disadvantage against a Romano-British force with mixed cavalry and infantry units. But then it must be remembered that cavalry will not charge against a solid mass of infantry, especially one armed with spears. However, it would be wrong to assume from selected examples of infantry battles that they *never* fought on horseback.

Chronicle entries for a defeat by the Picts in 672, a victory by Alfred the Great in 894 and Brunanburh in 937 all imply early Anglo-Saxon armies could, and did, fight on horseback at times.[52] Procopius in the sixth century describes Goth, Vandal, Lombard and Frankish armies as using cavalry, and Pictish and Irish carvings show mounted warriors. A ninth-century heroic poem describes a cavalry battle as beginning cautiously with thrown spears, followed by hand to hand fighting with swords somewhat similar to infantry battles.[53] One is reminded of the Battle of Hastings where the Saxons rode to the battle but dismounted to form a shield-wall. The Norman cavalry attacked with thrown spears before retreating several times. Despite the final outcome, the shield-wall was remarkably effective and resisted this for many hours. Another example of anti-cavalry tactics is in a sixth-century battle where the Thuringians dug pits to protect against Frankish cavalry.[54]

Having said that, the heroic poetry of the Dark Ages almost always describes fighting on foot.[55] While Germanic tribes quickly became proficient on horseback after coming into contact with eastern warfare, in the fifth and sixth centuries, the Franks and Anglo-Saxons still fought mainly on foot.[56] Procopius describes a Gothic army in 539 as being mainly infantry with swords, axes and shields. There were only a few horsemen, armed with spears, who protected the king. The infantry threw their axes first before charging with swords. In a sixth-century manual of war, *Strategicon*, the Franks and Lombards are said to dismount to fight on foot with shields, lances and swords. The following description could be instructive:[57] 'they fight according to families and not in regular troops…they charge swiftly with much spirit. They do not obey their leaders well. Headstrong, despising strategy, precaution of foresight, they show contempt for every tactical command especially cavalry.'

Such was the view in around 580. Yet these tactics were often successful. A different source describes the Franks' arms as simple: sword, shield, double-headed axe and barbed spear, with few wearing helmets or mail, or having horses. The leading men alone had long swords and they fought on foot, for which they are 'extremely well practised'.[58] Yet the Alamanni were renowned for their 'excellent' cavalry and most Germanic armies would have had a fifth to a third of their soldiers mounted. Procopius, describing Goths and Vandals, suggests the cavalry did not use missile weapons, but instead advanced quickly to use the spear as a thrusting weapon.[59] On balance, it would appear the Germanic settlers in Britain were familiar with horses, but certainly by the later Middle Ages, they tended to use them for transport and scouting rather than as a main force.

In summary, the sources imply Anglo-Saxons mainly fought on foot and deployed the shield-wall extensively. They used horses and may at times have engaged on horseback if caught in ambushes or in skirmishes. But their preference, and strength, seems to have been for infantry warfare. Yet there is no good reason why they would not have been aware of, and used, cavalry similar to other continental peoples. Their armour and shields were effective. Their main weapon was the spear but swords were prevalent too, especially among the elite. Almost all would have had a short *seax* to use at close quarters.

Tactics

We have already seen the main tactic of the Anglo-Saxons was the shield-wall. A wedge, or 'pig's-head' was a common tactic to break the line, but could be countered by forming a 'V' or 'pincer' to close in on both sides.[60] A twelfth-century Danish historian, Saxo, describes a wedge as having two warriors in the front, four in the second line, eight in the third and so on, doubling each time.[61] The Romans used the same tactic and, in all cases, the object was to break through the enemy line and attack the wings from the rear. The Anglo-Saxon tactics appear fairly simplistic although effective. What, then, of the Romano-British? Gildas states that the Romans, before they left for the last time, gave the British 'stirring advice and left them manuals on weapons training.'[62]

The 'Boar's Head' formation

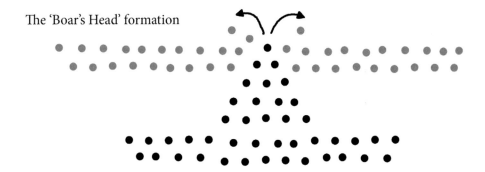

Defence against the 'Boar's Head' formation

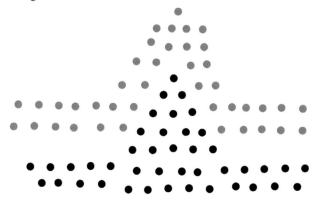

The 'Boar's Head' formation

One such manual may well have been Vegetius, who wrote in the fourth century and whose work survived to be read throughout the Middle Ages. It contained a number of military maxims such as: 'Skill and training are more important than numbers and a large untrained group are vulnerable to slaughter.'[63] We have already seen how the Roman army in Britain had been depleted, and are left to speculate how much of the training and discipline would have survived up to Arthur's day. But it is a useful place to start, giving us a glimpse of military thinking at the end of the fourth century.

Vegetius lays out the distances one would expect a force to cover in a day, usually beginning after dawn and completing in the afternoon. With the military step, 20 miles could be covered in 5 hours and at full step, 24 miles.[64] At this point, he bemoans the fact the necessity of building forts, along with the skills required, appear to have been forgotten in his day.[65] He states how camps should be built near a good supply of water, firewood and fodder, and how they should avoid swampy areas and those overlooked by higher ground. He describes three types:[66]

1. Where there's no immediate danger or for one night: a 3-foot-deep fosse or ditch is cut 5 foot wide with the turves stacked up on the inside edge.
2. A 'stationary camp': a temporary fosse 9 foot wide and 7 foot deep.
3. When more serious forces threaten, a 12- to 17-foot wide and 9-foot-deep fosse is built. Then inside, a 4-foot-high embankment overlooks the fosse, making it 13 foot deep.

In all cases, they fixed lines of stakes that the soldiers carried, along with tools. When under threat, half the infantry and most of the cavalry would draw up in front, while the remainder worked to complete the camp before evening. Ramparts could be reinforced with logs, and battlements and turrets constructed like walls. The engineering skills of the Romans were demonstrated at the siege of Alesia where Julius Caesar surrounded the hill fort with fortifications 10 miles long within three weeks, followed by an outer ring 14 miles long. In contrast, a fort could be constructed by a well-trained legion in a few hours, even while under enemy pressure. It's unlikely this practice and level of skill survived into the later fifth century, but nor can we dismiss the possibility. Indeed, Constantius's *Life of Saint Germanus*, recalling the first visit in 429, tells how the Britons marched out to meet raiders and after this 'were in camp'.[67] Scouts were then sent out from that camp to reconnoitre and report. In fact, the Briton scouts proved superior because they detected the raiders, while the raiders advanced but into a trap.

Some of the information in Vegetius is out of date by Arthur's time. For example, with the short Roman *gladius*, recruits were taught to strike with the point, rather than the edge. The wisdom at the time was that a cut seldom kills because the vitals are protected by armour, whereas 'a stab driven two inches in is fatal'.[68] The *gladius* was ideal for the fighting techniques and formation of the earlier Roman army. However, a solid shield-wall several men deep is harder to get through, and often the only openings would be over the top of the shield. The later *spatha* sword was designed more for a cutting blow than a stab. But the spear has greater reach and seems to be the weapon of choice, or certainly the most common.

In the early Roman army, the first five cohorts held the front line from right to left respectively. They had helmets, greaves, shields, long *spathae* swords, five lead-weighted darts slotted into their shields and two javelins: a short 4-foot one with a 5-inch tip and a longer 6-foot shaft with a 9-inch iron tip to transfix opposing shields. Five further cohorts formed the second line. Each cohort numbered 555 men with the first cohort on the right wing larger in number

(800). The third line was made up of light troops with javelins, slings and archers. Behind them were the reserve, *triarii*, armed similarly to the front ranks. The cavalry was posted on the wings. Usually, the light troops harassed the enemy first and if they ran, they would be pursued by the light troops and cavalry. If the enemy was provoked to attack, the light troops retreated. The two front ranks then stood like a wall of iron. If victorious, the light troops and cavalry pursued. As a rule, the heavy troops could 'not flee nor pursue easily.'[69] Vegetius also describes a six-line formation with the first two lines still being heavy infantry.[70] Then came the fast light infantry with javelins and archers, and the fourth line made up of 'light shield bearers' also with javelins and lead darts. The fifth line contained 'carriage ballistas' and 'sling staff men' discharging stones and bolts, followed by the *triarri* in reserve.

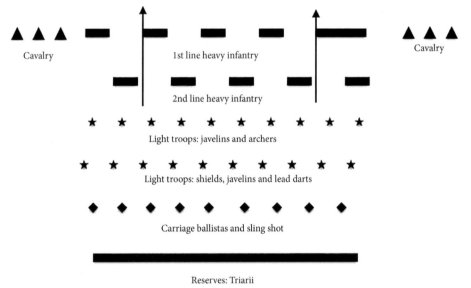

Early Roman army formation

Individual infantrymen occupy approximately three feet, hence, in a mile, 1,666 men could form a line. Between lines, a space of six foot was usual. Thus, Vegetius describes how 10,000 men could take up a position a mile wide and 42 foot deep.[71] In general, it's preferable to have depth to thinning a line out. The troops were trained to form a line, a wedge or a circle.[72] But this type of formation evolved over the decades. At the Battle of Catalaunian Plains against Attila in 451, the Romans formed what sounds identical to a Saxon shield-wall. While that battle in terms of size was comparable with the huge pitched battles of antiquity, we have seen that, in addition to the formations, the numbers involved also dwindled.

Cavalry was used for protecting and attacking flanks, and for pursuing a fleeing enemy. One interesting tactic is described by Vegetius:[73] when outnumbered, cavalry is mixed with light infantry, *velites*, with light shields and javelins, and he claims this 'cannot be matched' by an opposing cavalry force. To defend against cavalry, *caltrops* were often used, made of four spikes so that it rests on three on the ground with the remaining one sticking up. These could be scattered quickly to protect part of the line or flank. Vegetius describes how scythed chariots became a 'laughing stock' on the battlefield because of the ease of defending against them, partly due to the need for flat ground but mostly to the ease of defending against them with *caltrops*.[74] A defensive static line of troops expecting an attack, if they had the time and *caltrops* available, had a quick and easy defence against cavalry, aside from the fact that frontal cavalry attacks onto massed ranks of spearmen would likely be suicidal in the time of Arthur.

So, we see some changes in weapons and warfare, but some tactics are eternal such as outflanking the enemy. Vegetius lays out seven types of general battle tactics in his manual and we can see this in the diagrams:[75]

1. Rectangular formation with extended front. Should only be used with numerical superiority lest the flanks become enveloped. He describes this as the usual way to do battle in his day.
2. Oblique or angled formation engaging enemies' left flank with your stronger right and strongest cavalry to turn flank.
3. Same as no. 2 but engaging their right flank with your left.
4. Advance to 400–500 paces then spur on both wings having thinned out your own centre.
5. Same as no. 4, but place light troops and archers in front of centre to protect from breach.
6. He describes this as the best: a letter 'I' formation, oblique with the right flank attacking first, and cavalry and light troops outflanking enemy.
7. Use of terrain: simply by anchoring one flank against a mountain, forest or river, then placing all light troops and cavalry on the opposite wing.

A slight variation of these battle formations for the late Roman army in the fifth century might be as follows:[76] light units of infantry and cavalry, followed by a line of heavy infantry flanked by heavy cavalry; archers and slingers behind and a reserve force in the rear.

One last interesting point concerns battle standards. Given the various theories about the etymology of the name or title *pendragon*, Vegetius names three types of military signals: the voiced; the 'semi-voiced' with bugle, horn or trumpet; and the 'mute signals' with eagles, dragons, ensigns and plumes.[77] While the

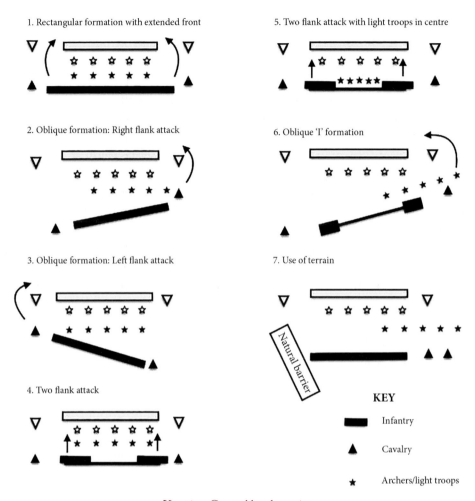

1. Rectangular formation with extended front

2. Oblique formation: Right flank attack

3. Oblique formation: Left flank attack

4. Two flank attack

5. Two flank attack with light troops in centre

6. Oblique 'I' formation

7. Use of terrain

Natural barrier

KEY

Infantry

Cavalry

Archers/light troops

Vegetius: General battle tactics

eagle was the standard of the entire Roman legion, each cohort had its own 'dragon-bearer.'[78] Geoffrey of Monmouth has a completely different story. He claims Uther witnessed a fiery comet on the eve of battle. From this, he acquired the title 'pendragon' or 'head dragon'. Gildas, we recall, calls one of his tyrant kings, 'dragon of the island.' Later genealogies name Uther as Uthr Pendragon or sometimes Bendragon. None of these are contemporary or can be trusted.

Swords

It's worth looking deeper into the subject of swords, given their prominence in the legend. The earliest reference to a named sword connected to Arthur is from the Welsh *Caledfwlch*, meaning 'hard cleft', in the tenth-century tale

Culhwch and Olwen. This possibly derives from the sword *Caladbolg*, from Irish mythology. Geoffrey of Monmouth Latinised the name to *Caliburnus*. In later French tales, this evolved into *Caliburc, Escaliborc, Escalibor, Excalibor* and finally *Excalibur*. The sword in a stone story only occurs after Geoffrey of Monmouth. It first appears in the twelfth-century poem *Merlin* by Robert de Boron. The sword is in an anvil on a stone in a London churchyard. In later stories, the anvil is dropped from the tale and the sword is in the stone itself. Thirteenth-century tales introduce the Lady in the Lake and from there, we get two swords and further confusion.

There are several possible explanations for the legend. A famous contemporary sword was that of St Galgano (1148–1181) which can be seen today, still embedded in rock in the Abbey of San Galgano in Italy. This may have influenced Robert de Boron shortly after the tale spread across Europe. Another possibility is the 'London Stone', a block of limestone that was once a well-known landmark in London in the Middle Ages. John Cade is said to have struck the stone with his sword, declaring himself Lord Mayor during his rebellion in 1450. Striking a stone with a sword may have been a sign of authority and one can imagine how this could have morphed into a sword 'in' a stone, rather than placed on it. A third option is the use of stone moulds to cast metal. Thus, afterwards, the sword would be drawn from the stone once cooled. This, though, is unlikely given that fifth- and sixth-century swords would have been pattern welded, as we shall see. Another possible confusion is between the Latin word for stone, *saxum* similar to *saxonum* for Saxon. The argument goes that Arthur pulled or got the sword from a Saxon and this became misinterpreted. I find this a rather convoluted and unlikely explanation. There are also various tribal myths from the east and west of magical swords embedded in the ground or trees. The last possibility is it was simply invented by the author, in the same way the original name *Caledfwich* may simply have been an addition by Welsh bards hundreds of years after Arthur lived. I would suggest the most likely explanation is the simplest. Robert de Boron, writing a generation after St Galgano became famous, simply used the story to embellish his work.

We do have evidence of named swords in many of the sagas. Over two hundred swords' names have been preserved in literary sources, although they are all relatively late with the earliest being in the tenth century from Anglo-Saxon poems.[79] In the fifteenth century, there was a Welsh tradition called 'The Thirteen Treasures of Britain.' One of these was *Dyrnwyn* ('white-hilt') owned by Rhydderch Hael. When drawn by a worthy man, it would come alight. There were examples in archaeology of inscriptions on blades, although they are more commonly found on hilts and scabbards. Often, they indicate who made or owned the sword.[80] Examples include: 'Sigimer named the sword'; 'Audmundr made me Asleikr owns me'; 'Biorhtelm made me Sigeberiht owns me'; or simply 'Leofric made me'.

We will now turn to the surviving physical evidence. We have three main sources of archaeological record for swords: the peat bogs of Denmark; lakes or rivers; and graves. In Anglo-Saxon cemeteries, the most common weapon is the spear with less than one in twenty containing swords.[81] In Kent, 66 out of 272 graves contained any weapons, with only 27 being swords. At Abingdon in Berkshire, only two swords have been found in 82 cremations and 119 burials. Bidford-on-Avon, in a rich cemetery of twenty-six men, had no swords at all. This, then, supports the idea of the spear being the primary and most common weapon in Anglo-Saxon armies at least. In Kent, 22 per cent of graves contained swords, yet only 3 per cent of Anglian graves in the north did so.[82] Earlier Anglian settlers would have been more likely to cremate their dead, but there may have been other cultural differences which would affect how swords were disposed of. Normal dimensions of swords from the migration period were 85 to 95cm long and 4.5 to 5.5cm wide.[83] Swords from the mid-fifth to early sixth century often had their grips covered in precious metal, similar to the sword of the Frankish King Childeric.[84]

By the seventh century, nearly all swords found were pattern welded made from several strips of iron twisted and forged welded; this design first appeared in the third century. At 86–94cm long and 5cm wide, it was similar to the late Roman *spatha* sword. The lower and upper guard were narrower than later swords and extended barely an inch either side of the hand, offering limited protection. The grip at around 10cm was wide enough for one hand and often, a pommel sat on the upper guard. Some swords have been found with a ring attached to the pommel or upper guard, and literary sources indicate that for some, at least, a cord was used to attach the sword to the wrist, presumably in case it was dropped in battle.[85] Stories of 'ring givers' are often assumed to refer to arm or finger rings, but it is at least plausible this is an alternative interpretation.

The earlier *gladius* was used as a stabbing weapon at close quarters, but the long *spatha*-type swords of the fifth century were usually employed as a cutting weapon, best used for hacking rather than thrusting.[86] However, mail armour would have offered reasonable protection against cutting or glancing blows.[87] Ammianus Marcellinus refers to swords of the Goths cutting through the head with such force that 'the severed halves hung down on each shoulder.'[88] Skeletal evidence from later medieval times confirm the horrific injuries with blows severing legs, and penetrating and cutting away parts of skulls.[89] A warrior protected with well-made good quality mail and helmet would have been at a considerable advantage over one without either.

Swords tended to be worn by a shoulder strap, with the belt becoming more popular from the seventh century.[90] So, Arthur would likely have employed the former method. Scabbards would have been wooden, leather-covered and lined with wool or fur soaked in oil to prevent rust. In the fifth century, Sidonius describes guests at a wedding of a Burgundian princess:[91] 'Green mantles… with crimson borders. Baldrics supported swords hung from their shoulders'. Shields had 'golden bosses' and 'silver borders'. In ninth-century Norway, Viking warriors wore 'scarlet cloaks with splendid borders, swords bound with silver, coats of ring mail, gilded baldrics and graven helmets, rings upon their arms.'

Some swords would have been a high-status weapon for the elite, costing as much in modern terms as a quarter of a million pounds or a Ferrari sports car.[92] In general, though, simple swords may not have been quite so expensive. The laws of the Ripurian Franks from around 500 set the cost of a sword and shield at two *solidus*, but a helmet at six and a mail shirt at twelve.[93] This contrasts with the *wergild* or 'man price' of a Frank set at 200 *solidus*. Experiments have shown it takes around 74 hours to manufacture a pattern welded sword, together with scabbards and fittings.[94] Breaking that down, it took approximately 43 hours to make the blade and a further 32 hours to finish the hilt, scabbard and belt fittings.[95] Two weeks' work for a master craftsman plus maybe an apprentice and materials makes the Ferrari analogy seem a little exaggerated.

A letter written by a secretary of Theodoric the Great, who reigned 493–526, describes swords 'capable even of cutting through armour, which I prize more for their iron than for the gold upon them.'[96] The implication is it is unusual and that armour would normally offer good protection. Yet poorer quality swords are also described. In a Norse saga, the warrior *Steinthor* found, when his sword came against a shield, he often had to straighten his sword out with his foot.[97] While a good workman should never blame his tools, one might forgive *Steinthor* cursing the blacksmith as he fought for his life. So prized were some swords that one belonging to Offa, King of Mercia, was still in the keep of the Kings of Wessex 200 years later.[98] It was originally a gift from Emperor Charles the Great and of Avar workmanship. One sword left by King Alfred to his son Aethelred, Earl of Mercia, cost 120 oxen.[99] In the Norse sagas, many swords have names and a long history covering the lives of many warriors, featuring in multiple tales.[100]

It is likely that Arthur, as a leader in battle, did carry a sword, with the scabbard attached to a shoulder strap. The Romans and Greeks did not name their swords, unlike their Germanic and Celtic counterparts. If Arthur descended from a Gallic-Roman family as Geoffrey of Monmouth claims, then he probably did not name his sword. But if he did, and it got handed down by bards to the tenth century, then it was likely a very different name from the familiar 'Excalibur'. The name *Caledfwich* would be the nearest we have. We can be more certain about its physical characteristics. We can dismiss later medieval swords or long swords with broad hand guards. It would have been a *spatha*-type sword around 90cm in length with a short handle and a narrow guard and pommel. Double-edged and ideal for hacking, rather than thrusting, it was more Roman than medieval in appearance, but more medieval than Roman in length.

Contemporary accounts of battles

Before we investigate the possible locations for Arthur's battles, it is useful to look at contemporary battles to get an idea of how a typical confrontation between the Anglo-Saxons and Romano-British may have panned out. We have already seen that pitched battles involving tens of thousands is unlikely. At the most, a few thousand is a likely scenario and at the lower end, as little as a few score. We will see that in Welsh traditions concerning Camlan, only seven survived suggesting a relatively minor conflict. The Welsh poem, *Y Gododdin*, states the British force numbered 303, of which only one returned. First, let us turn to a recurring theme in many a film or book – the single combat – and see how likely this is.

In the Gothic wars, Procopius tells of how the warrior *Valaris* rode out between two armies and challenged any of the Romans to face him in battle alone. In the eighth century, Paul the Deacon describes how a pitched battle between the Langobards and Assipitti was settled by single combat. So, we have historical proof it did occur. It certainly became very popular in sagas and poems. In the *Iliad*, Menalaus fights Paris outside the walls of Troy and later, Hector is slain by Achilles. In the Bible, David defeats Goliath with a sling. It has to be noted, though, that most battles were not decided in this way.

Yet Geoffrey of Monmouth can't resist the trope.[101] According to him, Arthur lands in Gaul which is under the jurisdiction of the tribune Frollo. Needless to say, no such person is recorded and Gaul had ceased to be under one authority by the mid-fifth century. Frollo marches out to meet him but is outnumbered, the battle turns against him and he retreats to Paris. Arthur besieges the city for a month and eventually, Frollo offers him single combat to decide the matter. They meet on an island outside the gates watched by the whole populace and both armies. He then describes a very twelfth-century fight with both men fully armoured on horses and armed with lances. Arthur strikes Frollo's chest and unseats him. He then rides forward, drawing his sword to deliver the final blow, leaving the more astute reader to wonder why he did not use the longer spear. But Frollo recovers, jumps to his feet and spears Arthur's horse in the chest, throwing him to the ground. Arthur now jumps up and with shield in hand, they exchange blows. Frollo found the first opening, hitting Arthur's helmet.

This saved him but he must have been wounded as his leather cuirass and round shield 'grew red', presumably with his own blood. Incensed, he raised Caliburn above his head and brought it down with such force that it severed helmet and head into two halves and Frollo fell dead with a rather poetic: 'drummed the earth with his heels and breathed his soul into the winds.' The townspeople threw open their gates and surrendered the city.

Turning away from fiction, at Adrianople in 378, Emperor Valens led 30,000 Roman troops against a Gothic force of around 15,000. Ammianus Marcellinus described the events:[102] after an 8-mile march in the midday sun, the Roman scouts came upon the Goths drawn up behind their wagons in a circular formation. The cavalry on the right wing had advanced the furthest, with much of the infantry and left wing some way behind. An attempt at negotiations was thwarted by an impulsive shower of arrows from the Roman side. This eventually brought on an attack by the Gothic cavalry that 'routed with great slaughter all that they could come to grips with.' Before the armies came together, arrows and javelins flew, and the lines pushed backwards and forwards 'like the waves of the sea.' The Roman left wing reached the wagons, but became exposed and fell back. The Roman infantry were then pressed so close together that a man could 'hardly wield a sword or draw back his arm once he had stretched it out'. Nor was it possible to 'see the enemy's missiles in flight and dodge them.' The Goths poured into the battle and the crush made ordered retreat impossible. We read of helmets and breast plates being split by battle axes, and of severed limbs. The infantry, having shattered their spears, had to 'make do' with their swords. Interestingly, the sword here is seen as a 'make do' weapon, secondary to the spear. The end, when it came, was quick. The Romans, 'weak from hunger, parched with thirst and weighed down by the burden of their armour', broke and ran. Roughly two-thirds of the Roman forces perished along with Valens.

The next battle is at the Catalaunian Plains in 451, in which the Roman general Flavius Aetius stopped Attila the Hun and forced his withdrawal. The result of the battle is disputed. Estimates vary from 30,000 to 80,000 on each side and interestingly, Aetius had Saxons as part of his allied force. The general placed the Visigoths on his right wing, while he held the left with the Roman forces placing the Alani in the centre. This was due to his mistrust of the Alan king, thus demonstrating the fragility of forming an alliance with many different tribes. Attila, on the other hand, took the centre with his strongest troops and placed his allies on the wings. So, we see here a change from the formation of the early Roman army. No longer are they in distinct units with specific jobs but in tribal units, and strength and loyalty become important factors. Both sides sought to gain a ridge in the centre of the plain. The Romans seized the heights first and Jordanes has Attila urging his men to attack the Romans who are 'forming in one line with locked shields.'[103] This line held and the Huns were driven back. So, we see here a description of a single line and a shield-wall being successful, perhaps a generation before the likely time of Arthur. It's being used by the last great Roman general in the west, implying that formal disciplined formations were now history.

Possibly contemporary with Arthur is the battle of Vouille in 507 between the Franks and the Goths, in which 'some of the soldiers hurled their javelins from a distance, others fought hand to hand.'[104] During the battle, two Goths attacked the Frankish king, Clovis, with spears. He was saved by 'the leather corselet... and sheer speed of his horse', although he was injured enough to be described as 'very near to death.'[105] It's interesting that the king is not wearing chainmail but a 'leather corselet'. Here, we get glimpses of the likely nature of warfare: throwing weapons used extensively and then hand to hand combat, while the king is mounted but close to the fighting.

An early sixth-century battle in Sweden is mentioned in *Beowulf* and Norse sagas. In 'The Battle on the Ice of Lake Vanern', Onela usurps the Swedish throne after his brother, the king's, death. The king's sons Eanmund and Eadgils seek refuge with the Geats. Onela pursues them, killing Eanmund and the Geatish king, Heardred. Beowulf vows to avenge Heardred and help Eadgils. A cavalry engagement on the ice is described which can't be verified historically. Yet it demonstrates that the audience would not have been too surprised by such a concept. Later Viking battles against the Saxons are almost all exclusively infantry affairs. Asser in the *Life of Alfred the Great* describes the Battle of Edington in 878 as being fought bravely by a 'close shield-wall against the whole army.'

At the Battle of Maldon in 991, a Viking raiding party of ninety ships was met by a similarly-sized Anglo-Saxon army of around 3,000. They rode to the battle but dismounted to fight. Such an army lining up six deep would stretch about 500 yards. The Vikings asked for gold to leave, but the Saxon leader Earl Byrhtnoth offers them 'spears, deadly darts and hard swords' instead. The battle is mainly fought with spears and arrows. But the leader Byrhtnoth is armed with a sword, 'broad and bright edged...ornamented', as are warriors in the second line when the battle descends into hand to hand fighting.[106] The earl formed his army into a war-wall or war-hedge then 'hard spears, sharp pointed, their shafts flew.'[107]

In 937 at Brunanburh in the north of England, Aethelstan, the grandson of Alfred the Great, met a combined army of Constantine of Scotland, Owen of Strathclyde and Olaf the Viking (King of Dublin). Battle was joined and 'they clove through the shield-wall and hewed through the linden wood defences' with 'hammered blades' and 'hewed down the fugitives with blades grindstone sharp.'[108] The *Anglo-Saxon Chronicle* records warriors as 'shot over shield, taken by spears' then later when the enemy broke the 'West Saxons with elite cavalry… hacked from behind those who fled battle.'[109] Five kings were 'put to sleep by swords' and the slaughter is described as the greatest ever in Britain of 'people felled by the swords edge.' Elsewhere, we hear of the 'meeting of spears, the mixing of weapons,' and the 'bloody survivors of darts.' We can visualise a meeting of shield-walls, spears and darts flying overhead, and spears and swords being used to stab and hack through. When the northerners broke, they were then pursued by cavalry. The Annals of Ulster record that several thousand died on each side, and that several kings and nobles also perished:[110] Cellach, son of King Constantine; Owen, king of Strathclyde; Gebeachan, Norse king of the Western Isles; two sons of Sihtric, king of York; Aelfwine and Aethelwine, cousins of Aethelstan; and other ealdormen and 'a multitude of lesser men.' This suggests strongly that kings and nobles of the time fought alongside their men, rather than positioning themselves out of danger.

In 1066, Harold Godwineson fought two battles, the last of which we have reasonable contemporary records for. For the first, he marched his army 200 miles north in less than a week to meet the threat of a Viking army, led by Harold's brother Tostig and the Norwegian King Harald Hardrada. Thus, demonstrating again that such distances were not unreasonable for a Dark Age warrior such as Arthur to cover. The Norwegians had already defeated one English army and captured York. The English arrived, found York undefended and marched through, catching the Viking army unawares at Stamford Bridge, a few miles east of the city on the River Derwent. Reports state the Vikings had their helmets and weapons, but had left their mail shirts on their ships as the weather was warm and sunny.[111] Yet the battle was fierce and lasted all day, which suggests a well-trained stubborn shield-wall could hold out against a force, even with superior armour. One unverified tradition has Harold approaching the enemy before the battle to ask his brother to change sides. Tostig asks how much he would be willing to pay Hardrada for the Viking army to leave, and Harold replies he would give seven foot of English ground as the Viking king was taller than most.

It's more likely this is myth, but whatever the case, the Norwegians were caught spread out on both sides of the river. Those on the west formed a defensive line, which was quickly destroyed. One version of the *Anglo-Saxon Chronicle* records how a single Norse axeman stood on the bridge and held up the advance, while those on the left bank quickly formed up.[112] Eventually, an enterprising Englishman came under the bridge and 'stabbed him through under the mail-coat.' Then the English army came over the bridge and made a 'great slaughter.' The Vikings fled back to their ships at Riccall, a few miles south of York, and the pursuing English 'fiercely attacked them from behind', while some were drowned and others burned, although how is not described. Out of 300 ships, only 24 could be manned for the return suggesting a fatality rate of over 90 per cent for the Vikings. Both armies are estimated at around 10,000 each. So, we have a picture of a 'very stubborn battle', as the *Chronicle* puts it: two shield-walls locked for some time until one breaks. The broken army is then extremely vulnerable, especially to cavalry. Three days later, William of Normandy arrived on the south coast at Pevensey where 575 years earlier, Aelle of the South Saxons was said to have slaughtered the Britons in the Roman fort of Anderitum. William moved quickly to occupy Hastings, a few miles to the east.

Harold marched south, 270 miles in two weeks, stopping for six days in London along the way. He attempted to catch William by surprise, as he had the Viking army three weeks earlier. He left London around 11 October and covered over 60 of the 70 miles by 13 October when William learnt of his approach. At dawn the next day, William set out from Hastings and caught Harold by surprise, 7 miles to the north-west at around nine in the morning. Both armies numbered roughly 7,000 men. The English are recorded as dismounting and leaving their horses to the rear. They formed a line along a ridge with forest on each flank. Harold took his place in the centre of this shield-wall. The Normans deployed in three lines: archers and crossbowmen in the front; infantry in mail shirts armed with spears and swords; and cavalry in the last line.

Contemporary accounts give us far more detail than in previous battles.[113] The battle started with trumpets and a 'thick cloud' of arrows, mainly from the Norman side. The heavy infantry then moved in to engage the English, 'crashing shield against shield'. The English responded by throwing 'javelins, missiles of various kinds, murderous axes and stones tied to sticks.' The Norman cavalry then engaged with swords to relieve the infantry, who were finding things difficult against the English shield-wall. There's then an apparent break in the fighting when a Norman cavalry man goads the English by juggling his sword. He challenges them to single combat. An Englishman breaks ranks and is quickly killed, his head hacked off and held aloft. But the English held their ground, 'rooted to the spot' as one writer states. The steepness of the hill and roughness of the ground made cavalry charges difficult, so the Normans resorted to riding close to hurl javelins or use their swords.

This exposed the attackers, and English weapons are said to have easily penetrated shields and armour, which is a possible reference to the large battle-axes of the housecarls. The battle raged all day and still the shield-wall held. Then two events occurred that proved pivotal. Firstly, the Norman left flank started to break, although some reports claim this was a ruse. Some of the English right flank pursued them down the hill, believing the battle to be won but weakening out their own line. Secondly, a rumour swept the battlefield that William was dead, causing nearly the whole army to start to give way. William rushed forward, removing his helmet, and extolled his men to re-engage. The pursuing English on the Norman left flank were quickly surrounded and killed. One source claims the tactic was repeated and it was certainly one utilised by the Normans in previous campaigns. The English line started to become weaker and arrows began to have more of an effect. The rumour then swept the English line that Harold was dead, and the truth of it caused the line to break. This is said to have occurred at nightfall, meaning the battle lasted all day, far longer than most conflicts. The story about Harold dying from an arrow to the eye is not actually supported by the contemporary accounts.[114] One account has the battle nearly won when Harold is cut down by four Norman knights. The explanation for the arrow to the eye story may be a biblical reference for oath-breakers, which was added later to show God's punishment.

Thus, the death of a king or battle leader could prove pivotal in medieval battles. We also saw how shield-walls could stand all day and withstand a huge amount of punishment. Armour, even leather and padded jerkins, did a surprisingly good job. Missile weapons were far more common than might be expected. Javelins, throwing axes, stones and archers were all utilised. Frontal heavy cavalry charges were for the future, and light cavalry tended to be confined to chasing down fleeing enemies once a formation broke. In terms of formation, the Anglo-Saxon tactics don't seem to have changed much from Arthur's time to the Battle of Hastings: a solid mass of spear and sword men behind a shield-wall. The question is: did the Romano-British retain any of the Roman tactics or formations? We can see by the Battle of Catalaunian Plains, in 451, that the use of a solid wall and allies taking up positions in tribal groups was common. At Hastings, William places his Breton allies on his left flank.

The *Historia* states 'Arthur along with the kings of Britain fought against them in those days, but Arthur himself was the military commander', which is reminiscent of Aetius commanding an allied army. Similarly, in 633, possibly a hundred years after Arthur, Cadwallon, King of Gwynedd, and Penda of Mercia defeated Edwin of Northumbria at the Battle of Haethfelth (possibly Hatfield Chase, Yorkshire). In 655, at the Battle of Winwaed, Penda was accompanied by 'thirty royal *ealdormen*.'[115] One such was Aethelhere, brother and successor to Anna, King of the East Angles. He died with 'all his *thegns* and followers' in the defeat, again suggesting that tribal groups or war-bands fought and died together within a formation.

Y Gododdin

The last battle we will cover is one we cannot verify. *Y Gododdin* is the closest contemporary account of a battle between Britons and Saxons. If the *Y Gododdin* is an authentic seventh-century account, then it would predate the *Historia* and be the first recorded reference of Arthur. It survives in the thirteenth-century *Book of Aneurin*. The men of the kingdom of Gododdin, around Din Eidyn (Edinburgh) are gathered together and feasted for a year to prepare for an attack on Angles of Deira and Bernicia at Catraeth (possibly Catterick). However, in the earliest version, Bernicia is not mentioned. Mynyddog Mwynfawr gathers warriors from all over Britain, and about eighty are named in eulogies. The battle is often dated to around the year 600, but there is no certainty. In fact, the absence of Bernicia in the earliest copies suggests it may have occurred before Ida began his reign in around the mid-sixth century.

Three hundred warriors set out and only one returned. Some start with the phrase 'men went to Catraeth at dawn.' Arthur is mentioned in passing in comparison to another warrior:

> He charged before three hundred of the finest,
> He cut down both centre and wing,
> He excelled in the forefront of the noblest host,
> He gave gifts of horses from the herd in winter.
> He fed black ravens on the rampart of a fortress
> **Though he was no Arthur**
> Among the powerful ones in battle,
> In the front rank, Gwawrddur was a palisade.

It's not at all clear if this charge was infantry or cavalry, but the reference to the front rank might suggest the former. The numbers are not always consistent: in three stanzas (56, 57 and 87), three hundred rode out and only one returned. Elsewhere, three hounds accompany the three hundred (19). The survivor must have lost his horse as, in stanza 88, three hundred horses and three hounds accompany the warriors, yet none return. The warriors are described as three hundred chieftains in stanza 46. But in two places, the number changes to three hundred three score and three, the first in stanza 22 and the second at the end. The former has three survivors and two battle hounds, and the latter has three alongside the author. The enemy is described as a hundred thousand in stanza 11: 'A hundred thousand and three hundred charged against each other.' This is surely an exaggeration, as is the claim they were outnumbered nine score to one in stanza 91, which would equate to over 54,000. Stanza 55 gives a more realistic figure claiming 'they slew seven times their number', which equates from 2,100 to 2,541 depending on which figure we use. It's at least credible a well-prepared heavily armoured force could devastate an unprepared lightly armoured army. Elsewhere, the inconsistencies continue (stanza 6): 'Of the men of Deira and Bernicia there fell a hundred score into oblivion in one hour.'

But we get the idea. Three hundred well-armoured warriors are outnumbered and eventually destroyed. Yet there are signs of initial victory (82): 'from our successful assault on the day of the mighty charge…the host was broken'. The Saxons were driven out 'without ceasing' (14). There are three references of approaching or attacking at the borderland (21, 24, 71). Perhaps there was an initial attack. It's simply not clear. In one place, there is a reference to the host plundering (75), which might suggest a border raid. Yet the whole thrust of the poem is that the force prepares for a year to attack the Angles. Whatever the case, the result is beyond doubt, yet we learn (4): 'Before the army of Gododdin there was flight, Hard pressure facing the land of Manawyd.' There are three references to fighting at a ford (18, 26 and 90), with the latter being called 'the defender at the ford'. Whether this is the same place or a reference to an earlier battle is unclear, but warriors are said to have fought around Catraeth (63).

Let us now turn to armour, weapons and the actual battle. Stanza 35 give us a vivid picture:

'A host of horsemen in dark blue armour with shields spear shafts held aloft with sharp points.' Their 'mail coated armour' (56) is coloured 'blood and dark blue' (51 and 59) over 'crimson garments' (72). Spears are described as being yellow in colour (51 and 53). Their shields are white and spear points 'square pointed' (12). Shields are also 'light and broad' (2). The battle begins and 'spears were shattered' (72). Some extracts are reminiscent of the Normans at Hastings: 'Marchlew cast spears in battle from a bounding, wide tracked charger…he threw spears from his steaming slender bay horse (28).'

In stanzas 41 to 43, the warrior Eithinyn casts spears between two armies and is described as a magnificent horseman attacking 'before the cattle herds of the eastlands', suggesting the east coast of Britain. We read of the 'surging fury of the horsemen' (54). Cynon 'with shattered shield…tore through armies his horses swift' (38). But in the next stanza, he is described as being on the flank where one might expect cavalry to be placed. Morien is said to 'set fire to the fleeing horsemen' (37), but this could be the pursuit of a fleeing army, rather than a cavalry engagement.

In other sections, we get the distinct impression of a shield-wall battle. The 'wall of battle' (1), close ranks (10), and a 'stronghold of shields' sounding 'like thunder' (15). Shields were shattered (3), spearpoints 'tore and cut' (15) while Cadfannan, 'defender of the border brandished javelins' (44). The warrior Graid also throws 'lances in the forefront of battle in the spear-fight' and 'formed a battle pen against the spears' (25). The battlefield is a 'place of spears' (12). Spears are splintered and shattered (31) and shields broken (33). Gwid's sword is said to resound 'above the rampart' (36), suggesting some sort of earthwork or fortified position, unless the rampart is the shield-wall. There is 'a charge of axe blows and sharpened sword's (83). A sword is described as a 'blue blade, fringes of worked gold' (2).

The warriors come from all over Britain: warriors from Eidyn, obviously (19); Geraint, with the men of Argoed and men of the south (83); Isag from the 'southern part' (29); Bubon...beyond the sea of Iddew (96); and Cydywal leads the men of Gwynedd (20). Interestingly, this last example is said to slay Athrwys and Affrai, two very British-sounding names. There is an Arthrwys in the Welsh genealogies, so there is a suggestion here that perhaps this wasn't a simple Briton versus Angle battle. There is an Athrwys ap Mor in the thirteenth-century copy of the *Bonedd Gwyr y Gogledd* (Descent of the Men of the North), but he seems too early for our battle. A recent analysis of the poem suggests there may have been more diverse enemies with Urien of Rheged suggested as a possible adversary.[116] It is possible that 'ethnicity was not determinant' in the sixth century and that the driving force was 'warlord animosity.' Ethnic alignments perhaps became more important later in the seventh century. Yet it must be remembered that Gildas certainly sees a distinction in the mid-sixth century.

John Koch makes some interesting observations about other poems that may reference the same battle, but from the other side.[117] *The Battle of Gwen Ystrad* is a Welsh heroic poem in which Urien is said to lead the 'men of Cattaeth.' In another early poem, the *Eulogy of Cadwallon*, 'fierce Gwallawg; is said to have caused the 'mortality at Cattraeth.' Later Welsh genealogies make Urien and Gwallawg cousins and the *Historia Brittonum* has them in alliance, fighting against the Angles of Bernicia with one of Ida's sons, just before Urien is assassinated while besieging Lindisfarne. If true, this would suggest an intriguing situation. Firstly, the *Historia* places the siege at Lindisfarne in the reign of Theodoric, son of Ida. If one trusts the reign lengths recorded in the *Historia*, this was c.571–578. If this is correct and Urien was 'Lord of Cattraeth', then Cattraeth was slightly earlier than first thought. The reader will notice this is still after Ida reigns in Bernicia. The implication is that Bernicia allowed or aided the attack or was too small at the time to prevent it.

Secondly, it gives a far different picture of the battle than in *Y Gododdin*. In that text, it is a simple Britons against Angles battle. But if these other poems contain some truth, then it is possible this is more of a civil war. If so, then we are left to consider some possibilities: the defenders of Catraeth utilised substantial Germanic mercenaries; or the attacking Gododdin war-band viewed the men of Urien and Gwallawg as different enough to be either labelled or insulted as Deirians. There are plenty of examples of civil wars referenced in the sources: Gildas refers to the many 'internal wars' and castigates his five kings for the same; the *Historia* has Urien murdered by his ally Morcant at the siege of Lindisfarne; the Battle of Camlan is mentioned numerous times in Welsh sources; and finally, the *Annales Cambriae* records the Battle of Arfderydd in 573. We also have examples of alliances between Britons and Anglo-Saxons, such as Penda and Cadwallon defeating Edwin of Northumbria in 633. In 655, Penda's defeated army was said to have comprised thirty war-bands and, again, contained Britons and Anglo-Saxon commanders from, for example, Gwynedd and East Anglia.

The army of the Gododdin also appears to have been made up of numerous war-bands. We recall the description of Germanic armies forming up into clans, rather than a traditional formation in functional units. We also remember Penda and Cadwallon in the seventh century, and the line in the *Historia:* 'Arthur along with the kings of Britain.' At Catraeth, there are 'three kings of the hosts' who, in the same stanza, fight against 'the tribes of the crafty Deirans' (19). At Catraeth, Ywain is named the battle leader (71), similar to Arthur being the *dux bellorum*.

Another interesting theme is reminiscent of Gildas describing one of his tyrant kings as a bear. The warrior Blaen is 'a bear in manner' (17); Merin is said to be a 'scatterer of the deirians…a fearful bear' (59); and Cibno is called a 'terrible bear' (100). We also have various references to boars and eagles, but given the etymology of Arthur's name and his association with bears, this does show that animal imagery, and bears in particular, was common.

So, we get a glimpse into a sixth-century battle. Warriors riding out, wearing dark-blue mail coats over crimson tunics, carrying white round shields and yellow spears with square spearheads. The Anglo-Saxons were very likely in a solid shield-wall. The battle starts with javelins and thrown spears. The cavalry of the Britons is more active than expected, although this may be a literary device. The spear and shield are prominent, though axes and swords are also used. The armies seem to be a collection of war-bands, rather than the disciplined formations of the early Roman Empire. A ford is mentioned, as is a rampart. If Catraeth is Catterick, then the abandoned Roman fort there might have offered refuge to either side. As we shall see from Arthur's battles, rivers and forts are likely locations for Dark Age battles. It is possible Arthur inherited a functioning army, supported by a Romano-British civilian provincial structure. Alternatively, it could have already fragmented into various petty kingdoms controlled by powerful warlords and kings, as in the late sixth century.

Perhaps Arthur's time was a combination or bridge between the two. However, Gildas suggests Britain is closer to the latter situation, and this is supported by the archaeology and other literary sources. We will now take a closer look at the war-band.

The war-band

By the time of Arthur, both the Britons and Germanic peoples came to share a common institution: the *comitatus* or war-band.[118] This term includes the Anglo-Saxon hearth-companions and Welsh *teulu* (family). It extended kinship groups and came to mean those warriors bound to their lord and who, in return for their loyalty, gave them shelter and food. By the seventh century, this social and personal structure gave way to one based more on territory. But in the sixth century, it appears to have been the dominant force. The principal function of the *comitatus* was warfare. We see many examples in Irish and Welsh Annals and the *Anglo-Saxon Chronicle*, as well as heroic sagas and poems.

Literary and archaeological evidence suggest that war-bands of both Britons and Germanic peoples would have likely numbered less than 100.[119] In the context of the Roman field army numbering in the low thousands by the year 400, it is unlikely the successor states, *civitates* or petty kingdoms could have raised a force of a thousand men.[120] Most Western Germanic tribes were based on similar power structures. A small number of farms or villages (often termed a *canton*) might be under the authority of one man. He would have a small retinue, *comitatus*, but perhaps be able to call upon 1,000 men from the farms and villages he controlled. This may be linked to the later military official *thusundifath* (leader of a 1,000). Ammianus, writing in the fourth century, attempted to translate one such example of structure by describing two kings followed by five subkings and ten princes with a long train of nobles and 35,000 troops. The loyalty was more personal and might dissolve on the death of a king.

With this type of warfare, strategy becomes less important and the fighting less organised compared to Roman legions. We have already seen references to Germanic armies being less disciplined and the Roman army changing its formation and tactics over time. The literary sources and poems suggest drawing infantry up into blocks or ranks to form a shield-wall was a common tactic for both Britons and Anglo-Saxons. One difference is suggested by the absence of horse-related equipment in the latter's graves. Chainmail and helmets seem to be rare with all but the wealthiest using leather jerkins and wooden shields for protection, while armed with spears rather than swords.

The organisation was along aristocratic lines in a 'thinly spread military elite.'[121] By the time Arthur fought, the bonds of the war-band had become more important than simple kinship ties. The following incident highlights the importance of such ties. In 786 in Wessex, Cyneheard and eighty-four warriors ambushed King Cynewulf of Wessex and killed him. Cyneheard offered his enemy's men mercy but all declined and fought to the death. The following morning, Cynewulf's followers heard of their lord's death and besieged Cyneheard. This time, Cyneheard's men were offered life but again, they all fought to the last man.

Gildas may well have been a contemporary of a historical Arthur and we get some clues as to his opinion of the behaviour of kings, though 'they are tyrants.'[122] He, too, speaks of them waging wars, 'civil and unjust' and of chasing thieves 'all over the country' but rewarding thieves who 'sit with them at table.' Their 'military companions' are 'bloody, proud and murderous men.' Aurelius Caninus is accused of an 'unjust thirst for civil war and constant plunder.' Cuneglasus also wages war against 'our countrymen.' This could be interpreted as meaning the remaining Romano-British as a whole. But perhaps it just refers to a province or former *civitas*.

Despite Gildas's 'tyrant kings' apparently murdering various family members, we also see how important kin was. Many warlords depended on family members to take responsibility. In 595, three of Aedan's sons died at Circhenn. Eight years later, he was defeated at Degsastan by Aethelfrith. But Aethelfrith's brother, Theobald, was also killed with 'all those he led' suggesting his entire war-band was wiped out. We have echoes of this in the Battle of Dyrham where three British kings were slain by Cuthwine and Caelwin of Wessex. Penda led thirty *duces* or royal commanders suggesting thirty war-bands. We recall the Battle of Catalaunian Plains where the opposing armies formed up in largely tribal groups.

As the custom evolved, loyalty to the war-band became even more influential than to kinship groups as warriors were attracted to success and the promise of great rewards. The tenth-century *Life of St Guthlac* concerns a late seventh-century saint. As a young man, he fought for Aethelred of Mercia and attracted warriors from 'various races' into his own war-band, presumably meaning Britons, as well as Angles and Saxons. King Oswine of Deira died in 651 but was said to have attracted 'noblemen from almost every kingdom.'[123] Lords were expected to distribute valuables such as armour, swords, treasure or gold. Sagas are full of references to 'ring givers'.

The lord's hall became an important concept and one wonders if this finally ended the Roman villa as the focus of civil administrative power. The halls ranged from 25 to 80 feet in length and up to 30 metres in width, like the one at Yeavering in Northumbria, a short distance from the River Glen.

Archaeology and literary sources suggest Britons and Anglo-Saxons shared many of the same building techniques, materials and constructions.[124] What some call 'hall life' became an important support mechanism for war-bands and their lords.[125] This included the distribution of gifts and the provision of food and shelter in return for service. We can see this in *Y Gododdin* where the king feasts the warriors for a year as he gathers his forces.

The court poet became an integral part of the war-band, whether the Welsh Bards or Anglo-Saxon *scops*.[126] Gildas complains that his tyrant kings prefer listening to the praises of 'criminals and raving hucksters'. He admonishes the clergy for preferring 'fabulous stories' from 'worldly men' to the word of God. The *Historia* makes the following statement in reference to the time of Ida who reigned from 547: 'Then Talhearn Tad Awen was famed in poetry, and Aneirin and Taliesin and Bluchbard and Cian, known as Guenith Guant, were all simultaneously famed in British verse.'

Taliesin praises military skill, courage and generosity in four Lords: Cynan Garwyn, Gwallawg, Urien and his son, Owain. Germanic sagas such as *Beowulf* show similar cultural values repaid by fierce loyalty. The social setting can be described as follows: a military aristocratic society in which the main interests of the nobility are warfare, courage and fierceness in war, generosity in peace, a longing for fame and a horror of disgrace.[127] In addition, an acceptance of death as a price worth paying for glory or to avoid shame. The court poet was a man to be respected as he could provide your immortality in song or dismiss you entirely. Worse, he could eviscerate you in words to your eternal shame.

One example is from the *Historia* again: Penda of Mercia, along with the kings of the British, was defeated by Oswy at Winwaed in 654.[128] The only survivor was Cadfael of Gwynedd who escaped with his army, 'rising up in the night.' Thus, he was called 'Cadfael the battle dodger.' The Welsh Triads include 'The three faithless/disloyal war-bands of the island of Britain.' So, we see traditions of poems and sagas entrenching particular views. Exile was considered one of the most terrible punishments and involved being stripped of all rights and help. Kings and others sent into exile were often followed by their retainers, again demonstrating the bond of loyalty was the stronger influence.

Fostering and hostage-taking were other important concepts. We see many examples from Bede and elsewhere of royal personages being fostered or held hostage. Oswald, son of Aethelfrith, had fled to the kingdom of Dal Riata when his father was killed by Edwin, himself having lived in exile. On Edwin's death, he returned and became king of Deira and a year later, Northumbria. Given this constant upheaval and warfare, boys were encouraged to learn the required skills early on. They were given weapons by the age of 14 or 15 and the archaeological record shows young adolescents buried with full-scale weapons and evidence of battle injuries.[129] So we have a fragmenting political context riven with internecine warfare and murder. The opportunity for tribute and booty also increased in importance.[130] Many of the sagas extol the virtues of stealing cattle and treasure, and raids on neighbouring kingdoms.

In the Welsh laws of Hywel Dda, the lord kept one-third of the treasure and was expected to distribute the remaining two-thirds. Gregory of Tours relates an interesting tale concerning Clovis, King of the Franks (481–511).[131] After the defeat of the last Roman enclave in northern Gaul, he had King Syagrius murdered. They then gathered in Soissons to distribute the booty to the troops which was 'placed in a heap before them.' The church had requested the return of a particular jug or ewer of 'great size and wondrous workmanship' that had been stolen by some troops. Clovis agreed but could not simply take it. He had to ask permission of his troops if it was included 'in his share.' They all agreed, bar one warrior who struck the ewer with his axe. Clovis accepted this, perhaps demonstrating the constraints such warlords experienced. But this act was neither forgotten nor forgiven. Gregory states 'at the end of the year', Clovis gathered his troops together on the pretext of an inspection and, coming face to face with the 'feckless fellow', castigated him for the state of his arms and threw the man's axe to the floor. When he stooped to retrieve it, Clovis raised his own battle axe and split his skull with it. The troops were 'filled with might dread' but no response is recorded. It seems killing someone could be considered fair game but breaking rules about who gets the share of what booty was taboo.

There is also evidence of the importance of tribute, as well as raiding.[132] Part of the Saxon tribute to the Franks in the late sixth century consisted of 500 cattle. Thuringians later paid Saxons 500 pigs a year. The praise poem of Cadwallon references cattle raiding. Leinster had to pay a cattle tribute to the Ui Neill and many Irish and Welsh poems allude to similar examples. Thus, Arthur lived in a world of constant warfare, revenge killings, cattle rustling and the emergence of petty kings and warlords supported by a retinue of loyal warriors and kinsmen. Underpinning all this was an agrarian society based on cereal grains, mainly barley, and the rearing of livestock, mostly cattle. Sufficient surplus meant not only a larger retinue of warriors could be maintained but also skilled craftsmen, in particular, jewellers and armourers. The strongholds of these petty kingdoms became the centre of manufacture and trade both locally and as far afield as Byzantium, as previous evidence has demonstrated. We see the beginnings of this process in the changing functions of the Roman villa and reoccupation of hill forts in the early fifth century. This is the case for both Britons and Anglo-Saxons. In general, the evidence suggests a high standard of living for the elites of all groups in Britain.[133] In fact, despite the evidence we have seen for upheavals, warfare and climatic change, there is also evidence for a higher calorific intake between the Roman and medieval periods across Western Europe. Archaeological finds show a marked increase of height over that period, 3 cm for men and 2 cm for women.[134] So some people at least were thriving.

In summary, the *comitatus* became the glue holding together many sixth-century petty kingdoms.[135] These war-bands would not have numbered more than a few hundred, and more likely much less. As time went on, the loyalty to the war-band became more important even than kinship bonds. At the same time, we see some continuity of a Romano-Brittonic identity alongside hints of surviving political structures from Gildas. As provincial authority contracted, some areas were forced to look to their own defences. At the *civitas* level, this may have accelerated to drift towards autonomy and eventual independence as a petty kingdom. At a more local level, this may have involved the reoccupation of hill forts or the building of earthworks to prevent raiding.

Roads, dykes and hill forts

Academics now accept the existence of prehistoric trackways and wheeled carts in Britain prior to the Romans.[136] These existing systems would have been usable during campaigning season (March to September) and the Romans would have naturally used these, sending detachments ahead to clear the way. One estimate of the initial invasion calculates 1,000 men would have taken 15 weeks to construct a temporary road from the Kent coast to the Thames.[137] We have already seen how the road networks evolved. What is perhaps less well known is how much of it survived and its connection to many later historical battles. M.C. Bishop's book, *The Secret History of the Roman Roads of Britain*, finds not only were many of the Anglo-Saxon battles associated with Roman roads, but so too were nearly all later battles on English soil.[138]

These include famous battles such as Stamford Bridge and Hastings (1066); Stirling Bridge (1297); Bannockburn (1314); Bosworth (1485); and Marston Moor (1644). Indeed, most of the battles of the War of the Roses and English Civil wars were fought on or near Roman roads. If *Y Gododdin* refers to Catterick, then that too was on Dere Street between York and Corbridge. Junctions and nodal points were also important. In the seventh century, Penda fought the West Saxons at Cirencester. In 633 near Hexham along Hadrian's Wall, Oswald's Bernicians defeated a British force led by Cadwallon of Gwynedd. Just to illustrate the problem of travel, it is estimated a cart travelling from Catterick to Corbridge, a little over 50 miles, might have taken five days.[139] Infantry might take two days while cavalry could do it in a day. Indeed, in the early fourteenth century, Edward III marched from Barnard Castle to Haydon Bridge in a day before retreating, a similar distance from Catterick to Corbridge.[140]

The distance from the heart of Gwynedd to Hadrian's Wall is roughly 250 miles so we can multiply these numbers by five for Cadwallon. At that distance, supplies might have been important so a month wouldn't be unreasonable. On the other hand, a raiding mounted force could achieve that in a week. However, this all assumes a reasonable road network. One should immediately see the problem of conducting campaigns if this did not exist. Yet we know as late as 1066, Harold marched south to meet William averaging 21 miles a day, undoubtedly using the surviving Roman roads. More impressive is his march north to York and on to Stamford Bridge which averaged 53 miles a day: a remarkable feat.[141] It is therefore not surprising early medieval armies utilised the network and so many battles occurred on or near to these roads.

The question then arises, how much did survive? Bishop estimates 40 per cent of the 3,000 miles survived into the medieval period.[142] The construction of the roads involved a foundation of coarse rubble or boulders covered with compacted sand or gravel forming a camber to remove water. Cobbles were rare. This was bordered by drainage ditches. There was no standard width, the range being 1.45 to 6.45 metres. The average wagon of the time, drawn by two yoked animals, was about 1.4 metres. It is estimated the 140 miles of Dere Street from York to Corbridge, at a width of 5 yards, would have taken 4,000 men a month to build. However, Tacitus refers to pairs of centuries being utilised for construction. Thus, 160 men would have taken 650 days to complete the same section.[143]

Once built, if roads are not maintained, then plants rapidly colonise them, especially blackthorn. It is likely the margins would have been cleared considerably to allow cavalry easier ground and to make ambush less likely. The Statute of Winchester in 1285 requested manorial landowners clear up to 200 feet so that there were no 'ditch, underwood or bushes where one could hide with evil intent.'[144] Water and frost would create potholes too so various legal measures were taken in the medieval period to address these. In another example, Henry I required that two wagons or sixteen knights could be able to pass side by side. It would thus appear that later medieval kings were interested in maintaining the roads, many of which had survived from Roman times. Edward I was one of the few we have records for undertaking limited road-building himself. In his North Wales campaign of 1274, he cleared about 30 miles from Chester to Rhuddlan in roughly thirty-four days using 1,500–1,800 woodsmen.[145]

We can compare this rate with our earlier estimate of Dere Street which is roughly 2 yards per man per day. This compares with other estimates of one and a half yards and the British Royal Engineers of 1 yard.[146] Edward I achieved the lower end of this range. The last section between Rhuddlan and Deganwy achieved over 3 yards per man per day. However, Edward was only clearing a route and not laying a permanent road. This should indicate just what an achievement the Roman road network was. Bishop ends with some important conclusions:

- The Romans didn't invent the entire network but used existing trackways, many of which survived into the early medieval period.
- The road network was built primarily for military purposes, but had unexpected benefits for trade and a profound effect on medieval Britain. 40 per cent survived beyond the fifth and sixth centuries.
- Most post-Roman battles were fought on or near roads. Importantly, for our purposes, the network is a valuable tool for assessing unknown battle sites.

In a fragmenting post-Roman Britain, one would not expect all roads to be maintained. A sufficient number fell into misuse to indicate, like the deterioration of urban life and towns, that the economy and civil administration was dysfunctional. Yet 40 per cent did survive. If we use our estimates, we might calculate the 18 miles from Gloucester to Cirencester might take 180 men a summer to construct. Maintenance is likely to be less arduous. It is possible to imagine functioning town councils organising such works in some regions. However, in areas where urban centres had collapsed or been abandoned altogether and where raiding had been endemic, we can see how roads could have deteriorated making wheeled transport and thus trade difficult. It follows that a functioning road is a valuable thing, worth defending and the most likely route an army might take.

Following on from that, we can also see why early medieval dykes started to appear across the countryside, often blocking roads. Erik Grigg, in *Warfare, Raiding and Defence in Early Medieval Britain*, describes over a hundred such dykes of the period ranging from as little as 100 metres in length to the much later Offa's Dyke at 59 miles. They are difficult to date but where they cross a previous roadway, we can be fairly sure they are post-Roman. Most examples are too short and in the wrong location to be associated with borders of documented kingdoms.[147] The vast majority appear to be defensive[148] and largely designed to control raiding.[149]

They were generally built on a downhill slope with a large bank fronted by a ditch. The average length was 10,331m (6.4 miles) and the median 3,235m (2.1 miles). The banks averaged at 1.8m high and 8.3m wide with 'v' shaped ditches at 2.1m deep and 6.2m wide, angled at 38–40 degrees.[150] There are no contemporary memorial stones or written evidence, no medieval coins found, and no evidence of any gateways or palisade. On this last point, examples in Jutland do indeed show such evidence, suggesting the absence of it in Britain means they were simply used without one.[151] Still this is a formidable barrier and difficult to navigate in armour with shields and spears while trying to defend oneself from above. Often constructed in open grassland with a good line of sight but lined with turf, they seem to have been designed to be seen from, rather than seen.[152] They were unlikely to be garrisoned but set back and patrolled to give defenders enough time to man the bank.

Examples include Bokerley Dyke in Hampshire which cuts a Roman road; Wansdyke in the West Country; and the Cambridgeshire Dykes. It may well be that prehistoric earthworks were used and that later medieval works further confuse matters. Yet we can estimate a range for some of the examples and many cover the period we are interested in.[153] What is clear is that many cut Roman roads or later Anglo-Saxon 'herepaths' (literally army paths).[154] The building of these dykes peaked in the late sixth and early seventh centuries.[155] It would appear the Germanic settlers may have brought these techniques from the continent. Grigg finds none in Brittany, for example. The Cambridgeshire Dykes seem to be defending East Anglia either against the Britons or later Mercians. Yet the Dykes do not match divisions in material culture.[156] Nor as previously stated do they appear to make sense as a boundary or border. Dykes protecting Britons seem no less sophisticated. One could speculate the later Arthur falls on our timeline, the more likely it is he would have encountered such defences, either defending from a dyke or attacking one.

We certainly have evidence of burials suggesting warfare in several locations. There are over 800 individuals found near six different earthworks with numerous burials dated to the sixth century near the Cambridgeshire Dykes.[157] At Heronbridge near Chester, between the River Dee and Watling Street, there is a 550m west-facing earthwork. Over 200 males of fighting age were found, half with head injuries and DNA indicating they came from north-east England.[158] The suggestion is these men could originate from the Battle of Chester in c.616 when Aethelfrith, King of Northumbria, attacked the Welsh of North Wales. This could be indicative of the size of armies. The *Anglo-Saxon Chronicle* records 200 priests from Bangor were killed while Bede claims the number was 1,200. Perhaps Bede has confused the Welsh Army size. If the victorious Northumbrians lost 200 men, this might suggest their total force was several times greater with perhaps 1,000 being the most likely and 2,000 the maximum. One could speculate a similar-sized force from Powys, Rhos and possibly Gwynedd breaking and being destroyed. Arthur, fighting possibly in the same area a hundred years earlier, might have had similar-sized forces. Of course, in this example he would be defending Chester from a deep penetrating raid. We are also reminded of *Y Gododdin* and warriors fighting on a 'rampart'.

The largest Dyke, Offa's, is outside our time period and it is estimated it would take 10,000 labourers 68 days to build. This is similar to estimates of numbers for Hadrian's Wall, although that would be over 240 days. In fact, Hadrian's Wall took six years. In contrast, most of the early medieval dykes could have been constructed by fewer than a hundred men in a single summer season.[159] Eighth-century Anglo-Saxon sources site obligations for military service, bridge repairs and building fortifications.[160] We can only speculate how organised some polities were in a complex, fragmenting, political and social situation. The further along the timeline, the more likely we have petty warlords and raiding and the less likely we have a central or regional authority to combat this. Indeed, as early as the mid-fifth century, St Patrick is complaining about raids from Coroticus. Gildas speaks of the raiding Picts and Scots and St Germanus helps defeat a raid from Saxons and Picts. Several decades later, the situation is likely to have been worse, not better.

The later tenth-century Burghal Hidage lays out how many men were required to defend a position, roughly one man for every four feet. The dyke at Heronbridge would thus need around 500 warriors. But this doesn't indicate how many were needed to build it. Grigg finds that most could be built by the inhabitants of a few villages.[161] As society fragmented and there was more reliance on cattle grazing, petty warlords and raiding became more common. One could interpret the later seventh-century Law Codes of Ine as reflecting this. Fewer than seven men were classed as thieves, while above that number was a 'band' and more than 35 a 'here' (army) with increasingly severe punishments. Grigg therefore concludes that the main reason for these early dykes was as protection from raiding, often cattle raiding which is a theme of many Irish and Welsh sagas and poems. One interesting point he makes is that it is estimated to take four times as many troops to storm a defended position such as a dyke. Nor could one go round if it was flanked by natural features such as rivers, woods or marsh. Raiders unfamiliar with the area might be aware of how far they needed to travel to get round it and leave themselves open to attack if they tried. If at Badon we have literary sources claiming Saxon casualties from up to nearly 1,000 down to nearly half that, then the attacking force would have likely been 2,000 to 4,000.

These problems are multiplied when attacking a hill fort. There are a number of reoccupied hill forts and other settlements from Cornwall to Strathclyde:[162] Trethurgy and Tintagel in Cornwall; Dinas Powys; Mote of Mark, Dumbarton and Doon Hill in Scotland; Cadbury Castle and Cadbury-Congresbury in the south; and Yeavering Bell in the north. Cadbury Castle has a number of ramparts, one of which appears to be post-Roman consisting of a dry-stone bank filled with Roman masonry, stone, pottery and roofing tiles.[163] Evidence of refurbishment of the inner rampart is thus fifth or sixth century.[164] Cadbury has long been associated with Camelot and Arthur as early as 1542 by John Leland. There is, of course, no evidence for such a claim and we cannot take seriously myths and legends thousands of years after the alleged events. What we can do is estimate how feasible such an endeavour would be. The British Army calculates one man can move 0.3 cubic metres of earth in one hour, half the amount in chalk or rocky ground.[165]

We can thus take the measurements of the ramparts at Cadbury, one of which measures 190m x 160m, giving a perimeter of 700m. The ditch and bank are roughly 2m deep and high respectively. Assuming they used the ditch material to form the bank and the bank was 2m wide, we can estimate 2,800 cubic metres of earth. It follows approximately 9,300 man-hours are required and assuming an eight-hour day, nearly 1,200 labour days. Or in other words a thousand labourers could achieve a reasonable defence in a day or forty labourers would take a month. One estimate for the entire Iron Age hill fort construction at Ravensburgh including timber work is 200 men in 109 days.[166]

This rough calculation gives us an idea of how long more extensive or higher earthworks would take to construct. Some of the ramparts at Cadbury are as high as 10m and 1.2km in length. We recall previous suggestions that early petty kingdoms might be able to field maybe 1,000 men with the later Tribal Hidage suggesting much more in places. What this demonstrates is that given the population at the time and the manpower available, it would have been feasible for even local powers to erect such defences in a relatively short time, certainly in one season. Returning to Cadbury Castle, the Burghal Hidage suggests around 700 men would be needed to defend the inner rampart, which implies a considerable force of 2,000 to 3,000 men would be needed to take it. In contrast, it has been calculated the 5 kilometres of Roman walls at London would have required 2,700 men to defend them.[167] A reduction in urban population may well have made some towns difficult to defend.

Returning to evidence of injuries, we do have some interesting finds.[168] Blade injuries were 'extremely uncommon' with only two examples in the west of Britain. In contrast, in Anglo-Saxon areas, there are four blade injuries per 300 inhumations for the early medieval period. This is over ten times higher than the current highest modern homicide rate (134 per 100,000 in Tijuana in Mexico). Of course, blade injuries don't equate to cause of death or murders so that may be a little unfair. To compare it to a more contemporary period, one would have been three times more likely to have been wounded with an edged weapon in these areas and time compared to fourth-century Roman Britain. At the same time, settlements in these areas are 'without exception' undefended by walls or earthworks, suggesting the majority of the population felt secure and confident.[169]

Summary

Post-Roman Britain did not collapse overnight. It is quite possible that the Diocese structure was maintained to allow a council or central authority to place *foederati* in the 'east of the island.' The economy, and thus towns and urban life, had already deteriorated. As time progressed, so the military and civilian authority structures fragmented. Ambrosius may have been the 'last Roman' who attempted to stabilise the remaining provinces after the initial revolt. A hundred years later, petty kingdoms had evolved alongside social and cultural identities. Warlords and raiding became endemic. At the start of our period, some centres such as Wroxeter, hill forts and parts of Hadrian's Wall had been refurbished. By the end, earthworks, some quite small, protected local areas. By the Middle Ages, half of the Roman road network had decayed. Yet half remained and was used extensively. It is important to note most later battles can be associated with a Roman road. We can speculate an early Arthur might have been similar to Ambrosius, fighting in the context of a crumbling provincial structure using the remnants of a Northern military command across the whole former Diocese. A later Arthur might be more likely to have lived in a world of petty kings and warlords fighting local wars. However, if earlier Roman or later medieval campaigns are anything to go by, there is nothing in theory that would have prevented a fifth- or sixth-century Arthur leading troops from the south coast all the way to Scotland.

What we can be more confident about is the size of armies and type of warfare. Battles as large as Hastings 500 years later would have been rare, but certainly not impossible. Far more likely are battles in the low thousands such as at Maldon in 991. It could be argued, as Britain fragmented, the average size of armies would have reduced accordingly, to perhaps the 300 suggested in *Y Gododdin*. Most battles would have involved shield-walls with the most common weapon a spear. Gildas suggests siege weapons are not unheard of, referring to battering rams. Indeed, Badon is described as a siege although on a hill and at least one other, Guinnion, is at a fort. Seven of the twelve battles are near or next to rivers.

We have laid out the historical background in great detail. It is a far more complex and nuanced picture than the one often portrayed. There was a fragmenting political and civilian structure at the same time as enormous change in cultural identities across a range of different groups: aristocratic elites; townspeople; rural peasants; the military and mercenary groups; and a disparate group of Germanic settlers. Alongside this change were economic, religious and social frictions. Into this context, we must place Arthur within a timeframe of c.450–550. We will now attempt to place the battles within this same context, perhaps narrowing Badon down at least to c.490–520.

Chapter 7

The Thirteen Battles of Arthur

The battles list in Chapter 56 of the *Historia* is one of the most discussed and controversial sections of the text. Some have decided the only safe conclusion is it is 'the author's own work.'[1] Alternatively, the list is 'impenetrable and cannot be treated as historical' or 'at best unproven, at worst implausible.'[2] The possibility of it being an authentic battle poem is described as 'an assumption' by some academic commentators and rejected by others.[3] Those that do entertain the possibility go only so far as to say the prospects of useful information from the list are 'poor...but cannot be ruled out' and, if it is based on such a poem, the date is entirely uncertain.[4]

Other academics argue that 'if such history is unhistorical, so also are all the major histories of the early Middle Ages.'[5] Indeed, the battle list has been 'perhaps rightly' suspected of being a Welsh battle poem.[6] There are a number of academics who view the list as coming from an 'early bardic poem.'[7] As this book is unashamedly based on that admired assumption, we will leave that debate to one side.

Several recensions – manuscripts – have survived. The earliest copy is probably the Chartres MS 98, a possible tenth-century version of the *Historia* that may even predate the consensus of an early ninth-century origin. The *Historia* can be divided into seven sections, although these divisions are not in the actual text: the six ages of the world, history of Britain, life of Saint Patrick, Arthur, Saxon genealogies, cities of Britain, the wonders of Britain. Only the Harleian rescission has all seven sections.[8] The forty manuscripts are known to exist and the excellent Vortigern Studies website details eleven that can be divided into five groups:[9] Chartres MS 98 (c. 900); Vatican manuscript (c. eleventh century); Harleian MS 3859 (c. 1100); Cambridge Corpus Christi manuscript 139 (c. 1164); and the twelfth-century British Library Cotton Caligula A VIII. It is worth noting that with the Chartres manuscript, there is some debate about dating. Unfortunately, this early version does not contain the battle list. What can be said is 'the *Historia Brittonum* may reflect an authentic (but very insecure) Welsh traditional history, which might even possibly date back to the fifth century as far as Vortigern is concerned.'

Keith J. Fitzpatrick-Matthews makes a slightly different distinction. Pseudo-Nennius and Pseudo-Gildas versions are as late as the Harleian recension.

The Vatican manuscript predates both, with Chartres being the earliest. The eleventh-century Lebor Bretnach is an Irish version attributed to the historian Gilla Coemain. Sawley is considered a twelfth-century composite with the Vatican recension and later additions. Importantly, he states 'the battle list appears to fossilise an Old Welsh rhyming structure.'[10] I will leave the debate about the historical veracity of the text to one side as this study is unashamedly based on the acceptance of its credibility. The question is: if authentic, can the locations be identified and how would that fit into the historical context?

The locations are described by some academics as 'unknown and unknowable'[11] claiming 'safe identification is impossible.'[12] As early as the twelfth century, Henry of Huntingdon in *Historia Anglorum* (1129) noted 'none of the places can be identified now.' Despite this, there is a consensus about some at least. We shall see that for at least one, *cat coit celidon*, there is some confidence. For battles two to five, there is also some consensus concerning the region of the *linnuis*, if not the River Dubglas. One further battle, at the city of the legions, only causes problems because there are two likely candidates and both have unlikely locations. It is not rejected on linguistic grounds, but because it's difficult to accept. So, unlike the other battles, it is very clear but it's thought improbable. One could therefore legitimately argue we can, in fact, identify five or six out of the twelve battles. A near 50 per cent strike rate is a long way from knowing nothing. So, we can proceed with some optimism.

As we shall see, it is possible to make a case for any one of several regions for the battles. Many theorists have attempted this and tried to shoehorn all the battles into their particular theory and favoured candidate. I intend to approach this in a different way. Firstly, I don't have a suspect for Arthur in mind, so I am not focused on any particular area. I will be guided by the archaeological record and likely political and military situation at the time. Gildas laments the 'unhappy partition' preventing access to the shrines of the martyrs. It must be acknowledged this doesn't necessarily mean a physical border. It could just refer to a break in the previous agreement with the *foederati*. But it cannot be ignored that a hundred years later, there was a definite distinction between emerging Anglo-Saxon and Romano-British kingdoms.

This should give us a rough guide or corridor within which conflict was likely. This wouldn't, of course, negate battle sites deep within one territory. Secondly, I will prioritise philology and linguistics over these other considerations. In short, if there is a conflict between an obvious or most likely etymology and the likely line of partition, I will favour the former over the latter. For example, we may unearth a claim that Arthur fought a battle at Portus Dubris. This may be unlikely. However, Dubris is clearly Dover and there is little point trying to pretend it's somewhere more likely and then trying to explain some complex etymology. It's far more honest to accept the location and try to explain how, and why, such a battle might have occurred there. It might be worth noting at this point what the list doesn't say. It doesn't say or even hint at Dover, Canterbury, Richborough or London. The former Diocese capital and cities and ports nearest to Gaul don't feature, although what this might mean can only be guessed at.

With that in mind, let us turn to the *Historia*. We can see from Table 12 there are various different versions of the battle list reflected in the surviving manuscripts. They reveal some variance in spelling, but also a significant consistency. Of these, the Vatican rescission is the earliest, followed by the Harleian.

Table 12: The battle list

Battle	Vatican c. eleventh century	Harleian c. twelfth century	pseudo-Gildas c. twelfth century	Lebor Bretnach c. eleventh century	Sawley c. twelfth century
1	Glein	Glein	Glem	Glein	Glem
2–5	Duglas Regione Linnuis	Dubglas Regione Linnuis	Duglas Regione Linnuis	Dubglassi	Duglas Regione Linnuis
6	Bassas	Bassas	Bassas	Bassa	Bassas
7	Silua Celidonis Cat Coit Celidon	Silua Celidonis Cat Coit Celidon	Silua Calidonis Cat Coit Celidon (Cat Toit Celidon)	Cailll Calidoin Cait Coit Cleduman	Silua Calidonis Cat Toit Celidon
8	Castellum Guinnion	Castello Guinnion	Castello Guinnon (Guinnion)	Guindoin	Castello Guinnion
9	Urbe Leogis Cair Lion	Urbe Legionis	Urbe Legionis	Cathraig Ind Legdin	Urbe Legionis
10	Traht Treuroit	Tribruit	Ribroit	Robroit	Ribroit
11	Monte breguoin bregion	Monte Agned	Monte Agned Cat Bregomion (Cath Regomion)		Monte Agned Cath Regomion
12	Monte Badonis	Monte Badonis	Monte Badonis		Monte Badonis

Before we begin, it is worth reminding ourselves of the likely situation. After the end of Roman Britain, there was a steady deterioration of urban life and fragmentation of the provincial structure, alongside an increase in Germanic material culture from 425 onwards. A major shift of power occurred in the middle of the fifth century, followed by evidence for increased Germanic settlement.

A fightback led by Ambrosius Aurelianus culminated in a partition separating some Britons from some areas. Either side of this line, significant change occurred in cultural identity across a range of different peoples, groups and regions. Arthur's Britain was one of political upheaval and fragmentation in a dynamic, complex and nuanced social and military context. According to the *Historia*, the battles occurred after some specific events, after both St Patrick and Hengest died. Octha came from the north to the kingdom of Kent. From him comes 'the kings of the kentishmen. Then Arthur fought against them…'

We will now examine each battle in turn while remembering the hypotheses set out in the introduction: the border or partition can be estimated; the location of at least some of the battles can be located on the balance of probabilities; and those locations are likely to be near that border. Hopefully, concerning the first, I have demonstrated we have a reasonable idea of the political and military situation. Regarding the second, we have some idea of the likely partition or border. Lastly, we have already seen that locating the battles is not as hopeless as some maintain. As we go through the list, it might be useful to note how confident we are with the locations. Some battle sites may be located on the balance of probability. Others we may have only a tentative clue about, while some may well be unknowable. It's not necessary to identify *all* the battles. Even identifying just one or two would be useful, but I hope we can do far better than that.

1. 'The first battle was at the mouth of the River Glein.'

Glein comes from the Brittonic *glanos* or *glano* meaning pure, clear or even holy, and thus there could have been many such named rivers in Britain. In modern Welsh, this would be *glân*. This might then become *glein* or *glain* and then possibly, glen. There are two rivers in England called Glen today. The first is the River Glen in Lincolnshire, north of Spalding, and is one of only two modern rivers of that name.[13] Spaldingas were an Anglian tribe mentioned in the Tribal Hidage with one of the smaller areas of 600 hides. It may be worth noting that battles two to five are on the River *Dubglas* meaning 'blackwater'. The peaty rivers of the Lincolnshire area, such as the River Welland, could have been dark and thus, a distinctive clear or pure river may have warranted a name describing it as such. In fact, the Glen and Welland have contrasting sources, with the former flowing from clays and limestone, which tended to be woodland and pasture, thus remaining relatively clear, unlike the Welland, which carries significant sediment. If the location of *Linnuis* given for the next four battles is indeed Lincolnshire, then it could be argued this battle is located elsewhere. Otherwise, why make the distinction between the first and next four? Or simply say the first five battles were in the region of the *Linnuis*?

The other *Glein* is mentioned by Bede and is near Yeavering Bell, running into the River Till, itself a tributary of the Tweed further north, about 4 miles from the hill fort. So, we have a near-contemporary named river. Bede, writing in 731, states that converts in Northumbria were baptised in the river after the conversion of King Edwin in 627. This is the same King Edwin the *Historia* claimed was baptised by Rhun, son of Urien, who, in turn, the Chartres manuscript claimed as its author. However, there is no evidence of Anglo-Saxon activity in this area prior to 550, despite the literary sources.[14] It is a little over 20 miles from Lindisfarne, whose etymology may well come from settlers from the Lincoln area, and 50 miles north of Hadrian's Wall, where Nennius claims Octha and Ebissa were sent to fight the Picts. The lack of evidence for Anglo-Saxon settlers at the right time in this location would suggest that Arthur would not have been attacking an Anglo-Saxon settlement. A more likely scenario would be an incursion of Germanic raiders from the coast or the River Till, or even an attack of Yeavering Bell hill fort. Having said that, absence of evidence is not evidence of absence. The *Historia* suggests Octha's force sent to the north was only about 1,200 strong. Archaeologically, an attack on a garrison of Germanic mercenaries located somewhere in the north would be like trying to find a needle in a haystack. So, the lack of archaeological evidence for early settlement does not negate this location.

A number of other sites have also been suggested:[15]

Glen Water, Strathclyde
River Glyme, Oxfordshire
Glynch Brook, Bewdley
River Gleiniant, Llanidloes, West Wales
Glynde Reach, Sussex
River Lune, Westmoreland
River Leven, Cumberland

None of these are as close linguistically to the Northumbrian or Lincolnshire Glens. Also, the Old Welsh *glinn* (valley), Irish *glenn* or Scottish *glen* are not seen as being connected linguistically. As we shall see, the following four battles are likely to be in Lincolnshire. If this is the case, then it might suggest the other battles were not. Otherwise, why make the point of the distinction? The archaeological record would favour an eastern or southern location if Arthur was attacking Anglo-Saxon areas. On the other hand, the literary sources and later historical record would negate the idea that any south-eastern areas were retaken. Given the probable boundary of the 'partition', the most likely location is the Northumbrian or Lincolnshire Glen, with the latter being much closer to areas of Germanic immigration.

A victory in the Northumbria area would explain the conflict between the literary sources and the archaeological evidence. If a relatively small number of

Anglo-Saxons were defeated and driven out of the north, this might explain why evidence is restricted to Deira until much later. It also might explain why the *Historia*, immediately after the battle list, brings us back to the north and makes a point of stating after they (the *Saxones*) had been defeated, they 'brought over their kings from Germany to rule over them in Britain, until the time when Ida reigned…He was the first king in Bernicia…'

Map 27: Battle 1 – The mouth of the River Glein

In fact, despite the lack of archaeological evidence for Saxon settlement in Bernicia in the fifth century, one is left to explain how Ida apparently became king in 547. By the beginning of the sixth century, Aethelfrith was powerful enough to defeat Dal Riata at Dagestan in c.603; possibly the Gododdin at Catraeth in around 600; conquer Deira in 604; defeat Powys at Chester between 613 and 616; and conquer the British kingdom of Elmet. Throughout the fifth century, the British appear to have been strong enough to prevent any Germanic takeover of Bernicia. But the Angles didn't just appear in 547. Support for Ida must have come from some part of the population. Nor is this an unlikely place for a battle: battles in 1402 (Humbleton Hill), 1415 (Geteryne), 1465 (Yeavering) and 1513 (Flodden Field) were all nearby.

One other criticism we can also dismiss. The word *ostium* is sometimes assumed to refer to a mouth of a river at a coast, rather than an inland confluence into another river. However, elsewhere in the text such as the 'Wonders of Britain', the same word is used to describe just that, concerning tributaries into the Severn and Humber. In summary, we have two likely possibilities and a variety of others that rely on corruption of meaning, misspellings, mistranslations or other errors. Given the near contemporary use of the same name in Bede, the archaeological record, the likely political and military situation at the time, and the fact Linnuis is connected to the next four battles and not this one, I would favour the Northumbria Glen as the location for this battle. I wouldn't say I am confident in this. I'd estimate it at certainly less than 50 per cent, but it is significantly ahead of the other claimants. Bede's reference is the clincher for me on this one. I will put this down as tentative, with the Lincolnshire Glen as another possibility.

2–5. 'The second, third, fourth and fifth were on another river, called the Dubglas which is in the country of Linnuis.'

This has a fairly straightforward etymology coming from the Brittonic *duboglasso* – 'black blue/black green'.[16] There are no doubt hundreds of rivers that could have previously been called 'Black Water' or some other derivative. Douglas is another form, such as a tributary of the Ribble in Lancashire or another of the River Clyde in South Lanarkshire. There's also a River Blackwater in Hampshire, near to some of Cerdic's supposed battles recorded in the *Anglo-Saxon Chronicles*. Another Blackwater is in Essex close to where the Anglo-Saxons were defeated by a Viking army in 991. There are also several other derivatives, such as twelve Dulas rivers in Wales, Dawlish in Devon, and Hampshire, and various black/dark/devil's waters. Blackburn, in Lancashire, literally means 'black stream' and there are, of course, many such bourne/bourn/burn ending names for towns and rivers. Yet the phrase 'in the region of the *Linnuis*' gives additional clues.

There are only three credible theories for this area: Lincolnshire, Lennox (in Scotland) or Dorset. The first is the most likely, both linguistically and in the political and military context of the time. Late British *Lindes* becomes *Lindissi* in Old English, *Linnes* in archaic Welsh and *Linnuis* in Old Welsh. Identification of *Linnuis* with Lincoln is thus claimed to be 'beyond reasonable doubt'.[17] However, the second-century Roman geographer Ptolemy named the Roman fort of *Drumquhassle* in the Lennox area of Scotland as Lindum too.[18] Nearby is the Douglas Water in Glen Douglas, flowing into Loch Lomond. Also close by is the Cobbler, 884m high and originally called Ben Arthur. This would place Arthur fighting north of the Antonine Wall and therefore, his likely opponents would be Picts or the Dal Riata. But Ptolemy aside, we have no record of this area ever being referred to in this way.

The Hampshire option requires a corruption for the Roman name for Ilchester, Lindinis. Two inscriptions at Hadrian's Wall refer to *Durotriges Lindinsienses*. This would have led to *Lininuis* and thus a simple spelling mistake or misunderstanding converted it to *Linnuis*. Nearby are the Rivers Divelish and Devil's Brook, and the village of Dewlish, the latter deriving from 'dark stream'.[19] This area is some 30 miles west of Cerdic and Cynric's activities recorded in the *Anglo-Saxon Chronicles*. However, we must remember the dating for their arrival appears to have been artificially pushed back from 532, and the West Saxons, or Gewisse, originated in the Thames Valley, and didn't penetrate so far west until the latter part of the sixth century. Having said that, an arc from Dorset, through the concentration of early Saxon cemeteries in the Thames Valley to north of St Albans, would be consistent with battles either side of a border area. It would also be close to other suggested battle sites, such as Mount Badon.

Another possibility is rather a long shot. In the poem *Y Gododdin*, the meaning of *lynwyssar* could be translated as 'bloodied bodies' or a variant of *llynwysawr*: 'wounded/injured person.' Yet, it is at least possible this, too, has been corrupted from 'men of linnuis'.[20] Given the etymology of Lindisfarne, and the possibility it was settled by Angles originally from the Lincoln area, it could be argued that, at some point in the distant past, the area on the coast opposite the Holy Island was settled, and known, as the land of the *Linnuis*. Looking at the word more closely, *Llyn* is a lake or pool and the ending *-uis*, or later Welsh *-wys*, meaning 'the people of', thus making *Linnuis* or *lllynwys* the 'people of the pool.' Given the topography of the region around Lincoln, Lindsey certainly fits, though not with complete certainty. There is also a Lydney near the English-Welsh border, about 25 miles north-east of Caerleon. Other place names have equally dubious claims: Lindsey, Suffolk; Lindley, Yorkshire; Liney, Somerset; and ten Lintons, to name just a few. Geoffrey of Monmouth, writing in the twelfth century, places one of his battles at Lincoln, possibly as a nod to the *Historia*. Given the likely line of partition, the areas settled by Anglo-Saxons and the views of academics, I think the most likely location is, indeed, the Lincoln area. It is the only one that does not require some sort of corruption or error in previous texts. We are then left with a river whose name has changed. Any slow-moving river flowing through wetlands, such as the Fens, can become darkened by the decaying vegetation. This is perhaps slightly easier to believe than picking a River Douglas and then trying to manipulate *Linnuis* out of a local regional name. Many eminent academics, such as Jackson, identify *Linnuis* with Lindsey with some confidence.[21] Thus, the balance of probability suggests Lindsey while we perhaps retain the other two areas as less likely possibilities. If correct, then we can narrow down four out of the twelve battles to a region at least. We can thus be reasonably confident, even without locating the actual river.

Map 28: Battles 2–5 – River Dubglas in the region of the Linnuis

6. 'The sixth battle was on the river called Bassas.'

Brittonic in origin, the name 'Bassas' contains the element *basso-*, which gives the modern Welsh for shallow, *bas*. It is possibly related to the Latin *bassus* for low. The most popular theory seems to be Baschurch in Shropshire. One of the arguments is that all the *Bassing*-type locations suggest an Anglo-Saxon etymology, yet we are looking for a place that was called *Bassas* or *Bassus*, not just in the time of the *Historia* in the ninth century, but when the battle list was compiled. As this could, in theory, have been in the sixth or even fifth century, we are therefore more likely looking for a Brittonic place name. There is a ninth-century Welsh poem, *Canu Heledd*, that refers to *Eglwyssau Bassa* (Churches of Bassa), and the same name appears in the nearby village of Baschurch, which appears in the Domesday Book of 1086 as *Bascherche*.

One popular theory cites a local legend identifying Berth Pool, just outside the village, as the final resting place of Arthur.[22] Another place that has a local legend is Dinas Basing in Flintshire. A stone carries the imprint of Arthur's horse as he jumped from a nearby crag. The stone can still be seen on the road between Mold and Loggerheads. The area did have a castle at one point, but only the ruins of Basingwerk Abbey remain. There are also three Basfords in England – in Cheshire, Staffordshire and Nottinghamshire – although none of the rivers nearby are known to have been called Bassas.

If English in origin, then perhaps it's from *Basingas*, or 'Basa's people', connected with Basingtoke in Hampshire, or Old Basing just 7 miles to the east. There's also a Bassingthorpe in Lincolnshire, a *thorpe* place name ending that means 'small village'. Bassingbourn, in Cambridgeshire, literally the stream of Bassa's people, is recorded in the Domesday Book as containing thirty-nine households in the eleventh century. The Roman fort at Cambuslang in Glasgow seems a long shot, as does Bass Rock off the Lothian coast. Another theory focuses on Caracalla, who was campaigning in Scotland with his father Emperor Septimus Severus when he died at York in AD 211. Caracalla's birth name was Lucius Septimius Bassianus and the suggestion is that he lent his name to a river crossing. This is a very tenuous argument and not one that can be sustained through any close inspection.

I'm torn between Baschurch and one of the Bass-type Anglo-Saxon names in the south or east. On balance, Baschurch does seem the most likely linguistically. However, in terms of any likely border clash, Old Basing is perhaps the best placed, being near Winchester and Silchester, both of which may have had some continuity of British occupation but with significant Saxon presence nearby. In fact, if one runs a straight line between Winchester and Silchester, just to the east of this by a couple of miles is Old Basing. Similarly, the Bassing-type names in Lincolnshire and Cambridgeshire may well have been on the northern or western edge of growing Anglo-Saxon powers pushing out from the Fens. If forced, I would choose Baschurch as we have an early reference to the churches of Bassa, and the Anglo-Saxon etymologies are unlikely to be traced back to the sixth century. Unfortunately, I have no confidence in this choice. It could easily be an as yet unknown site. We must leave this to one side.

Map 29: Battle 6 – River Bassas

7. 'The seventh battle was in the Celidonis forest, that is the battle of Coit Celidon.'

The Latin *silua celidonis* is accepted to be 'wood of Celyddon', with Celyddon being derived from *Calidonia*. The usual explanation is the Caledonian Forest which covered a huge area, but it is also the Roman name for what is now Scotland. Sometimes it referred to just the Highlands, north of the Antonine Wall, but often included the southern part as well. In the *Annales Cambriae*, we read 'The battle of Armterid between the sons of Eliffer and Gwenddolau son of Ceidio; in which Gwenddolau fell; Merlin went mad.'[23] The accepted translation is Arfderydd, which is considered to have been near Arthuret, north of Carlisle.

The book of Taliesin, the *Dialogue of Taliesin and Myrddin*, makes the following statement about the battle's aftermath: 'To the forest of Celyddon they fled.' In the *Life of St Kentigern*, a certain Lailoken is said to have fled into woods in a fit of madness, and his story is very similar to Myrddin Wylit, or 'Merlin the Wild'. He, too, fled a battle 'which took place in the plain lying between Lidel and Carwannok.' The latter has not been identified, but Liddel Water is a day's march north of Hadrian's Wall. The argument is thus, that the Celidonis Forest at that time covered much further south, and was known at the time by that name. The name for the forest comes from the first-century Roman, Pliny the Elder. He names it *Silua Caledonia*. In the second century, Ptolemy placed the forest far in the north above the Antonine Wall, which would make a scenario of Arthur fighting Saxons unlikely. If the *Historia* is wrong about who Arthur was fighting, then this could undermine the whole narrative.

However, there is another explanation. Nennius seems very careful to give the Welsh name for the forest, which would suggest he was trying to be specific. In fact, it could be translated as meaning the forest of Celidon, and we do have a figure called Celyddon in Welsh legend. In *Culhwch and Olwen*, Celyddon Wledig is the grandfather of Culhwch and is based in Gwent, South Wales. It is at least possible that Nennius is referring to the wood belonging to a figure called Celidon that a ninth-century audience would have recognised. This, of course, means it could be anywhere. But we have to remember how an early medieval audience would interpret it.

The simplest, and most likely, explanation is that the forested area north of Hadrian's Wall was known as *Coit Celidon* to a ninth-century audience. Geoffrey of Monmouth has Arthur's fourth battle at Caledon Wood after pursuing the Saxons north from Lincoln, although he doesn't give a clue as to how far north. A battle just north of Hadrian's Wall wouldn't be unlikely, and a victory in that area might explain why Bernicia had to wait until 547 to have its first Anglian ruler. In fact, battles in the later decades occurred in the same region: Arfderydd

(573); Degsastan (603); and Hexham (633). It became a battleground between competing Brittonic, Northumbrian, Pictish and Dalriadian kingdoms: an area that Gildas suggests was lost when the Picts captured the north up to the wall. Perhaps he meant the Antonine Wall, but the reference to destroyed towns and a scattered people suggest it affected a Romano-British area. One is then left to wonder what brought about a change so that powerful Brittonic kingdoms such as Rheged, Strathclyde and Gododdin not only emerged, but held back the Angles, Picts and Irish for many decades.

The linguist Kenneth Jackson is 'certain' it is the forest known to the Welsh as *Coed Celyddon*, which, in turn, is a memory of the older *Silva Caledoniae*.[24]

Map 30: Battle 7 – Celidonis Forest

Thus, I am satisfied this battle was the Caledonian Forest. The exact location is a little more difficult. I would suggest the area just north of the western part of Hadrian's Wall. There's always room for doubt, of course, but I'm as close to being sure as I can be. What I am certain of is suggestions that none of the battle list can be identified are grossly unreasonable. Here's one. Even if it's only one, it's better than none and it places Arthur, at one point in time at least, north of Hadrian's wall. Additionally, if 'fighting them' means the Angles, then it places an Anglian force in an area for which we have no archaeological support for that time. Either we have the remnants of Octha's mercenaries being driven out, or we have an incursion from further south, most likely Deira. Nor would a raiding party from either coast be impossible to imagine. Lastly, this could just as easily be a battle against Picts, Scots or fellow Britons. Regardless of the exact political and military background, we can be confident about the rough location.

8. 'The eighth battle was in Castello Guinnion, and in it Arthur carried the image of the holy Mary, the everlasting virgin, on his shoulders and the heathen were put to flight on that day, and there was a great slaughter upon them.'

Castello implies a Roman fort rather than a hill fort, town or city. Temporary forts built by legions were also called castella.[25] *Gwen* or *Gwyn* means 'white' or 'holy' in the sense of 'pure'. The Brittonic *uindo-* is linked to the Old Welsh *guinn-*, and the likely meaning is the people, rather than the fort, are being described, hence, 'fort of the white people', rather than 'white fort'. *Guinnion* would certainly have become *Gwynion* in later Welsh. One example is Caer Carreg Gwynion hill fort in the Berwyn Mountains. There are many other Gwyn-type names in Wales, and there would likely have been many across what is now England. This may have been changed to *Wen-* or *Wan-* by Anglo-Saxon settlers and again, we have a variety of *Wan*-type place names. Equally, Car- or Caer-type names followed by *win* or *wyn*, such as Carwynnen in Cornwall. Caerguidn at Land's End seems an unlikely location.

Burgh Castle in Norfolk was one of the Saxon Shore Forts and its Latin name, Gariannonum, may have been corrupted by settlers unfamiliar with the Latin pronunciation. Winchester was also called Caer Guinn in Brittonic, or Guinntguic in the *Historia*. Winchester would have originally been Uenta Belgae (town of the Belgae) in Brittonic. One wonders, though, why the *Historia* spelled it differently in the battle list and didn't clarify what other names it was known as, like with the other battles. By the time of writing, Winchester had been the seat of Wessex bishops for over a hundred years and was well known as Wintan-ceastre. For those reasons, I find this option very unlikely.

One of the most favoured sites is the Roman fort at Binchester, near Durham. Vonovium was refortified and still in use in the fifth century, and was known as Uinouion in Brittonic. The argument goes that a simple evolution to a *Gwyn-*type pronunciation would give us *Guinnion*. The Old Welsh comes from the Brittonic *uindo-* but *uin-* is unknown. Interestingly, a small town to the south-west of Badbury Rings was known as Uindocladia and we have a Uindonio at Neatham, East Hampshire, and Uindolanda at Chesterholm on Hadrian's Wall. A little south of Leicester is Venonae or Venonis. This could have evolved from *Uenonis* to *Guoinon*, and then possibly to *Guinnion*.

Map 31: Battle 8 – Castello Guinnion

Most view this as unidentifiable and all the suggestions above do require some sort of corruption from the original form. Binchester Roman fort is 32 miles south of Corbridge on Hadrian's Wall, and 70 miles north of York. However, it is only 10 miles north of the River Tees, which was the traditional boundary between Deira and Bernicia. If Bernicia was a Brittonic kingdom in Arthur's time and Deira was under Angle control, it would be a likely place for a border clash. This is highly speculative and I put it forward as the best choice of a bad bunch. I am as confident as I am with Bassas, which is to say not at all.

9. 'The ninth battle was fought in the urbe legionis (city of the legion).'

The traditional options tend to be Chester or Caerleon in South Wales. The former is named *Caer Legion* by the *Historia* in the list of twenty-eight cities, with the latter called *Caer Legion Guar Usic*. Chester was also called *Deva* and *Deverdoeu* in the twelfth century. Later, Anglo-Saxons used *Legacæstir* eventually dropping the first part to simply *Caester* or Chester. Some have suggested this is a copy of the Battle of Chester when Aethelfrith of Northumbria defeated a Welsh force, killing 200 priests. The *Anglo-Saxon Chronicles* date this to 605–606, although Bede suggests it was between 613 and 616. Bede gives both the English name *Legacaestir* and, as he puts it, the 'more correct' British name: *Caerlegion*. It would be odd to include a well-known defeat in Arthur's battle list. Strange, too, to include a battle that an audience would associate with the seventh century. Unless, of course, the ninth-century audience would know full well this was a different battle entirely. There are, of course, plenty of examples in history of battles being fought in the same area twice.

The Roman fortress at Caerleon was named Isca Augusta probably from the Welsh *Wysg*, the name for the River Usk. The town later derived its name from the Welsh for 'fortress of the legion', *Caerleon* with the *Guar Usic* being added to differentiate it from *Caer Legion*, Chester. Geoffrey of Monmouth places Arthur's court at Caerleon and, if there was any truth in this, it would be a target for an enemy force. However, the Welsh Triads actually place his court in three different locations: Mynyw (St David's in Wales); Celliwig in *Cernyw* (possibly Cornwall); and Pen Rhionydd 'in the North', although the earliest surviving copy of the Triads are from the thirteenth century. There is also the suspicion that Geoffrey, writing around six hundred years after Arthur lived, may have had political and personal reasons for placing him in South Wales. Both these locations seem far away from early Anglo-Saxon settlements and thus unlikely sites for a battle. One could speculate about a Saxon force attempting to destroy an enemy's base. The distance to Chester, at least, was no barrier as Aethelfrith demonstrated a hundred years later.

There is one other option that makes more sense in terms of location. The etymology for York can be traced back to Brittonic *Eburakon*, Roman *Eboracum* to Norse *Jorvik*. It was home to two legions at different times: the Ninth Legion Hispania and the Sixth Legion Victrix. York has the advantage of actually being an *Urbs*, that is a city. It is also the headquarters of the *Dux Britanniarum*, who would have commanded the forces along Hadrian's Wall, plus the reserves including forces at York. The *Notitia Dignitatum* does record units still being stationed at York at the end of the fourth century, unlike at Chester and Caerleon. It is thus possible, in the fifth century, York, rather than Chester or Caerleon, was known as the 'city of the Legion.' We have already seen how Gildas's reference to being unable to visit graves is not likely to mean Caerleon, despite later medieval traditions and a ninth-century shrine.

Against this is the inconvenient fact there is no record of York being known by such a title. The *Historia* calls it *Cair Ebrauc*. Neither Chester or Caerleon was commonly known as *Urbe*. York, on the other hand, was one of the major cities in Britain, the headquarters of the command of the *Dux Britanniarum*, and later an Episcopal See. Given the first Anglo-Saxon king of Bernicia was Ida in 547 and Deira was settled before that, it is possible York was lost to Germanic control at the time of Arthur. No such thing could be said for Caerleon or Chester.

Another possibility is *Caer Lerion* (as Nennius names it) or *Legorum Urbs*, meaning 'city of the *Legores*', which would likely make it Leicester. This would require a spelling mistake or misunderstanding on the part of copyists. Similar to this is a whole variety of theories which place Arthur in parts of the country, far away from the likely suspects. Any fort, *coloniae*, town or city that could have a unit of soldiers is used to support a pet theory. This leads to a long list of tenuous and speculative suggestions. There is even a Chesters Roman fort on Hadrian's Wall near Hexham, although it was known as Cilurnum by the Romans; I only include it to demonstrate how names can change over time and later be confused with other sites.

The fact remains only one location was ever named in the way the *Historia* does in the battle list. The *Annales Cambriae* refers to the Battle of Chester as *Cair Legion*. It also dates a Synod in 601, shortly before the battle, at *Urbis Legion*. The earliest copy of the *Annales* is attached to a copy of the *Historia*, so one might expect the spellings to be similar, although a nagging doubt remains about the word *Urbis* rather than *Caer*. It is unlikely this Synod refers to the Roman church, so a British Synod at Chester would make sense. While St Augustine did arrive in Kent in 597, Paulinus, the first bishop of York, did not do so until 604; he then spent many years in Kent before travelling north in the 620s with Ethelburg, sister of King Eadbald of Kent, to marry King Edwin of Northumbria. The latter was baptised by Paulinus around 627. Thus, the Synod recorded in the *Annales Cambriae* is likely, unsurprisingly, to refer to Chester or Caerleon, and not York. Nor could this be confused with the meeting between Augustine and the British bishops in his effort to convert them to Roman ways. Bede places this after 605 at Augustine's Oak, on the borders of the Hwicce and West Saxons, probably in Gloucestershire.

What this means is the Synod referred to in the *Annales Cambriae* cannot be York because it was in Pagan Northumbrian hands at the time. It therefore likely demonstrates an occasion when Chester was referred to as *Urbis*, rather than *Caer*, which supports this location. Additionally, the Vatican recension of the *Historia* is arguably closer to the original version and uses the spelling *cair legion*, which again supports Chester. It is true that York makes far more sense in terms of the likely military and political situation at the time. It's likely to be near to any line of partition. As a *civitas* capital, headquarters of the northern command of the *Dux Britanniarum* and its strategic position, York would be my preference. But as unlikely as Chester seems, that does appear to be what the text is telling us. In fact, this is one of the locations we can be most certain of linguistically.[26]

It is at least possible a copyist meant Caerleon, but neglected 'on-Usk'. As a location, Caerleon has similar problems to Chester. Both locations are well away from any early Germanic settlement. Both lie on a good road network and are within emerging Brittonic kingdoms of Powys and Gwent, which lay in the former Britannia Prima. Thus, the likely explanation for either would likely hold for both: it indicates either a defensive battle against a raid, by land or sea, deep inside Brittonic territory; or possibly the removal of former mercenaries or settlements based at former legionary fortresses. Locations such as York and Lincoln have known Brittonic names, and if we apply Occam's razor, we should dismiss them.

In summary, I am very satisfied this refers to Chester. I am in good company as Kenneth Jackson describes this identification as 'certain'.[27] The reason for academics and theorists holding against this is purely its geographical location. One could use that argument to negate the credibility of the entry or the whole list, but not to claim it doesn't mean Chester. Someone writing *urbe legionis* in the ninth century meant Chester. How such a battle may have come about is a different question. The most likely scenario is an Anglo-Saxon attack over land from the Trent Valley or Lincolnshire, or more likely down the Roman road from York. But we now have two locations that we can be reasonably confident about: Chester and just north of the east end of Hadrian's Wall. Interestingly, both are well away from areas of early Anglo-Saxon finds. Plus, we have identified another four battles, in the region of the Linnuis, most likely near Lincoln. Two out of twelve is far from the hopelessness many portray. Six out of twelve is cause for optimism.

Map 32: Battle 9 – Urbe Legionis

10. 'The tenth battle was fought on the bank of the river called Tribuit.'

The Middle Welsh word *Tryfrwyd* derives from two elements *tri-* and *bruit*, which, when compounded, give 'pierced/very/excessive through/broken', which most commentators write as 'pierced through'. It could also derive from *tribreito-*, which is Brittonic for 'speckled'. It has proved one of the most difficult to locate. The mid-thirteenth-century Black Book of Carmarthen contains the possibly tenth-century poem *Pa Gur yv y porthaur*, translated as 'What man is the gatekeeper?' Arthur is asked to vouch for his men before being allowed in. These include Cai, Bedwyr and Mabon, son of Mydron, a servant of Uthr Pendragon. There is a reference to a battle at Eiddyn, which is the Brittonic for Edinburgh. It goes on to describe 'pierced shields at Trywuid', which many have identified as the equivalent of the *Historia's Tribuit*. A second reference mentions the 'strands of *Trywuid*.' We get a further clue from the line: 'Did not Manawyd bring Perforated shields from *Trywruid*?' In the poem *Y Gododdin* there is a reference to Manawyd: 'Before the army of Gododdin there was flight, Hard pressure facing the land of Manawyd.'

This suggests Manawyd was close to Catterick, or somewhere bordering Deira or Bernicia. This, in turn, would support the idea of a warrior called Manawyd located in the north, which supports the idea of *Trywuid* also being in the north. However, *Pa Gur* also references locations in Wales, such as Anglesey, so it's not clear where exactly the author means.

The Vatican recension contains the word *traith*, which means 'shore' or 'beach'. This could indicate it's the beach or shore of the river, which, in turn, could suggest the mouth of a river on the coast. Theories concerning the Firth of Forth, or further east at Frew, are based on alleged previous names, Traeth Gwruid or Bruit respectively. Another theory is it's related to the hunt for the boar *Twrch Trwyth* in *Culhwch and Olwen* and there is, indeed, a River Twrch in South Wales. The River Brue in Somerset, the Ribble in Lancashire or the Northumbrian Teviot have also been suggested. The latter is the most likely geographically.

The Latin *tribui* means 'tribe' but could also be a form of the verb to bestow, give, allow, ascribe, attribute or allot: *tribuo, tribui, tribuere, tributum. Tributum* as a noun means 'tribute' or 'tax'. It is unfortunate the Latin dictionary doesn't include the definition for 'grants' because in Welsh the word would translate as *grantiau*. We do, indeed, have one river that has an apparent Brittonic etymology called Granta in Cambridgeshire. But this is just speculation, as is any attempt at using the suffix *tri-* to locate the confluence of three rivers, of which there are many examples.

None of the suggestions carry any weight and many are based on false etymologies. The only hint is that it may be connected in some way with the north through the reference in *Pa Gur*. If this is the case, then we are likely looking at the Kingdom of the Gododdin and its surrounding borders. To the north would mean fighting against the Picts; to the south, the early Angle settlers north of the Wall. If one dismisses the relevance of the poem *Pa Gur*, written hundreds of years after, then we are left with no clues at all. It could quite simply be anywhere. It is quite possible the word is not a place name at all and is, in fact, an adjective. I will grasp at straws and place it in the north somewhere. If forced to choose, the Fords at Frew near Stirling is a possibility, though the likelihood of a battle against Angles is low. Perhaps it was a raiding party or a garrison at the reoccupied Antonine Wall. The alternative spellings, *Treuroit* or *Ribroit* are often ignored, but they offer little help. This is the battle I have the least confidence in locating. But on balance, I'd take a wild guess at somewhere north of Hadrian's Wall and not far from the likely seventh battle in the Caledonian Forest. But I have no confidence, aside from a vague hunch, that it's in the north. We must place this with Bassas as unknown.

Map 33: Battle 10 – River Tribuit

11. 'The eleventh battle was on the hill called Agned.'

Some manuscripts record the eleventh battle as *Breguoin, bregion* or *bregomion*, and others combine both names: *Agned* and *cath regomion*. A rough translation of the pair together might be the *battle of (b)regomion* on *mount Agned*. Geoffrey of Monmouth, in the twelfth century, identifies Agned with Din Eidyn, Edinburgh. Other suggestions include Bravonium, the Roman fort at Leintwardine in Hertfordshire. The fort is also recorded as Branogenium in one record. Another

Map 34: Battle 11 – Mount Agned/Breguoin

suggestion, Bremetennacum, at Ribchester in Lancashire, lies on the banks of the Ribble. A note in the margin of one manuscript of the *Historia* gives us Cathbregyon in Somerset, which has been identified as Catbrain in Bristol.[28] I'm not sure how much credence we should give to such an addition made centuries after the alleged battle.

If we view *Agned* as corrupt, then there is a consensus that the best candidate for Breguoin is *Bremenium*, the Roman fort at High Rochester in Northumberland. There is a separate record of a battle known as *kat gellawr brewyn* – 'the battle of the cells of *brewyn*' – which is attributed in Welsh poetry to Urien of Rheged. Respected academics identify *breguoin* with *Bremenium*, the Roman auxiliary fort.[29] Or at least there's no reason why it can't be linguistically. This seems to be the best we can do with this location. We can be slightly more confident than with the River Tribuit, but the bar there is set very low. *Bremenium* Roman fort at High Rochester in Northumberland is about 25 miles north of Corbridge on Hadrian's Wall. If this theory is correct, then it places this battle close to the Caledonian Forest and potentially, *Castello Guinnion* if that battle is at Binchester, 35 miles south of Corbridge. It is another location which, although is possibly northern, is more correctly described as unknown.

12. 'The twelfth battle was on Monte Badonis and in it 960 men fell in one day, from a single charge of Arthur's, and no-one laid them low save him alone; and he was victorious in all his campaigns.' Or as the *Annales Cambriae* puts it dating it to the year 516: 'The battle of Badon, in which Arthur carried the Cross of our Lord Jesus Christ for three days and three nights on his shoulders and the Britons were the victors.'

Gildas describes it as 'the siege of Badon Hill, pretty well the last defeat of the villains but certainly not the least.' Bede states 'the siege of Mount Badon when the Britons slaughtered no small number of their foes.' Geoffrey of Monmouth describes the Saxons as besieging Bath. Arthur arrives and after a day's fighting, the Saxons retreat to a nearby hill and the battle rages on the next day. A number of points are worth noting: the battle is on a hill or mount. It is not described as a *caer*, hill fort, town or city; it may have been the culmination of a campaign (the last defeat); it was a heavy defeat, although not the least, with no small number being slaughtered. The impression this gives is that Arthur is the attacker, rather than the defender. Geoffrey of Monmouth's version is therefore not unlikely. Most of the likely suggestions are in British-controlled areas, which might suggest a raiding army did indeed retreat to a hill and was overwhelmed. We get no clues from the earlier sources, other than it was a siege and several hundred Saxons were slaughtered. In terms of location, we have the opposite problem from many of the other battles. We have too many potential sites, rather than too few.

While we cannot be sure where Gildas was writing, it is probable his five kings were all in the western province of Britannia Prima. Ambrosius is also linked to sites in the south and the *Historia* places both Vortigern and Ambrosius in the same province. This, coupled with the archaeological evidence, suggests the south is the most likely location for these particular events. I would therefore agree with Higham that Gildas was likely to have been writing in the south somewhere in the province of Britannia Prima.[30] Higham places him specifically in the *civitas* of the Durotriges or around the modern-day Dorset. The historian Kenneth Jackson agrees, placing Badon 'somewhere in Wessex'[31] and Chambers, too, states Badon is 'likely in Wessex'.[32]

A section of the *Historia* talks about 'The Wonders of Britain': 'The third wonder is the hot lake, where the baths of Badonis are in the country of the Huich.' One notices the same spelling as in the earlier battle list. The Huich surely means the Hwicce, located on the east bank of the Severn and likely covering the same area as the *civitas* of the Dobunni. This would indicate the author does, indeed, mean Bath. Geoffrey of Monmouth certainly regarded it as such. In Welsh tradition, Caer Faddon is the name for Bath such as in the twelfth-century *Dream of Rhonabwy*. Arthur camps below Caer Faddon half a day's ride of the ford at Rhyd-y-Groes which means 'the ford of the cross'. One such location is near Welshpool, a few miles west of Shrewsbury. This gives rise to suggestions of Breidden Hill, an Iron Age hill fort, a few miles to the east. This is actually over 100 miles north of Bath, which might suggest earlier traditions had a different location in mind. There are other Rhyd-y-Groes-type names. One, Pont-rhyd-y-groes is in Ceredigion, West Wales. Another is in Bangor, North Wales. It is possible that there were many fords named after the cross.

The *Historia* goes on to describe the baths of Badon as follows: 'It is surrounded by a wall made of brick and stone, and men may go to bathe at any time, and every man can have the kind of bath he likes. If he wants it will be a cold bath and if he wants a hot bath it will be hot.' It is thus likely he means Bath. The first recorded Anglo-Saxon name for Bath was Hat Bathu in a seventh-century charter. Later names include Badum, Badan and Badon. The *Anglo-Saxon Chronicle* names it Badanceastre. All this suggests the Anglo-Saxons referred to Bath as Badon as early as the seventh century. The question is: did they invent this or copy the name from the locals?

Both the *Historia* and Geoffrey of Monmouth could have assumed Gildas meant Bath. Our first reference to Badon is Gildas writing in around 540. He is certainly writing before the later Wessex expansion, which captured Bath after the Battle of Deorham in 577. Why would Gildas, a Briton writing in Latin, give a later Saxon name to what was then a British town? The 'd' in Gildas's *Badonici montis* should be a hard 'd' sound as in 'bad', not a softer 'th' sound as it would be if spelled 'Baddon'. Old English would have had its own letter to represent this Old Welsh 'dd' soft 'th': 'ð' as in Baðon, which would produce a soft 'th' sound.[33] The 'bad'-type names, as in Badbury or Baddanbyrig, of which there are many such examples, form an arc from Dorset to Lincolnshire. Bennett and Burkitt, writing in 1985, found that Badan was the most commonly used medieval term for Bath, and they see no objection to Gildas dropping a 'd' to Latinise it to Badonis. They also point out that, in the seventeenth century, the hill to the north of the Roman City walls was known as Badonca.[34]

Badonicus could come from a place name of some variation of Badon. In Brittonic, this would be related to *boddi* or *baditi* meaning 'drown/flood/submerge',[35] similar to Old Irish *baided* or *badun* meaning 'fortified enclosure'. Baddon in Welsh is bath in English. Either way, it's possible that badon- was 'the very wet place'. The consensus is that Badon was indeed Brittonic and that Gildas was Latinising a Brittonic place name. With this in mind, we have a distinction in Latin between a long versus short 'a' sound in Latin. This is indicated by a line above the 'a' called a macron. Thus, Bādon versus Badon as in father versus fatter. It is possible Gildas, or a copyist, neglected the macron, thus Badon could be Bardon as at Bardon Hill, Leicestershire. Baþan or Baþum are Old English meaning 'at the Baths', evolving into the later Baþanceaster. If Gildas had Latinised an earlier 'Bath' type sound, it would more likely take a different form such as '*bathama*'. One possible explanation would be if there was already a large Germanic community that far west, and/or much of the south was already bilingual with Brittonic language already under pressure. However, the fact remains Bath was known as Aqua Sulis by the Romans and there is no record of any British name.

There was one other Roman Spa town in Britain: Buxton, in Derbyshire, known as Aqua Armemetiae, which is surrounded by much larger hills than Bath. Interestingly, the Roman road from Buxton towards Doncaster was, and still is, called Batham Gate, running from the north-east into the town. A force coming from Lincolnshire or Deira towards Wroxeter would certainly follow this route. So might a force that was attacking Chester, one of the few battles we are confident in locating. If we assume a hard 'd' sound, then we start looking at the very many 'bad'-type names, mostly across the south. One of the most respected experts, Kenneth Jackson, writing in 1959, finds Badon must be somewhere on the border near the Salisbury Plain and suggests the following: Badbury, Swindon; Badbury Hill, Farringdon; Badbury Rings, Blandford.[36] A variety of other theories can be seen below:

- Baumber in Lincolnshire was called Badeburg in the Domesday Book of the eleventh century
- Bannerdown Hill on the Avon, north of Bath
- Badbury Rings hill fort in Dorset
- Badbury Hill in Berkshire
- Badbury (Baddeburi in Old English) and Bedwyn in Wiltshire
- Baydon in Wiltshire means the 'hill where berries grow' in Old English
- Braydon forest, Wiltshire, lies west of the Roman road from Winchester to Cirencester. Ringsbury camp is an Iron Age hill fort overlooking the area near the village of Purton
- Beedon, West Berkshire
- Bladon, Oxfordshire
- Breedon on the Hill, Leicestershire
- Bardon Hill, Leicestershire
- Bierton in Buckinghamshire is recorded in the Domesday Book as Bortone, meaning 'farmstead near the stronghold'
- Mynydd Baedan, near Bridgend in South Wales
- Badden, west of Loch Lomond in Scotland
- Dumbarton (fort of the Britons) in Scotland

Bath was also known as Acemannesceaster to the Anglo-Saxons, and this leads us to wonder where they might have got the alternative: Hat Bathu, Badum, Badan and Badon? The question follows why the latter persisted and why we don't know the town today as Acemannchester or a derivative of Aqua Sulis? It is quite possible the early Saxons were simply copying an earlier and unknown Brittonic name. Equally, it's possible that there was widespread immigration and bilingualism before the time Gildas was writing, and that Bath was already known as Badon long before the later Wessex expansion. Even if we ignore Geoffrey of Monmouth, we have the simple fact that the composer of the *Historia* clearly refers to Bath as Badon in the 'Wonders of Britain.'

However, in one way it makes little difference if Badon is Bath or a 'bad'-type location on the Gewissae/Brittonic border. Once we can be reasonably confident we have at least one battle in the south and one in the north, this paints a vivid picture: one of a military force operating across the length of any partition and the island in general. All the sources are consistent: Monte Badonis refers to the name of a place, rather than the name of a hill. Thus, it is not Badon's Hill but a hill belonging, or near, to a place called Badon. We get another clue from the *Annales Cambriae* record for the year 665: 'The first celebration of Easter among the Saxons. The second battle of Badon. Morgan dies.'

It is not clear if this second Badon is in the same location, or means a similar defeat of the Saxons by the Britons, or even a similar defeat of the enemy but by someone else. There is no clue as to who Morgan is from this or what, if any, connection there is to Badon. The 'B' text version simply refers to the first celebration of Easter among the Saxons and doesn't mention the battle. Both versions place the event four years before the death of Oswy, King of Northumbria who, in fact, died in 670. It is often stated this is an error as the *Anglo-Saxon Chronicle* gives the year 634 for when Bishop Birinius first 'preached baptism to the West Saxons.' The year before Cadwallon, the King of Gwynedd had joined forces with Penda of Mercia to defeat King Edwin of Northumbria at the Battle of Heathfield. It is possible a battle in this campaign could be described as a 'second Badon'. However, there is a more likely connection.

The *Anglo-Saxon Chronicle* does have an entry for 661: Wulfhere, King of Mercia, the son of Penda, raids as far as Ashdown. He stands godfather to Aethelwald, King of the South Saxons. He raids Wight, gives it to Aethelwald and had 'received him at Baptism.' Elsewhere, Eoppa 'the mass priest' is commanded by Wulfhere to bring baptism to the inhabitants of Wight. So here we have an entry that appears to correspond to the reference in the *Annales Cambriae* for the first baptism of the Saxons. The *Annales* simply says Saxons and makes no reference to which Saxons. Clearly, the only Saxons who received their first baptism shortly before Oswy dies are the South Saxons and those on the Isle of Wight.

There is, unfortunately, no Battle of Badon in the *Anglo-Saxon Chronicles*. However, there are some possible clues. In the same year, 661, Cenwalh, King of West Saxons, fights at *Posentes byrg* (possibly Posbury, Devon or Pontesbury, Shrewsbury). It's not recorded as a victory, so it's possibly a setback. Wulfhere, in raiding from Mercia to Wight, would have passed through many of the possible locations for Badon, from Bath to Badbury. It's possible that, like his father Penda, he had allied British kings who might record a great victory against the West Saxons in the same place the great Arthur won. Another possibility is recorded for 675, five years after Oswy's death, rather than before: 'Here Wulfhere Penda's offspring, and Escwine, fought at Bedan (or Biedan) Heafde.'

Again, a battle between the Mercian and West Saxon kings is likely to be near to several of the suggested locations for Badon. Bedan or Biedan Heafde is translated as Bieda's or Beda's Head. Sadly, this has not been located either. But if it is connected, it would count against Bath as the identification. Whatever the case, if any of the entries from the *Anglo-Saxon Chronicle* could be connected, it would point to a southern location.

There is one possibility we need to remind ourselves of at this point. We have already seen that the earliest Welsh stories and poems rarely connect Arthur with Badon at all, and Gildas implied it was the culmination of the campaigns of Ambrosius. We have also seen that many of the other battles have likely locations further north, with *Linnuis* and Chester on the southern border of the northern province, and *Celidonis* to the north. It is possible the battle list was

Map 35: Battle 12 – Monte Badonis

from a northern source and Badon was attributed to Arthur much later. This would allow a Badon c.490s and a 'late Arthur' c.510–540.

The *Historia* is also quite clear that it regards *Badonis* as Bath, and the fact early Germanic speakers were calling it the same within a hundred years of Gildas cannot be dismissed easily. I don't see Gildas's use of an apparent Saxon name as problematic. Saxons had settled there for a hundred years, the Belgae were a Germanic tribe, and we've seen from previous evidence that some areas would have been bilingual. An apparent Germanic name for Bath is not necessarily a barrier. In many of the other battles, the *Historia* gives the Latin and the Brittonic name. With Badon, it doesn't bother and later refers to it again by the same name, locating it at Bath.

In summary, I find no good reason to ignore the obvious and seek corruptions, misspellings and other twisted etymologies. It is one of the few locations that does indeed have a later attested equivalent, albeit in Old English. Even if we cannot be sure of Bath, on the balance of probabilities, the siege of Badon Hill was somewhere in later Wessex. If the battle list accurately reflects Arthur's battles, then it is very likely he was not a localised petty warlord. It follows it is more likely he was able to lead forces from north to south across the whole of the former Diocese.

13. 'The battle of Camlann, in which Arthur and Medraut fell: and there was plague in Britain and Ireland.' (From the *Annales Cambriae* entry for the year 537)

Text 'A' of the *Annales* records it as *Gueith cam lann* with the last 'n' added. Text 'B' gives us *Bellum camlam*. Geoffrey of Monmouth spells it *Camblan* and other Welsh sources give us *Gamlan*. This could stem from the Brittonic *camboglanno-*, meaning 'bent or crooked river bank'. Or it could possibly be *cambolando-*, meaning 'bent or crooked enclosure'. The *Ravenna Cosmography*, an eighth-century Italian list of place names, records a *cambroianna*, which seems to be a corruption of *Camboglanna*. We do, indeed, have a Roman fort of that name on Hadrian's Wall. Originally thought to be at Birdoswald, there is now a consensus it is located at Castlesteads, 15 miles east of Carlisle. Two other locations exist further north near the Antonine Wall: Cambuslang, south of Glasgow, and Camelon, near Falkirk. However, the second 'n' is significant, suggesting the scribe realised the mistake and corrected it. It is important because *Camboglanna* would give *Camglann* in the tenth century, so *Cam lann* is more likely derived from Cambolanda which means 'crooked/twisting enclosure'.

There are possibilities in Wales too:[37] firstly, the area of Camlan near Mallwyd, on the River Dyfi (or Dovey in English), and Afon Gamlan, also in Gwynedd. Camlann Isa, Camlan Uchaf, Bron Camlan and Maes y Camlan all survive on modern maps but unfortunately, the name Camlan only goes back to 1571 as a small village or township in the lordship of Mawddwy. The area lies on the Gwynedd/Powys border about 50 miles, or around two to three days' march, west of Wroxeter. Afon Gamlan runs from north of Dolgellau, a few miles to the west. The Afon Gamlan lies 10 miles to the north-west where it meets the River Eden at Ganllwyd, north of Dolgellau.

Near Cwmllan in Snowdonia, there is a tradition that Arthur and his men set out from Dinas Emrys near Beddgelert.[38] They found the enemy in a pass between Snowdon and Y Lliwedd. Arthur, in the vanguard, came to a pass called Bwlch y saethau, meaning 'the pass of arrows', so called because here Arthur fell to a shower of arrows. Nearby is a cairn called Carnedd Arthur where Arthur is alleged to have been buried. Indeed, there is a further legend of Arthur's men sleeping in a cave nearby in their armour, waiting for the time to awake. This all seems very hopeful but unfortunately, we have no early record to confirm these locations.

Geoffrey of Monmouth places it on the River Camel in Cornwall, although Slaughterbridge appears to be named after a battle in 823 between Wessex and the Britons. A nearby stone is also often mistranslated and, in fact, is a burial stone for a 'Latinus son of Mogari.'[39] It's likely Geoffrey chose this because of the proximity to Tintagel, which he also cited as connected to Arthur. In addition, we have the River Cam in Somerset that passes near to Cadbury Castle, which we know had continued occupation right through the period we are looking at. John Leland, in the sixteenth century, located Camlann at Queen Camel, a few miles to the west. It may well derive from the nearby Camel Hill as the Brittonic *cantmael* means 'bare ridge'.

Camlann is mentioned in a number of Welsh poems and tales, albeit from many centuries after. *Culhwch and Olwen* names three survivors, Morfran ail Tegid, Sandde Bryd Angel and Cynwyl Sant, plus another who plotted the battle, Gwyn Hywar. 'The Stanzas of the Graves' in the *Black Book of Carmarthen* names Camlann as the site of the grave of Osfran's son. In *The Dream of Rhonabwy*, Iddog Cordd Prydain, the Churn of Britain, kindled strife before the battle and scuppered peace talks by delivering insults, instead of the given message of peace. The Welsh Triads have a number of references as shown in Table 13.[40]

Table 13: Camlann and the Welsh Triads

Number	Triad	Details
30	Three faithless/ disloyal war-bands	The war-band of Alan Fyrgan that fled the night before the battle and he was slain at Camlann.
51	Three men of shame	Description of Medrawd that follows Geoffrey of Monmouth's story resulting in Camlann.
53	Three sinister (ill omened) hard slaps	'Gwenhwyfach struck upon Gwenhwyfar and because of that there took place afterwards the conflict of the battle of Camlann'
54	Three violent (costly/ reckless) ravagings	The first where Medrawd came to Arthur's court at Celliwig and dragged Gwenhwyfar from her chair and struck her. The second describes Arthur coming to Medrawd's court and 'leaving neither food nor drink in the court or the cantref.'
59	Three unfortunate counsels	Arthur's threefold division of his men with Medrawd at Camlann
84	Three futile battles	'The third was the worst': Camlann, caused by the contention between Gwenhwyfar and Gwenhwyfach

Unfortunately, none of these Triads gives a clue as to location. But they do show a tradition separate from Geoffrey of Monmouth as to the cause of Camlann. Geoffrey's tale describes Mordred betraying Arthur with Guinevere and joining with Saxons, Picts and Scots. These Welsh tales suggest Gwenhwyfach and Gwenhwyfar (Guinevere) were sisters, and their quarrel caused the issue between their respective husbands, Medrawd and Arthur. Personally, I find this a more intriguing story than the traditional one involving a love triangle with Lancelot or the betrayal of Mordred. But what these tales do demonstrate is that Camlann, or Gamlan as it is sometimes spelled, featured quite often in Welsh tradition. Indeed, in a fourteenth-century code of Welsh laws, it states when the queen wills it 'let the bard sing a song respecting Camlann.'[41]

We cannot trust Geoffrey of Monmouth because much of his writing appears to have political motives in light of his benefactors. The academics seem to favour *Camboglanna*, the Roman fort at Castlesteads. I am drawn to the Welsh Camlan and Afon Gamlan, but we have no early confirmation of these place names. Camboglanna overlooks the River Irthing, which could indeed be described as 'crooked' at that point. Intriguingly, a day's march to the west is the Roman fort at Burgh-by-Sands known as Aballava. The *Ravenna Cosmography* records this as Avalana, which many have pointed out is very similar to Avalon. On balance, I prefer the River Gamlan or the nearby Camlan in Mallwyd, Wales. It's far simpler to accept the obvious. I can't say I am convinced but I'm slightly more confident than with the battles of *Tribuit* or *Breguoin*. Which is to admit, very little.

Map 36: Battle of Camlann

Conclusion

What becomes apparent with this list of battles is that identification isn't quite as hopeless as one is led to believe. Firstly, there is some consensus that battle 7, *Silua Celidonis*, is the Caledonian Forest north of Hadrian's Wall. This is not a small thing. We know from archaeology that there was some continuation of occupation at some sites. We also know there is little to no Germanic settlement, until much later in the sixth century, in many western or northern regions. However, the *Historia* states Octha was given land by the wall to fight the Picts, and later came down 'from the north' to the land of the Kentishmen. We also know that northern British petty kingdoms were relatively strong and resisted Angle expansion until the latter half of the sixth century. Thus, an Arthur active in the north in the former military command of the *Dux Britanniarum* would not be inconsistent with this.

Similarly, there is some consensus that the most likely etymology of *Linnuis* is Lindum, and is thus a reference to Lindsey, the area north of modern-day Lincoln. The lack of a River Dubglas is a problem, but not a major one if we can locate the region with some confidence. If we had an unknown river, but the source was clear about the region of the Cantii, for example, then I'd be quite content to say Arthur fought in Kent. The lack of identification for the river or likelihood of that area would not detract from it. The fact he seems to have fought four battles in Lincolnshire, given the archaeological evidence, is very significant. Firstly, it's in an area surrounded by early Angle and Saxon burials and settlement. Secondly, there appears to have been a British enclave into the sixth century, covering all the likely periods for Arthur's activity. So, we have five battles located out of twelve, which is certainly not the picture often painted.

The last battle for which there is a consensus is the ninth battle at the City of the Legions. Logically, it should be York, but no amount of wishful thinking will make it so. There is simply no record of it ever being called by that name. Caerleon is possible but that has a distinctive name. In any other context, it would be accepted as Chester. In the *Historia* itself and the later *Annales Cambriae*, Chester is referred to as Caer Legionis, and the only reason to doubt it is the unlikely location for a battle. But that is a secondary issue. If the list named Londinium as a battle location, this might be viewed as unlikely as it appears to have been unoccupied by 500. But that shouldn't prevent us from identifying Londinium as London. Caerleon is the only other possibility, but relies on a copyist's error. Both sites are well away from early Germanic settlement, and far enough from battles north of the Hadrian's Wall to imply a force existed that extended over a wide area of the former provinces. Indeed, the text only gives us these two choices and we have no good reason to ignore the obvious, which is Chester. So, we now have six of the twelve battles in the *Historia* located.

The next battle is the one most talked about, but I feel many ignore the simplest answer. Mount Badon is associated with Bath, not just by later writers but in the *Historia* itself. The 'Wonders of Britain' section make it quite clear the author identifies Badon with Bath. Additionally, here is a location that we know was referred to much later as Badon. The reason this is not accepted is usually for two reasons. Firstly, it's in the wrong place with the *Anglo-Saxon Chronicle* recording Bath being taken much later in 577. Secondly, why would Gildas be using an apparent Old English name for a British location?

I have attempted to offer a reasonable explanation to these points. However, it is clear what the *Historia* says. It regards Badon as Bath and therefore Mount Badonis as a hill outside the city. It is possible there was significant Germanic settlement in the area and that the Belgae spoke a Friesian dialect, thus Badon was in common usage by the time of Gildas. It's certainly far easier to accept that conclusion than to scour the country for Badon-type names and then fit an explanation to it. It is possible the ninth-century author of the *Historia* simply assumed Badon was Bath. However, the evidence points to a southern location for the region in which Gildas is writing. We can have some confidence in agreeing with the experts and accepting Badon was 'somewhere in Wessex'.

A battle in the north, one in the south, one in the west and four in the east. I am therefore fairly comfortable with locating seven of the battles. The others are more problematic but we must differentiate again from those we have some clue about, and those for which we are scrambling in the dark. With that in mind, there are two battles I think we have a reasonable suggestion for. The first is battle 1 at the River Glein, purely because Bede, a hundred years before the *Historia*, names the Glen in the *Ecclesiastical History of the English People*. The second is battle 11 at *breguoin*, which linguistically seems to derive from Bremenium, the Roman auxiliary fort north of Hadrian's Wall.

I am not nearly as confident as others in identifying Baschurch for battle 6 on the River Bassas. However, I am persuaded it is more likely a Brittonic name, rather than a Saxon one and we do have the reference to the 'Churches of Bassa' in the *Canu Heledd*. This isn't much but it's the best we have, so I will stick with Baschurch or the nearby Basford in Cheshire. Regarding Castle Guinnion, I think the use of the word *Castello* suggests a Roman fort. I am far more comfortable stating where it isn't. Winchester, for example, appears as Guinntguic. The nearest candidate appears to be the Roman fort at Binchester, near Durham, which has evidence for continued occupation in the fifth century. Vonovium was also known as Uinouion in Brittonic. I am even less comfortable with this identification than with Bassas. Battle 10 on the River Tribuit is the most difficult one. The reference in the poem *Pa Gur* suggests a northern location. Beyond that, it's impossible to say. None of the theories are particularly convincing. Camlan is slightly different in that we do have a number of different theories, but with no good reason to pick any one over another. Map 37 represents my opinion of the most likely locations.

Some theorists have made a case for placing all twelve battles from the *Historia* and Camlan in one particular region. Modern authors have put forward a whole plethora of different theories. Unfortunately, many depend on substantial leaps of logic, convoluted etymologies and a loose reading of genealogies, aside from the uncomfortable fact that none of the sources or genealogies are contemporary or can be relied upon. Higham lists just a few of the best-known theories:[42]

Map 37: Most likely battle locations

- Scotland and the north: Carroll, Ardrey, Stirling, Breeze, Moffatt, Goodrich, Johnson
- The north: Keegan, Field, Bromwich
- North Wales: Blake and Lloyd
- South Wales: Blackett & Wilson, Gilbert, Barber
- Shropshire: Phillips and Keatman
- West Country: Alcock
- Devon and Cornwall: Dunning, Castledon
- Lincolnshire: Green, Leahy
- Essex, Middlesex, East Anglia: Storr, Morris, Laycock

We can see the lack of consensus, which perhaps demonstrates why academics such as Dumville, Higham and Halsall are sceptical.

Table 14: Regional locations for battle list

Battle	Northern Arthur	Lincolnshire	Central and Eastern Wales and West Midlands	South Wales, Wessex and the West Country
1 River Glein	River Glen, Northumberland Glen Water, Strathclyde	River Glen, Lincolnshire	River Gleiniant, Llanidloes, Wales	Glynde Reach, Sussex
2–5 River Dubglas, Linnuis	Douglas Water in Glen Douglas. Lennox area	Unknown river, Lincoln area	Any of the Dulas-type river names in Wales	River Divelish near Lindinis/Ilchester
6 Bassas	Cambuslang, Glasgow	Bassingbourn, Cambridgeshire	Baschurch, Shropshire	Old Basing, Hampshire
7 Silua Celidonis Cat Coit Celidon	Caledonian Forest, north of Hadrian's Wall	Relies on a misinterpretation of forest of someone called Celidon	Relies on a misinterpretation of forest of someone called Celidon	Relies on a misinterpretation of forest of someone called Celidon
8 Castello Guinnion	Binchester Roman fort	Unknown	Unknown	Gwynion, Powys; Winchester
9 Urbe Legionis	York	York	Chester	Carleon
10 River Tribruit	Frew, Scotland River Teviot	Unknown	Unknown	River Twrc, Wales
11 Monte Agned/Breguoin	Edinburgh. High Rochester Roman Fort	Unknown	Leintwardine, Herefordshire	Catbrain, Bristol
12 Monte Badonis	Bowden Hill	Baumber	Buxton	Bath
13 Camlan	*Camboglanna*, Castlesteads. Cambuslang, Glasgow. Camelon, Falkirk.	Unknown	Camlan, Mallwyd. Afon Gamlan	River Camel, Cornwall. River Cam, Somerset.

Many of these are rather far-fetched and there are some gaps, but it is a useful exercise because it tells us something rather important. If the battle list is a poem and to be treated as a whole, then it is unlikely Arthur was a local leader fighting battles in one region. The only area that one could argue dominates and has the most credible identifications is the north. This has led some to nominate a northern leader based on the Roman Command of the *Dux Britanniarum*. One

Map 38: Main areas of interest

example of a northern version of the battle list comes from Stephen Holden from the Facebook group, 'King Arthur and the Lords of the North'. He lists the battles as follows: 1. White Lyne; 2–5. Black Lyne; 6. Possibly around King Water, Banks Burn or Burtholme Beck; 7. The woods extending and from Little Salkeld on the Eden and Inglewood; 8. Probably one of the mile castles on Hadrian's Wall (Whinshields, Castle Nick, Chesterwood, Cumquencath or Ninekirks); 9. Carlisle & Stanwix or perhaps Corbridge; 10. About Thirwall Castle, Greenhead; 11. Possibly Beacon Hill, Penrith, near Brougham; 12. Cross Fell, Cumbria; Camlan at Castlesteads (Camboglanna after Crawford, 1935) and Avalon, perhaps nearby was meant to be Brampton Old Church, only

9 miles from 'Arthur Lives at Merrie Carlisle'. There are, of course, many other similar lists from a range of theorists in articles and blogs.

However, the general consensus from academic historians is we cannot improve much on the analysis of Jackson:[43]

1. *Glein*, possibly Northumberland or Lincolnshire Glen but 'highly uncertain'.
2–5. *Duglas regione Linnuis*, 'probably' Lindsey.
6. *Bassas*, unknown.
7. *silua celidonis, cat coit celidon*, 'certainly' *silva caledoniae* in Strathclyde.
8. *Castellum Guinnion*, unknown.
9. *Urbe legos, cair lion*, 'certainly' Chester.
10. *Traht treuroit*, unknown
11. *Monte breguoin, bregion*, 'probably' High Rochester.
12. *Monte Badonis*, 'somewhere in Wessex'.

We can see here that expert opinion does not believe that none of the battles can be identified at all. The oft-quoted and well-respected Guy Halsall states: 'The locations of all these battles are unknown and unknowable'.[44] But he precedes this emphatic statement by saying: 'With the exception of the battle of the Caledonian Forest, which ought to be somewhere north of Hadrian's Wall and Linnuis which *might* be Lindsey…' Personally, I agree with Jackson and would include Chester. But for argument's sake, if we agree with Halsall, then we can still say one battle was likely in the north and another four 'might' be in Lincolnshire. That, at least, is something.

It is worth looking at the north in more detail. It is unlikely any formal structure survived beyond the mid-fifth century. We do have evidence of continued use of some areas and, notably, some forts. We also have the existence of powerful British kingdoms such as Rheged, Elmet and Gododdin. It is interesting Geoffrey of Monmouth has Ambrosius making his base at York after he defeats the Saxons, rather than London, but we can't trust that source. It is possible a powerful warlord was able to keep the north under one authority throughout the period in which Arthur would have lived. It's equally possible the northern province was able to retain its political authority, even as its neighbours fragmented. Battles in Linnuis and at Chester, and even as far north as the borders of the *Gododdin*, would be in line with this. The one outlier is probably Badon, which is difficult to place in the north.

Another suggestion often put forward to identify Arthur is Artur Mac Aedan. This is even more problematic than the northern British warlord. The placing of *Urbe Legionis* is a major stumbling block as there is no suggestion from Adomnán or Bede that such an event occurred at the end of the sixth century. Sites such as Dumbarton or the legionary fortress at Inchtuthill, north of the Tay, have been suggested. One could pick any site in Britain that had a Roman military presence using that logic. The main problem with Artur as a candidate is that he is in the wrong time: at least fifty years too late. Additionally, we are left to explain why an obscure prince of the Dal Riata became a hero for the Britons, from Wales to Cornwall, and for the Bretons in Armorica. There is nothing in Adomnán's *Life of St Columba* to suggest Artur is Arthur. It is possible that the author of the *Historia* found a battle poem concerning Artur and assumed it was Arthur, and thus added Badon. But then we would still be left with a convoluted explanation for *Urbe Legionis*. A more credible possibility is that the battle poem is of a northern Arthur and Badon was added to his exploits. But there is absolutely nothing to prevent an early sixth-century Arthur being based anywhere in the west or north, or indeed, across the whole land with several different bases, as the Triads suggest. The fact one area predominates in battle locations would not necessary mean that was where he was based.

Let us return to the sources. The *Historia* was written around 300 years after Arthur lived. It may have been a copy of an earlier manuscript and, in turn, may reflect a late sixth-century battle poem. Whatever the case, it is not unreasonable to state that a ninth-century audience would have accepted it. Similarly, a tenth-century scribe would expect his entries for Badon and Camlan in the *Annales Cambriae* to be believed. They would have known that there was a Battle of Chester in the early seventh century that had nothing to do with Arthur. It follows that they would view this as a separate battle. It also shows that Arthur is already associated with Badon by this time. Additionally, Badon was already an accepted name for Bath by then.

The author is clear when he places Arthur: after the death of Hengest and St Patrick, and before Ida reigns in Bernicia. He is reasonably clear who Arthur is fighting. Octha comes down from the north to Kent, then Arthur fights against *them*. So, it was possibly the Angles in the north, those in the south-east and/or Anglo-Saxon immigrants, settlements or mercenaries in general. We must remember that the land lost in the partition likely included the whole of the former province, Maxima Caesariensis. '*Them*' could just as easily be a catch-all phrase for all Germanic settlements, including Saxons. One could speculate that Arthur also fought against Picts and Irish, and this got lost over the centuries. But that's not what the text says. He's not titled a king, but he leads the kings of the Britons into battle. This implies, in Arthur's time, the provinces had already fragmented into petty kingdoms, probably based on *civitates*.

Arthur then fights twelve battles. There's no reason to assume they are in order, or that they were on one campaign. Despite what others have claimed, two are easy to locate: the Caledonian Forest and Chester. If we only knew this, we could make a reasonable hypothesis of a northern leader based at York, or in one of the military forts of the old command of the *Dux Britanniarum* or the northern Roman province. The next group of battles are in the region of the Linnuis. Whether this is in Lincolnshire or Lennox, it would still be on the border of the northern province. Lincolnshire is far more likely linguistically and historically. There are significant Angle settlements and evidence for a British enclave surviving into the sixth century. Badon is the last battle location I have any confidence about. In Bath, we have an area that was populated by the Belgae, was later known as Badon and remained in British hands until 577. We can accept that for the rest, at best, we have highly speculative suggestions and, at the worst, no clue at all. But if we just plot these four locations on a map, they give us an interesting picture, especially if we include the likely boundary of the south-eastern province and the line showing early Anglo-Saxon settlements.

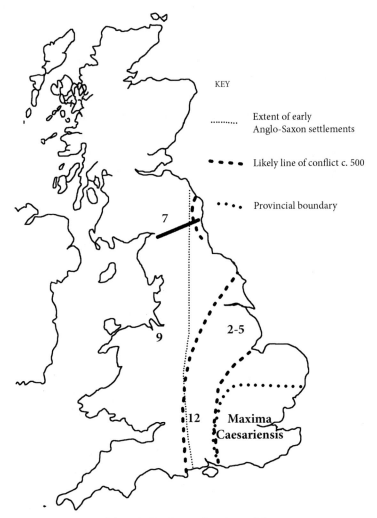

KEY

.... Extent of early
Anglo-Saxon settlements

- • - • - • Likely line of conflict c. 500

• • • • Provincial boundary

Map 39: Battles sited with confidence

We can see that these battles, at least, all appear to be outside the south-eastern province. The hypothesis was that these battles would likely be along, or near, any border or partition. Yet Chester and the Caledonian Forest are outliers. Indeed, many of the suggestions for the more difficult sites are in the north. We thus have a pattern pointing to some battles in areas outside early Anglo-Saxon settlements. Perhaps having lost Kent and the surrounding areas, other *civitates* were keen on pushing their Anglo-Saxon settlements out. Alternatively, *foederati* were forced out of their garrisons, which would make any location from the northern command, Hadrian's Wall, Chester or around Lincoln a reasonable suggestion.

It is true the *Historia* is not trusted as a reliable source. Yet it was written for a purpose and would have likely been accepted by a ninth-century reader. It is interesting that none of the characters in that part of the work are knowingly fictitious. It is likely a ninth-century audience accepted Arthur was a historical figure and that the battle list was genuine. Working on that admitted assumption, we have come to two interesting conclusions based on the historical background and likely context. Some of the battles, at least, were not in areas of early settlement. There are a number of possibilities: we simply haven't yet found evidence of settlement; some battles were defensive against raids deep inside Brittonic territory; it reflects the clearing out of *foederati* garrisons; or the conflicts included civil wars or battles against Picts and Irish, wrongly attributed to Anglo-Saxons.

The second point is if the whole list is valid, it is far more likely it reflects a wide-ranging leader, fighting from the south of the former Britannia Prima to the north on the borders of the Gododdin: an alternative someone in the former northern province or fragmented military command of the *Dux Britanniarum*. There would be nothing impossible about such a figure leading forces down the surviving road networks to fight southern Germanic groups. It's equally possible all the battles were within, or around, the borders of the northern province. If, as is more likely, Badon was in the south, it could have been erroneously attributed to the list.

Apart from the battle list, Arthur's mention is confined to one line: 'Then Arthur fought against them in those days, together with the kings of the British, but he was their leader in battle.' A similar line is used in Chapter 62 for another warrior: 'At that time Outigern then fought bravely against the English nation.' We get no further information as to who Outigern was. He seems to have lived after the time of Ida when 'Aneirin and Taliesin...were famed in British verse.' This suggests the second half of the sixth century. Yet we have no legends of Outigern, no tales of magical swords or knights. Geoffrey of Monmouth, writing 300 years later, chose Arthur to focus on. No doubt there were many stories at the time that inspired him, but much of the legend we know today was an invention of later centuries. Let us now turn to Geoffrey of Monmouth and other legends to see if we can get any further clues.

Chapter 8

Battles and Locations from Other Sources

For the sake of completeness, we will look at some other sources. They are all much later than the *Historia Brittonum* and shouldn't be considered historically accurate. But they do indicate which traditions had been handed down and survived 600 years or more.

Geoffrey of Monmouth: *The History of the Kings of Britain*

The *Historia Regum Britanniae* (The History of the Kings of Britain) was written in 1136 and attempts to trace a detailed history of Britain over nearly 2,000 years. Geoffrey is thought to have been Welsh or Breton and seems to have a connection with the area of Monmouth, as he mentions Caerleon-on-Usk several times and places Arthur there. The book is dedicated to the son of Henry I, Robert (Earl of Gloucester), and to Waleron, Count of Mellent. It begins with the foundation of Britain by a Trojan prince, Brutus, after the fall of Troy. Brutus defeats many giants that lived on the islands and gives Britain its name. We then get a very ahistorical account with many plainly fictitious entries, most notably Brennus, the Gaulish chieftain, who captured Rome in 387 BC, becoming two British brothers, Belinus and Brennius.

When we get to the period we are focusing on, Geoffrey roughly follows the narrative in the *Historia Brittonum*. He adds further details though. After the Romans leave, the Britons request help from King Aldoneus of Armorica. His brother Constantine comes instead and is made king. He has three children: Constans, Ambrosius Aurelianus and Uther Pendragon. Constantine dies and Vortigern encourages Constans to leave holy orders and become king. He then conspires to have him assassinated and has the murderers killed to cover up the crime. The two younger brothers, Ambrosius and Uther, are whisked off to Armorica to escape the same fate. He then invites Hengest and Horsa, and their Saxon mercenaries, to settle in Lindsey, near Lincoln, where Hengest builds a fortress.

At this point in the story, the implication is that Britain is still controlled by the Romano-British. The arrival of Hengest's daughter, Renwein, causes Vortigern to ask for her hand in marriage and give Hengest Kent in return.

Hengest advises Vortigern to allow his son Octa and his cousin Ebissa to arrive with 300 ships, and settle near the wall to fight the Picts. This, in turn, leads to Vortigern's son Vortimer deposing his father and forcing the Saxons to leave after four battles. Renwein poisons Vortimer, Vortigern retakes the crown and Hengest returns with an implausible 300,000 men.

The subsequent peace conference results in the murder of 300 British nobles, the imprisonment of Vortigern and the capture of London, York, Winchester and Lincoln. We recall that the *Historia* confines the area to Essex, Sussex and Middlesex. Vortigern escapes but shortly after, the now-grown-up Ambrosius and Uther land and burn him alive inside Castle Generou in South Wales. Ambrosius becomes king and defeats the Saxons at Maisbeli and Kaerconan, both sites unidentified. Hengest is executed which, if we believe the *Anglo-Saxon Chronicle*, occurred in 488. Ambrosius rules from York, interestingly, not from London. Octa and Ebissa surrender and are given Bernicia. Later, a surviving son of Vortigern invades with an Irish king and is defeated by Uther, who becomes king after Ambrosius is poisoned. On the eve of battle, Uther sees a two-headed dragon in the sky with a fiery tail, from which he gets his title 'head dragon', hence Pendragon (or in some sources, Bendragon).

We then get the tale of Merlin aiding Uther to change appearance to seduce Ygraine at Tintagel, where Arthur is conceived. In terms of dates, there is a comet recorded for 497 in a fourteenth-century text, *Flores Historiarum*. The only date Geoffrey does give is 542 for Camlan so, working back with the timeframes he also provides, gives the year 521 for Badon, which occurs shortly after Arthur's coronation at the age of 15. This, then, places Arthur's birth in 506, which places his floruit at the latter end of the range that is considered likely. The references of various saints, St Samson (c. 485–565) and St Dubricius (465–555) seem to tie in with this, as do the various *Saints' Lives* in other sources. Yet Arthur's Roman war, as claimed by Geoffrey, is associated with figures dated to the second half of the fifth century. Perhaps he simply stole the career of Riothamus (c.470) and added it to Arthur's.

When we get to Arthur's battles, we can see Geoffrey appears to use some of the locations from the *Historia* list. Arthur is crowned at Silchester and he immediately marches on the Saxons, now led by Colgrin and Baldulf, based at York. There then begins a series of battles:

1. The first battle is on the River Douglas, which one assumes is on the way to York. Arthur is victorious after a closely fought battle.
2. The second battle has Arthur besieging York, which is possibly a reference to the City of the Legions in the *Historia*. He wins a battle against a relief force, but is forced to retreat to London due to the arrival of Childeric and

600 ships. He requests assistance from Hoel of Brittany, son of Arthur's sister and King Budicius.

3. The third battle is a victory at Kaerluideoit, Lincoln. Arthur relieves a siege on the town, killing 6,000 and forcing them to flee.
4. The fourth is at Caledon Wood, another nod to the battle list. After three days, the Saxons finally surrender. There is a mention of a 'foray' against the Picts and Scots, but no details of a battle.
5. The fifth is the Battle of Badon: the Saxons, having promised to leave, break the treaty and sail to Devon before marching on Bath. Arthur's cousin, Cador, Duke of Cornwall, pursues the Saxons to Thanet, reminiscent of Vortimer's four battles, although Arthur is not involved.

Arthur then fights a series of battles against the Picts. He relieves his nephew, Hoel, under siege at Alclud, Dumbarton, in the Kingdom of Strathclyde, although it's not clear if a battle was fought. He then advances to Moray where the Scots and Picts are under siege. Three times Arthur defeats them 'in this particular district.' The Picts seek refuge on islands in Loch Lomond. Arthur besieges them for fifteen days, forcing their surrender although, presumably, without a battle. Gilmaurius, a king of Ireland, lands to assist the Picts under siege at Loch Lomond and is defeated. So, this could be four to six battles, depending how we count it. It is likely the much later *Scottish Chronicles*, and other sources identifying the north or Scotland, derived from Geoffrey. Arthur then marries Guinevere before invading Ireland, winning a battle, followed by another victory in Iceland. The Orkneys and Gotland surrender.

Twelve years go by, meaning Arthur is at least 27 years of age at this point. He invades Norway, wins a battle and conquers Denmark too. Next, he invades Gaul, wins another battle, then defeats their leader, Frollo, in single combat outside Paris and subdues the whole province. None of these foreign escapades have a shred of evidence. In fact, we can safely say at this point that this part, at least, is all a figment of Geoffrey's vivid imagination. A further nine years pass. Arthur is now at least 36 when we come to a part of the tale often forgotten in later retellings, and always left out of more modern renditions.

Messengers from the Roman Procurator, Lucius Hiberius, arrive at Arthur's court at Caerleon-on-Usk, demanding tribute and submission. Arthur refuses and, egged on by his generals, leads an army to Gaul to fight the Romans, leaving Mordred in charge of Britain. There is a short story of Arthur defeating a giant at Mont St Michel, in which he remembers another giant-killing act. Arthur marches towards Autun, some 200 miles south-east of Paris. En route, near the River Aube, he meets the Romans and talks quickly turn into a skirmish, then a battle. Next, an attempted ambush on the road to Paris is thwarted and

7-9 Moray: Three battles

10 Besieges Picts in Loch Lomond
11 Defeats Irish army

6 Dumbarton:
Relieves siege

4 Caledon Wood

2 York

1?

3 Lincoln

London
5 Badon Silchester

Map 40: Geoffrey of Monmouth – Arthur's battles

results in a British victory. Arthur is not present at either of these battles. Lucius retreats to Langres, on the road to Autun. Arthur marches ahead and blocks the road in the valley of Saussy, near Dijon in Eastern France. A huge battle ends in Arthur's victory and he prepares to invade Italy and take Rome.

We then return to battles in Britain. Mordred betrays Arthur, seizes the crown and allies himself with Saxons, led by Chelric. He records 'the treacherous tyrant was living adulterously and out of wedlock with Queen Guinevere who had broken the vows of her earlier marriage.' Arthur returns to Britain and defeats Mordred in a series of battles.

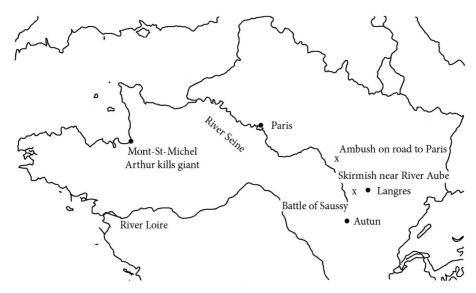

Map 41: Arthur's war against the Romans in Gaul

1. Mordred met Arthur as he landed at Richborough in Kent. Both armies suffered 'great slaughter' but Arthur occupied the shore and drove Mordred away.
2. Mordred retreated to Winchester where Arthur besieged him. Again, there was immense slaughter outside the city but again, Mordred fled, this time by ship to Cornwall.

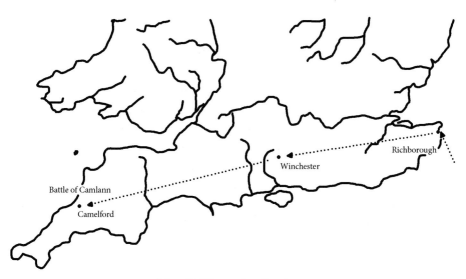

Map 42: The road to Camlann

3. Arthur followed and caught up at the River Camblam, which Geoffrey identifies as near Slaughter Bridge at Camelford on the River Camel. Mordred is killed and Arthur is mortally wounded. He is carried to the Isle of Avalon so that his wounds may be attended to. No further details are given.

Geoffrey states the Battle of Camlann was in 542, which implies Arthur was about 36 when he died. He places the battle in the time of the Eastern Emperor Justinian, when the Romans were trying to reconquer Italy and the sons of Clovis ruled in Frankia. We thus have five initial battles against the Saxons, five battles against the Picts and one against the Irish. There then follows a victory in Ireland, Iceland, Norway and France, before his 'Roman war' and the epic battle at Saussey. Lastly, he fights three battles against Mordred.

Saints' Lives

There are a number of saints' lives that mention Arthur. None of them can be considered historical. They are often written to enhance the status of the saint, or to justify rights to land by including a story of a king granting property to the saint or monastery. An eleventh-century *Life of St Goeznovius* concerns a sixth- or seventh-century saint from Cornwall. If the date of 1019 is to be believed, and it is controversial, it predates Geoffrey of Monmouth by a hundred years. This is important as it is the only other reference that places Arthur in Gaul. In the preface, it refers to the Saxons invited by Vortigern: 'Presently their pride was checked for a while through the great Arthur, king of the Britons. They were largely cleared from the island and reduced to subjection. But when this same Arthur, after many victories which he won gloriously in Britain and in Gaul...'

No locations are given. An eleventh-century Breton tale places Arthur in Brittany and receiving help from St Efflam in killing a dragon, which Arthur had been battling with. There's a hint of Tristan and Iseult about this tale, although St Efflam is thought to have lived in the last half of the fifth century, so may not have been contemporary with the other saints.

The *Life of St Cadoc* (c.497–580) was written in around 1086 in South Wales. In the prologue, a battle occurs in South Wales between King Gwynllyw and King Brychan, on the border between Gwynlliog and Brycheiniog. Arthur, accompanied by Kai and Bedwyr, witnesses the battle and joins forces with Gwynllyw. Later in the tale, St Cadoc gives refuge in Gwynlliog to a fugitive from Arthur, who killed three of Arthur's men. Arthur then comes to the River Usk with a 'very great force' and demands the man. Cadoc intercedes, negotiates compensation and is granted certain land rights.

The *Life of St Carannog* (sixth century) was written in the twelfth century. The saint travelled from Wales across the Severn sea to Devon with a magic altar, which he later loses: 'In those times Cadwy and Arthur were reigning in that country, dwelling in Dindraithov [Dunstan Castle, Exmoor]. And Arthur came wandering about that he might find a most formidable serpent, huge and terrible, which had been ravaging twelve portions of the land of Carrum.' Arthur agrees to find the altar if the saint captures the dragon. This comes to pass and the saint is granted land rights in Carrum, thought to be Carhampton in Somerset. So here, Arthur is associated with the West Country.

The *Life of St Padarn* (c.500–550) is set in Ceredigion in West Wales. Arthur, 'a certain tyrant', attempts to steal a red tunic from the saint. The saint causes the earth to 'swallow him up' and Arthur is forced to beg for forgiveness. The *Life of St Illtud* was written in Wales in the twelfth century and there is one reference concerning the saint travelling from Brittany to Arthur's court. The location isn't given but Illtud leaves shortly after to visit the king of Glamorgan.

There are two versions of the *Life of St Gildas*. The first, written in Rhuys in the ninth century, fails to mention Arthur. The second is a twelfth-century Welsh tale which has Arthur killing Hueil, the brother of Gildas. This is later used by Gerald of Wales, writing in around 1190, to explain why Gildas ignores Arthur in his tract. In the story, King Melvas of 'the summer country' captures Gwenhwyfar, Arthur's wife. Arthur besieges Glastonbury and Gildas intercedes, brings peace and conveniently gains extensive land rights to give to the Abbot of Glastonbury.

In summary, we have seven saints' lives. One source may support Geoffrey in having Arthur fighting in Gaul, although there's doubt as to when it was written. A second places him in Brittany fighting dragons. The other five all place him in South Wales or the West Country, interacting with early sixth-century saints.

Map 43: Saints' Lives

Welsh legends

Preiddeu Annfwn (The spoils of Annfwn) has Arthur with three boatloads of warriors, sailing to the underworld to capture various treasures, one of which is a magical cauldron guarded by nine maidens. There are echoes here of the nine maidens of Avalon. There are also similarities with the tale of *Culhwch and Olwen* where Arthur sails to Diwrnach in Ireland to steal a cauldron. In this latter tale, Arthur is enlisted to help in completing various tasks so that Culhwch can marry the daughter of a giant. One of the main tasks involves the hunt for the boar, Twrch Trwyth. This starts in Ireland and moves through South Wales, across the River Severn then through the West Country, before disappearing into the sea off Cornwall. The earliest copy is from the fourteenth century, but it is thought to originate from the eleventh and thus predates Geoffrey of Monmouth.

The *Elegy for Geraint son of Erbin* is from the thirteenth-century *Black Book of Carmarthen*, but may stem from as early as the ninth century. It celebrates Geraint's deeds at the Battle of Llongborth: 'In Llongborth I saw Arthur, And brave men who hewed down with steel, Emperor and conductor of the toil.' Langport in Somerset or Portsmouth in Hampshire have been suggested. A 'Geraint of the South' is mentioned in *Y Gododdin*, so it's possible we have a southern or West Country location. Another tale, *Geraint and Enid*, from the thirteenth-century *Red Book of Hengest*, concerns the son of Erbin of Dumnonia, which was Devon and Cornwall combined.

The Dream of Rhonabwy is another text from the *Red Book of Hengest* although it's thought to have originated from the twelfth century. In this tale, Rhonabwy falls asleep and dreams he is back in Arthur's time. He dreams he is travelling towards Rhyd-y-Groes on the River Severn. He then meets Iddawg, 'the Churn of Britain', named because he caused the Battle of Camlann. He deliberately changed the messages between Arthur and his enemy Medrawd. At the ford, they come upon Arthur's camp prior to the Battle of Badon. Yet the ford is over a hundred miles north of Bath. It is, in fact, just 20 miles south-west of Shrewsbury, near Welshpool and the border between England and Wales. At the end of the tale, a truce is declared for a 'fortnight and a month', and the army leaves for Cornwall with Kai proclaiming 'whosoever will follow Arthur, let him be with him tonight in Cornwall.' This is rather difficult to imagine as it's over 200 miles.

These tales are not, of course, historical and they are full of mystical and magical elements. The most we can say is, like in the *Saints' Lives*, there are hints of Wales and the West Country in terms of locations. The last story we get any clues from is *Pa Gur yv y porthaur?* (Who is the gatekeeper?), from the *Black Book of Carmarthen*. Arthur is refused entry until he tells of his exploits and those of his companions. We get the following lines throughout the poem (locations in square brackets):

Did not Manawyd bring, perforated shields from Trywruid? [River Tribuit]

And Anwas Adeiniog, And Llwch Llawynnog--Guardians were they, On Eiddyn Cymminog, [Edinburgh]

Arthur distributed gifts, The blood trickled down. In the hail of Awarnach, Fighting with a hag, he cleft the head of Palach [unknown]

In the fastnesses of Dissethach, In Mynyd Eiddyn, He contended with Cynvyn; By the hundred there they fell, There they fell by the hundred, Before the accomplished Bedwyr. [Edinburgh]

On the strands of Trywruid, Contending with Garwlwyd, [River Tribuit. Garwlwyd also appears in Welsh Triads and is translated as 'man-dog/ rough-grey'. Possibly synonymous with a werewolf in mythology.]

The heights of Ystavingon Cai pierced nine witches [Unknown location but nine witches similar to the poem Peredur, the Life of St Samson and nine maidens of Annwn, or Avalon]

Cai the fair went to Mona, To devastate Llewon. His shield was ready Against Cath Palug When the people welcomed him [Anglesey]

If we ignore the mythical elements, we get but one clue: Eiddyn is mentioned just before, or just after, Trywuid, twice. If there is a connection and Trywuid is the River Tribuit in the *Historia*, then we have confirmation that Tribuit is close to Edinburgh and Arthur would be linked to the Kingdom of the Gododdin. The River Teviot would also be fairly close to the Gododdin border, which, in turn, would explain why a northern author of *Y Gododdin* would reference Arthur. Unfortunately, none of these Welsh legends are in any way historical. The earliest dates to many hundreds of years after Arthur's time.

Camelot

Camelot is mentioned for the first time, in passing, by Chrétien de Troyes in the twelfth century. He distinguishes it from Arthur's chief court at Caerleon, which Geoffrey of Monmouth's earlier work names as Arthur's main base in South Wales. In the thirteenth century, the French Romances increase the importance of Camelot to the detriment of Caerleon. The earliest written source, in the eleventh century, *Culhwch and Olwen*, names Celliwig ('forest grove') in Cornwall as Arthur's court. The Welsh Triads name three of Arthur's courts: Pen Rhionydd in the north; Celliwig in Cornwall; and Mynyw in Wales (St David's). The first two are unidentified although there are numerous suggestions. Other tales and legends name different sites: Quimper in Brittany in *Lancelot Romance*; Carduel, Wales in Chrétien's *The Knight and the Lion* (unidentified); Cardigan in Chrétien's *Eric and Enide*; and Stirling in Beroul's twelfth-century *Tristan*.

Suggested identifications include Camulodunum (Colchester); Carlisle; Caerleon; Cadbury Castle in Somerset; Camelon, near Falkirk in Scotland; and Winchester, among many others. But the disappointing fact is none of the early Welsh legends or Geoffrey of Monmouth mention Camelot. It is therefore quite possible it was an invention of Chrétien de Troyes that was copied by later writers.

Avalon

Avalon is first mentioned by Geoffrey of Monmouth. Arthur is taken to be healed by Morgan Le Fay after Camlan. Insula Avallonis means 'Isle of fruit (or apple) trees'. Later Welsh texts use the name Ynys Afallon or Afallach, which could be linked to Emain Abhlach, a mythical island paradise, possibly identified with the Isle of Man or Arran. In Geoffrey's Vita Merlini, a sea voyage is taken to the 'Isle of Apples'. The French Romances identified it with Glastonbury and in 1190, there was a 'discovery' of a burial on the site of the abbey, with a cross inscribed referring to Arthur and Avalon. This discovery is believed to be a fake by the monks to drum up money from visitors after a destructive fire.

There is an Avallon in Burgundy, close to the west of where Riothamus was defeated. Aballava, or Avallana, is a Roman fort at the western end of Hadrian's Wall, not far from one of the candidates for Camlan, the Roman fort called Camboglanna. Another suggestion is Ile d'Aval off the coast of Brittany. In AD 45, Mela gave an account of an island off Brittany, which was home to nine priestesses. This reminds us of the nine maidens in *The spoils of Annwfn*. Similar to Camelot, we have the very real possibility this is a late addition to the legend from the imagination of a twelfth-century writer. In fact, I am going to commit 'Arthurian heresy' here and state I have come to the conclusion that Avalon, Camelot and mythical ladies in lakes holding swords are all later inventions, and have nothing to do with a historical Arthur if he lived.

Miscellaneous

There are also many topographical features all over Britain: twenty-two Arthur's stones, thirty Arthur's Quoits (discus-shaped stones); five tables and three round tables; eight seats; six halls, camps or other types of residence; five graves; and fifteen other sites referring to Arthur.[1] We can see these on Map 43, along with Arthur's courts from the Welsh Triads and Caerleon from Geoffrey of Monmouth. I have also added the path of the boar, *Twrch Trwyth*, in *Culhwch and Olwen*. They support what we already know. Arthur is associated with, and connected to, the landscape and culture of Wales, the West Country and the north.

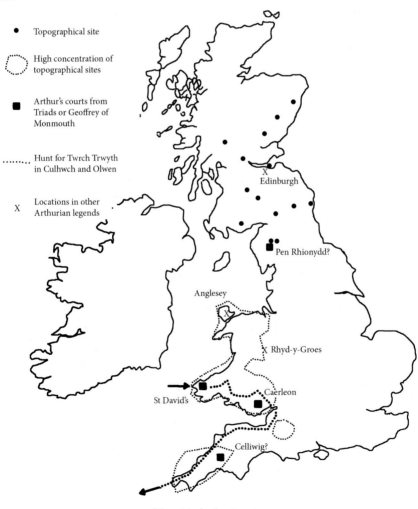

KEY

●   Topographical site

⬭   High concentration of topographical sites

■   Arthur's courts from Triads or Geoffrey of Monmouth

⋯⋯⋯   Hunt for Twrch Trwyth in Culhwch and Olwen

X   Locations in other Arthurian legends

Edinburgh

Pen Rhionydd?

Anglesey

Rhyd-y-Groes

St David's

Caerleon

Celliwig?

Map 44: Arthurian sites

The name

Regarding the name, Arthur, there are two main theories: the first is a native, Celtic, derivation.[2] The second regards a Latin source, from Artorius, as more likely.[3] In fact, this has been described as 'phonologically perfect'.[4] However, the sources never refer to Artorius but rather the Brittonic form, Arthur or Arthurus.[5] The earliest version of the name from the *Historia Brittonum* is *Arturus* which, along with Arcturus, would be a correct Latin version.[6] This could be translated as Bear (Art-) and guardian, which would be understood as a star in the constellation of Ursa Major – The Great Bear; hence, 'Guardian of the Bear'.

In Welsh, such as *Y Gododdin*, *Arth* is also Bear, but the ending '-ur' is not common in Brittonic languages. I summed up the problem in my previous book: 'The ending 'ur' may have come from 'gwr', meaning 'man', which would translate Arthur as 'Man of the Bear' or 'Bear-man'. However, the '-wr' and '-ur' sounds are different and in Welsh poetry, Arthur is always rhymed with -ur endings.'[7] Additionally, by the tenth century, this would be most likely written as *Artgur*, which is never seen. By this time, it is Arthur, and some versions of the Harleian Rescension spell it *Artur*. This is likely the oldest Brittonic version and the Latin would be *Arturus* as mentioned. This would suggest a Latin etymology is the most probable, yet we have seen how four Irish-influenced dynasties named their sons 'Artur'.

Indeed, to both Latin and Brittonic speakers, Arthur or Arturus would be understood as meaning 'bear-man'. Frustratingly, it could simply be a nickname. We can, however, dismiss similar-sounding names, such as Arthwys, as these have a different and well-documented root.[8] Unfortunately, this has not prevented myriads of theories built around such false etymologies. To conclude, we cannot decide. It could be Latin or Celtic, or even a nickname. Even if we found it was more likely a Roman name, this would not rule out someone in the later Welsh genealogies because there are numerous examples, as we shall see.

Genealogies

There are three main genealogies and they are as follows: firstly, the Harleian genealogies, held in the British Library (MS 3859), containing the *Annales Cambriae* and *Historia Brittonum* dated to 1100. As it contains the paternal and maternal genealogy of Owain Hywel Dda, who died in 988, they were likely compiled in the tenth century. They include descendants of Cunedda, who founded many of the Welsh kingdoms and from whom many of the Welsh saints descended. Secondly, the *Bonedd Gwyr y Gogledd* (Descent of the Men of the

North) showing the kings of *Hen Ogledd* (the Old North) in the sixth century. The earliest manuscript is late thirteenth century. It shows the descendants of Coel Hen, including Urien of Rheged. Some of these figures feature in the siege of Lindisfarne recorded in the *Historia Brittonum* (c.572–9) or the Battle of Arfderydd (573), mentioned in the *Annales Cambriae*, when Myrddin went mad. These figures are placed a generation after Arthur, yet are dated perhaps a little later than one might expect. Thirdly, we have genealogies from Jesus College (MS 20) compiled in the late fourteenth century, including a number of Welsh lineages, especially those of South Wales. It has to be acknowledged first that none of the earliest Welsh genealogies contain Arthur.[9]

The genealogical tables can be quite complex and there are some contradictions. For our purposes, it is sufficient to simplify these late sources. We can view it as two houses: the first, Cunedda, in North Wales, who came from Manaw Gododdin in the north. From Cunedda, we get various Welsh saints and founders of kingdoms. Importantly, certain saints and Maelgwn of Gwynedd are great-grandsons. The second house is the Coelings from the north. From Coel Hen, we get various northern lines.

The later genealogies add Arthur into the same generation as Maelgwn and the saints he interacts with in the various *Saints' Lives*. If Cunedda had several offspring, then they could be spread over a twenty-year period and this

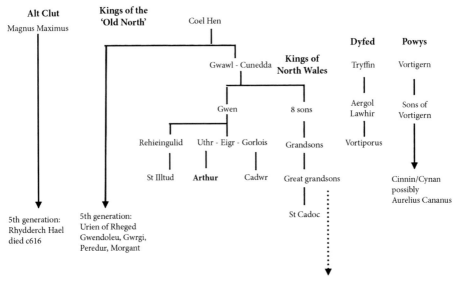

Arthur in the genealogies

is compounded by future generations. This might explain why Arthur could be placed before 500, while Maelgwn reigned c.534–547. It is very difficult to fit them all together in a coherent chronology without assuming some very long lifespans. This difficulty was discussed in greater detail in my previous book.[10] However, we can see on the family tree a hopefully simple illustration of where Arthur was placed by medieval copyists.

Let us now look at Arthur's alleged pedigree in more detail, firstly from Geoffrey of Monmouth's early twelfth-century story. At first glance, it looks like Constantinus might be Constantine III. However, aside from the name and one son, Constans, there are no other similarities. Additionally, we can calculate the implied floruit from the alleged settlement of Conanus in Armorica in around the 380s. It is unclear if Geoffrey means Budicus of Armorica marries Arthur's sister or Ambrosius's. But the Breton link is repeated time and again, with both Constantinus and Hoel providing military assistance. It is quite possible Geoffrey added the continental link, as well as Arthur's Roman war, for political purposes. This is also the first time Ambrosius is added to Arthur's family. But taken at face value, Geoffrey is claiming Arthur is the grandson of a Breton, who is crowned as a king of Britain, not of any particular petty kingdom. His floruit is implied at between 505 and 542.

In later centuries, we get a number of different versions. The French and post-Vulgate Romances change the role and familial links of Morgana and Mordred's

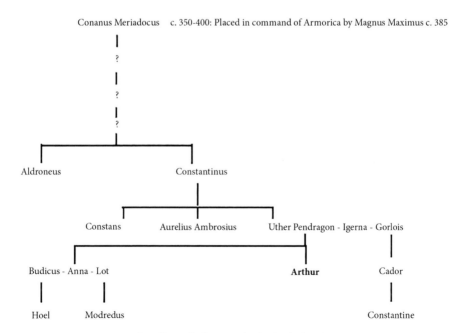

Geoffrey of Monmouth: Arthur's family tree

parentage. It is perhaps best to view such changes as transparent additions to the legend. We can see this transformation most clearly with the development of Morgan Le Fey. From Geoffrey of Monmouth, where she is the leader of the nine sisters of Avalon or takes Arthur to the fortunate Isle to be healed, to Chrétien de Troyes, who makes her Arthur's half-sister; later, she becomes a sorceress and seducer, and eventually, Mordred's mother. Mordred begins in the tales as Arthur's nephew. We must remember that Geoffrey was writing 600 years after any historical figure and much of his story was fanciful. All the later legends and stories that post-date Geoffrey are therefore suspect, especially when we can see the addition and evolution of characters over the centuries.[11]

The earliest Welsh legend is likely *Culhwch and Olwen*. The earliest copy is from the fourteenth century but it is thought to derive from an eleventh-century original. Other sources have various different spellings for Arthur's grandfather, Geoffrey's Constantinus:[12] for example, Custenin Gornev or Kustennin vendigeit. The former links Custenin with Cornwall.[13] However, we recall the links between regions in Cornwall and those of Brittany. The latter comes from the thirteenth-century *Brut Y Brenhinedd*. Bartrum finds there is 'no good reason to doubt the pedigree'. We, however, should doubt Geoffrey's tale of them coming from Armorica, although it is likely he got it from an existing genealogical table.[14] We can see the family tree from this source with missing generations from later genealogies.[15]

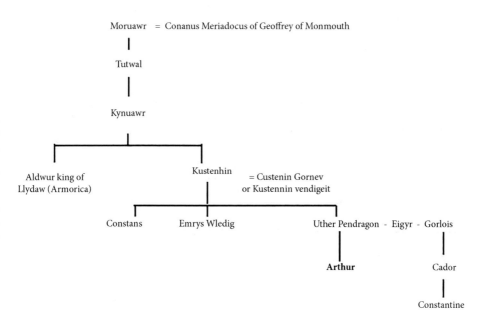

Welsh sources: Arthur's family tree

There is some consistency in the earliest stories.[16] Arthur's father is Uthr, his mother, Eigr (or Igraine) and Medrod, his nephew. He has a daughter Archfedd and, depending on the source, sons, Amhar, Llacheu, Gwydre, Cydfan and Smerbe. We can create a more detailed family tree, while remembering none of these sources are even close to being contemporary. Having said that, some academic historians, such as Chadwick, have found 'no valid reason for doubting the authenticity of the genealogy recorded in the *Bonedd y Saint*'.[17] This relates to the dynasty of Dumnonia, which makes Custennin Goreu king and Uther's father. But the line flows to Erbin, Geraint and Cadwy.

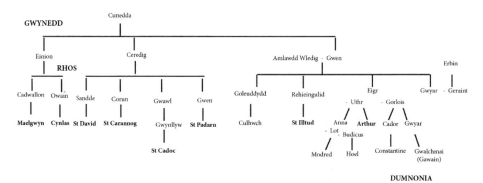

Detailed family tree from Welsh sources

We recognise Cadwy as Cador, father of Constantine who succeeds Arthur, according to Geoffrey. Many late genealogies follow Geoffrey and list the kings of Britain. One fourteenth-century source gives us:[18] Gwrtheyrn (Vortigern), Gwertheuyr Vendigeit (Vortimer), Emrys Wledic (Ambrosius), Vthur (Uther), Arthur and Constantinus (Constantine). We are left to speculate if this is one of Gildas's five tyrant kings: Constantine, 'whelp of the filthy lioness of Damnoniae'. What is interesting is that none of the traditions make Arthur king of a particular kingdom. If we accept some accuracy was maintained through several hundred years, and Geoffrey of Monmouth did not corrupt or misrepresent any of the sources, then we could make some tentative suggestions.

He is not in any of the Welsh or northern genealogies. He is connected to the south-west, Dumnonia, through his mother's side. Geoffrey connected him with Armorica and there are indeed historical links between Cornwall and regions in Brittany. He is also connected to various saints of South Wales, some of which feature him in their *Saints' Lives*. There is a level of consistency in both his family tree and timeline, despite some chronological concerns for some figures and later additions and contradictions. Unfortunately, we have insufficient evidence to support this.

Summary

We have a number of legends, saints' lives and topographical features, none of which are historical. However, they do show a heavy concentration in Wales, and South Wales in particular; the West Country, especially Cornwall; and the north. Indeed, the story *Pa Gur* does suggest a northern location for at least one of the battles and implies a connection with Edinburgh and south-east Scotland. This is interesting given the reference in the possibly seventh-century poem *Y Gododdin*. It's also of interest that Geoffrey of Monmouth places so much activity in Scotland, although the insertion of battles across north-west Europe suggests he cannot be trusted. This might cause one to consider whether the four battles in the 'region of the Linnuis' are in Lennox, rather than Lincolnshire. If so, then Arthur would more likely be fighting Picts or Irish settlers of the Dal Riata.

Overall, though, I'm tempted to accept the implication of the widespread nature of the stories and legends, as well as the topographical features. An Arthur operating along the border of a partition from the south to the north could leave such an impression from Devon to Edinburgh. The genealogies suggest a familial connection with the south-west, which might account for legends persisting in South Wales, the West Country and Cornwall, with links to north-west France. He might well have several bases, as described in the Triads. Battle sites could range from north to south. If, in addition, he led kings of the Britons from the former northern military command or province, then he might well be remembered by sixth-century northern bards.

We could also take a crude mid-point from all the regions that maintained an Arthurian tradition, through topography or legends. An Arthur operating mainly from Central England would be able to reach all the areas mentioned reasonably quickly. A hundred years later, his main area of activity may have fallen to Anglo-Saxon control, or perhaps more accurately, Romano-British-Germanic control. Perhaps it simply evolved through dynamic change in cultural or political identity. According to the *Anglo-Saxon Chronicles*, the Gewissae fighting to the north of the Thames Valley were still battling Britons towards the end of the sixth century. Yet two generations later, Penda of Mercia was also fighting with the kings of the British.[19] This would suggest, at the time of Arthur, the Midlands was under British control, despite significant settlement, especially in the Trent Valley and in the East Midlands. Whatever the case his exploits were remembered, embellished and drifted into legend.

Chapter 9

Conclusion

This investigation was based on two assumptions. Firstly, Arthur was a historical figure and secondly, the battle list in the *Historia Brittonum* is a genuine Welsh battle poem that survived in an oral tradition before being written down in the seventh or eighth centuries. There are a number of facts we can be confident about that are worth repeating. At the start of the fifth century, Britain was a fairly prosperous Diocese with a largely Roman identity, and with Christianity as the dominant religion. By the end of the sixth century, the Diocese and provincial structures had disintegrated and petty kingdoms had emerged, many based on *civitates* and/or tribal areas. Cultural identities had also changed and evolved considerably.

It's worth separating facts from speculation. The sources tell us Constantine III left with a substantial proportion of the army in 407. We then hear from both the *Gallic Chronicles* and Zosimus that in c.409, Britain was devastated by an incursion of the Saxons. The appeal to Honorius is uncertain but the *Notitia Dignitatum* suggests Britain was still considered to be Roman, if not under Roman authority. The visit of St Germanus suggests even in 429, and possibly 437, Britain was stable and still seen as a 'Roman island' by Prosper of Aquitaine. Our last record about which we can have some confidence is the *Gallic Chronicle* for 440: 'Britain fell to the power of the Saxons.'

On this, Gildas's chronology cannot be trusted. It is possible Bede followed him and erroneously dated the *adventus Saxonum* to 449. On the balance of probabilities, we have two options. Either the *Gallic Chronicle* is correct and Gildas caused Bede (and many sources afterwards) to misdate the events. Or Bede had access to other sources that allowed him to date the event accurately. If this is the case, it is likely we are seeing two different events reflected in different sources. Ironically, the much-maligned *Historia Brittonum* provides a perfectly reasonable, and entertaining, narrative to address this discrepancy.

Archaeology has demonstrated the presence of Germanic material culture from c.425, and evidence of settlements through burial practices. This increased throughout the fifth century and we see a marked difference, broadly supporting Bede's statement concerning Saxons in the south and Angles in the east. However, he mentions other groups and Procopius suggests Friesians were a significant group. Yet DNA studies imply there was not an invasion as such. In fact, we see significant continuation of both population and land use. Assimilation of incomers, alongside acculturation by the indigenous population, appears to have been significant factors.

We can use the example of Gaul to speculate on the changes in cultural identity, and perhaps put to one side the simplistic Romano-British fighting against waves of invading Anglo-Saxon warriors. It is likely provinces, *civitates* and peoples evolved different political, economic, social and cultural patterns. No doubt fragmentation of the Diocese, provincial and other structures caused friction and conflict. It is into this context Arthur is placed. We started with three options: an early, middle or late Arthur. I have suggested that the early option, c.450–480, is perhaps the least likely. This brings us to dating the Battle of Badon.

It is generally accepted Gildas is writing in the second quarter of the sixth century. In this instance, his chronology is more certain. He dates either the first victory of Ambrosius or Badon to forty-four years earlier, thus in the 490s. Bede, with his other sources, places Ambrosius c.474–491 and Badon in 493, forty-four years after the Saxons' arrival. The *Annales Cambriae* places Badon over twenty years later. It may be that one, or both, sources are mistaken. Alternatively, Badon might have been erroneously added to Arthur's exploits. In fact, many of the later genealogies suggest a late Arthur, c.510–540. Whatever the case, we can say nothing we have covered undermines the traditional timeframe: the Romans left, and sometime later, Vortigern invites Saxon mercenaries who subsequently rebel. A fightback ensues, led first by Ambrosius Aurelianus. Arthur then rules during a period of relative peace. After his death, the Anglo-Saxons expand once more before their first historically-attested kings appear towards the end of the sixth century.

We then saw that some of the battles could, indeed, be identified. The evidence seems to negate a localised Arthur confined to one region. Even the most sceptical of historians accept two or three locations are likely. Battles at Chester and in the Caledonian Forest suggest, at the very least, a provincial authority operating on the borders of the former northern military command. The identification of Linnuis in Lincolnshire adds to this. It also suggests links between provinces and *civitates* still existed at that point. Additionally, there is nothing preventing a force fighting a battle in the south at Badon, and utilising the road networks to reach beyond Hadrian's Wall. This would suggest a force operating across the whole of the former Diocese. It is interesting none of the likely locations are in the south-east, which is the most likely area to have broken away first. None, for example, at Verulamium, which Gildas complains cannot be visited, or at London, where the Britons fled to from the Battle of Crecganford in 457. The other battles are more difficult but two, *Guinnion* and *Breguoin* could be former Roman forts in the northern command. The first battle, at the River *Glein*, has likely suspects in Northumbria or Lincolnshire. If *Trueroit* is in the north and *Bassas* between Wroxeter and Chester, then we have two further sites near the border of the northern province.

But it is not necessary for the purposes of this investigation to locate *all* the battles. What I hope we have done is shown that at least three sites and six battles can be located on the balance of probabilities. It is then necessary to place those sites within the historical context. It is likely the Diocese structure collapsed sometime around the mid-fifth century. The south-east province appears to have been the first to break away, or to be partly taken over by Germanic elements. The remaining provinces and bordering *civitates* appear to have fragmented, especially down the centre of the island. Perhaps Ambrosius attempted to stabilise this situation. Yet Gildas seems to suggest there is still some sort of civilian structure and later, early kingdoms appear to be based on earlier *civitates* or tribal areas.

However, Gildas also refers to a partition, although it's not clear if this is a physical border. The forming of different cultural identities between Britons and Anglo-Saxons points to distinct areas. We thus estimated a 'zone of fragmentation' or 'line of likely conflict'. We expected to find our battles in that zone. It is worth looking at the three hypotheses from the introduction.

1. There is a reasonable amount of evidence to estimate the political, cultural and military situation. From this, we can attempt to draw the border or partition that Gildas alluded to and the later emerging kingdoms imply.
2. Despite claims to the contrary, some of the battles can be located on the balance of probabilities.
3. These locations will make sense in the context of the political and military situation, and the archaeological and literary evidence. They will more likely be on, or near, any boundaries or borders within the fragmenting political situation.

The first two have some reasonable support. Yet the third hypothesis is not completely supported. The two battles with the strongest support, Chester and Caledonian Forest, undermine this. That leaves us with some possible options:

- A border war between two distinct polities, combined with fighting off Pictish and Irish raiders. The subsequent oral battle poem remembered only the locations and not the enemy.
- A defensive war with Arthur pushing back Germanic incursions, some of which were quite deep.

- A war of ethnic cleansing with Arthur clearing out Germanic settlers and/or *foederati* within Romano-British *civitates*.
- A civil war scenario that is later seen as Romano-British versus Anglo-Saxons.

I would suggest the following likely scenario. Firstly, prior to the events of the mid-fifth century, *foederati* troops were posted to various forts, especially in the northern command, to defend against Pictish raids. Chester, too, might be an obvious staging point to defend against Irish raiders. At the time, significant levels of immigration into the east added to social, economic and cultural change through the decline of urbanisation and the break from Rome. The subsequent revolt resulted in significant areas falling under Germanic influence, mainly in the south-east. These upheavals resulted in further weakening of provincial and *civitas* authority. Some remnants survived, including the church. Ambrosius Aurelianus attempted to stabilise the situation, culminating in two distinctive zones. There was a Germanic Romano-Brittonic zone in the south-east with pockets along the east coast, while in the west and north, there was a Romano-Brittonic zone. These were marked by urban-based *civitates*, some of which moved to reoccupied hill forts. Other areas were based on tribal groups.

Petty kings and warlords emerged, although they were loosely connected through a sense of shared identity and the remaining threads of civic and church authority. When Arthur appears, he takes over the role of Ambrosius. The *civitates* along the 'unhappy partition' were in the process of fragmenting. When military aid was requested, Arthur had to rely on, in effect, autonomous rulers: from the petty kings of North Wales, *civitas* and bishoprics of Wroxeter and Lincoln; individual commanders of the former northern command forts; and civic leaders from the remaining urban centres and hill forts. He can be truly said to lead the kings of the Britons.

Arthur had a number of tasks. He needed to clear out pockets of Octha's mercenaries, left scattered across the north. He had to react to raids from the Picts and Irish, but also from rival *civitates* from the east. The battles in the region of the Linnuis reflects an attempt to clear out non-loyal Germanic groups from around the former provincial capital at Lincoln. But the level of migration and political change was too great. None of his campaigns appear to have been directed at the south-east. Most were directed internally, in what was left of the crumbling provinces. In fact, in some of his battles, he was likely facing more indigenous Britons than Angles or Saxons. Not everyone viewed the former Roman identity as positive. Not everyone wished to fight for the former civic and military leaders. After stabilising the north and the East Midlands, he marched south to prevent the Atrebates from disintegrating. He was only partly successful and a partition was created, splitting east from west.

Arthur's exploits were only half-remembered in far-flung corners from the north to Brittany, often fuelled by those Britons who chose, or were forced, to move. I would suggest he comes from an area lost early to polities that developed a Germanic cultural identity. If he was from any of the Welsh or northern kingdoms, it is very likely he would not only appear unequivocally in the genealogies, but his descendants would have left written records. Lindsey or early Bernicia might be likely areas, but also Central England. The second Battle of Badon might be more significant than many have realised if the *Annales Cambriae* entry could be linked to that in the *Anglo-Saxon Chronicles*. So, too, might the comment regarding Penda of Mercia fighting alongside the kings of the Britons. The *Chronicles* imply the Gewissae were fighting Britons to their north, many decades after Arthur. An Arthur in the Midlands would have good links with all the areas that later maintained a tradition. If Arthur inherited a civic or military role, then it's unlikely that would be remembered. If provincial governors or a council leader survived to the time of Gildas, they had disappeared by the end of the sixth century. No-one would remember an obscure title. They might call him a king or a general, or simply remember a warrior leading the kings of Britain.

In summary, we can say with some confidence that some of the battles from the list in the *Historia Brittonum* can, indeed, be identified: Chester, north of Hadrian's Wall, and four in Lincolnshire. In addition, Badon is likely located in the south. Some of the other battles suggest the north might be a fruitful place to investigate. But the Welsh sources connect him to the south-west, notably Cornwall and South Wales. However, Arthur is not to be found in any of the genealogies. There are no 'Arth'-type names or complex etymologies. Even if we take the sources at face value, they do not claim he rules in any particular early kingdom. Rather, he is related to kings through his mother's side. With Cornwall having significant Irish immigration, perhaps that connects the relative popularity of the name in Irish genealogies. However, the fact there is no similar tradition there makes a direct link unlikely. Alternatively, Arthur comes from Romano-Gaul, as Geoffrey claimed. Many centuries later, he is imagined to be king of the whole of Britain. Perhaps the council of the surviving provinces did indeed elect a king.

If there was a direct connection with any of the surviving Brittonic kingdoms, we would likely have evidence. It is far more likely Arthur ruled in an area that later evolved a Germanic-Brittonic identity, and had no use for a fifth- or sixth-century Romano-British hero. I would suggest the most likely scenario is that he held a post similar to Ambrosius, whatever that may have been, leading the remnants of the military forces from the crumbling provincial and *civitate* structures. It is hoped, one day, we may have more definitive evidence about the locations and battles themselves, perhaps in some long-forgotten manuscript. Or an inscription on a stone buried in the foundations of a medieval church or castle. Let us hope this eventually leads us to identify the man who led the Britons in these conflicts. I will end with a series of maps. The first reflects Arthur's Britain c.500 with likely battle locations added. There follows a series of eight smaller maps, showing the chronology from the end of Roman Britain to c.600.

Map 45: Britain c. AD 500

AD 410 Roman Britain

AD 450 Vortigern's Britain

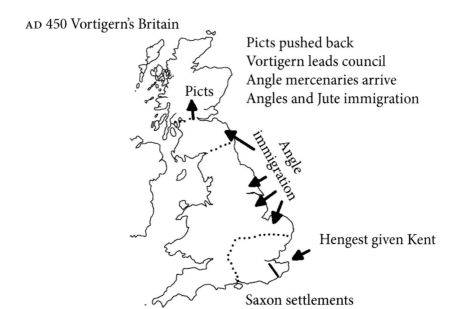

Picts pushed back
Vortigern leads council
Angle mercenaries arrive
Angles and Jute immigration

Picts

Angle immigration

Hengest given Kent

Saxon settlements

Maps 46–49: Britain c. AD 410–460

AD 440 The power of the Saxons

Picts capture 'up to wall'
Kings appointed
Provincial structure breaks down
Council formed
Political change

Saxon
immigration

c. AD 460 Rebellion

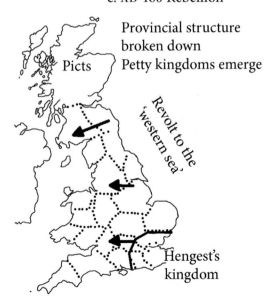

Provincial structure
broken down
Petty kingdoms emerge

Revolt to the
'western sea'

Hengest's
kingdom

474-491 Ambrosius's war

Pro- Romano -
British *civitates*

Pro-Germanic-British *civitates*

Ambrosius
'High-King'
or council leader

Aelle 'Bretwalda'

Hengest's
Kingdom

490-500 Arthur's battles

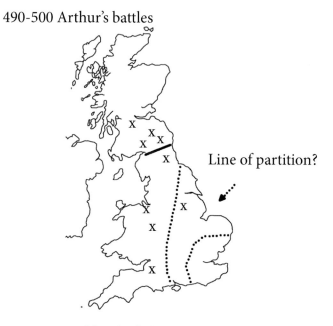

Line of partition?

Maps 50–53: Britain c. AD 470–600

550 Early kingdoms

c. AD 575-600 Expansion

1 Battle of Arferydd 573
2 Siege of Lindisfarne c.572-9
3 Battle of Catraeth ?
4 Battle of Chester 606
5 Elmet destroyed c. 616

Notes

Introduction
1. Sullivan, 2020
2. http://www.vortigernstudies.org.uk/artsou/chron452.htm
3. Dark, 2000: 229
4. Dark, 2000: 43
5. Evans, 2000: 148
6. Morris, 1980: 45
7. Morris, 1980: 35

Chapter 1: Roman Britain
1. http://www.vortigernstudies.org.uk/artsou/chron452.htm
2. Rippon, 2018: 352
3. Halsall, 2014: 480
4. Wilson, 1980: 271
5. Bédoyère, 2006: 181
6. Bishop, 2020: 70–71
7. Laycock, 2008: 24
8. Laycock, 2008: 40
9. Gerrard, 2016: 215
10. Rippon, 2018: 327
11. Bédoyère, 2006: 89
12. Salway, 2001: 230
13. Bédoyère, 2006: 143–7
14. Crabtree, 2018: 18
15. Crabtree, 2018: 5–6
16. Gerrard, 2016: 246
17. Halsall, 2014: 457
18. Charles-Edwards 2014: 31
19. Dark, 1994: 10
20. Dark, 1994: 15
21. Dark, 1994: 16
22. Gerrard, 2016: 55
23. Salway, 2001: 277
24. Goldsworthy, 2010: 344
25. Dark, 2000: 17
26. Dark, 1994: 25
27. Bédoyère, 2006: 183
28. Halsall, 2014: 363
29. Bédoyère, 2006: 207
30. Higham, 2014: 21
31. Salway, 2001: 280–281
32. Gerrard, 2016: 23–25
33. Salway, 2001: 293
34. Salway, 2001: 297
35. http://www.vortigernstudies.org.uk/artsou/orosius.htm
36. http://www.vortigernstudies.org.uk/artsou/chron452.htm
37. http://www.vortigernstudies.org.uk/artsou/zosim.htm
38. Oosthuizen, 2019: 27
39. http://www.vortigernstudies.org.uk/artsou/procop.htm
40. Salway, 2001: 243
41. Hughes, 2020: 34–35
42. Goldsworthy, 2010: 337
43. Evans, 2000: 26
44. Salway, 2001: 316
45. Gerrard, 2016: 168
46. Higham and Ryan, 2015: 42

Chapter 2: Post-Roman Britain AD 410–450
1. Higham and Ryan, 2015: 42
2. Hills, 2011: 9
3. Clearly, 2011: 13
4. Gerrard, 2016: 73–78
5. Gerrard, 2016: 114–117
6. Wallace-Hadrill, 1961: 992
7. Charles-Edwards, 2014: 43
8. Gerrard, 2016: 163
9. Halsall, 2014: 358
10. Gerrard, 2016: 255–258
11. Gerrard, 2016: 60
12. Crabtree, 2018: 22–23
13. Wacher, 1995: 150
14. Green, 2012: 27 & 32

15. Wacher, 1995: 149
16. Wacher, 1995: 241
17. Wacher, 1995: 271
18. Wacher, 1995: 289–290
19. Wacher, 1995: 301
20. Crabtree, 2018: 29
21. Bédoyère, 2006: 207
22. Crabtree, 2018: 42
23. Wacher, 1995: 322
24. Wacher, 1995: 335
25. Wacher, 1995: 342
26. Wacher, 1995: 362
27. Wacher, 1995: 377
28. Halsall, 2014: 359
29. Crabtree, 2018: 41
30. Crabtree, 2018: 42
31. Wacher, 1995: 188
32. Wacher, 1995: 401, 406–407
33. Carver, 2019: 37
34. Carver, 2019: 169
35. Bédoyère, 2006: 258–259
36. Dark, 2000: 33
37. Dark, 2000: 36
38. Bédoyère, 2006: 263
39. Salway, 2001: 347
40. Salway, 2001: 348
41. Crabtree, 2018: 31
42. Webb, 2011: 132
43. Naismith, 2019: 43
44. Webb, 2011: 132
45. Bailey in Bassett, 1989: 110
46. Crabtree: 2018: 47
47. Dark, 1994: 10
48. Dark, 1994: 16
49. Eagles, 2018: 14
50. Salway, 2001: 345
51. Wacher, 1995: 81
52. Clearly, 2011: 22
53. Clearly, 2011: 22
54. Crabtree, 2018: 40
55. Collins, 2012: 1
56. Collins, 2012: 110
57. Collins, 2012: 103
58. Collins, 2012: 138
59. Collins, 2012: 139
60. Collins, 2012: 106–110
61. Arnold, 2000: 214
62. Collins, 2012: 132
63. Pearson, 2010: 9
64. Pearson, 2010: 168
65. Pearson, 2010: 169
66. Goldsworthy, 2010: 341
67. Gerrard, 2016: 55
68. Bédoyère, 2006: 256
69. Dark, 2000: 33
70. Gerrard, 2016: 242
71. Salway, 2001: 347
72. Oosthuizen, 2019: 96
73. Green, 2012: 44 & 48
74. Manco, 2018: 126
75. Rippon, 2018: 3–4
76. Gerrard, 2016: 208
77. Oosthuizen, 2019: 30
78. Carver, 2019: 19
79. Oosthuizen, 2019: 34–35
80. Salway, 2001: 341
81. Bédoyère, 2006: 267
82. Carver, 2019: 189
83. Carver, 2019: 192
84. Carver, 2019: 176
85. Carver, 2019: 145
86. Carver, 2019: 144
87. Crabtree, 2018: 42
88. Crabtree, 2018: 84
89. Wood in Dumville and Lapwood, 1984: 8
90. http://www.vortigernstudies.org.uk/
    artsou/prosp.htm
91. Thompson, 1968: 39–46
92. Hughes, 2020: 93
93. Eagles, 2018: 14
94. Oosthuizen, 2019: 29
95. Charles-Edwards, 2014: 227
96. O Cróinín, 2017: 46
97. O Cróinín, 2017: 47
98. Dumville, 1999
99. Bury, 1998: 192
100. Mortimer, 2011: 173
101. Lapidge and Dumville, 1984: 52
102. Lapidge and Dumville, 1984: 47
103. Lapidge and Dumville, 1984: 50
104. Morris, 1978: 19
105. Hughes, 2020: 144
106. Hughes, 2020: 130
107. Dark, 2000: 20
108. Cunliffe, 2013: 411
109. Charles-Edwards, 2014: 370
110. Halsall, 2014: 361–366
111. Higham, 2015: 107
112. Arnold, 2000: 29
113. Halsall, 2014: 361–366
114. Manco, 2018: 128
115. Halsall, 2014: 17

116. Rippon, 2018: 167
117. Lewis in Mitchell and Greatrex, 2000: 77
118. Eagles, 2018: 2
119. Oosthuizen, 2019: 59
120. Matthews in Mitchell and Greatrex, 2000: 31
121. Mathisen, 1993: 42–43
122. Mathisen, 1993: 41
123. Mathisen, 1993: 2
124. Mathisen, 1993: 106–107
125. Mathisen, 1993: 111
126. Mathisen, 1993: 59
127. Mathisen, 1993: 60
128. Mathisen, 1993: 11
129. Mathisen, 1993: 13–14
130. Mathisen, 1993: 20
131. Mathisen, 1993: 32
132. Mathisen, 1993: 25
133. Mathisen, 1993: 50
134. Mathisen, 1993: 68–69
135. Mathisen, 1993: 70
136. Mathisen, 1993: 78
137. Mathisen, 1993: 51
138. Matthews in Mitchell and Greatrex, 2000: 32
139. Oosthuizen, 2019: 76
140. Mathisen, 1993: 132–139
141. Mathisen, 1993: 72
142. Mathisen, 1993: 134–135
143. Mathisen, 1993: 136
144. Matthews in Mitchell and Greatrex, 2000: 34
145. Harries in Mitchell and Greatrex, 2000: 48
146. Mathisen, 1993: 34
147. Mathisen, 1993: 142–143
148. Mathisen, 1993: 6
149. Mathisen, 1993: 119
150. Mathisen, 1993: 121
151. Halsall, 2014: 42
152. Greatrex in Mitchell and Greatrex, 2000: 278
153. Crabtree, 2018: 47
154. Gerrard, 2016: 262
155. Halsall, 2014: 472
156. Thomas, 1981: 198
157. Goldsworthy, 2010: 338, 345
158. O Cróinín, 2017: 37
159. Dark, 1994: 30 & 32
160. Charles-Edwards, 2014: 227
161. O Cróinín, 2017: 46
162. Mathisen, 1993: 93
163. Bede, Book 1.15
164. Mathisen, 1993: 33
165. Mathisen, 1993: 90–91
166. Drinkwater in Drinkwater and Elton, 2002: 217
167. Drinkwater in Drinkwater and Elton, 2002: 210–211
168. Drinkwater in Drinkwater and Elton, 2002: 208–217
169. Mathisen, 1993: 64
170. Wallace-Hadrill, 1961: 29
171. Stenton, 1989: 12
172. Charles-Edwards, 2014: 70–71
173. Charles-Edwards, 2014: 71
174. Mathisen, 1993: 129
175. Halsall, 2014: 34
176. Elton in Drinkwater and Elton, 2002: 176
177. Halsall, 2014: 66
178. Mathisen, 1993: 81
179. Mathisen, 1993: 82
180. Mathisen, 1993: 93

Chapter 3: The Anglo-Saxons

1. Oosthuizen, 2019: 3
2. Halsall, 2014: 17
3. Manco, 2018: 7 & 111
4. Manco, 2018: 93
5. Manco, 2018: 112
6. Manco, 2018: 115
7. Arnold, 2000: 23
8. Hills, 2011: 10
9. Zaluckyj, 2018: 2
10. Brugman, 2011: 32
11. Charles-Edwards, 2014: 48
12. Zaluckyj, 2018: 6
13. Arnold, 2000: 23
14. Bede, Book 5.9
15. Arnold, 2000: 59
16. Arnold, 2000: 104–107, 116–118
17. Eagles, 2018: xxxiv
18. Arnold, 2000: 60
19. Oppenheimer 2007: 380
20. Hills, 2011: 6
21. Green, 2012: 93 & 94
22. Arnold, 2000: 29
23. Higham, 1992: 74
24. Cunliffe, 2013: 413

25. Manco, 2018: 126
26. Eagles, 2018: xxvi
27. Manco, 2018: 129
28. Manco, 2018: 127
29. Manco, 2018: 130
30. Manco, 2018: 128
31. Eagles, 2018: 6
32. Laycock, 2011: 173
33. Arnold, 2000: 214
34. Higham, 2015: 80
35. Halsall, 2014: 361–366
36. Higham, 2015: 107
37. Crabtree, 2018: 57
38. Higham, 1992: 8
39. Oosthuizen, 2019: 7
40. Sykes, 2006: 325 & 338
41. Higham and Ryan, 2015: 91
42. Higham and Ryan, 2015: 91
43. Moffatt, 2013: 177
44. Higham and Ryan, 2015: 91
45. Manco, 2018: 30
46. Higham and Ryan, 2015: 107
47. Eagles, 2018: xxx
48. Moffatt, 2013: 182
49. Cunliffe, 2013: 242
50. Cunliffe, 2013: 424
51. Manco, 2018: 124
52. Carver, 2019: 3
53. Carver, 2019: 7
54. Oosthuizen, 2017: xiii
55. Green, 2012: 109
56. Carver, 2019: 56
57. Arnold, 2000: 20 & 21
58. Oosthuizen, 2019: 59
59. Manco, 2018: 193
60. Higham and Ryan, 2015: 98
61. Higham and Ryan, 2015: 98
62. Carver, 2019: 34
63. Oosthuizen, 2017: 46
64. Oosthuizen, 2017: 43
65. Carver, 2019: 38
66. Gerrard, 2016: 180
67. Cunliffe, 2013: 419

Chapter 4: Timelines and Partitions

1. http://www.vortigernstudies.org.uk/artsou/chron452.htm
2. Wood in Lapidge and Dumville, 1984: 19
3. Muhlberger in Drinkwater and Elton, 2002: 34–35
4. Wood in Lapidge and Dumville, 1984: 16–20
5. Dumville in Lapidge and Dumville, 1984: 59
6. Dumville in Lapidge and Dumville, 1984: 52
7. Morris, 1978: 20–36
8. http://www.vortigernstudies.org.uk/artsou/zosim.htm
9. Hughes, 2020: 209
10. Oosthuizen, 2019: 24
11. Dumville in Lapidge and Dumville, 1984: 67
12. Dumville, 1993: II.83
13. Morris, 1978: 28
14. Halsall, 2014: 55
15. Morris, 1978: 26
16. Wright in Lapidge and Dumville, 1984: 104
17. Lapidge in Lapidge and Dumville, 1984: 47
18. Lapidge in Lapidge and Dumville, 1984: 50
19. Morris, 1978: 45
20. Dumville in Lapidge and Dumville, 1984: 52
21. Higham, 1994: 141
22. Charles-Edwards, 2014: 215
23. Morris, 1978: 70
24. Woods, 2014: 226–34
25. Chadwick in Chadwick et al, 1959: 21
26. Bede, Book 1.15
27. Hughes, 2020: 210
28. http://www.vortigernstudies.org.uk/artsou/bede.htm
29. Wright in Lapidge and Dumville, 1984: 96
30. Morris, 1978: 92
31. Charles-Edwards, 2014: 438
32. Higham, 2009: 120
33. Green, 2009: 9
34. Charles-Edwards in Bromwich et al, 1995: 21
35. Chadwick in Chadwick et al, 1959: 31
36. Halsall, 2014: 63
37. Chadwick in Chadwick et al, 1959: 21–33
38. Morris, 1980: 33

39. Wood, 1987: 75
40. Bartrum, 1993: 269
41. Morris, 1978: 28
42. Yorke, 2013: 131
43. Beard, 2005: 263
44. Higham, 2009: 194
45. Higham, 2009: 209
46. Charles-Edwards, 2014: 347
47. Morris, 1980: 45
48. Higham, 2009: 209–217
49. Higham, 2009: 195
50. http://www.vortigernstudies.org.uk/
    artgue/guesthoward.htm
51. Green, 2009: 16
52. Padel, 2013: 10
53. Sullivan, 2020: 113–127
54. Ashe, 1985: 103
55. Charles-Edwards, 2014: 71
56. Ashe, 1995: 15–18
57. Bartrum, 1993

58. https://www.arthurlegends.com/vita-
    sancti-euflami-life-of-saint-efflamm/
59. Padel, 2013: 35
60. Sullivan, 2020: 208
61. Sisam, 1953: 328
62. Thorpe, 1966: 19
63. Sullivan, 2020: 219
64. Eagles, 2018: 32
65. Eagles, 2018: xxv
66. Eagles, 2018: 111
67. Eagles, 2018: 106 and 115
68. Eagles, 2018: xxxii
69. Eagles, 2018: 24
70. Eagles, 2018: 20–21
71. Eagles, 2018: 30
72. Eagles, 2018: 138
73. Dark, 2000: 207
74. Dark, 2000: 200
75. Gerrard, 2016: 179

Chapter 5: *Civitas* to Kingdom

1. Dark, 2000: 50
2. Rippon, 2018: 42
3. Rippon, 2018: 107
4. Eagles, 2018: 2
5. Dark, 2000: 191
6. Loveluck and Laing, 2011: 537
7. Dark, 2000: 53
8. Eagles, 2018: 185
9. Dark, 2000: 103
10. Oosthuizen, 2019: 76
11. Brooks in Bassett, 1989: 55
12. Brooks and Harrington, 2010: 24
13. Manco, 2018: 131
14. Yorke, 2013: 26
15. Brooks and Harrington, 2010: 42
16. Crabtree, 2018: 46
17. Brooks and Harrington, 2010: 36
18. Yorke, 2013: 27
19. Yorke, 2013: 27
20. Morris, 1980: 31
21. Brooks in Bassett, 1989: 64–67
22. Tolkien, 1998: 167
23. Yorke, 2013: 46
24. Rippon, 2018: 269
25. Rippon, 2018: 284
26. Rippon, 2018: 352
27. Rippon, 2018: 285
28. Rippon, 2018: 103
29. Rippon, 2018: 240

30. Yorke, 2013: 46
31. Bailey in Bassett, 1989: 122
32. Bailey in Bassett, 1989: 111
33. Blair in Bassett, 1989: 97
34. Welch in Bassett, 1989: 75–81
35. Welch in Bassett, 1989: 83
36. Charles-Edwards, 2014: 444
37. Carver in Bassett, 1989: 156
38. Oosthuizen, 2019: 96
39. Newton, 1994: 13
40. Newton, 1994: 27 & 29
41. Newton, 1994: 109
42. Newton, 1994: 116–117
43. Newton, 1994: 142–144
44. Manco, 2018: 183
45. Rippon, 2018: 318
46. Rippon, 2018: 266
47. Rippon, 2018: 284
48. Rippon, 2018: 327
49. Eagles, in Bassett, 1989: 212
50. Green, 2012: 62
51. Green, 2012: 100
52. Oosthuizien, 2017: 42
53. Oosthuizien, 2017: 39
54. Green, 2012: 122
55. Bede Book 2.16
56. Oosthuizien, 2017: 47
57. Rippon, 2018: 239
58. Rippon, 2018: 229

59. Loveluck and Laing, 2011: 539
60. Yorke, 2013 :74
61. Loveluck and Laing, 2011: 541
62. Dumville in Bassett, 1989: 215
63. Dumville, 1993: III.5
64. Newton, 1994: 30
65. Dumville, 1993: III.9
66. Carver, 2019: 639
67. Dumville in Bassett, 1989: 218
68. Dumville, 1993: III.9
69. Marsden, 1992: 27
70. Dumville, 1993: III.7
71. Dumville, 1993: III.7
72. Bede, Book 3.7
73. Yorke, 2013: 131
74. Yorke in Bassett, 1989: 89
75. Yorke, 2013: 132
76. Eagles, 2018: 185
77. Eagles, 2018: 43
78. Eagles, 2018: 22
79. Eagles, 2018: 139
80. Dumville in Bassett, 1989: 140
81. Zaluckyj, 2013: 21
82. Bede, Book 2.2
83. Bede, Book 4.13
84. Bede, Book 4.23
85. Hooke, 1985: 17
86. Hooke, 1985: 17
87. Bede, Book 5.23
88. Bede, Book 1.15
89. Bassett, 1989: 26
90. Carver in Bassett, 1989: 158
91. Carver, 2019: 637–641
92. Gerrard, 2016: 179
93. Gerrard, 2016: 155–156
94. Gerrard, 2016: 245
95. Morris, 1978: 28
96. Collins, 2012: 1
97. Clarkson, 2010: 19
98. Collins, 2012: 110
99. Collins, 2012: 103
100. Clarkson, 2010: 19
101. Collins, 2012: 106–110
102. Collins, 2012: 139
103. Clarkson, 2010: 32
104. Dumville, 1993: III 7
105. Charles-Edwards, 2014: 385
106. Morris, 1980: 37
107. Clarkson, 2010: 32
108. Bartrum, 1993: 290
109. Charles-Edwards, 2014: 386
110. Bartrum, 1993: 634
111. Clarkson, 2010: 75
112. Clarkson, 2010: 39
113. Charles-Edwards, 2014: 13
114. Morris, 1980: 38
115. Bartrum, 1993: 565
116. Blair in Chadwick, 1959: 151
117. Dumville, 1993: III 4
118. Dumville, 1993: III 9
119. Dark, 2000: 191
120. Charles-Edwards, 2014: 17
121. Dark, 1994: 76
122. Dark, 1994: 78
123. Zaluckyj, 2013: 8
124. Charles-Edwards, 2014: 18
125. Dark, 1994: 79–83
126. Dark, 1994: 83–86
127. Bartrum, 1993: 321
128. Lapidge and Dumville, 1984: 53–59
129. Bartrum, 1993: 153
130. Sullivan, 2020: 165
131. Higham, 2009: 130
132. Chadwick in Chadwick, 1959: 25
133. Charles-Edwards, 2014: 21
134. Dark, 1994: 89
135. Charles-Edwards, 2014: 22
136. Dark, 1994: 90
137. Dark, 1994: 94–95
138. Dark, 1994: 91–92
139. Wade-Evans, 1988
140. Bartrum, 1993: 104
141. Green, 2009: 276
142. Chadwick in Chadwick et al, 1959: 53
143. Green, 2009: 20
144. Chambers, 1966: 18
145. Gregory of Tours, Book II 17–18
146. Charles-Edwards, 2014: 59
147. Charles-Edwards, 2014: 71
148. Charles-Edwards, 2014: 26
149. Charles-Edwards, 2014: 72
150. Charles-Edwards, 2014: 60
151. Morris, 1978: 27
152. Hughes, 2020: 144
153. Charles-Edwards, 2014: 59
154. Charles-Edwards, 2014: 58
155. Bromwich, 1991:251
156. Barber, 2016: 206
157. Bromwich, 1991:262
158. Clarkson, 2019: 1
159. Clarkson, 2019: 17
160. Clarkson, 2019: 27

161. Morris, 1978: 23
162. Clarkson, 2019: 31
163. Clarkson, 2019: 34
164. Clarkson, 2019: 66
165. Foster, 2014: 4
166. Clarkson, 2019: 73
167. Foster, 2014:136
168. O Cróinín, 2017: 38
169. O Cróinín, 2017: 39
170. O Cróinín, 2017: 8
171. O Cróinín, 2017: 9
172. Clarkson, 2019: 4
173. O Cróinín, 2017: 14
174. O Cróinín, 2017: 47
175. O Cróinín, 2017: 47
176. Foster, 2014: 139
177. O Cróinín, 2017: 71
178. O Cróinín, 2017: 72
179. O Cróinín, 2017: 74
180. Clarkson, 2008: 90
181. Carver, 2019: 36
182. Gerrard, 2016: 262

183. Manco, 2018: 124
184. Oppenheimer, 2007: 382
185. Manco, 2018: 119
186. Rippon, 2018: 241
187. Rippon, 2018: 327
188. Rippon, 2018: 136
189. Rippon, 2018: 352
190. Rippon, 2018: 197
191. Rippon, 2018: 352
192. Rippon, 2018: 219
193. Halsall, 2014: 34
194. Halsall, 2014: 66
195. Halsall, 2014: 19
196. Halsall, 2014: 34
197. Halsall, 2014: 484
198. Halsall, 2014: 482
199. Gerrard, 2016: 276
200. Collins, 2014: 10
201. Halsall, 2014: 484
202. Halsall, 2014: 495
203. Halsall, 2014: 472
204. Manco, 2018: 120

Chapter 6: Weapons, Armour and Warfare

1. Goldsworthy, 2003: 205
2. Goldsworthy, 2003: 206
3. Goldsworthy, 2000: 168
4. Goldsworthy, 2000: 175
5. Goldsworthy, 2000: 168
6. Goldsworthy, 2003: 169
7. Goldsworthy, 2003: 206
8. Esposito, 2018: 56–57
9. Esposito, 2018: 71
10. Goldsworthy, 2000: 169
11. Goldsworthy, 2003: 169
12. Mortimer, 2011: 192
13. Bédoyère, 2001: 74
14. Halsall, 2003: 174
15. Halsall, 2003: 198
16. Mortimer, 2011: 192–194
17. Halsall, 2003: 173
18. Storr, 2016: 56
19. Goldsworthy, 2010: 337
20. Hughes, 2020: 19
21. Higham, 1992:9
22. Marren, 2006: 3
23. Marren, 2006: 153
24. Goldsworthy, 2000: 178
25. Goldsworthy, 2000: 197
26. Halsall, 2003: 130–132
27. Mortimer, 2011: 189

28. Higham, 1992:8
29. Higham, 1992:79–80
30. Marren, 2006: 153
31. Gerrard, 2016: 45
32. Underwood, 1999: 41 & 47
33. Underwood, 1999: 24
34. Underwood, 1999: 25
35. Esposito, 2018: 73–74
36. Underwood, 1999: 32–34
37. Esposito, 2018: 111
38. Underwood, 1999: 73
39. Underwood, 1999: 70
40. Hughes, 2020: 53
41. Underwood, 1999: 77
42. Underwood, 1999: 63
43. Esposito, 2018: 93
44. Underwood, 1999: 94
45. Marren, 2006: 10
46. Mortimer, 2011: 169
47. Hughes, 2020: 45
48. Evans, 2000: 136
49. Esposito, 2018: 93
50. Newton, 1994: 33
51. Underwood, 1999: 127
52. Halsall, 2003: 185
53. Halsall, 2003: 196
54. Halsall, 2003: 207

55. Davidson, 1998: 189
56. Davidson, 1998: 189
57. Davidson, 1998: 192
58. Davidson, 1998: 189
59. Hughes, 2020: 50–51
60. Milner, 2011: 103
61. Underwood, 1999: 133
62. Morris, 1978: 22
63. Milner, 2011: 2–3
64. Milner, 2011: 10
65. Milner, 2011: 89
66. Milner, 2011: 24 & 80–81
67. Thompson, 1988: 133
68. Milner, 2011: 13
69. Milner, 2011: 50
70. Milner, 2011: 95–6
71. Milner, 2011: 97
72. Milner, 2011: 26
73. Milner, 2011: 98
74. Milner, 2011: 112
75. Milner, 2011: 104
76. Esposito, 2018: 71
77. Milner, 2011: 72
78. Milner, 2011: 44
79. Davidson, 1998: 103
80. Davidson, 1998: 80
81. Davidson, 1998: 9
82. Marren, 2006: 9
83. Davidson, 1998: 38
84. Davidson, 1998: 59
85. Underwood, 1999: 56–57
86. Underwood, 1999: 50
87. Marren, 2006: 10
88. Davidson, 1998: 197
89. Davidson, 1998: 197
90. Davidson, 1998: 95
91. Davidson, 1998: 104
92. Marren, 2006: 9
93. Underwood, 1999: 119
94. Underwood, 1999: 119
95. Davidson, 1998: 28
96. Davidson, 1998: 108
97. Davidson, 1998: 165
98. Davidson, 1998: 109
99. Davidson, 1998: 118
100. Davidson, 1998: 138
101. Thorpe, 1966: 223–225
102. Hamilton, 1986: 435
103. Mierow, 1908, 66
104. Thorpe, Lewis, 1977: 153
105. Thorpe, Lewis, 1977: 154
106. Davidson, 1998: 149
107. Marren, 2006: 156
108. Davidson, 1998: 150
109. Swanton, 2001: 106
110. Marren, 2006: 135
111. Morris, 2013: 164
112. Swanton, 2001:198
113. Morris, 2013: 180
114. Morris, 2013: 183
115. Bede, Book 3.24
116. Carver, 2019: 609
117. Koch, 2013: 187–8
118. Evans, 2000: 1
119. Evans, 2000: 28
120. Evans, 2000: 26
121. Evans, 2000: 42
122. Morris, 1978: 29
123. Bede, Book 3.14
124. Evans, 2000: 91
125. Evans, 2000: 105
126. Evans, 2000: 74
127. Evans, 2000: 84
128. Morris, 1980: 38
129. Evans, 2000: 119
130. Evans, 2000: 126
131. Gregory of Tours: Bk II. 27
132. Charles-Edwards in Bassett, 1989: 30
133. Evans, 2000: 131
134. Gerrard, 2016: 242
135. Evans, 2000: 135
136. Bishop, 2020: 3
137. Bishop, 2020: 17
138. Bishop, 2020: 70–71
139. Bishop, 2020: 66
140. Bishop, 2020: 85
141. Bishop, 2020: 76
142. Bishop, 2020: 104
143. Bishop, 2020: 20–21
144. Bishop, 2020: 99
145. Bishop, 2020: 80
146. Bishop, 2020: 20
147. Grigg, 2018: 28–29
148. Grigg, 2018: 31
149. Grigg, 2018: 20
150. Grigg, 2018: 77–78
151. Grigg, 2018: 46
152. Grigg, 2018: 81
153. Grigg, 2018: 55
154. Grigg, 2018: 122
155. Grigg, 2018: 135
156. Grigg, 2018: 60

157. Grigg, 2018: 48–49
158. Grigg, 2018: 53
159. Grigg, 2018: 86
160. Grigg, 2018: 67
161. Grigg, 2018: 33
162. Carver, 2019: 189–193
163. Alcock, 1989: 221

164. Harding, 2012: 164
165. Grigg, 2018: 72
166. Dyer, 1992: 24
167. Gerrard, 2016: 48
168. Gerrard, 2016: 68–69
169. Gerrard, 2016: 59

Chapter 7: The Thirteen Battles of Arthur

1. Higham, 2009: 146
2. Higham, 2009: 146–147
3. Green, 2009: 54
4. Bromwich et al, 1995: 29
5. Charles-Edwards in Bromwich et al, 1995: 20
6. Charles-Edwards in Bromwich et al, 1995: 28
7. Bartrum, 1993: 26
8. Fitzpatrick-Matthews 2017
9. Vermaat, Robert http://www.vortigernstudies.org.uk/artsou/historia.htm
10. Fitzpatrick-Matthews, http://www.historiabrittonum.net/wp-content/uploads/2018/09/The-Arthurian-battle-list-of-the-Historia-Brittonum.pdf
11. Halsall, 2014: 67
12. Padel, 2013: 3
13. Green, 2012: 182
14. Green, 2012: 182
15. Ashley, 2005: 134–5
16. Ashley, 2005: 135
17. Green, 2012: 60
18. Rivet and Smith, 1982: 393

19. Ashley, 2005: 137
20. Green, 2012: 96
21. Higham, 2018: 191
22. Phillips, 2016
23. Morris, 1980: 45
24. Jackson, 1959: 4
25. Milner, 2011: 83
26. Jackson, 1959: 4
27. Jackson, 1959: 4
28. Ashley, 2005: 148
29. Jackson, 1959: 4
30. Higham, 1994: 112–3
31. Jackson, 1959: 4
32. Chambers, 1966: 199–201
33. Alcock, 1989: 69–70
34. Bennett & Burkitt, 1985: 5–8
35. Hatfield, 2016
36. Jackson, 1959: 2–3
37. Lloyd, 2017: 193
38. Bartrum, 1993: 98
39. Ashley, 2005: 154
40. Bromwich, 2014: 150, 153, 166, 217
41. Bartrum, 1993: 98
42. Higham, 2018: 265
43. Jackson, 1959: 4
44. Halsall, 2014: 67

Chapter 8: Battles and Locations from Other Sources

1. Green, 2009: 101
2. Green, 2009: 27
3. Higham, 2009: 80
4. Higham, 2009: 74
5. Green, 2009: 26
6. Griffin, 1994: 82
7. Sullivan, 2020: 183
8. Green, 2009: 30
9. Green, 2009: 20
10. Sullivan, 2020: 158–181
11. Sullivan, 2020: 129–142
12. http://christophergwinn.com/wp-content/uploads/2016/09/achArthur.png

13. Bartrum, 1993: 158
14. Bartrum, 1993: 157
15. http://christophergwinn.com/wp-content/uploads/2016/09/achArthur.png
16. Bartrum, 1993: 28
17. Chadwick, 1959: 52–3
18. http://christophergwinn.com/arthuriana/arthurs-pedigree/#genealogies
19. Morris, 1980: 38

References and Bibliography

Adomnán of Iona, *Life of St Columba*, (Penguin, London, 1995).

Ardrey, A., *Finding Arthur*, (Overlook Press, New York, 2013).

Arnold, C.J., *An Archaeology of the Early Anglo-Saxon Kingdoms*, (Routledge, London, 2000).

Ashe, Geoffrey, *The Discovery of King Arthur*, (The History Press, Stroud, 2010).

Ashe, Geoffrey, *The Landscape of King Arthur*, (Anchor Press Doubleday, London, 1985).

Ashley, Mike, *The Mammoth Book of King Arthur*, (Constable and Robinson Ltd, London, 2005).

Baring-Gould, Sabine, *The Lives of British Saints Volumes 1–4*, (Forgotten Books, London, 2012).

Bartrum, Peter, *A Welsh Classical Dictionary*, (National Library of Wales, 1993).

Bassett, Stephen, *The Origins of the Anglo-Saxon Kingdoms*, (Leicester University Press, London, 1989).

Beard, D, 'Astronomical references in the Anglo-Saxon Chronicles' in *Journal of the British Astronomical Association*, (Vol. 115, No. 5, p.261, 2005).

Bede, *The Ecclesiastical History of the English People*, (Oxford University Press, Oxford, 1994).

Bédoyère, Guy, de la, *Eagles over Britannia*, (Tempus Publishing, Stroud, 2001).

Bédoyère, Guy, de la, *Gladius: Living Fighting and Dying in the Roman Army*, (Little Brown, London, 2020).

Bédoyère, Guy, de la, *Roman Britain: A New History*, (Thames and Hudson, London, 2006).

Bennett, A., and Burkitt, T., 'Badon as Bath' in *Popular Archaeology*, (Volume 6 (6), 1985).

Bishop, M.C., *The Secret History of the Roman Roads of Britain*, (Pen and Sword, Barnsley, 2020).

Breeze, Andrew, *The Name of King Arthur*, (Mediaevistik, Internationale Zeitschrift für interdisziplinäre Mittelalterforschung, Peter Laing, 2015).

Bromwich, Jarman and Roberts, *The Arthur of the Welsh*, (University of Wales Press, Cardiff 1995).

Bromwich, Rachel, *The Triads of the Island of Britain*, 4th ed., (University of Wales Press, Cardiff, 2014).

Brookes, S. and Harrington, S., *The Kingdom and People of Kent AD 400–1066 Their History and Archaeology*, (The History Press, Stroud, 2010).

Brugman, B., 'Migration and Endogenuous Change' in Hamerow, H., Hinton, D., and Crawford, S., *The Oxford Handbook of Anglo-Saxon Archaeology*, (Oxford University Press, Oxford, 2011).

Bury, John, *The Life of St Patrick and His Place in History*, (Dover Publications, London, 1998).

Carver, Martin, *Formative Britain: An Archaeology of Britain Fifth to Eleventh Century AD*, (Routledge, Abingdon, 2019).

Chadwick et al, *Studies in Early British History*, (Cambridge University Press, Cambridge, 1959).

Chambers, E.K., *Arthur of Britain*, (Sidgwick and Jackson, London, 1966).

Charles-Edwards, T.M., *Wales and the Britons 350–1064*, (Oxford University Press, Oxford, 2014).

Clarkson, Tim, *The Men of the North*, (Birlinn Ltd, Edinburgh, 2016).

Clarkson, Tim, *The Picts: A History*, (Birlinn Ltd, Edinburgh, 2019).

Clearly, S., 'The Ending(s) of Roman Britain' in Hamerow, H., Hinton, D., and Crawford, S., *The Oxford Handbook of Anglo-Saxon Archaeology*, (Oxford University Press, Oxford, 2011).

Clemoes, Peter, *Anglo-Saxon England: Volume 5*, (Cambridge University Press, Cambridge, 1976).

Collins, Rob, *Hadrian's Wall and the End of Empire*, (Routledge, New York, 2012).

Cornwell, Bernard, *Excalibur*, (Michael Joseph, London, 1997).

Crabtree, Pam, *Early Medieval Britain: The Rebirth of Towns in the Post-Roman West*, (Cambridge University Press, Cambridge, 2018).

Cusack, Mary Francis, *History of Ireland from AD 400 to 1800*, (Senate, London 1995).

Cunliffe, Barry, *Britain Begins*, (Oxford University Press, Oxford, 2013).

D'Amato, R. and Negin, A., *Decorated Roman Armour: from the Ages of the Kings to the Death of Justinian the Great*, (Frontline Books, Barnsley, 2017).

Dark, K.R., *Civitas to Kingdom: British Political Continuity 300–800*, (Leicester University Press, London, 1994).

Dark, Ken, *Britain and the End of the Roman Empire*, (Tempus Publishing Ltd, Stroud, 2000).

Davidson, Hilda, Ellis, *The Sword in Anglo-Saxon England*, (Boydell Press, Woodbridge, 1998).

Davies, Hugh, *Roman Roads in Britain*, (Shire Archaeology, Oxford, 2008).

Dumville, David, *Britons and Anglo-Saxons in the Early Middle Ages*, (Variorum, Aldershot, 1993).

Dumville, David, *Saint Patrick*, (Boydell Press, Woodbridge, 1999).

Dyer, James, *Hillforts of England and Wales*, (Shire Archaeology, Risborough, 1992).

Eagles, Bruce, *From Roman Civitas to Anglo-Saxon Shire: Topographical Studies on the Formation of Wessex*, (Oxbow Books, Oxford, 2018).

Esposito, Gabriele, *Armies of the Late Roman Empire AD 284–476: History, Organisation and Equipment*, (Pen and Sword Books, Barnsley, 2018).

Evans, Stephen, *Lords of Battle*, (Boydell Press, Woodbridge, 2000).

Field, P.J.C., 'Gildas and the City of the Legions' in *The Heroic Age*, (Issue 1, Spring/Summer 1999)

Fitzpatrick-Matthews, Keith, J., *The textual history of the Historia Brittonum*, (http://www.historiabrittonum.net/wp-content/uploads/2018/09/The-textual-history-of-the-Historia-Brittonum.pdf, 2017).

Fitzpatrick-Matthews, Keith, J., *The Arthurian Battle list of the Historia Brittonum*, (http://www.historiabrittonum.net/wp-content/uploads/2018/09/The-Arthurian-battle-list-of-the-Historia-Brittonum.pdf)

Foster, Sally, *Picts, Gaels and Scots: Early Historic Scotland*, (Birlinn Ltd, Edinburgh, 2014).

Gantz, Jeffrey, *The Mabinogion*, (Penguin Books, London, 1976).

Geoffrey of Monmouth, *The Life of Merlin, Vita Merlini*, (Read a Classic, USA, 2011).

Gerrard, James, *The Ruin of Roman Britain: an Archaeological Perspective*, (Cambridge University Press, Cambridge, 2016).

Gilbert, Wilson and Brackett, *The Holy Kingdom*, (Bantam Press, London, 1998).

Goldsworthy, Adrian, *The Fall of the West*, (Phoenix, London, 2010).

Goldsworthy, Adrian, *The Complete Roman Army*, (Thames and Hudson, London, 2003).

Goldsworthy, Adrian, *Roman Warfare*, (Phoenix, London, 2000).

Green, T., *Britons and the Anglo-Saxons, Lincolnshire 400–650 AD*, (History of Lincolnshire Committee, Lincoln, 2012).

Griffen, T., *Names from the Dawn of British Legend*, (Llanerch, Dyfed, 1994).

Grigg, Eric, *Warfare and Raiding and Defence in Early Medieval Britain*, (Robert Hale, Marlborough, 2018).

Guy, Ben, *Medieval Welsh Genealogy*, (The Boydell Press, Woodbridge, 2020).

Halsall, Guy, *Barbarian Migrations and the Roman West 376–568*, (Cambridge University Press, Cambridge, 2014).

Halsall, Guy, *Warfare and Society in the Barbarian West 450–900*, (Routledge, London, 2003).

Halsall, Guy, *Worlds of Arthur*, (Oxford University Press, Oxford, 2014).

Hamerow, H., Hinton, D., and Crawford, S., *The Oxford Handbook of Anglo-Saxon Archaeology*, (Oxford University Press, Oxford, 2011).

Hamilton, Walter, *Ammianus Marcellinus: The Later Roman Empire AD 354–378*, (Penguin Books, London, 1986).

Harding, Dennis, *Iron Age Hillforts in Britain and Beyond*, (Oxford University Press, Oxford, 2012).

Harrington, Sue and Welch, Martin, *Early Anglo-Saxon Kingdoms of Southern Briton AD 450–650: Beyond the Tribal Hidage*, (Oxbow Books, Oxford, 2018).

Hatfield, Edward, *Pritanica: A Dictionary of the Ancient British Language*, (Whiskey and Beards Publishing, 2016).

Higham, N.J., *King Arthur: Myth-Making and History*, (Routledge, Abingdon, 2009).

Higham, N.J., *King Arthur: The Making of the Legend*, (Yale University Press, New Haven, 2018).

Higham, N.J., *Rome, Britain and the Anglo-Saxons*, (Seaby, London, 1992).

Higham, N.J., *The English Conquest, Gildas and Britain in the Fifth Century*, (Manchester University Press, Manchester, 1994).

Higham, N. and Ryan, R., *The Anglo-Saxon World*, (Yale University Press, New Haven, 2015).

Hills, C., 'Anglo-Saxon Identity' in Hamerow, H., Hinton, D., and Crawford, S., *The Oxford Handbook of Anglo-Saxon Archaeology*, (Oxford University Press, Oxford, 2011).

Hobbs, R., & Jackson, R., *Roman Britain*, (The British Museum Press, London, 2015).

Hooke, Della, *The Anglo-Saxon Landscape: The Kingdom of the Hwicce*, (Manchester University Press, Manchester, 1985).

Hughes, Ian, *Aetius: Attila's Nemesis*, (Pen and Sword Books, Barnsley, 2020).

Jackson, K.H., 'The Arthur of history' in Loomis, R. S. (ed.), *Arthurian Literature in the Middle Ages: A Collaborative History*, (Clarendon Press, Oxford, 1–11, 1959).

Jarman, A., *Aneirin: Y Gododdin*, (Gomer Press, Ceredigion, 1990).

Keegan, Simon, *Pennine Dragon*, (Newhaven Publishing, 2016).

Keys, David, *Catastrophe: An Investigation into the Origins of the Modern World*, (Arrow Books Ltd, London, 2000).

Koch, John, *Waiting for Gododdin: Thoughts on Taliesin and Iudic-Hael, Catraeth, and Unripe Time in Celtic Studies* in *Beyond the Gododdin: Dark Age Scotland in Medieval Wales: the proceedings of a day conference held on 19 February 2005 [St. John's House papers, no. 13.]*, (The Committee for Dark Age Studies, University of St Andrews, St Andrews, Fife, 2013).

Lapidge, Michael and Dumville, David, *Gildas: New Approaches*, (Boydell Press, Woodbridge, 1984).

Laycock, Stuart, *Britannia: The Failed State*, (The History Press, Stroud, 2011).

Lloyd, Scott, *The Arthurian Place Names of Wales*, (University of Wales Press, Cardiff, 2017).

Loveluck, C., and Laing, L., 'Britons and Anglo-Saxons' in Hamerow, H., Hinton, D., and Crawford, S., *The Oxford Handbook of Anglo-Saxon Archaeology*, (Oxford University Press, Oxford, 2011).

Low, D.M., *Gibbon's The Decline and Fall of the Roman Empire*, (Chatto and Windus, London, 1981).

Manco, Jean, *The Origins of the Anglo-Saxons*, (Thames and Hudson, New York, 2018),

Mathisen, Ralph, *Roman Aristocrats in Barbarian Gaul: Strategies for Survival in the Age of Transition*, (University of Texas Press, Texas, 1989).

Matthews, John, *Taliesin: The Last Celtic Shaman*, (Inner Traditions, Vermont, 2002).

Marren, Peter, *Battles of the Dark Ages*, (Pen and Sword, Barnsley, 2006).

Marsden, John, *Northanhymbre Saga: History of the Anglo-Saxon Kings of Northumbria*, (Kyle Cathie Ltd, London, 1992).

Mierow, Charles, *Jordanes: The Origin and Deeds of the Goths*, (Dodo Press, Princetown, 1908).

Mills, A.D., *A Dictionary of British Place Names*, (Oxford University Press, Oxford, 2011).

Milner, N.P., *Vegetius: Epitome of Military Science*, 2nd ed., (Liverpool University Press, Liverpool, 2011).

Mitchell, Stephen, and Greatrex, Geoffrey, *Ethnicity and Culture in Late Antiquity*, (Duckworth and The Classical Press of Wales, London, 2000).

Moffat, Alistair, *The British: A Genetic Journey*, (Birlinn, Edinburgh, 2013).

Morris, J., *Arthurian Period Sources Volume 3 Persons: Ecclesiastics and Laypeople*, (Phillimore, Chichester, 1995).

Morris, J., *Arthurian Period Sources Volume 7 Gildas*, (Phillimore, Chichester, 1978).

Morris, J., *Arthurian Period Sources Volume 8 Nennius*, (Phillimore, Chichester, 1980).

Morris, Marc, *The Norman Conquest*, (Windmill Books, London, 2013).

Mortimer, Paul and Bunker, Matt, *The Sword in Anglo-Saxon England from the 5th to 7th Century*, (Anglo-Saxon Books, Ely, 2019).

Mortimer, Paul, *Woden's Warriors: Warriors and Warfare in 6th–7th Century Northern Europe*, (Anglo-Saxon Books, Ely, 2011).

Naismith, Rory, *Citadel of the Saxons*, (I.B. Tauris and Co., London, 2019).

Newton, Sam, *The Origins of Beowulf and the Pre-Viking Kingdom of East Anglia*, (D.S. Brewer, Cambridge, 1994).

O Cróinín, Dáibhí, *Early Medieval Ireland 400–1200*, 2nd ed., (Routledge, London, 2017).

Oosthuizen, Susan, *The Anglo-Saxon Fenland*, (Oxbow Books, Oxford, 2017).

Oosthuizen, Susan, *The Emergence of the English*, (Arc Humanities Press, Leeds, 2019).

Oppenheimer, Stephen, *The Origins of the British*, (Robinson, London, 2007).

Padel, O.J., *Arthur in Medieval Welsh Literature*, (University of Wales Press, Cardiff, 2013).

Pearson, Andrew, *The Roman Shore Forts*, (The History Press, Stroud, 2010).

Pennar, Merion, *The Black Book of Carmarthen*, (Llanerch Enterprises, 1989).

Phillips, Graham, *The Lost Tomb of King Arthur, Bear and Company*, (Rochester, Vermont, 2016).

Procopius (translated by Williamson, G. & Sarris, P.), *The Secret History*, (Penguin Books, London, 2007).

Rippon, Stephen, *Kingdom, Civitas, and County: The Evolution of Territorial Identity in the English Landscape*, (Oxford University Press, Oxford, 2018).

Rivet, A.L.F. and Smith, Colin, *The Place-Names of Roman Britain*, (Batsford, London, 1982).

Salway, Peter, *A History of Roman Britain*, (Oxford University Press, Oxford, 2001).

Sisam, Kenneth, *Anglo-Saxon Royal Genealogies*, (The British Academy, London, 1953).

Stenton, Frank, *Anglo-Saxon England*, (Oxford University Press, Oxford, 1989).

Sullivan, Tony, *King Arthur: Man or Myth*, (Pen and Sword, Yorkshire, 2020).

Swanton, Michael, *The Anglo-Saxon Chronicles*, (Phoenix Press, London, 2000).

Sykes, Brian, *Blood of the Isles*, (Corgi Books, London, 2006).

Syvanne, Ilkka, *Military History of Late Rome 425–457*, (Pen and Sword, Yorkshire, 2020).

Thompson, E.A., *Saint Germanus of Auxerre and the end of Roman Britain*, (Boydell Press, Woodbridge, 1988).

Thornton, D., *Kings, Chronicles and Genealogies: Studies in the Political History of Early Medieval Ireland and Wales*, (Linacre College, Oxford, 2003).

Thorpe, Lewis (translator), *Gerald of Wales*, (Penguin Books, London, 1988).

Thorpe, Lewis (translator), *Gregory of Tours: The History of the Franks*, (Penguin Books, London 1977).

Thorpe, Lewis (translator), *Geoffrey of Monmouth: The History of the Kings of Britain*, (Penguin Books, London, 1966).

Tolkien, J.R.R., *Finn and Hengest: The Fragment and the Episode*, (Harper Collins, London, 1998).

Underwood, Richard, *Anglo-Saxon Weapons and Warfare*, (Tempus Publishing Ltd, Stroud, 1999).

Vermaat, Robert, *Nennius: The Historia Brittonum*, (http://www.vortigernstudies.org.uk/artsou/historia.htm).

Wacher, John, *The Towns of Roman Britain*, (BCA, London, 1995).

Wade-Evans, A.W., *The Lives and Genealogies of the Welsh Saints*, (Ashley Drake Publishers, Cardiff, 1988).

Wallace-Hadrill, J.M., *The Barbarian West 400–1000*, (Blackwell, Oxford, 1999).

Wallace-Hadrill, J.M., *The Long-Haired Kings*, (Methuen & Co., London, 1962).

Webster, L. & Brown, M., *The Transformation of the Roman World AD 400–900*, (British Museum Press, London, 1997).

Webb, Simon, *Life in Roman London*, (The History Press, Stroud, 2011).

Wilson, Roger J.A., *A Guide to the Roman Remains in Britain*, (Constable & Company, London, 1980).

Wood, Michael, *Domesday: A Search for the Roots of England*, (Book Club Associates, London, 1987).

Woods, David, 'Gildas and the Mystery Cloud of 536–537' in *The Journal of Theological Studies*, (NS, 2010, University of Southern California, April 5, 2014).

Yorke, Barbara, *Kings and the Kingdoms of Early Anglo-Saxon England*, (Routledge, London, 2013).

Zaluckyj, Sarah, *Mercia: The Anglo-Saxon Kingdom of Central England*, (Logaston Press, Logaston, 2013).

Zosimus (translation), *Zosimus Historicus*, (Green and Chaplin, London, 1814).

www.vortigernstudies.org.uk

Index